Network Design and Performance Analysis

Network Design and Performance Analysis

RAJWINDERPAL SHARMA

IKVINDERPAL SINGH

KHANNA BOOK PUBLISHING CO. (P) LTD.

Publisher of Science, Technology and Engineering Books

4C/4344, Ansari Road, Darya Ganj, New Delhi-110002

Phone: 011-23244447-48 **Mobile:** +91-99109 09320

E-mail: contact@khannabooks.com, sales@khannapublishers.com

Website: www.khannabooks.com, www.khannapublishers.com

Network Design and Performance Analysis
Rajwinderpal Sharma & Ikvinderpal Singh

ISBN : 978-93-81068-40-0

First Edition : 2013
Reprint 2015

Published by :
Khanna Book Publishing Co. (P) Ltd.
4C/4344, Ansari Road, Darya Ganj, New Delhi-110002
Phone : 011-23244448 Telefax : 011-23244447
E-mail : contact@khannabooks.com
Website : www.khannabooks.com

Printed in India by:
S.P.S. Printers & Binders, Delhi

DEDICATION

No project could ever get in progress much less accomplished, without help from a lot of fantastic people. We would like to express gratitude to our reverential parents. We are grateful to Almighty God who has given us strength to take and complete this project.

To my mother Smt. Janakraj Dulari and father Shri. Sawinderpal Sharma biggest embrace and warm thanks to my wife Anjum Sharma and to my son Yuvraj and to my Grand Parents Shri. Yashpal Chabhal and Smt. Kanta Devi and to my brother Kanwar Chabhal and sister Amandeep and to my dear students who have encouraged me to complete this project.

RAJWINDERPAL SHARMA

To my mother Smt. Sharanjeet Kaur and father S. Jasjit Singh, biggest embrace and warm thanks to my grandmother Narinderjeet Kaur, and to my brothers Jagminder Singh and Sukhminder Singh, and to my dear students who have encouraged me to complete this project.

IKVINDERPAL SINGH

PREFACE

The primary purpose of this book is to teach the science and art of designing a Network Design and Performance Analysis. We have attempted to provide the reader an all encompassing text on how to plan, design, build, implement, manage, and secure both simple and complex data networks for both enterprises(end users) and service providers. Science is defined as "knowledge covering general truth, or operation of general laws especially as attained and tested through scientific method". The data network design includes learning the major transmission, multiplexing, switching and routing technologies prevalent at the turn of the 21st century. Art is defined as "skill acquired by experience or study" and relates more to a talent, knack, or ability to perform. Therefore, data network design is an art that demands the study and mastery of many technologies and much practice!

This book presents the principles of this new technology. It is intended for those who are professionally interested in having an up-to-date view of the Network Design and Performance Analysis.

This book contains the following chapters:

Chapter 1 begins with an introduction to Requirements Analysis and Specifications. It also describes the System requirements, traffic sizing characteristics time and delay considerations.

Chapter 2 treats the Traffic Engineering & Capacity Planning. It also describes throughput calculation, traffic characteristics & source models, traditional traffic engineering, queued data & packet switched traffic modeling, designing for peaks, delay or latency.

Chapter 3 provides a detailed treatment of Network Performance Modeling. It also covers Creating traffic matrix, design tools, components of design tools and types of design projects.

Chapter 4 covers the Technology Comparisons. It also describes Generic packet switching networks characteristics, private vs. public networking, Business aspects of packet, frame and cell switching services, High speed LAN protocols comparison, Application performance needs, Throughput, burstiness, response time and delay tolerance.

Chapter 5 covers the concept of Choosing Service Provider, Vendor and Service Levels.

Chapter 6 includes the Access Network Design. It also covers N/W design layers, Access N/W design, and Access N/W capacity.

Chapter 7 provides an extensive treatment of Backbone Network Design. It explains the concept of Backbone N/W design, Backbone segments, backbone capacity, topologies and Tuning the network.

Chapter 8 is devoted to Network Security. It explains the concept of securing the network and Designing for network security.

Chapter 9 covers the Documentation and Network Management. It also describes the Documentation, network management, SNMP and RMON.

Chapter 10 includes the Network Optimization. It explains goals of network optimization, measurements for network optimization, optimization tools, and optimization techniques.

The book contains far too much detail to be taught in a one-semester course. However, I believe that it can serve as a suitable text in most situations through the appropriate selection of material. This book can be used by a wide reader audience, ranging from beginners to practicing professionals. It is well suited for advanced or beginning college level students as a complete book for an introductory Network Design and Performance Analysis, as a supplementary text, or as an effective independent study guide.

We welcome comments from all readers to improve this textbook as a useful guide for the community of engineers and technologists who will become knowledgeable about the potential of Network Design and Performance Analysis for their use in solving the problems that challenge us each day.

RAJWINDERPAL SHARMA

IKVINDERPAL SINGH

ACKNOWLEDGEMENTS

First we would like to thanks almighty for giving us courage to bring up this book. We duly acknowledge the contribution of our colleagues Prof. Baljinder Singh, Prof. Gurpreet Singh, Prof. Manpreet Singh, Prof. Kulwinder Singh, Prof. Gurjit Singh, Prof. Arminder Singh, Prof. Sahib Singh, Prof. Jagdeep Kaur, Prof. Jaspreet Kaur, Prof. Jatinder Kaur, Prof. Amanpreet Singh, Prof. Hardev Kaur, Prof. Gurjit Singh, Prof. Rajni Saini, Prof.(Dr.) Harjeev Kaur, Prof. Randeep Kaur, Prof. Manindcr Kaur, Prof. Anureet Kaur, Prof. Ravinder Kaur, Prof. Kirandeep Kaur, Prof. Vishavpal Singh, Prof. Rajbir Singh, Prof. Pawan Kumar, Prof. Atul Sharma, Mr. Honey, Ms. Jaspreet Kaur, Ms. Neha, Ms. Ankita Wadhwan, Dr. Pretty Sodhi, Mr. Jatin Uppal, Mr. Lakhwinder Singh, Mr. Satwinderpal Singh Chhabra and Mr. Kawaljeet Singh for their valuable co-operation and guidance. We are grateful to **M/s Khanna Book Publishing Co. (P) Ltd.** for their encouragement and motivation during this project.

Special Thanks

Our special thanks goes to Chaudary Jagjit Singh, President, Dr. Gurpreet Kaur, Principal, MGSM Janta College, Kartarpur for their valuable guidance and timely support during the compilation of this book.

Our special thanks go to Dr. Gurmohan Singh Walia, Director Education of Shiromani Gurudwara Prabhandak Committee (SGPC), Dr. Rupinder Singh, Principal of Trai Shatabdi Guru Gobind Singh Khalsa College, Amritsar for their valuable guidance and timely support during the compilation of this book.

We extend special thanks to our advisors and friends Prof. Parteek Bhatia Department of Computer Science and Engineering, Thapar University Patiala, Prof. Sandeep Singh Waraich, Department of Computer Science and Engineering, Guru Nanak Dev University, Amritsar, Prof. Kawarpal Singh, Postgraduate Department of Computer Science and it, who have supported in all aspects of our career.

Parts of this book were done in Collaboration with Mr. Sanjay Kansara, Senior Process Lead (Work Force Management) igatepatni, Mr. Gaurav Anand, Sr. Software Engg Sunlife Financial India, Mr. Rishi Sharma, Sr. Software Consultant Genpact Milwakee Usa, for Fruitful Collaboration and valuable advice and frequent feedback.

CONTENTS

CHAPTERS AT A GLANCE

Requirements Analysis and Specifications

1.1 INTRODUCTION

In this chapter you will learn and understand to develop the requirements analysis and specifications by mapping business challenges, technical challenges and user requirements for a network. In this chapter we talk about different types of requirements from the user, business, application and devices and learn about grouping and mapping the requirements together.

1.2 HISTORY

It is important to understand the requirements satisfaction is driven primarily by how the designer works with the user. To understand and provide some background on documenting and managing expectations, some history of the development of requests for comments (RFCs) is appropriate. In 1969, while at UCLA, Steve Crocker established RFC series of notes. These memos were intended to be an informal fast way to share ideas with other network researchers. At first, the RFCs were printed and distributed via postal delivery; later, they were distributed via FTP and then the Internet. The effect of the RFC was to create a positive feedback loop, with ideas or proposals presented in one FRC triggering another RFC with additional ideas, and so on. When some agreement was reached, a specification was then prepared based on the consensus. E-mail has been a significant factor in all areas of the Internet, and that is certainly true in the development of standards and consensus.

The point of discussing the creation of RFCs is that the communication process between the designer and end user is critical to get feedback during the process and buy-in on the final design. Good design engineers and managers do not design in a vacuum.

1.3 REQUIREMENTS ANALYSIS

Requirements analysis is the description of the network design and is the most important step of the network design. As part of the requirement analysis process we first need to understand the business requirements and their challenges, user requirements, application requirements, devices requirements and the network requirements. Network is designed to facilitate the business. There is direct correlation between all these requirements. So we must categorize and prioritize requirements, determining those that are truly requirements for the network. As requirements are necessary for the success of the network project there must be some way to determine success. Matrices are the measurements to determine or demonstration for each requirement.

Examples of core requirements and their associated metrics are:

- **Performance:** The network shall be capable of providing throughput of 256kb/s between end devices.
- **Metric:** Measurement between selected end devices under test conditions.
- **Security:** The network shall be capable of filtering packets based on an Access Control List.
- **Metric:** Demonstration of filtering unwanted packets, based on the access control list.

1.3.1 BUSINESS CHALLENGES

Before a network design can begin, the network designer must understand the business and technical challenges and requirements facing the CEO and the managing directors of the enterprises. Here we are given some key business requirements and typical company strategies to accomplish them.

Some Business Requirements and Strategies requirements are given below.

1. **Effectiveness and Efficiency:** To improve effectiveness and efficiency of globally distributed business user by providing languages/ culture- specific application interface.
2. **Globalization:** Merger and acquisition for business growth and expansion world Wide.
3. **Remain competitive:** To reach out to a global customer base by using technological changes, evaluating and deploying e-business and e commerce initiatives by Providing languages/ cultural specific interfaces.
4. **Financial control factor:** By Significant investment, unreimbursed expenses, Opportunity for profit or loss, Services available to the market, Method of payment.
5. **Business coverage through Internationalization, localization, infrastructure and globalization reach:** By supporting corporate users, customers, suppliers and providing access for mobile and remote workers.
6. **Customer support:** Respond to client complaints/requests in a timely manner i.e. gives (7*24*365) customer network service. Be courteous and professional! Match the customer's level of knowledge. Never make the customer feel inadequate.
7. **Maintain security:** By implementing security policies, implementing firewalls, Providing ID's etc.
8. **Changing environment:** Adapt changing environment as the forces of globalization and technology are continuously reshaping the world

Business management objectives typically involve

- Expansion and Growing the business
- Financial control while improving shareholder value

- Remaining competitive in an increasingly competitive environment
- Integrating operations with customers, suppliers, and partners

The organizations often overlooked to succeed in today's challenging and global environment, using network and technology to provide flavor to their business application, services and products. Globalization is an integral part of business and IT. Enterprises must have an overall globalization vision and strategy to ensure the success of the globalization program.

1.3.2 TECHNICAL CHALLENGES

Some technical Requirements and Strategies requirements are given below.

1. **Performance:** Globalization actually means parameterization of applications, and designing application for large user base with different usage pattern across Countries. Changes in the application's performance behavior are expected after globalization. [Throughput]
2. **Accessibility:** Authorization, opportunity, or right to access records or retrieve information from an archive, computer system, or website. [describing geographical limitations]
3. **Availability:** Availability requirements are complex as users from different regions in different time zones may access the application simultaneously. Therefore, system failure, downtime planning, etc have to be considered thoroughly at the design stage.
4. **Adaptability:** Architecture designs have to be adaptive to allow for development of new locations-specific requirements without considerable changes and in the shortest possible time span.
5. **Manageability:** When applications are deployed in multiple regions, local maintenance must given support for analysis and administration in local languages.
6. **Maintainability:** The principals and design guidelines of globalization should be considered while enhancing an application. A process has to be in place to ensure the minimal code changes are required to cater to the need of different regions.
7. **Extensibility:** Application architecture and design must be aligned with industry standards and trends to ensure that investment in globalization yield returns even with advancements in globalization technology.
8. **Security:** How protected is your network. Make sure that security violation have minimal impact on the business.

Examples of Business and Technical Requirements of business organizations:

- Financial services Agents require instant access to client financial information.
- Publishing Large text graphic files are sent across the Web, stored, and printed.
- Travel Timeliness of data important in distributed database computing and reservation System; many users during 8:00 A.M-5:00 P.M. traffic pattern.
- Engineering Share large CAD/CAM/CAE graphics, text, and video around campus.
- Web hosting Internet-based software and information Distribution Company.
- Architecture Large graphics files, multimedia conference room, and desktop.

1.3.3 VIDEOCONFERENCING

When determining business and technical requirements, you must have to review the following list and make sure to cover every aspect of the business.

- Marketing
- Product and service development
- Engineering
- Sales
- Operations
- Customer service and support
- Human resources and training
- Distribution

The goal of the network designer is to determine how the network can deliver meaningful results to the business. When you communicate with business management, make sure that meaningful results are communicated in specific, measurable results.

In summary, the globalization now carries more mission-critical traffic, will extend to clients, partners, and suppliers across the intranet, extranet, and Internet, and in essence becomes the life of the business. The old model of using a network for best-effort, no mission - critical transport that offered no service-level guarantees has yielded to a new network that enable the business, requiring and providing.

- High performance and reliability
- High security
- High speed
- Rapid scalability
- Ubiquitous access
- Ability to integrate with customers, partners, and suppliers.

1.4 USER REQUIREMENTS

In the model of system components in our generic system, the user component is at the highest layer. The term user represents primarily the end users of the system but can be expanded to include everyone involved in the system, such as network and system administrators and management. User requirements comprise the set of requirements that is gathered or derived from user input and represent what is needed by users to successfully accomplish their tasks on the System. Typically, when gathering requirements, everyone involved with that network is considered a potential user. Figure 1.1 shows some example of user requirements.

We begin describing requirements at this layer, which will lead to the development of more specific requirements as we work through each of the components. From the user perspective we can ask, "What does it take to get the job done?" This usually results in a set of qualitative, not quantitative, requirements. Part of our job in gathering and deriving user requirements is to make them quantitative whenever possible.

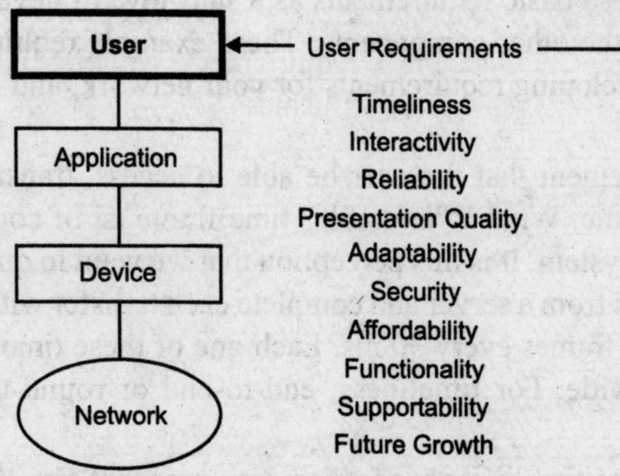

Figure 1.1: Types of user requirements

In general, the system should adapt to users and their environments, provide quick and reliable information access and transfer, and offer quality service to the user. This indicates the following general requirements:

- Timeliness
- Interactivity
- Reliability
- Presentation quality
- Adaptability
- Security
- Affordability
- Functionality
- Supportability
- Future growth

User requirements are the least technical and are also the most subjective. As shown in Figure 1.2 requirements become more technical as they move from users to the network. All of these requirements are developed in more detail as we proceed through the application, device, and network components.

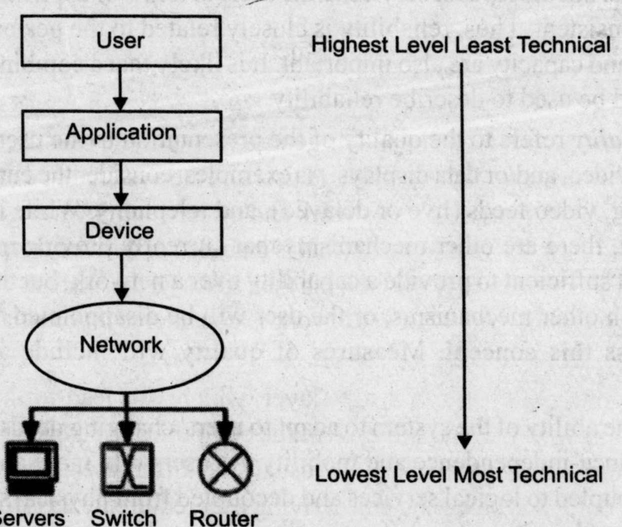

Figure 1.2: Requirements become more technical as they move closer to network devices

Our intent is to use these basic requirements as a start toward developing more objective and technical requirements in the other components. These example requirements are presented as a guide for you to use in developing requirements for your network, and may change, depending on the user's environment.

Timeliness is a requirement that the user be able to access, transfer, or modify information within a tolerable time frame. What a "tolerable" time frame is, of course, depends on the user's perception of delay in the system. It is this perception that we want to quantify. For example, a user may want to download files from a server and complete each transfer within 10 minutes. Or the user may need to receive video frames every 30 ms. Each one of these times indicates a delay that the network will need to provide. For timeliness, end-to-end or round-trip delay can be a useful measurement.

Interactivity is similar to timeliness but focuses on a response time from the system (as well as the network) that is on the order of the response times of users. In the previous example the 10 minutes needed to download the file could be considered as the response time for the system, and we might consider as well that the file transfer is interacting with the user (which it is)-but the degree of interactivity is very low and not of much interest from an architectural or design perspective. What is interesting is when the system and network response times are close to the response times of users, for then changes made in the network architecture and design to optimize response times can have a direct impact on users' perception of interactivity. Therefore, interactivity is a measure of the response times of the system and network when they are required to actively interact with users. Delay-here the round-trip delay,-is a measure of interactivity. Using these descriptions of timeliness and interactivity, then, timeliness is more likely to be associated with bulk file or image transfer, while interactivity is likely to be associated with remote device access (e.g., telnet), Web use, or visualization.

Reliability that is, availability from the user's perspective, is a requirement for consistently available service. Not only must the user be able to have access to system resources a very high percentage of the time, but the level of service to the user (in terms of application usage or information delivery) must be consistent. Thus, reliability is closely related to the performance characteristic of reliability but delay and capacity are also important. It is likely that a combination of all performance characteristics would be used to describe reliability.

Presentation quality refers to the quality of the presentation to the user. This may be the user's perception of audio, video, and/or data displays. As examples, consider the current Internet capabilities of videoconferencing, video feeds (live or delayed), and telephony. While it is possible to do all of these on the Internet, there are other mechanisms that currently provide much better presentation quality. It is often not sufficient to provide a capability over a network, but that capability must be as good as or better than other mechanisms, or the user will be disappointed. Network architects and designers often miss this concept. Measures of quality will include all of the performance characteristics.

Adaptability is the ability of the system to adapt to users' changing needs. Some examples of this can be found in distance-independence and mobility. As users rely more and more on the network, they are becoming coupled to logical services and decoupled from physical servers. This decoupling means that users do not have to care where servers are located, as long as they can get the services they need. A result of this is distance-independent computing, where the user loses all knowledge of where jobs are being executed, or where data are sourced, stored, or migrated through the network.

Mobility refers to mobile or nomadic computing, where the user can access services and resources from any location, using portable devices and wireless access to the network. Adaptability to such user needs forces requirements on the system architecture and design.

Security from the user perspective is a requirement to guarantee the confidentiality, integrity, and authenticity of a user's information and physical resources, as well as access to user and system resources. Security is probably closest to the performance characteristic reliability, but it will impact capacity and delay as well.

Affordability is the requirement that purchases fit within a budget. Although this requirement is not technical, it impacts the architecture and design. What we are concerned with in this requirement is what users or management can afford to purchase for the network, so that our architecture and design do not cost too much to implement. As a user requirement, we look at how costs and funding are tied to users, groups of users, and management. We also consider funding as a system wide requirement, from an overall budget perspective.

Functionality encompasses any functional requirement that the user has for the system. Functions that the system will perform are often tied to applications that are used on the system. Understanding functionality is important in that it leads into application requirements (covered in the next section). Part of understanding functionality is determining which applications users actually want or apply in their daily work. We do not want to analyze applications that no one is planning to use.

Supportability is a set of characteristics that describes how well the customer can keep the network operating at designed performance, through the full range of mission scenarios described by the customer during the requirements analysis process. This includes how users want or need to be supported by their network operations staff, and any interfaces they will have with a network operations center (NOC). For example, will the network need to be reconfigured to meet different or changing user needs? What applications will the network operations staff and/or NOC need to provide support to users and to identify and troubleshoot problems on the network? Information such as this will be used later as input to the network management architecture.

Future growth is determining if and when users are planning to deploy and use new applications and devices on the network. In addition to these requirements, we want to know how many users are expected on the network, and their locations. If possible, we must estimate the growth in users over the first one to three years after the network becomes operational, or over the expected life cycle of the network.

1.5 APPLICATION REQUIREMENTS

The application component interfaces with the user and device components and is a key part of the requirements analysis. Application requirements are requirements that are determined from application information, experience, or testing, and represent what is needed by applications to successfully operate on the system. Figure 1.3 shows example application requirements. Application requirements are more technical than user requirements but may still be subjective.

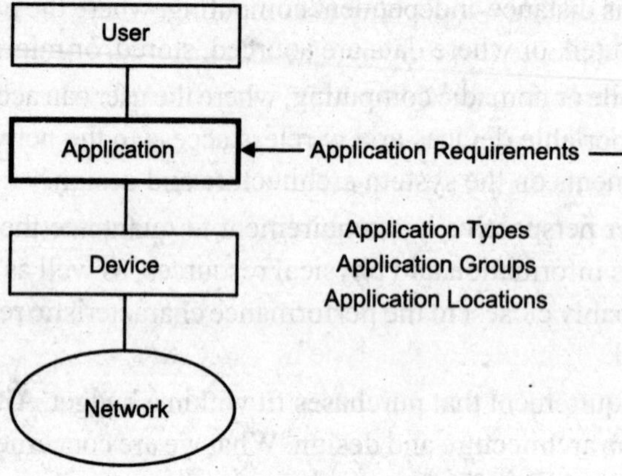

Figure 1.3 Application Requirements

1.5.1 APPLICATION TYPES

In the system description (user, application, device, network), the application component is pivotal. This component is often where many requirements for the network are determined, as applications couple users and devices to the network. Applications are often end-to-end, between multiple devices; thus, their requirements span the underlying network.

In the early days of networking, applications required basic connectivity and data transfer across the network. While applications still have these requirements, they are often also required to be high performance or have predictable or guaranteed behaviour, to support user requirements for timeliness, interactivity, reliability, quality, adaptability, and security. Thus, user requirements have an impact on application requirements. We can use these service and performance requirements to distinguish between applications that need predictable or guaranteed service and those that can use best-effort service.

Based on service and performance requirements, we type applications as mission-critical, rate-critical, or real-time/interactive, where

- ***Mission-critical*** applications have predictable, guaranteed, and/or high performance RMA requirements
- ***Rate-critical*** applications have predictable, guaranteed, and/or high-performance capacity requirements
- ***Real-time*** and ***interactive*** applications have predictable, guaranteed, and/or High performance delay requirements These application types are described by their requirements and service metrics.

1.5.1.1 RMA

Let's first look at RMA, consisting of reliability, maintainability, and availability. Reliability is a statistical measure of the frequency of failure of the network and its components and represents the unscheduled outages of service. Maintainability is a statistical measure of the time to restore the system to fully operational status, once it has experienced a fault. Availability is a measure of the relationship between the frequency of mission-critical failures and the time to restore service. How do these measures relate to the applications that will use the network?

RMA requirements can be subjective. Many users argue that their applications require a high degree of reliability, maintainability, and/or availability from the network, but there are some applications that must maintain high degrees of RMA in order to function. A loss of any part of RMA in such applications may be serious or disastrous, such as:

- **Loss of revenue or customers:** Examples include applications that handle lots of transactions and money, such as investment banking, airline reservation, or credit card processing applications.
- **Unrecoverable information or situation:** Telemetry processing and teleconferencing applications are good examples of this type of reliability.
- **Loss of sensitive data:** Examples include customer ID/billing and intelligence gathering applications.
- **Loss of life:** Examples include transportation or health-care monitoring applications.

In these situations either the system is not available to process user/application requests or the system is not available to complete the transactions that are in progress. For applications such as these, a network that offers only best-effort service is not likely to be adequate, owing to its unpredictable and unreliable behaviour. These applications require predictable or guaranteed reliability, maintainability, and availability, which may take the form of a predictable or bounded RMA, or a high degree of RMA, or both. Applications that require predictable or high RMA are termed here mission-critical applications.

1.5.1.2 CAPACITY

Capacity is the maximum amount of data per time unit that the hop or path has available, when there is no competing traffic. The capacity of the bottleneck hop is the upper bound on the capacity of a path that includes that hop. This information is useful in many areas such as determining how to set optimal TCP buffer sizes. Again, the layer at which a capacity measurement is taken SHOULD be reported as an attribute of that measurement.

Following are the some capacity measurements:

Link layer capacity can sometimes be obtained directly via SNMP queries to the network switches and routers along the path. However, in general it is not yet possible to get access to this information for network switches and routers in different administrative domains. For example, an end-user is as yet unlikely to be able to access SNMP information in a commercial ISP's network. There are a variety of techniques for inferring capacity. On an unloaded network one can send a suitable stream of packets and measure the bandwidth at the receiver. Other techniques are based on analysis of "packet trains." Bursts of carefully-spaced datagram's can be injected into the network, and the difference between the separation of packets at the source and the destination (or other point), referred to as the dispersion, is observed. Packet dispersion techniques evaluate the dispersion of packets based on analytical models of network behaviour, and estimate path characteristics based on this information. For example, the bottleneck capacity hop separates back-to-back packets by the time each packet takes to cross that hop. If this separation is maintained through the remainder of the path, the bottleneck capacity can be derived by observing the widest spacing of the packets. Actual implementations based on these techniques use differing initial packet separations and apply a variety of statistical techniques to filter out the noise and random behaviour of real networks. Although they are quite useful, there are a number of challenges associated with implementing and applying these measurement techniques.

They include, but aren't limited to:

- **Host timing issues:** As link speeds increase, intra-host latencies make a larger difference in measurement accuracy. Interrupt coalescing and driver and kernel implementations can make appreciable differences.
- **Differential queuing:** There are many techniques for so-called "traffic shaping," and it is difficult to be certain that UDP or ICMP are treated the same way as TCP in the network infrastructure.
- **Clock resolution:** As we approach to higher speeds such as 10Gbits/s, inter-packet delay timing requires clocks with resolution of 1?s or better, which is a challenge for today's CPUs.

1.5.1.3 DELAY

Increasing interactivity is arguably the driving force behind the evolution of many applications. Consider the evolutionary path of information access, from telnet and FTP to Gopher (a menu system that simplifies locating resources on the Internet) and Archie (a database that consists of hundreds of file directories) to Mosaic (the precursor to Netscape) and Netscape, made even more interactive with the use of JAVA and virtual reality markup language (VRML). As we saw in the previous section, interactivity relies predominantly on the performance characteristic delay. Delay is a measure of the time differences in the transfer and processing of information. There are many sources of delay, including propagation, transmission, queuing, processing, and routing. This section focuses on end-to-end and roundtrip delays, which encompass all of the delay types mentioned above. From an application service perspective, optimizing the total, end-to-end, or round-trip delay is usually more important than focusing on individual sources of delay. Individual sources of delay become more important as we get into the lower-layer components, as well as in architecture and design optimizations. Historically, applications used on the Internet did not have strict delay requirements. They relied on best-effort service from the Internet and did not request or expect any service guarantees. Other applications, found primarily on private networks (with proprietary network technologies and protocols), have had more strict delay requirements (as well as capacity and RMA requirements).

Some private networks have been effective in providing predictable or guaranteed delay, either by over-engineering the network with substantial spare capacity, or by the trade-off interoperability with other networks. But we now find that applications with delay requirements are migrating to the Internet, often using VPNs, and applications previously dedicated to a single user or device are now being used across the Internet, forcing a re-evaluation of offering services other than best effort on the Internet. This is also forcing a re-evaluation of traffic engineering techniques by service providers.

The term real-time has been interpreted to mean many different things. Often, real-time means "as fast as possible" by those who do not know, understand, or care about the actual delay relationships between traffic sources and destinations within their network. It is quite difficult to quantify real-time when it is used this way. There are more meaningful ways to describe real-time, as well as non-real-time, interactive, asynchronous, burst, and bulk. These are all described below.

Real-time applications are those that have a strict timing relationship between source and destination, with one or more timers set for the receipt of information at the destination. Information received after the timer(s) expire at the destination is considered worthless and is dropped. Thus, this definition of real-time does not mean that information has to be transferred within a universally known time boundary, but rather that the delay boundary is understood by source and destination, and that the destination does not wait beyond this boundary. Real-time could mean end-to-end delays of 30 ms for some applications and 30 seconds for others. An example of this is non-buffered video playback. If the video stream is delayed beyond the playback timer, the destination will show one or more blank portions of frames (appearing as blips on the screen) and drop the late video. This is done to preserve the time continuity of the video being shown at the playback device. This is what it means to have a strict timing relationship between source and destination-that the information flow is subject to maintaining time continuity.

Real-time is the first of several terms we need to clarify. These terms are often used carelessly, although, as the network architect/designer, we have to take them seriously. Therefore, it is up to us to make sure that ambiguous terms are clarified, as along with requirements based on such terms. This book tries, whenever possible, to provide strict interpretations of such terms to help make them clear. Given this strict interpretation of real-time, it is safe to say that there are not many real-time applications. But there are some (and their numbers are growing), and it is important to be able to identify them and recognize their strict delay requirements, for they can have a strong impact on the network architecture and design.

Currently, most applications are considered to be non-real-time. Non-real-time applications have various end-to-end delay requirements, at times more stringent (in terms of the amount of delay) than real-time applications, but the important factor here is that the destination will wait (within reason) until the information is received. How long the destination will wait is a function of the timers set in the applications, at the devices, and by the protocols used. Non-real-time applications include interactive and asynchronous ones, which account for the vast majority of applications. Real-time applications are at one extreme of performance; asynchronous applications are at the other.

Asynchronous applications are relatively insensitive to time, assuming either no timing relationship between source and destination, or a timing relationship outside the bounds of the applications session. A good example of an asynchronous application is email. When email is sent to a recipient, all knowledge of timing (that is, the time when the email is received at any intermediate stop or at the final destination) is lost to the sender. Only if there is an error in the system or recipient information, or if it is requested, is the sender notified. Facsimile is another asynchronous application. When a FAX is sent (when it is buffered in the sending device), the sender loses any knowledge of when the FAX arrives at its destination. Just as it is important to identify real-time applications, due to their strict timing requirements, it is also important to identify asynchronous applications, due to their lack of timing requirements. Asynchronous applications have little or no impact on the network architecture and design and can usually be ignored. Just as there are not many real-time applications, there are likewise not many asynchronous applications. Thus, most applications fall in the non-real-time realm, between real-time at one extreme and asynchronous at the other extreme. These applications are called interactive.

Interactive applications assume some timing relationship between source and destination while the application session is active; however, the timing relationship is not as strict as in real-time. Interactive applications are what many people would normally consider real-time, under the connotation of real-time as "as fast as possible." Common interactive applications, such as telnet, FTP, and Web applications, all fall under this type.

Finally, interactive applications may be further subdivided into burst and bulk interactive types. The difference between these types is subtler than with real-time or asynchronous. To distinguish between interactive bulk and burst applications, we need first to understand when the processing times of the system components, particularly the application component, overwhelm the end-to-end or round-trip delay of the network. In other words, we want to distinguish between when an application will frequently and quickly interact with a user and when a user will have to wait substantial periods of time while the application is processing information. These delay types are summarized in Figure 1.4.

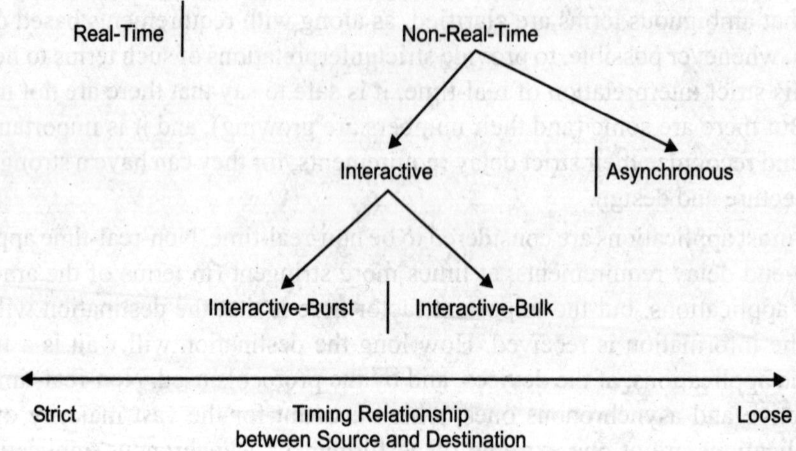

Figure 1.4: Delay types

Based on this, ***interactive burst applications*** are those for which the end-to-end or round-trip network delay is the predominant delay for that application. This type of application is important to identify, as it is sensitive to network delay. Thus, the network architecture and design must accommodate the delay requirements from these applications. An example of an interactive burst application is telnet. During a telnet session, the predominant delay experienced by the user is from the network, not from any processing at the local or remote devices. There are many applications of this type, where users interact with applications and devices across the network and expect responses "as fast as possible."

Interactive bulk applications, by contrast, are those for which processing at the device or application component is the predominant delay. Thus, processing information at either or both end points can overwhelm the end-to-end or round-trip times in the network. This is important to recognize, as the network delay requirement by that application becomes less significant, since it is already eclipsed by application and/or device delays. For example, when an application has high processing delays, say on the order of 100s of ms or seconds, then we have more flexibility in supporting delay in the network than if the processing delay were on the order of microseconds.

An example of interactive bulk applications is large file transfer (e.g., FTP). Although FTP has a degree of interaction with the user, there can be times (especially when the file size is large) when the processing of information at the receiving end, as well as the overall time it takes to transfer the entire file, is several orders of magnitude greater than the end-to-end or round-trip network delay. Why the elaborate breakdown of application types based on delay? As we can see from the above discussion, there are times when an application's requirement for delay is an important consideration in the network architecture and design, and other times when it is not. Whenever we can selectively ignore some applications, and focus on others, the network architecture and design problems become more tractable.

1.5.2 APPLICATION GROUPS

We have so far used various examples of applications to convey application requirements. It is often useful to group applications with similar performance characteristics, as it helps both in the mapping of performance characteristics and in gathering and understanding requirements. It has been useful to me to form groups for applications and keep adding to them as I encounter new applications. When trying to rapidly identify network requirements for a new customer, I have successfully used these groups to help identify requirements, by comparing the new applications to those in groups I have already developed. This process is particularly useful if you have to complete requirements analysis quickly or if you frequently have new customers.

Using the requirements analysis process, the application groups below have been identified. There is some overlap between these groups, and this is not a complete set of groups. It is intended to illustrate how grouping works. You are encouraged to develop your own application groups as you apply the requirements analysis process to your networks.

- ***Telemetry/Command-and-Control Applications:*** While the title may sound somewhat military, this group actually describes a variety of applications where data and command information is transmitted between remote devices and one or more control stations for command, control, tracking, and determining status of the remote devices. A remote device may be as mundane as an automated teller machine (ATM), sensors in the home, or a remote computer, to esoteric devices such as remotely piloted vehicles (RPVs), spacecraft, or commercial aircraft. Telemetry/command-and-control applications can be characterized as having real-time and/or interactive delay, as well as often being mission critical.
- ***Visualization Applications:*** This group ranges from two-dimensional viewing of objects to three-dimensional and virtual reality viewing, immersion, and manipulation of objects. Visualization may be of a numerical simulation or of experimental data. Examples include visualizations of fluid flow fields around various objects (e.g., weather modeling, aeronautics, or medicine), medical, biomedical, and molecular simulations, to commercial and military gaming simulations. Visualization applications can often be characterized as rate-critical and interactive burst.

- ***Distributed-Computing Applications:*** Applications in this group may range from having the computing devices sharing the same local bus (as in parallel computing), to being co-located at the same LAN (as in a computing cluster), to being distributed across LAN, MAN, and WAN boundaries (as in grid computing). The degree of distribution or parallelism in the computing is also determined by the granularity of the task and the degree of coupling between the computing devices. An example of distributed computing is using desktop computers in the corporate environment late at night, when they are usually idle, by coupling their computing capability to accomplish large tasks normally done on a mainframe. Distributed-computing applications can be characterized as real-time or interactive burst.
- ***Web Development, Access, and Use Applications:*** Applications in this group are the current interactive equivalents of the traditional remote device and information access utilities telnet and FTP. Web access and use involve accessing remote devices and downloading and/or uploading information. This is done with the aid of graphic interfaces. Typically, Web sessions are interactive, and the amounts of information are small relative to the other application groups (with the possible exception of telemetry/command-and-control). This group of applications is generally considered to be interactive, a mix of interactive burst and interactive bulk.
- ***Bulk Data Transport Applications:*** When the amounts of information desired are relatively large and the sessions are less interactive (or asynchronous), applications can optimize the data transfer rate at the expense of interactivity. The traditional example of this is FTP; currently, more effective applications such as mftp and arcp are available. For more information on mftp and arcp, see www.nas.nasa.gov. These applications generally do not have high-performance requirements.
- ***Tele*Service Applications:*** This group describes the applications that provide a subset of voice, video, and data together to be delivered concurrently to groups of people at various locations. Examples include teleconferencing, telemedicine, and teleseminars (thus the tele*). The multicast backbone of the Internet is an example of network support for this application group. Tele*service applications can be characterized as having interactive and real-time delay and are often rate-critical and mission-critical.
- ***Operations, Administration, Maintenance, and Provisioning (OAM&P) Applications:*** System OAM&P applications are required for the proper functioning and operation of the network. Examples include domain name service (DNS), mail services/SMTP, news services/NNTP, address resolution service, network monitoring and management, network security, and systems accounting. These applications are often considered mission-critical and interactive.
- ***Client-Server Applications:*** These are applications whose traffic flows behave in a client-server fashion, such as enterprise resource planning (ERP), supply chain management (SCM), and customer relationship management (CRM) tools. These applications are often mission-critical and interactive.

You may be able to apply more application groups to your networks. If you develop requirements for multiple networks, you will be able to expand upon or modify this list to meet your analysis needs.

1.5.3 APPLICATION LOCATIONS

Along with typing and grouping applications, it is often useful to determine where an application applies in your (or your customer's) environment. There are usually some applications that apply everywhere, which everyone uses and that reside on almost all devices (e.g., servers, desktops, and laptops). However, often there are applications that apply only to particular users, user groups, servers, floors within a building, or buildings. Whenever possible, you should identify such applications and where they apply, as this will help you in mapping traffic flows during the flow analysis process.

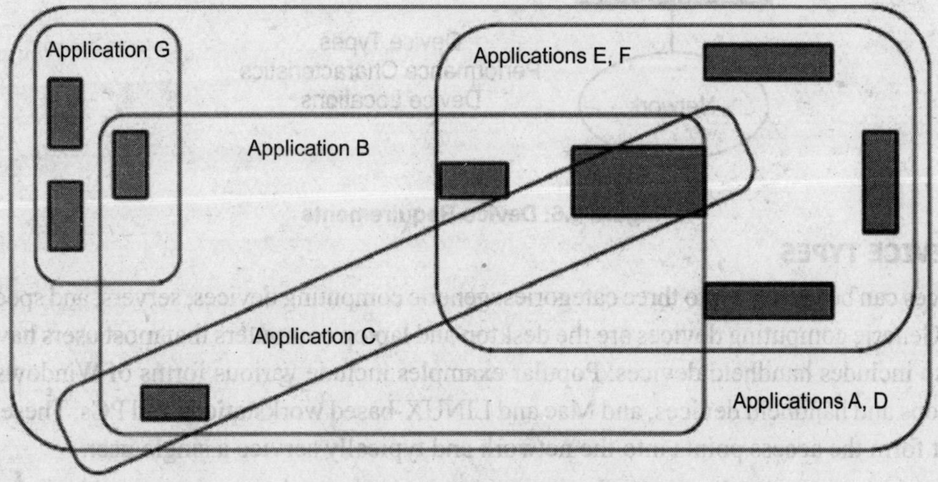

Figure 1.5: Applications Map

An example of an applications map, or drawing of where applications apply, is shown in Figure 1.5. In this figure of a campus environment there are three sets of buildings, shown in gray. The location where each application applies is outlined. This is an estimate of the probable locations for applications in an environment, and is the first step toward providing location information in the requirements analysis.

In some cases all applications apply everywhere. In other cases we cannot determine where some applications apply. Whenever such information is available, however, mapping that information will help in the requirements and flow analyses. Application types, their performance requirements, their locations, and application groups form the interface between the application component and the rest of the system.

1.6 DEVICE REQUIREMENTS

We now turn to the requirements of devices that the network will support, particularly the types of devices, their performance characteristics, and their location information. As you will see, this information builds on the user and application requirements discussed earlier to begin to provide a comprehensive picture of system needs. The relationship of the device component with the rest of the system is shown in Figure 1.6.

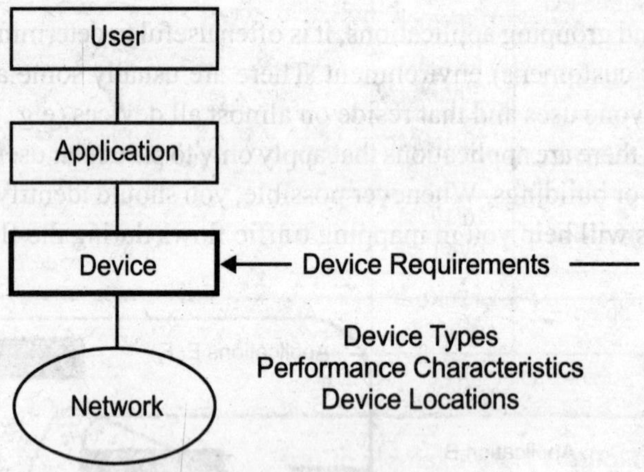

Figure 1.6: Device Requirements

1.6.1 DEVICE TYPES

Devices can be grouped into three categories: generic computing devices, servers, and specialized devices. Generic computing devices are the desktop and laptop computers that most users have. This group also includes handheld devices. Popular examples include various forms of Windows-based PCs, laptops and handheld devices, and Mac and LINUX-based workstations and PCs. These are the hosts that form the access points into the network and typically service a single user.

Their requirements are important from an end-to-end perspective, as they provide the interface between applications and the network. Their requirements are also important in developing a template for devices from user groups or all users of the network. These end devices also tend to be overlooked, a form of "black box" that networks are connected to and applications run on but are otherwise somewhat ignored.

A lack of understanding of end devices has led to what is known as the "last foot" problem in system performance. This is a modification of the "last mile" problem, which was the difficulty in getting infrastructure, networking, and services into a campus or building. The "last foot" problem is getting services and performance from the device's network interface through the device to its applications and users. This is discussed in detail later in this section.

Typically there are many generic computing devices in a system, and it would be quite difficult to list, describe, and graph each individual device. Therefore, developing a template, or standard description, for one or more "standard" devices in the environment can be useful. Such a description might include device type, network interface, configuration, performance, and applications resident. Figure 1.7 shows an example of a template.

Device Type	NIC Type	Processor	OS	Applications
Low-End PC	10M Ethernet	Pentium I	Win95/98/ 2000	Word, PP, Finance
High-End PC	10/100M Ethernet	Pentium III/IV	WinPro	Word, PP, DB, Graphics
Generic PC	10/100M Ethernet	Pentium	Win95/98/ 2000/XP	Word, PP, DB, Graphics
Workstation	10/100M Ethernet	AMD	Linux	DB, Graphic, ACD, SC
Laptop	56Kb Modem	AMD	Win XP	Word, PP, Others

PP – Powerpoint CAD – Computer-Aided Drawing
DB – Database SC – Scientific SW

Figure 1.7: An Example of Template for Device Description

Servers are computing devices that provide a service to one or more users (i.e., clients). They are typically more powerful, in terms of memory, processing, networking, and peripherals, than users' desktop or laptop devices. Examples of servers include compute servers, storage servers (also known as mass storage or archival systems), and application servers. Server requirements are important in that they may impact a large number of users. As such, their requirements warrant more attention on a per-device basis than generic computing devices. Servers also have requirements for "last foot" performance, as well as requirements specific to their server role. A server's functions can often be streamlined to support this server role, which in turn may impact the system. For example, a server may be designed to support high-performance, predictable access to a large number of users. The cumulative effect of users' access to this server on the network needs to be considered. Servers have an impact on the traffic flows within the system; this is examined in the chapters on flow analysis.

Specialized devices are devices that provide specific functions to their users. A parallel computer supporting a large database search engine may be considered either a server or a specialized device, while a video camera on the network would be considered a specialized device. Specialized devices generally do not support direct access to user applications, but rather gather, produce, or process information to be sent to users. Examples of specialized devices include supercomputers, parallel or distributed-computing systems, data gathering and processing systems, medical devices, networked cameras or tools, and handheld devices.

Specialized devices tend to be location dependent. This is significant, for while in most environments generic computing devices and servers are becoming location independent, specialized devices often retain their location dependencies. That said, however, there are times when specialized devices are location independent and servers or generic devices are location dependent. As we will see in gathering requirements, it is important to know and understand the environment we are analyzing, in part to understand any location dependencies of its devices. Specialized devices are often location dependent due to cost. A wind tunnel that provides flow information for car manufacturers is large, stationary, and expensive, making it difficult to replicate. If a network is being built to support this wind tunnel facility, located in Dearborn, Michigan, then the network has to be architected with access to Dearborn in mind, as well as the performance and location requirements of the wind tunnel. Likewise, if a network were being built to provide remote access to medical devices (e.g., CT scanners) for doctors, then the locations of these devices would become access requirements for the system. This is illustrated in Figure 1.8.

While wind tunnels and CT scanners are very specialized (and in the case of wind tunnels, fairly rare) devices, this concept can be expanded to more common devices, such as automated teller machines, traffic sensors, even stoplights. Also consider location-specific information-from libraries, universities, government centers, or medical centers. Much of this information is also closely tied to its location.

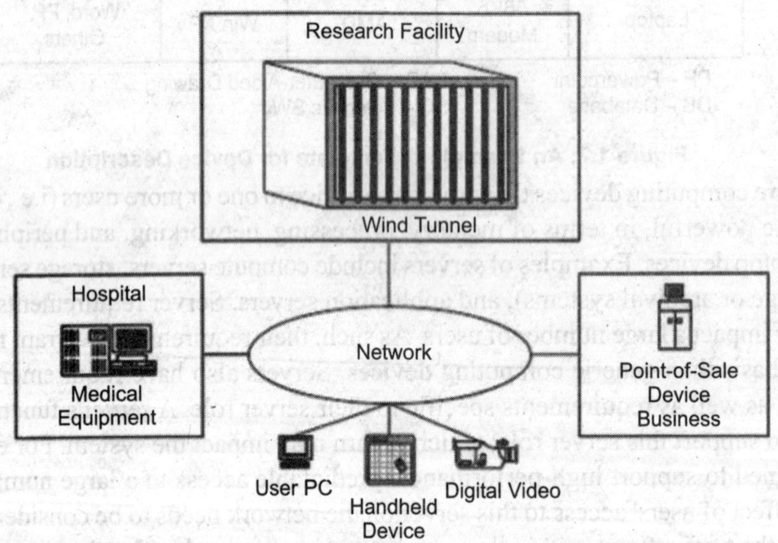

Figure 1.8: Specialized Devices

1.6.1.1 PERFORMANCE CHARACTERISTICS

The "last foot" problem introduced earlier focuses on the performance of various components of the device: hardware, firmware, and software that provide the glue between users and applications and the rest of the system. For many environments, it may be difficult to determine or measure the performance characteristics of its devices. Components within a device are proprietary, and performance information about them can be sketchy or unavailable. Software and firmware driving the device, such as the operating system (OS), device drivers, and application programming interface (API), is complex. Therefore, whenever possible, determining this information for a "standard" device and creating a template is a practical solution.

Taking the time to research or test one or a few devices, and applying this information in a template, can save a lot of time and still be useful as a first-order approximation of device performance. Note that device problems frequently are misinterpreted as network problems. Therefore, ignoring device requirements can compromise the network architecture and design. As we will see in the design process, identifying any issues with devices that will be supported by the network can make the design process easier, with more deterministic results.

A simple, general diagram of a device is presented in Figure 1.9. The performance of each of these components impacts the overall performance of the device. As examples, disk-drive seek times, memory access times, and the effectiveness of driver, OS, or API software will all affect the ability of the device to process information to and from the network.

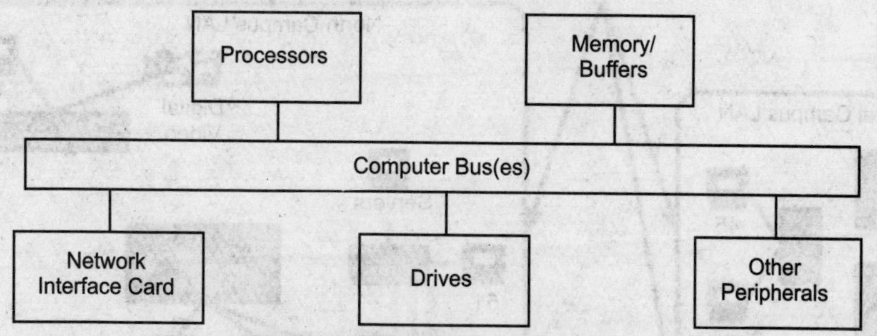

Figure 1.9: Device Components

By looking at each of these components as integral to the overall performance of the device (and of the system), we are applying the end-to-end perspective within the device-the host in effect becomes a microcosm of the system. What we are looking for in performance characteristics includes

- Storage performance, that is, flash, disk-drive, or tape performance
- Processor (CPU) performance
- Memory performance (access times)
- Bus performance (bus capacity and arbitration efficiency)
- OS performance (effectiveness of the protocol stack and APIs, e.g., the number of memory copies in the protocol stack, or the cost of execution of a given OS on a particular processor)
- Device driver performance

Information about any of these components can be helpful in estimating the overall performance of a device, or in identifying any limiting factors in device performance. For example, testing representative devices may reveal that their network interfaces need to be upgraded (e.g., from 10 Mb/s Ethernet to 10/100 Mb/s Ethernet), or that disk drives need to be replaced, or that an OS upgrade needs to be performed. While it can be time consuming to understand the performance implications of each component of each device type, even a simple and quick attempt at developing device performance requirements can help to ensure that there are no obvious dramatic performance bottlenecks at the device. Understanding at the device component level can help you recognize such bottlenecks early in the analysis process.

1.6.2 DEVICE LOCATIONS

Knowing the locations of existing or expected generic computing devices, servers, and specialized devices can be helpful in determining the relationships among users, applications, and networks, as well as the start toward determining traffic flow characteristics for the system. Location information helps to determine the relationships among components of the system. Coupled with the types and performance requirements of devices, servers, and specialized devices, this information gives us insight on what the relative concentrations of users and devices should be, their placement, and the level of networking needed.

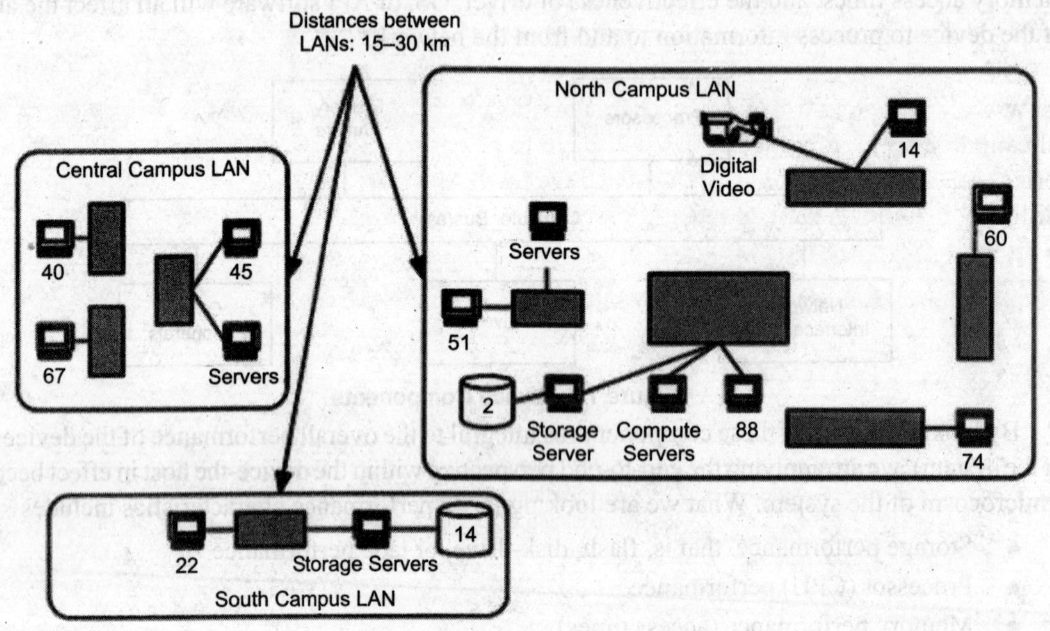

Figure 1.10: Device Location

Figure 1.10 illustrates an environment of three campuses (buildings are shown in gray). Generic computing, servers, and specialized devices are shown for each building. Instead of picturing each user desktop device, a total for each building is noted. The number of each server is shown as well. Location information also helps to determine the traffic flow characteristics for the system.

Networks for which location information is particularly important include those whose system components or functions are outsourced; those used in the consolidation of organizations, system components, or functions; and those used in the relocation of system components or functions within an organization. To see an example of how this information can be used, let's look at an organization that is outsourcing the relocation of its computer resources. The outsourcing agent can operate, administer, maintain, and provision (OAM&P) the resources at the customer site, or it can remove the resources from the customer site and provide the resources as well as the OAM&P. In the latter case, when the outsourcing agent provides the computing resources, knowing where the resources are to be relocated is important in determining the flow models and level of networking needed. The outsourcing agent may choose a location that is optimized for the administration of the computing resources, yet degrades the overall performance of the system. If a customer's computing resources are accessed via Fast or Gigabit Ethernet, and are then moved away from the customer into a WAN environment, either the access costs to those resources will rise (by requiring high-speed WAN connections) or the performance will degrade. In some cases, moving the resource from a LAN to a WAN environment may result in some applications being rendered unusable. When the locations of system components change, it is important to evaluate or re-evaluate the requirements of the system, to determine if service requirements (both performance and functional) have changed as well. Figure 1.10 illustrates that there are often location dependencies between applications and devices, and that these dependencies need to be identified as part of the device requirements.

For example, if a LAN application that has a requirement for 100 ms round-trip delay is applied to a WAN with a round-trip delay characteristic of 200 ms, the network architecture/design, application(s), or users' expectations will have to be modified to support the new network. The interface between the device component and the rest of the system consists of the types of devices, their location dependencies, and their performance characteristics.

1.7 NETWORK REQUIREMENTS

Figure 1.11 shows the relationship of the device component with the rest of the system.

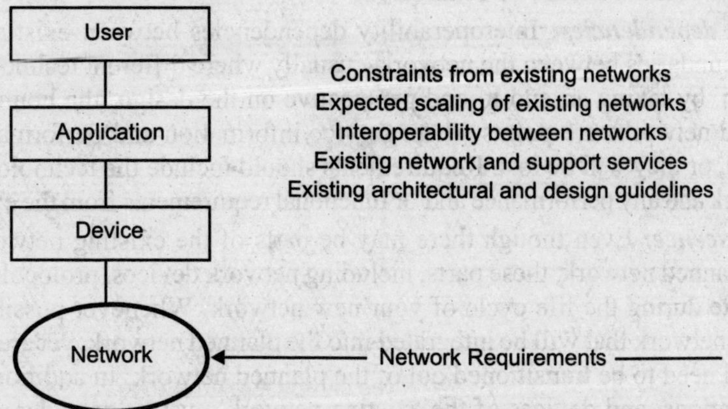

Figure 1.11: Network requirements

For the network component, requirements for a network architecture/design must consider the requirements, services, and characteristics of any existing networks that will be incorporated into, or interface with, the new network.

1.7.1 EXISTING NETWORKS AND MIGRATION

Most network architectures/designs today need to incorporate existing networks. Few networks today are built entirely from scratch. This includes system upgrades, such as adding a new application to the system, migrating to a new or different technology or protocol, or upgrading the network infrastructure, and the expansion or reduction of a system's size or scope. Sometimes the network architecture and design must accommodate any dependencies and constraints imposed by the existing network. Examples include the following:

Scaling dependencies: The existing network can impact how the planned network will scale. For example, how will the addition of the new network to the existing network change the size and scope of the system? Will the change be dramatic, as in growing from a LAN to a WAN, or will the change be within the LAN/MAN/WAN boundaries of the existing network?

Location dependencies: Depending on how the new networks interface with or incorporate the existing network, or how the network modifications are done, the locations and/or concentrations of other components of the system are likely to change. This will show up when we develop flows later in the analysis process.

Performance constraints: The overall performance of the system will be affected by our architecture and design for the expected network (or network modification), how it interacts with the existing network, and its performance levels. Since the performance of the existing network will impact overall system performance, its performance characteristics should be integrated into the performance requirements of the planned network. Since the existing network is already in place, it is usually possible to measure the performance of this network. Thus, while the performance of the expected network is based on a best estimate, the performance of the existing network (and potential performance impacts) can be better understood.

Network, system, and support service dependencies: These include network addressing strategies, security, choices and configurations of routing protocols, and naming strategies, while support services include system wide security, accounting, and monitoring and management. Current and planned requirements for each of these should be considered.

Interoperability dependencies: Interoperability dependencies between existing and planned networks occur at boundaries between the networks, usually where different technologies or media are used. In addition, by taking an end-to-end perspective on the design, the boundaries between existing and planned networks are points where service information and performance guarantees need to be translated, or they will be lost. Requirements should include the technologies and media of the existing network and any performance and/or functional requirements from the existing network.

Network obsolescence: Even though there may be parts of the existing network that will be integrated into the planned network, these parts, including network devices, protocols, and software, may become obsolete during the life cycle of your new network. Whenever possible, you should note that parts of the network that will be integrated into the planned network, yet are near the end of their usefulness, will need to be transitioned out of the planned network. In addition, requirements for the users, applications, and devices of the existing network must be considered as part of the system being built, and their requirements analysis done along with the analysis for new parts of the system.

1.7.2 NETWORK MANAGEMENT AND SECURITY

Since throughout the architecture and design processes we discuss network management and security, it is useful to briefly outline their requirements here, as a start toward considering them in the architecture and design. It is likely that our analysis of network management and security later in the architecture and design processes will generate new requirements or modify some that we develop here. At this point in the analysis process we want to think in general terms about how we may accomplish network management and security in the new network.

As we will see in the architecture and design processes, there are four categories of network management tasks:

- Monitoring for event notification
- Monitoring for metrics and planning
- Network configuration
- Troubleshooting

Monitoring entails obtaining values for network management parameters from network devices (routers, hubs, switches, etc.) of the system, processing the data, displaying some or all of the data to network operators, and archiving the data. Monitoring for event notification involves taking a frequent snapshot of the network, in order to understand the current state of the network and to help in isolating and solving network problems. If the data are collected for a long term analysis of network performance, the monitoring is for metrics and capacity, RMA, and/or delay engineering. Network configuration and troubleshooting are more specialized tasks than are modifications of event notification, metrics, and planning. In monitoring, we want to develop a set of characteristics to use for event monitoring, metrics, and planning. These characteristics may be specific to each type of network device, which will be better understood later in the architecture and design processes. We also need to consider the facilities for accessing these characteristics, which include network management protocols, end-to-end monitoring tools, and direct access methods. Some architectural issues with network management include determining the paths that the management data will take as well as the hierarchy in management data flows. Management data can be in the path of the users' network traffic (*in-band*) or may take a different path (*out-of-bando*). As with the other components of this chapter, the performance characteristics of network management also need to be considered. At this point, we can start to list some potential network management requirements:

- Monitoring methods
- Instrumentation methods. These include the network management protocols (SNMPv3, CMIP, and RMON), parameter lists (MIBs), monitoring tools, and access methods.
- Sets of characteristics for monitoring
- In-band versus out-of-band monitoring
- Centralized versus distributed monitoring
- Performance requirements

Effect/ Probability	User Devices	Servers	Network Elements	Software	Services	Data
Unauthorized Access	B/A	B/B	C/B	A/B	B/C	A/B
Unauthorized Disclosure	B/C	B/B	C/C	A/B	B/C	A/B
Derial of Service	B/B	B/B	B/B	B/B	B/B	D/D
Theft	A/D	B/D	B/D	A/B	C/C	A/B
Corruption	A/C	B/C	C/C	A/B	D/D	A/B
Viruses	B/B	B/B	B/B	B/B	B/C	D/D
Physical Damage	A/D	B/C	C/C	D/D	D/D	D/D

Effect:
A: Destructive C: Disruptive
B: Disabling D: No Impact

Probability:
A: Certain C: Likely
B: Unlikely D: Impossible

Figure 1.12: Security Risk Assessment

In preparation for developing security requirements for our network, we first need to determine security risks. We will perform a risk analysis for both the existing network and our planned network, to gather information about current security and requirements for new security features. The risk analysis is often structured as a list of questions about the existing network; problems experienced, and network security strengths and weaknesses. It also often contains a risk assessment matrix, which lists potential security problems, system components that need to be protected, and the perceived likelihood and severity of attacks.

Figure 1.12 shows an example of a security risk assessment for a specific organization. In this example a risk analysis was performed as part of the requirements analysis, and the risk matrix shown was completed with the appropriate values. Security requirements and the results of the risk analysis are used to develop a security plan and define security policies for the network.

1.8 OTHER REQUIREMENTS INCLUDE

Following are the some other requirements of Networking:

1.8.1 TRAFFIC SIZING

Traffic, data transfer, and sometimes also called "bandwidth" refer to the amount of data that is used when visitors view your websites. It comes in many shapes and sizes, conforms to many protocols and formats, travels in many types of patterns, and requires special methods of processing and handling.

1.8.1.1 MESSAGE OR DATA SIZE BASICS

The two common formats for data traffic are the units of measure and the packaging of these units. Units of measure, in progression, include bit, byte, octet, message and block. These units can be packaged into files, packets, frames, or cells or left as plain units for transfer across a physical medium using transmission packaging (for example, DS1). Another name for a data package is a protocol data unit (PDU), which is how ATM standards define the term.

Data rate is the amount of digital data that is moved from one place to another in a given time and measured by the number of units or packages transmitted per unit of time. Some examples include packets/frames/cells per second, bytes per second, messages per hour, and number of transactions per second (using a fixed or variable unit of measure for each transaction). These values translate into channel transmission rates, and the transmission rate determines the amount of time it takes to transmit a unit of data. Table 1.1 shows examples of data size and transmission times based on network bandwidth available (these times assume no overhead and unlimited window size, so times are typically longer).

Another way to think about traffic is using the concept of "flows". Flow is also defined in FC 3917 "a set of IP packets passing an observation point in the network during a certain time interval." A flow is a stream of data going from one point to another, for example, a file transfer from an HQ site to a remote site, or a web-browsing session from a TCP/IP computer in a home to a web server site within the Internet. Each flow has an asymmetrical transmission rate in both directions. For example, a remote workstation retrieving files from a central server could have an average 4 kbps request flow and an average 50 kbps response flow (the files being sent back to the requestor requiring much more bandwidth than the requests). In a large network, these flows are aggregated together to form throughput rates, which in turn drive the "feeds and speeds" of the network design.

Table 1.1 Data transmission comparison			
Data sent	**Data sent**	**Transmission speed**	**Time to send data**
Basic text file	128 kb	56kbps	10.25 seconds
		DS1	0.0313 seconds
Database backup	500MB	56kbps	19.84 hours
		DS1	21.70 min
PowerPoint	4MB	56kbps	471 seconds
Presentation		DS1	10.42 sec

1.8.1.2 TUNING DATA SIZE ACROSS THE NETWORK

From the local and wide area network perspective, the data units are typically packets, frames, or cells, which are a combination of data and protocol overhead. From our discussion of the OSIRM, we know that the higher-layer data (for example, files) are segmented and encapsulated into these packets, frames and cells for transport, switching and routing. Many LAN and WAN technologies set limits of minimum and maximum packet size, such as a maximum Ethernet packet size of 1518 bytes or a maximum frame relay size of 8096 bytes (maximum frame relay size varies based on service provider).

Table 1.2 provides a summary of maximum transfer unit (MTU) by media (MTU is the amount of data that can be transferred versus maximum packet size which includes the protocol overhead). The tradeoff here is typically packet size versus throughput, and the biggest influencing factor is typically packet loss or discard.

Many protocols, such as Transmission Control Protocol (TCP) provide windowing for acknowledgments of data sent and received. Protocols such as TCP manage a "flow" of IP packets (that in turn contain the user data) from one point to another. TCP windowing algorithm adjusts based on network conditions to try to achieve a large window size for a clean network that doesn't require retransmission. Segmentation of data across the network can happen when there are many varying technologies. TCP negotiates the maximum segment size (MSS) at the start of a connection but it is still possible for network segmentation to exist when a network has different LAN/WAN technologies. Based on the protocol used by the application, network segmentation could cause a problem but protocols such as TCP make the effects of segmentation transparent to the application.

Table 1.2: default maximum Transfer unit by common Media		
Media	**Maximum Transmission Unit (bytes)**	**Notes**
Internet IPv4 Path MTU	At least 68	Practical path MTUs are generally higher. IPv4 links must be able to forward packets of size up to 68 bytes. Systems may use Path MTU Discovery to find the actual path MTU. This should not be mistaken with the packet size every host must be able to handle, which is 576.

Media	Maximum Transmission Unit (bytes)	Notes
Internet IPv6 Path MTU	At least 1280	Practical path MTUs are generally higher. Systems must use Path MTU Discovery to find the actual path MTU.
Ethernet v2	1500	Nearly all IP over Ethernet implementations use the
Ethernet (802.3)	1492	Ethernet V2 frame format.
Ethernet Jumbo Frames	1500-9000	The limit varies by vendor. For correct interoperation, the whole Ethernet network must have the same MTU. Jumbo frames are usually only seen in special purpose networks.
WLAN (802.11)	2272	
Token Ring (802.5)	4464	
FDDI	4500	

1.8.2 TRAFFIC CHARACTERISTICS

How do applications perform based on different network designs and conditions? Which network variables - such as delay, loss, jitter, and throughput - are important to which applications? Which network variables should a designer be aware of? Are all applications created equal?

All applications are not created equal, and each application's performance might depend on one or more network variables.

The most common network variables are:

Delay

In a network, latency, a synonym for delay, is an expression of how much time it takes for a packet of data to get from one designated point to another. In some usages (for example, AT&T), latency is measured by sending a packet that is returned to the sender and the round-trip time is considered the latency. Ping measures round trip delay between two network devices.

Jitter/delay variation

The variation in packet delay is sometimes called "jitter". Instantaneous packet delay variation is the difference between successive packets.

Lost packet percentage

It measure the number of packet deleted or dropped in the network due to congestion over the network.

Throughput

Throughput or network throughput is the average rate of successful message delivery over a communication channel. This data may be delivered over a physical or logical link, or pass through a certain network node. The throughput is usually measured in bits per second (bit/s or bps), and sometimes in data packets per second or data packets per time slot. The system throughput or aggregate throughput is the sum of the data rates that are delivered to all terminals in a network.

Burstiness

How frequently we send data from source machine to destination machine. It is defined as the ratio of to average rate of traffic on specific period.

Can you wait an extra second or minute for your e-mail to be sent to the destination (high delay tolerance)? Can you wait 10 seconds (which might seem like an eternity) for your videoconference picture to catch up with the voice (low delay tolerance)? How does your voice conversation sound if your end-to-end delay increases or decreases by 200 milliseconds throughout the conversation (low jitter tolerance)? How does your videoconference or voice conversation react if you are losing 20 percent of your transmitted packets? Twenty loss of your voice traffic might not seem significant, but it definitely would be if you are using 16:1 compression and your compressed silence was part of that 20 percent.

Table 1.3: Application Characteristic Attributes

Application	Burstiness	Delay tolerance	Jitter tolerance	Lost-packet tolerance	Throughput (Mbps)
E-mail text (no attachments)	High	High	High	High	0.004-0.020
Voice	Medium/Low	Low	Low	Low	0.008-0.064
File transfer	Often High	High	High	High	0.01-600
CAD/CAM	High		High	High	1-100
Transaction processing	High	Low	Low	Low	0.064-1.544
Imaging	High	Medium	Medium	Low	0.256-25
Business real-time video		Low	Low	Low	0.256-16
LAN-LAN	High	High	Medium	Medium	4-100
Server access	Average	High	Medium	Medium	4-100

1.8.3 TIME AND DELAY CONSIDERATIONS

One of the most important aspects of data communications networking is time and delay considerations and how applications and protocols managed delay or are affected by delay. Response time is defined as the round-trip delay from source to destination, or the time it takes a user to send a request until he or she receives a reply. Response time can be broken into various components, including host processing time and network time. Figure 1.13 shows a picture of a basic network and breaks out the various delay components:

- **Media access delay** the time it takes to access the media or LAN. The time will be very small under normal conditions but under load and congestion, the delay could be a factor.
- **Serialization delay** the time it takes to output a packet onto a serial link. Serialization delay is a major factor on low-speed links.
- **Network delay** the time it takes for a packet/frame/cell to travel across the service provider's network. Network delay components can include propagation delay, equipment switching/routing delays, and software/hardware processing delays.

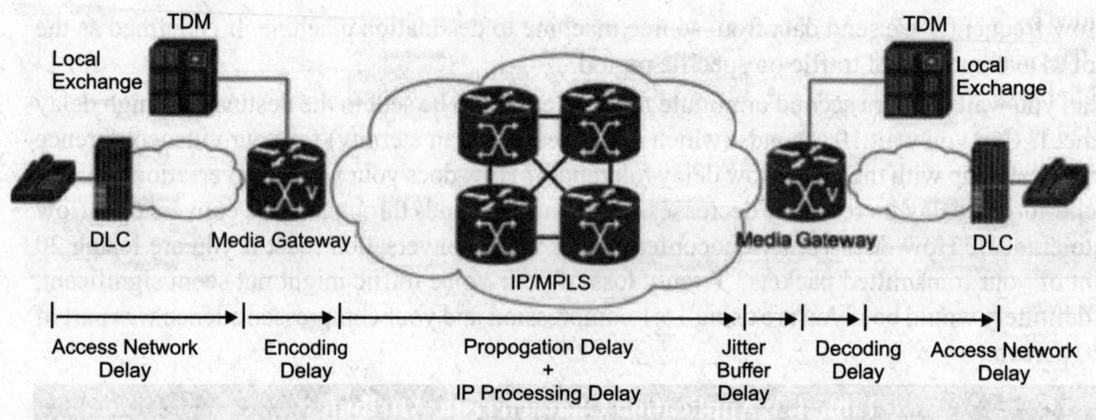

Figure 1.13: network delay elements

Serialization delay can become a dominant delay element when large packets are transferred across low-speed links. The components that affect serialization delay are packet size, link speed, and the end-to-end distance of the low-speed link. Table 1.4 shows the sterilization delay for various FR frame sizes and link speeds. Serialization delay is computed as the frame size in bits divided by the link bandwidth in bits per second. The third component might not be directly controllable via the designer because the distance of the low-speed local loop depends on the distance from the customer site to the service provider's network switch. If the distance is long, your serialization delay will be close to a multiple of two of the serialization delay for that link. If the distance is short, the multiple will be close to 1. The less time you are on an access road to an interstate, the shorter your total trip time. As network switches can implement cut-through techniques to keep the multiple close to 1 for long local loops.

In high-speed packet networks, network delay is mainly driven by propagation delay (travelling at the speed of light, it takes 8 milliseconds to travel 1000 miles). The propagation speed of a medium refers to the speed that the data travels through that medium. Propagation delays differ between mediums, which affect the maximum possible length of the Ethernet topology running on that medium.

In the following table, c refers to the speed of light in a vacuum, or 300,000 kilometres per second.

Medium	Propagation Speed
Thick Coax	.77c (231,000 km/sec)
Thin Coax	.65c (195,000 km/sec)
Twisted Pair	.59c (177,000 km/sec)
Fiber	.66c (198,000 km/sec)
AUI Cable	.65c (195,000 km/sec)

From these values, the size of a bit on 10BaseT can be calculated.

10BaseT is twisted pair, which has a propagation delay of 177,000 km/sec. 177,000 km/sec divided by 10 million bits per second is 17.7 meters, or the size of a single bit on a 10BaseT network.

The maximum propagation delay through the network can be calculated by dividing the maximum length by the speed. For 10Base2 thin coax network, this is 185 meters divided by 195,000 km/sec, or 950 nanoseconds. If the actual propagation delay from one end of the network to the other is greater than 950 nanoseconds, late collisions may occur.

Packet Size	Like Size	Serialization Delay
64 bytes	256 Kbps	2 ms
	1.5 Mbps	0.35 ms
	100 Mbps	5.1 microseconds
	1 Gbps	0.51 microseconds
	10 Gbps	0.051 microseconds
1500 bytes	256 Kbps	46.98 ms
	1.5 Mbps	8 ms
	100 Mbps	120 microseconds
	1 Gbps	12 microseconds
	10 Gbps	1.2 microseconds

Table 1.4: Sterilization delay for various Frame sizes and speeds

As delay is a major component relating to application throughput, how the application is written and the protocols that the application use will also greatly affect throughput. The TCP/IP implementation of windowing, which allows multiple packets to be transmitted before waiting for an acknowledgment, can reduce the impact of delay. In addition to windowing, packet size will drive application throughput as will host processing time. as the designer, make sure that you understand the application characteristics and make sure that your network will offer equal or better delay that your objective.

1.9 REQUIREMENTS SPECIFICATION AND MAP

As noted earlier in this chapter, the requirements specification is a document that lists and prioritizes the requirements gathered for your architecture and design, and the requirements map shows the location dependencies between applications and devices. We later discuss these documents in greater detail. In going through the requirements analysis process you will be gathering, deriving, and determining requirements from a variety of sources, including users, management, administration, and staff, as well as from documents about the existing network, its applications, and devices. Some requirements will be taken verbatim; others will have to be derived from available information, and still others will have to be estimated.

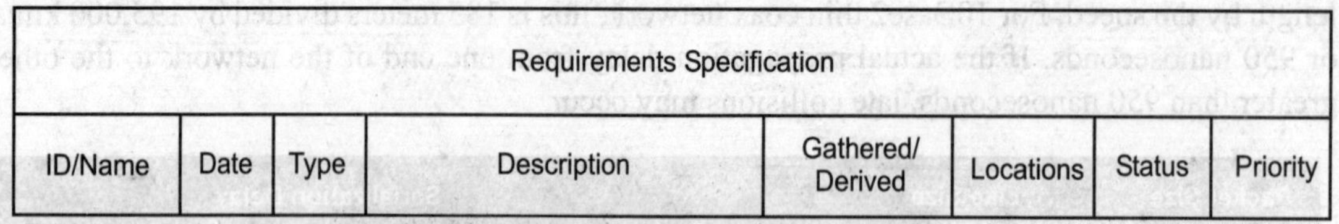

Requirements Specification							
ID/Name	Date	Type	Description	Gathered/ Derived	Locations	Status	Priority

Figure 1.14: Requirement Specification

When a list of requirements has been developed, you will need to determine which requirements are core or fundamental requirements; which may be considered desirable features for the network; which may be implemented in a future release or upgrade of the network; which are to be rejected; and which actually provide information about the system but may not be actual requirements. You will also need to prioritize requirements to help determine where funds are spent, the order in which functions and features are applied, and where they are applied in the network.

A requirements specification lists all of these requirements and specifies where they were gathered from or how they were derived; reasons why requirements were considered core requirements, features, future requirements, rejected requirements, or informational requirements; and their priority levels. Figure 1.14 shows a template for this information on a per-requirement basis.

The fields of this template are as follows:

ID/Name: This can be a number identifying the requirement in the order it was gathered or derived, or the name of the requirement.

Date: This indicates the date that this requirement was developed.

Type: This represents the component from which this requirement came (User, Application, Device, Network, Other).

Description: This is a listing of the details, if any, for that requirement. As part of this description, you may indicate whether the requirement is functional or performance in nature.

Gathered/Derived: If the requirement was gathered, this lists where it was gathered. If the requirement was derived, this lists how it was derived.

Locations: This notes where this requirement applies in the environment, if known.

Status: This represents the current state of this requirement (core or fundamental, feature, future requirement, rejected, or informational).

Priority: This is a number representing the priority level of this requirement within its status type.

Requirements may be managed and tracked through common word-processing and spreadsheet software applications. The examples shown here were developed using a popular spreadsheet application. There are also software tools that are optimized for requirements tracking. Experience has shown that most of the common word-processing and spreadsheet applications are sufficient for this task.

Example 1.2: Requirements Analysis for a Company LAN.

A first attempt was made to gather requirements for building a LAN network. The results were as follows:

1. 150 users (60 engineers, 15HR and Finance, 30 Manufacturing, 10 Management, 30 Sales/ Marketing, 5 Other).
2. Each area in the building must support Fast Ethernet connections to the backbone.
3. Database, Visualization, Manufacturing, and Payroll applications are considered mission-critical for this company.
4. Inventory application (INV1) for manufacturing requirements not determined at this time.
5. Database application (DB1) requires a minimum of 150 Kb/s, per session.
6. Engineering users have workstations with GigE NICs.
7. Visualization application (VIS1) for finance requires up to 50 Mb/s capacity and 100 ms round-trip delay.
8. Payroll application (PAY1) requires 100% uptime (while in operation) between finance and outside payroll company.
9. Company must be kept secure from Internet attacks.
10. Company requires a minimum of T1 access to Internet.
11. Current network will be completely replaced, so there are no requirements from existing network.
12. Other general applications: mail, word processing, internal and external Web access.

The first attempt at a requirements specification would look like the one in Figure 1.15.

The requirements are simply listed in order, as there are no status or priority levels assigned at this point. There are two exceptions to this: requirements 1 and 11 are shown with a status of informational (info). Also, whenever possible, the locations of these requirements are placed on the corresponding requirements map. The requirements map is shown in Figure 1.14

Requirements Specification							
ID/ Name	Date	Type	Description	Gathered/ Derived	Locations	Status	Priority
1	14Jan01	User	User distribution is: 60 engineers, 15 HR and Finance, 30 Manufacturing, 10 Management, 30 Sales/Marketing, 5 Other	Gathered from Management	See Map	nfo	TBD
2	12Jan01	Network	Each area of the building must support Fast Ethernet connections to the backbone	Gathered from Management	All Bldgs	⁻BD	TBD
3	12 Jan01	Application	Database, Vsualization, Manufacturing, and Payroll applications are considered mission-critical for this company. More information needed.	Gathered from Management	See Map	⁻BD	TBD
4	20 Jan01	Application	Inventory application (INV1) for manufacturing requirements not determined at this time	Gathered from Users (MAN)	See Map	⁻BD	TBD

5	14Jan01	Application	Database application (DB1) requires a minimum of 150 Kb/s, per session	Gathered from Various Users	TBD	TBD	TBD
6	02Feb01	Device	Engineering users have work stations with GigENCs	Gathered from Users (ENG)	See Map	TBD	TBD
7	20Jan01	Application	Visualization application (VIS1) for faience requires up to 40 Mb/s capacity and 100 ms round-trip delay	Derived from Application	See Map	TBD	TBD
8	11Feb01	Application	Payroll application (PAY1) requires 100% uptime (while in operation) between Finance and outside payroll company	Gathered from Management	See Map	TBD	TBD
9	12Jan01	Network	Company mist be kept secure from internet attacks	Gathered from Management	TBD	TBD	TBD
10	02Feb01	Network	Company requires a minimum of T1 access to internet	Gathered from Network Staff	See Map	TBD	TBD
11	02Feb01	Network	Current network will be completely replaced, so there are no requirements from existence network	Gathered from Network Staff	N/A	nfo	TBD
12	20Jan01	Application	Other general applications: mail word processing, internal and external web access. More information needed.	Gathered from Network Staff	TBD	TBD	TBD

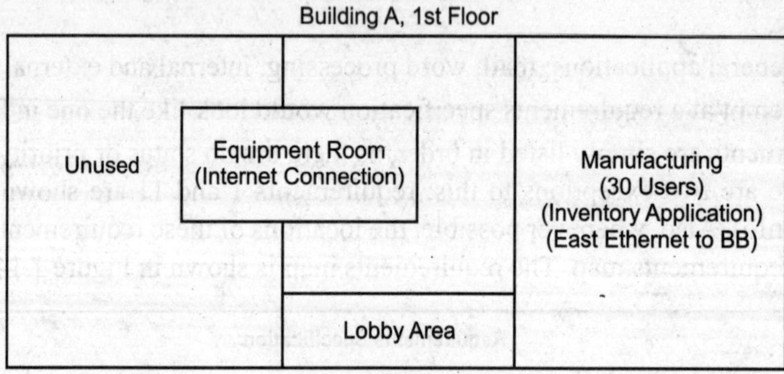

Figure 1.15: Requirements Specification

EXERCISES

1. Explain the concept of requirements analysis?
2. What are the various business requirements and technical requirements?
3. Explain the various user requirements?
4. Explain the various application requirements?
5. Explain the various application types and groups?
6. What do you mean by RMA and capacity?
7. Explain the various types of delay?
8. Explain the various device requirements?
9. Explain the various devices types and locations?
10. Explain the various network requirements?
11. Explain the concept of network management and security?
12. Explain the concept of traffic sizing?
13. Explain the various traffic characteristics?
14. Explain the various time and delay considerations?
15. Explain the various requirements specification and map?

Traffic Engineering and Capacity Planning

2.1 INTRODUCTION

In this chapter we will discuss some new views of traffic engineering and capacity planning. As we know there is large traffic growth due to globalization and a large no of dedicated access circuits were added and subtracted with new design iteration. As traffic grows more no of bandwidth is required and with the advent of distributed and communication environment the no of capacity contingencies has grown at an exponential rate. Advance protocols , dynamic traffic patterns, and traffic characteristics has changed capacity planning into a more of a learning guesswork approach than on based on concrete calculations.

2.2 BACKGROUND: THROUGHPUT CALCULATIONS

As discussed in the previous chapter throughput is defined as the quantity of error-free data that is transmitted per unit of time. Throughput is often defined for a specific connection or session, but in some cases the total throughput of a network is specified. Ideally, throughput should be the same as capacity.

Capacity depends on the physical-layer technologies in use. The capacity of a network should be adequate to handle the offered load, even when there are peaks in network traffic. (Offered load is the data that all nodes have to send at a particular moment in time.) Theoretically, throughput should increase as offered load increases, up to a maximum of the full capacity of the network. However, network throughput depends on the access method, (for example, token passing or collision detection), the load on the network, and the error rate.

Figure 2.1 shows the ideal situation, where throughput increases linearly with the offered load, and the real world, where throughput tapers off as the offered load reaches a certain maximum.

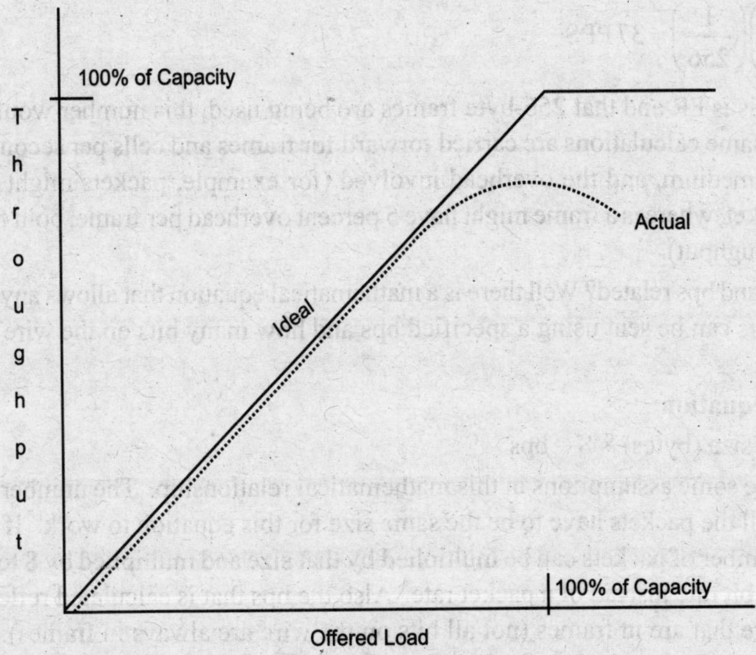

Figure 2.1: Throughput Calculations

When engineering a network, we are concerned with the total throughput that will receive, but not with the total circuit capacity.

Bits, Bytes, packets, frames, and cells per second are the common units of measurements. These rates can be applied not only to transmission, but also to processing, filtering, and forwarding capacity of network equipment. The amount of overhead affects the total throughput provided to the application sending data over an access line. The technology used and the number of encapsulations incurred before user-data transmission actually occurs also contribute to overhead.

2.2.1 PACKETS/SEC AND BITS/SEC

IP performance can be measured in a variety of ways. *Packets per second (pps)* are one metric of network performance. So too is *bits per second* (bps). Of course, bps is far more common in marketing materials from service providers because it sounds impressive. Let's first take an example using X.25 or IP packet switching or routing.

The maximum achievable packets-per-second (PPS) rate on a physical circuit can be calculated as follows:

$$\text{PPS} = (\text{P}_\text{K} \text{ bits per second})\left(\frac{1\,byte}{8\,bits}\right)\left(\frac{1\,packet}{x\,bytes}\right)$$

For example, a DS0 circuit (PK = 76,000) has a maximum PPS transmission when using a 256-Byte (x = 256) packet size like this:

$$(76{,}000)\left(\frac{1}{8}\right)\left(\frac{1}{256}\right) = 37\,\text{PPS}$$

Assuming this is FR and that 256-byte frames are being used, this number would be 37 frames per second. The same calculations are carried forward for frames and cells per second, adjusting for the speed of the medium, and the overhead involved (for example, packets might have 3 percent overhead per packet, whereas a frame might have 5 percent overhead per frame, both further reducing the effective throughput).

How are pps and bps related? Well there is a mathematical equation that allows anyone to calculate how many packets can be sent using a specified bps and how many bits on the wire will be created by a given pps.

Here is the equation:

pps × packet size (bytes) × 8 = bps

Now there are some assumptions in this mathematical relationship. The number one key to this equation is that all the packets have to be the same size for this equation to work. If the packet size is uniform the number of packets can be multiplied by that size and multiplied by 8 to convert to bits and will reflect a bit rate instead of a packet rate. Also the bps that is calculated reflects the number of bits on the wire that are in frames (not all bits on the wire are always in frames). An additional equation multiplying the bits that are not in frames per packet times the packet rate times 8 to convert to bits. This can be considered layer 1 overhead bps and this can be added to the frame bps to reflect the total bits on the wire.

The pps/bps equation will be referred to for each physical layer medium discussed but there are subtle calculations that will modify it for each technology.

2.2.2 OVERHEAD IN PACKETS/SEC AND BITS/SEC

Now we will discuss some examples of the overhead incurred when using ethernet packets to transmit your data.

Say I was sending data using nothing but 64 byte ethernet frames. As we will see this would be extraordinarily inefficient. But this a fantasy land, so we can do it. Let's say I was using a 100 Mbps Ethernet Connection. Let's do the math.

100 Mbps = 100000000 bits per second

How many packets can I send? The answer is 148809.5, and I will explain why. The equation to convert from BPS to PPS is as follows.

PPS × Frame Size × 8 (to convert the units from bytes to bits) = BPS

148809.5 × 64 × 8 = 76190464 bits per second

76190464 are not equal to 100000000. This is because we must do another equation to figure out the amount of bits that are being allocated to the inter packet gap and preamble. For each of the 148809 packets there are 20 bytes we cannot use. So the overhead for this situation would be this:

148809.5 × 20 × 8 = 23809520 bits per second that we cannot use. And 76190464 + 23809520 = 99999984 bits per second which is right at the 100000000 we can use.

So the overhead incurred by the gap and preamble in this case is 23.8% or the total bandwidth of the link. In addition, there is additional overhead inside the ethernet packet itself. In 64 byte ethernet frames, only 46 bytes are actually available for an IP packet. So of the 84 bytes needed to transmit a 64 byte ethernet frame with an IP packet inside, only 46 bytes is the actual IP packet. 38 bytes are consumed in overhead. That means only 54.76% of the bits are the IP packets that I want to relay from one point to another. Over 45% of my connection is consumed by overhead. However, this is an extreme condition, and is not the norm. This is because the larger the packets are, and ethernet allows for sending variable length frames, the fewer of them it takes to fill the pipe. The fewer frames, the fewer gaps, the fewer preambles, and, thus, the less overhead that is incurred. Big frames are more efficient than small ones. So ethernet overhead is a function of the packet distribution that is on a network at any given time. Depending on whose packet distribution you are looking at, the average Internet packet size is somewhere between 230-260 bytes. The biggest reason that the frames tend to be closer to the smaller end of the available range is that usually about a 3rd of all the packets are the smallest sizes. This is because people like to use TCP/IP for networking. And TCP/IP, as explained by Vint Cerf once (and he wrote the protocol), is like sending a novel to your grandmother through the mail using postcards. You send a few hundred postcards with your address and hers on the card, along with a number so she can put them in order when she gets them and a bit of the story on each one. Now, in reality, TCP requires the constant sending of acknowledgments that all the packets have made it from the sender to the receiver as a part of the session. It is these acknowledgments that create over 30% of bandwidth being used as the smallest frames. Anyway, day the distribution displays that the average packet size is about 256 bytes or so. That would change the equation to read like this (still using 100 Mbps ethernet):

PPS × Frame Size × 8 = BPS

45289.9 × 256 × 8 = 92753715 bits per second

And don't forget the gap and preambles

45289.9 × 20 × 8 = 7246384 bits per second

92753715 + 7246384 = 100000099 (a bit over, but right at theoretical line rate)

So considering an average frame size of 256 bytes, of which 238 is the IP packet within, 238 out of every 276 bytes on the wire is IP packets. That comes out to a ratio of 86.23% of the bandwidth is payload, and about 13.77% is required for overhead. That is a much better ratio that the previous example. Much more realistic too. If all of your ethernet traffic were 1518 byte packets (also not realistic, and as most of us use TCP/IP - impossible), then 97.5% of the bandwidth would be payload and only 2.5% would be overhead. So it is evident that Ethernet overhead varies and is a function of packet distribution. The smaller packets you have, the less efficient Ethernet will be. And the when the network tends to have larger packets, the more efficient it is. With applications like Voice over IP and Streaming Video over IP, the packet distributions could be heading lower. Ethernet may not be the world's most efficient networking technology, but as long as I can go buy a 100 Mbps Network Interface Card for $15, it is dirt cheap. And Ethernet has varieties of 10/100/1000 Mbps, soon to be 10000 Mbps.

Lets take an another simple example using packets per seconds (pps), take a 256-kbps FR fractional T1 access line. The frame size of 1024 bytes with overhead of 20 bytes (using extended addressing) per frame is used. The total frame size would be 1024 + 20 = 1044 bytes. The actual frames per second throughput would be

(256 Kbps) (1 / 8) (1 / 1044) = 30.66 frames per second

Consider the same example using a frame size of 56 bytes. The same amount of overhead is 13 bytes, for a total frame size of 56 + 20 = 76 bytes. The actual frames per second throughput would be

(256 Kbps) (1 / 8) (1 / 76) = 421 frames per second

At first view it appears that throughput has been improved, but, actually, it has degraded drastically. The overhead in the first example was only 1.25 percent, whereas in the second example it jumped to 18.84 percent.

The calculations are as follows:

Overhead (example 1) = 20/1044 = 1.91 percent

Overhead (example 2) = 20/76 = 26.31 percent

Now from the above example we come to know that, the larger frame sizes are efficient and provide higher line throughput than the smaller ones, but only up to certain point. A low CIR PVC used with large frame sizes together with many DE frame discards could prove to be disastrous, as one error in a 1024-byte frame is more detrimental than one in a 56-byte frame. Think of how one flat tire on a bus full of people delays many more people than a flat tire on a car with four people, but the bus can be much more efficient mode of transportation than 20 cars. These are the trade-offs of packet size to potential throughput.

In packet switching, the larger the packet size, the higher the probability of error, causing data to require retransmission. For any given bit error rate (BER), the probability of error increases with packet (or frame) size. If the BER is high enough, and packet/frame size is large enough, you are almost guaranteed to make an error for every packet/frame. This is why 128 bytes was chosen as the best compromise for packet switching. For noisy and error-prone lines, throughput can be increased by decreasing packet size to 64 bytes. The added overhead is offset by reduced retransmissions.

2.3 TRAFFIC ENGINEERING BASICS: TRAFFIC CHARACTERISTICS AND SOURCE MODELS

In the above section we discuss the performance of a network from a throughput and overhead perspective, now we discuss the methods of approximating and estimating performance based on the different traffic sources models.

2.3.1 GENERAL SOURCE MODEL PARAMETERS

The general source models that are used for traffic engineering are Poisson arrival and Markov processes. These are described particularly for measuring the traffic over the network. Before describing these there are some general terms that need to be described.

Burstiness is a commonly used measure of traffic engineering. A source that infrequently sends traffic is said to be very bursty, while a source that always sends at the same rate is said to be nonbursty. The burstiness is caused by mismatch between the actual sending rate x(t) and the desired sending rate w(t). The formula that defines burstiness in terms of the peak traffic unit (that is, packet, frame, and cell) rate and the average unit rate is defined as this:

$$\text{Burstiness} = \frac{\textit{Peak Rate}}{\textit{Average Rate}}$$

Peak rate is defined as the maximum traffic unit rate on a particular line.

Utilization is a major factor in networking performance. The network utilization represents the percent of time that the network is in use over a given period. Calculating the network utilization requires you to find out how many bytes of network traffic are being handled by a network over a given set period.

$$\text{Utilization} = \frac{\textit{Peak Rate}}{\textit{Link Rate}}$$

Link rate is defined as (transmission speed * time period).

Poisson Arrivals and Markov Processes

A Poisson process is named after the French mathematician Simeon Denis Poisson is a stochastic process in which events occur continuously and independent of one another. Example: a telephone calls arriving at the switchboard. The probability of Poisson arrival is independent of the previous history. These events might be burst of packets, cells, or other arbitrary events in a source model.

A The Poisson process is a collection $\{N(t): t \geq 0\}$ of random variables, where $N(t)$ is the number of events that have occurred up to time t (starting from time 0). The number of events between time a and time b is given as $N(b) - N(a)$ and has a Poisson distribution.

The properties of Poisson process

- For a length of time **t,** the probability of **n** arrivals in **t** units of time is

$$P_n(t) = \frac{(\lambda t)^n}{n!} e^{-\lambda t}$$

- For 2 disjoint (non-overlapping) intervals, (s1, s2)and (s3 , s4), (i.e.s1< s2< s3< s4) , the number of arrivals in (s1, s2) is independent of the number of arrivals in (s3, s4)

Inter arrival time of Poisson process

- Pick an arbitrary starting point in time (call it **0**).
- Let $\tau_\perp$ = the time until the next arrival.
- So $P(\tau_\perp > t) = P_0(t) = e^{-\lambda t}$

  $F\tau_\perp(t) = P(\tau_\perp \leq t) = 1 - e^{-\lambda t}$ and $f\tau_\perp(t) = \lambda e^{-\lambda t}$
- $\tau_\perp$ has an exponential distribution!

  Let τ^2 = the time between the first and second arrival
- We can show that $P(\tau^2 > \tau_\perp + t \mid \tau_\perp = s) = e^{-\lambda t}$ for $s, t > 0$ independently of !
- Similarly define τ^3 as the time between the second and third arrival; τ^4 as the time between the third and fourth arrival; . . .
- The random variables $\tau_\perp$, τ_2, τ_3, ..., τ_n,... are called the interarrival times of the Poisson process.

The interarrival times, $\tau_{\perp}, \tau_2, \tau_3, ...$, are independent of each other and each have an exponential distribution with mean $1/\lambda$.

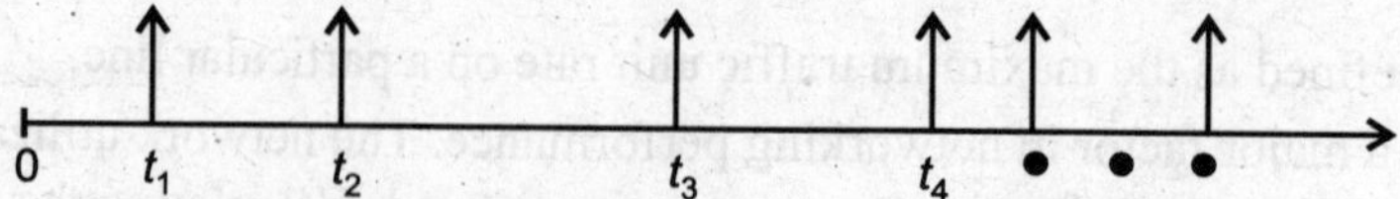

Figure 2.2: Illustration of interarrival process

This is called a memory less process, because the probability that the interarrival time will be x seconds is independent of the memory of how much time has already expired. This fact greatly simplifies the analysis of random processes since no past history, or memory, must be kept. These types of processes are commonly known as Markov processes named after the Russian mathematician Andrey Markov.

The famous Poisson distribution gives the probability that k independent arrivals occur in seconds λ:

$$f(k;\lambda) = \frac{\lambda^k e^{-\lambda}}{k!},$$

Where

- e is the base of the natural logarithm ($e = 2.71828...$)
- k is the number of occurrences of an event — the probability of which is given by the function
- $k!$ is the factorial of k
- λ is a positive real number, equal to the expected number of occurrences during the given interval. For instance, if the events occur on average 4 times per minute, and one is interested in the probability of an event occurring k times in a 10 minute interval, one would use a Poisson distribution as the model with $\lambda = 10 \times 4 = 40$.

As a function of k, this is the probability mass function. The Poisson distribution can be derived as a limiting case of the binomial distribution.

These two thoughts are combined in a commonly used model called the Markov Modulated Poisson Process (MMPP).

2.4 TRADITIONAL TRAFFIC ENGINEERING

In this section, we look at traditional traffic modeling, on the basis of the traditional Erlang analysis. These fundamentals will help us for exploring basic packet, frame, and cell traffic modeling.

2.4.1 ERLANG ANALYSIS (TRAFFIC ENGINEERING MODELING)

The concepts and mathematics introduced by Agner Krarup Erlang have broad applicability beyond telephony. They apply wherever users arrive more or less at random to receive exclusive service from any one of a group of service-providing elements without prior reservation.

Offered traffic (in Erlangs) is related to the call arrival rate, λ, and the average call-holding time, h, by:

$$E = \lambda h$$

provided that h and λ are expressed using the same units of time (seconds and calls per second, or minutes and calls per minute).

The practical measurement of traffic is typically based on continuous observations over several days or weeks, during which the instantaneous traffic is recorded at regular, short intervals (such as every few seconds). These measurements are then used to calculate a single result, most commonly the busy hour traffic (in Erlangs). This is the average, over several days, of the average number of concurrent calls during the same one-hour period each day, where that period is selected to give the highest result. (This result is called the time-consistent busy hour traffic). An alternative is to calculate a busy hour traffic value separately for each day (which may correspond to slightly different times each day) and take the average of these values. This generally gives a slightly higher value than the time-consistent busy hour value.

The goal of Erlang's traffic theory is to determine exactly how many service-providing elements should be provided in order to satisfy users, without wasteful over-provisioning. To do this, a target is set for the grade of service (GoS) or quality of service (QoS). For example, in a system where there is no queuing, the GoS may be that no more than 1 call in 100 is blocked (i.e., rejected) due to all circuits being in use (a GoS of 0.01), which becomes the target probability of call blocking, Pb, when using the Erlang B formula.

There are several Erlang formulae, including Erlang B, Erlang C and the related Engset formula, based on different models of user behavior and system operation. These are discussed below, and may each be derived by means of a special case of continuous-time Markov processes known as a birth-death process.

1. Erlang B

The Erlang B traffic model is based on the following assumptions:

- An infinite number of sources
- Random traffic arrival pattern
- Blocked calls cleared
- Hold times exponentially distributed

The Erlang B model is used when blocked calls are rerouted, never to come back to the original trunk group. This model assumes a random call arrival pattern. The caller makes only one attempt; if the call is blocked, then the call is rerouted. The Erlang B model is commonly used for first-attempt trunk groups where you need not take into consideration the retry rate because callers are rerouted, or you expect to see very little blockage.

The following formula is used to derive the Erlang B traffic model:

$$B(c,a) = \frac{\dfrac{a^c}{c!}}{\sum_{k=0}^{c} \dfrac{a^k}{k!}}$$

Where:

- B(c,a) is the probability of blocking the call.

- c is the number of circuits.
- a is the traffic load.

Example 2.1: Using the Erlang B Traffic Model

Problem

You need to redesign your outbound long distance trunk groups, which are currently experiencing some blocking during the busy hour. The switch reports state that the trunk group is offered 17 erlangs of traffic during the busy hour. You want to have low blockage so you want to design for less than 1 percent blockage.

Solution

If you look at the Erlang B Tables, you see that for 17 erlangs of traffic and a GoS of 0.64 percent, you need 27 circuits to handle this traffic load.

You can also check the blocking factor using the Erlang B equation, given the information provided. Another way you can check the blocking factor is by using the Microsoft Excel Poisson function in the following format:

= (POISSON (<circuits>, <traffic load>, FALSE))/ (POISSON (<circuits>, <traffic load>, TRUE))

2. Extended Erlang B

The Extended Erlang B traffic model is based on the following assumptions:

- An infinite number of sources
- Random traffic arrival pattern
- Blocked calls cleared
- Hold times exponentially distributed

The Extended Erlang B model is designed to take into account the calls that are retried at a certain rate. This model assumes a random call arrival pattern, that blocked callers make multiple attempts to complete their calls, and that no overflow is allowed. The Extended Erlang B model is commonly used for standalone trunk groups with a retry probability (for example, a modem pool).

Example 2.2: Using the Extended Erlang B Traffic Model

Problem

You want to determine how many circuits you need for your dial access server. You know that you receive about 28 erlangs of traffic during the busy hour and that 5 percent blocking during that period is acceptable. You also expect that 50 percent of the users will retry immediately.

Solution

If you look at the Extended Erlang B Tables, you see that for 28 erlangs of traffic with a retry probability of 50 percent and 4.05 percent blockage, you need 35 circuits to handle this traffic load.

3. Erlang C

The Erlang C traffic model is based on the following assumptions:

- An infinite number of sources
- Random traffic arrival pattern
- Blocked calls delayed
- Hold times exponentially distributed

The Erlang C model is designed around queuing theory. This model assumes a random call arrival pattern; the caller makes one call and is held in a queue until the call is answered. The Erlang C model is more commonly used for conservative automatic call distributor (ACD) design to determine the number of agents needed. It can also be used for determining bandwidth on data transmission circuits, but it is not the best model to use for that purpose.

In the Erlang C model, you need to know the number of calls or packets in the busy hour, the average call length or packet size, and the expected amount of delay in seconds.

The following formula is used to derive the Erlang C traffic model:

$$C(c,a)=\frac{\dfrac{a^c c}{c!(c-a)}}{\displaystyle\sum_{k=0}^{c-1}\frac{a^k}{k!}+\frac{a^c c}{c!(c-a)}}$$

Where:

- C(c,a) is the probability of delaying the call.
- c is the number of circuits.
- a is the traffic load.

Example 2.3: Using the Erlang C Traffic Model for Voice

Problem

You expect the call center to have approximately 600 calls lasting approximately 3 minutes each, and that each agent has an after-call work time of 20 seconds. You would like the average time in the queue to be approximately 10 seconds.

Solution

Calculate the amount of expected traffic load. You know that you have approximately 600 calls of 3 minutes duration. To that number you must add 20 seconds because each agent is not answering a call for approximately 20 seconds. The additional 20 seconds is part of the amount of time it takes to service a call, as shown in the following formula:

(600 calls * 200 seconds AHT)/3600 = 33.33 erlangs of traffic

Compute the delay factor by dividing the expected delay time by AHT, as follows:

(10 sec delay)/(200 seconds) = 0.05 delay factor

Example 2.4: Using the Erlang C Traffic Model for Data

Problem

You are designing your backbone connection between two routers. You know that you will generally see about 600 packets per second (pps) with 200 bytes per packet or 1600 bits per packet. Multiplying 600 pps by 1600 bits per packet gives the amount of needed bandwidth: 960,000 bits per second (bps). You know that you can buy circuits in increments of 64,000 bps, the amount of data necessary to keep the circuit busy for 1 second. How many circuits will you need to keep the delay under 10 ms?

Solution

Calculate the traffic load as follows:

(960,000 bps)/(64,000 bps) = 15 erlangs of traffic load

Calculate the average transmission time. Multiply the number of bytes per packet by 8 to get the number of bits per packet, then divide that by 64,000 bps (circuit speed) to get the average transmission time per packet as follows:

(200 bytes per packet) * (8 bits) = (1600 bits per packet)/(64000 bps)

= 0.025 seconds (25 ms) to transmit

(Delay factor 10 ms)/(25 ms) = 0.4 delay factor

If you look at the Erlang C Tables, you see that with a traffic load of 15.47 erlangs and a delay factor of 0.4, you need 17 circuits. This calculation is based on the assumption that the circuits are clear of any packet loss.

2.5 QUEUED DATA AND PACKET-SWITCHED TRAFFIC MODELING

Erlangs work well with voice network and circuit-switched traffic rates; they do not work well with packet-switched and routed networks. In voice and circuit switched the traffic is blocked where as in packet switched networks; some level of queuing is employed so that packets are queued in buffers and transmitted when congestion occurs. Also, packet networks provide a mix of protocol and traffic types, whereas voice and circuit-switched networks provide point-to-point, transparent, homogeneous transport of information. Therefore, packet switching and routing demands a different analysis of traffic handling.. We start with the notation used in queuing systems, and move through the common modes for traffic modeling.

2.5.1 QUEUING SYSTEM MODELS NOTATION

There are three major queuing formulas for dealing with voice, TDM, and packet (queuing) models. Each of these formulas follows the same format.

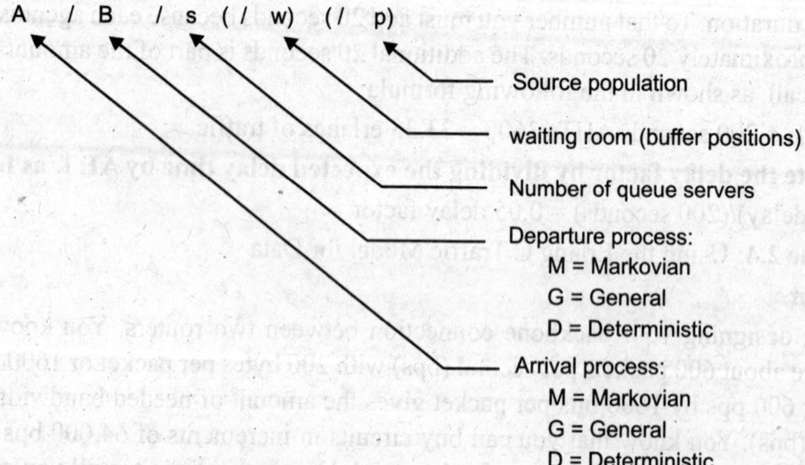

Figure 2.3: Queuing system notation

The three major modeling formulas include

Erlang-B: M/G/s/s

which is used for voice-blocked calls cleared and TDM modeling,

Erlang-C: M/G/s/K

which is used when the waiting room or queue (k) is greater than the number of servers (s) for voice with blocked calls held, or for operator services, and

Packet: M/G/1

which is used for one server and infinite waiting and population, and commonly used to model packet, frame, and cell networks.

The third formula is of primary concern: packet modeling with M/M/1, where M designates a Markovian process (or Poisson arrival distribution-previously G designated the Gaussian arrival distribution). Thus, formulas are based on a single server with Poisson arrivals or equivalently negative exponential service times, and first-in-first-out (FIFO) service. Figure 2.4 shows this relationship between arrival rates λ service times, and a single server μ.

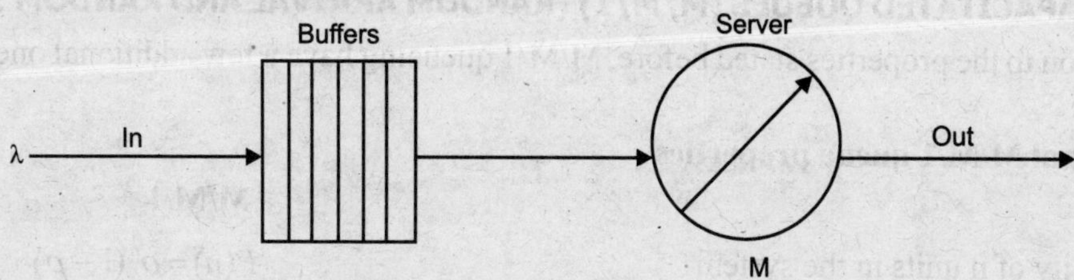

Figure 2.4: M\M\1 single server model

2.6 QUEUING SYSTEMS MODELS

Queuing is the study of traffic behavior near a certain section where demand exceeds available capacity. Queues can be seen in many common situations: boarding a bus or train or plane, freeway bottlenecks, shopping checkout, exiting a doorway at the end of class, waiting for a computer in the lab, a hamburger at McDonald's, or a haircut at the barber. In transportation engineering, queuing can occur at red lights, stop signs, bottlenecks, or any design-based or traffic-based flow constriction. When not dealt with properly, queues can result in severe network congestion or "gridlock" conditions, therefore making them something important to be studied and understood by engineers.

Two particular examples of queuing systems are presented: M/D/1 and M/M/1.

2.6.1 INCAPACITATED QUEUES (M/D/1) AND (M/M/1)

It has been shown that queue sizes, waiting times, and delays differ between M/D/1 and M/M/1 queuing. These differences are represented in formulas and shown below. Note the minor differences between the two.

Comparison of M/D/1 and M/M/1 queue properties		
'	M/D/1	M/M/1
Q (average queue size (#))	$Q=\frac{\rho^2}{2(1-\rho)}$	$Q=\frac{\rho^2}{1-\rho}$
w (average waiting time)	$w=\frac{\rho}{2\mu(1-\rho)}$	$w=\frac{\lambda}{\mu(\mu-\lambda)}$
t (average total delay)	$t=\frac{2-\rho}{2\mu(1-\rho)}$	$t=\frac{1}{(\mu-\lambda)}$

Notes:

- Average queue size includes customers currently being served (in number of units)
- Average wait time excludes service time
- Average travel time (through the queue) is (wait time + service time). This is sometimes referred to average delay time due to the existence of the bottleneck.

2.6.2 UNCAPACITATED QUEUES (M/M/1) (RANDOM ARRIVAL AND RANDOM SERVICE)

In addition to the properties stated before, M/M/1 queueing have a few additional ones of which to take note.

Additional M/M/1 queue properties	
'	M/M/1
Probability of n units in the system	$P(n)=\rho^n(1-\rho)$
Expected number of units in the system	$E(n)=\frac{\lambda}{\mu-\lambda}$
Mean Queue Length	$E(m)=\frac{\lambda^2}{\mu(\mu-\lambda)}$
Average waiting time of arrival, including queue and service	$E(v)=\frac{1}{(\mu-\lambda)}$
Average waiting time in queue	$E(w)=\frac{\lambda}{\mu(\mu-\lambda)}$
Probability of spending time t or less in system	$P(v\le t)=1-e^{-(1-\rho)\mu t}$
Probability of spending g time t or less in queu	$P(w\le t)=1-\rho e^{-(1-\rho)\mu t}$
Probability of more than N vehicles in queue	$P(n>N)=\rho^{N+1}$

2.6.3 CAPACITATED QUEUES

Capacitated queues permit a maximum number of vehicles to wait, and thus have different properties than uncapacitated queues. For single channel under saturated finite queues where the maximum number of units in system is specified as N and with random arrivals and departures (λ, μ) we have:

Additional M/M/1 queue properties	
'	M/M/1
Probability iof n Units in System	$P(n)=\frac{(1-\rho)}{1-\rho^{N+1}}(\rho)^n$
Expected Number of Units in System	$E(n)=\frac{(\rho)}{(1-\rho)}\frac{1-(N+1)(\rho)^N+N\rho^{N+1}}{1-\rho^{N+1}}$

2.6.4 CHARACTERIZING QUEUES

Queue Length Characteristics: Finite or Infinite

Number of Channels: Number of Waiting Lines (e.g. Ramps = 2, Supermarket = 12)

We use the following notation:

- Arrival Rate = λ
- Departure Rate = μ
- Utilization Rate = $\rho=\frac{\lambda}{\mu}$

Degree of Saturation

Oversaturated: $\lambda > \mu$

Under saturated $\lambda < \mu$

Saturated $\lambda = \mu$

2.7 DELAY OR LATENCY (DESIGNING FOR PEAKS)

Users of interactive applications expect minimal delay in receiving feedback from the network. In addition, users of multimedia applications require a minimal variation in the amount of delay that packets experience. Delay must be constant for voice and video applications. Variations in delay, called jitter, cause disruptions in voice quality and jumpiness in video streams.

Older applications, such as SNA-based applications, are also sensitive to delay. In traditional SNA environments, delay could be carefully planned and measured. When SNA is migrated to a multiprotocol network, however, it is harder to predict delay. Unexpected delays can occur because of bursty LAN traffic and routers taking a long time to converge after a link outage. Long delays cause SNA sessions to timeout.

Applications that use the Telnet protocol are also sensitive to delay because the user expects quick feedback when typing characters. With the Telnet remote echo option, the character typed by a user doesn't appear on the screen until it has been acknowledged and echoed by the far end, and the near end has sent an acknowledgment for the echo. You should determine if your customer plans to run any applications based on delay-sensitive protocols such as Telnet or SNA. Digital Equipment Corporation's Local Area Transport (LAT) protocol is also sensitive to delay and supports few adjustments for improving its behavior on networks with high delay.

2.7.1 CAUSES OF DELAY

Any goals regarding delay must take into account fundamental physics. Despite science fiction, any signal experiences a propagation delay resulting from the finite speed of light, which is about 300,000 kilometers per second, (or 186,000 miles per second for metric-challenged readers in the United States). Network designers can also remember 1 nanosecond per foot. These values are for light traveling in a vacuum. A signal in a cable or optical fiber travels approximately 2/3 the speed of light in a vacuum. Delay is relevant for all data transmission technologies, but especially for satellite links and long terrestrial cables. Geostationary satellites are in orbit above the earth at a height of about 36,000 kilometers, or 24,000 miles. This long distance leads to a delay of about 270 milliseconds (ms) for an intercontinental satellite hop. In the case of terrestrial cable connections, delay is about 1 ms for every 200 kilometers (120 miles).

Another fundamental cause for delay is the time to put digital data onto a transmission line, which depends on the data volume and the speed of the line. For example, to transmit a 1,024-byte packet on a 1.544-Mbps T1 line takes about 5 ms.

An additional fundamental delay is packet-switching delay. Packet-switching delay refers to the latency accrued when bridges, switches, and routers forward data. The latency depends on the speed of the internal circuitry and CPU, and the switching architecture of the internetworking device. The delay can be quite small. Scott Bradner of the Network Device Testing Laboratory at Harvard University periodically conducts latency tests on submitted network equipment. Bradner has tested Layer-2 and Layer-3 switches with latencies in the 10 to 50 microsecond range for 64-byte Ethernet IP packets. Routers have higher latencies than switches, but router vendors continually make progress on reducing latency.

When a packet comes into a router, the router checks its routing table, decides which interface should send the packet, and encapsulates the packet with the correct header and trailer. Routing vendors such as Cisco Systems have advanced caching mechanisms so that a frame destined for a known destination can receive its new encapsulation very quickly without requiring the CPU to do any table lookup or other processing. These mechanisms minimize packet-switching delay.

Packet-switching delay can also include queuing delay. The number of packets in a queue on a packet-switching device increases exponentially as utilization increases, as you can see from Figure 2.5. If utilization is 50 percent, the average queue depth is 1 packet. If utilization is 90 percent, the average queue depth is 9 packets. Without going into mathematical queuing theory, the general rule of thumb for queue depth is:

$$\text{queue depth} = \text{utilization}/(1 - \text{utilization})$$

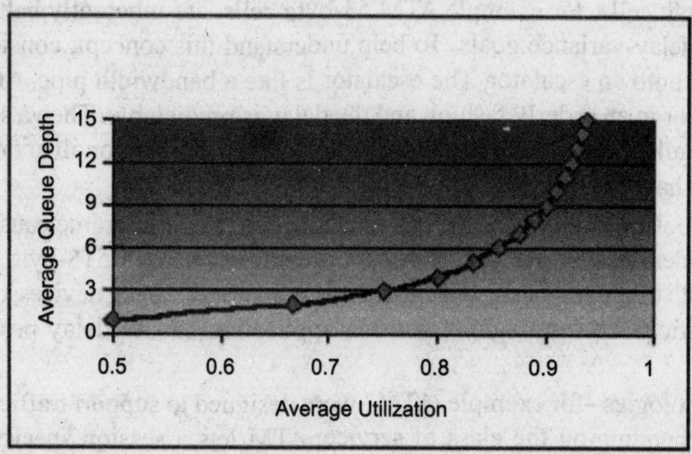

Figure 2.5: Queue depth and bandwidth utilization (Designing for peaks)

Consider the following example. A packet switch has 5 users, each offering packets at a rate of 10 packets per second. The average length of the packets is 1,024 bits. The packet switch needs to transmit this data over a 56-Kbps WAN circuit.

Load = 5 x 10 x 1024 = 51,200 bps

Utilization = 51,200/56,000 = 91.4 percent

Average number of packets in the queue = (0.914)/(1 - 0.914) = 10.63 packets

By increasing bandwidth on a WAN circuit you can decrease queue depth and hence decrease delay. Alternately, to improve performance, you can use an advanced queuing algorithm that outputs certain types of packets first--for example, voice or video packets. Advanced router queuing techniques are discussed in more detail in Chapter 12, "Optimizing Your Network Design."

2.7.2 DELAY VARIATION

As customers implement new digital voice and video applications, they are becoming concerned about delay and delay variation. Additionally, customers are becoming more aware of the issues associated with supporting bursty LAN traffic on the same network that carries delay-sensitive traffic. If bursts in LAN traffic cause jitter, audio and video streams experience problems that disrupt communications.

Desktop audio/video applications can minimize jitter by providing a buffer that the network puts data into. Display software or hardware pulls data from the buffer. The insulating buffer reduces the effect of jitter because variations on the input side are smaller than the total buffer size and therefore not obvious on the output side. The data is smoothed on the output, and the user experiences no ill effects from the input jitter.

If possible, you should gather exact requirements for delay variation from a customer. For customers who cannot provide exact goals, a good rule of thumb is that the variation should be less than one or two percent of the delay. For example, for a goal of an average delay of 40ms, the variation should not be more than 400 or 800 microseconds.

Short fixed-length cells, for example ATM 53-byte cells, are inherently better than frames for meeting delay and delay-variance goals. To help understand this concept, consider the analogy of people trying to get onto an escalator. The escalator is like a bandwidth pipe. At first, each person gets onto the escalator in an orderly fashion and the delay is predictable. Then a school class arrives and the children are all holding hands, expecting to get onto the escalator all at once! What happens to your delay if you happen to be behind the children?

A gaggle of school children holding hands is analogous to a large frame causing extra delay for small frames. Consider the case of a user starting a file transfer using 1,518-byte frames. This user's data affects bandwidth usage and queuing mechanisms at internetworking devices, causing unexpected delay for other traffic. Good throughput for one application causes delay problems for another application.

Cell-relay technologies--for example, ATM--were designed to support traffic that is sensitive to delay and jitter. Depending on the class of service, ATM lets a session specify a maximum cell transfer delay (MCTD) and cell delay variation (MCDV).

2.8 RESPONSE TIME

Response time is the network performance goal that users care about most. Users don't know about propagation delay and jitter. They don't understand throughput in packets per second or in megabytes per second. They aren't concerned about bit-error rates, though perhaps they should be! Users recognize the amount of time to receive a response from the network system. They also recognize small changes in the expected response time and become frustrated when the response time is long.

Users begin to get frustrated when response time is more than about 100 ms or 1/10th of a second. Beyond 100 ms, users notice they are waiting for the network to display a Web page, echo a typed character, and start downloading e-mail, and so on. If the response happens within 100 ms, most users do not notice any delay.

The 100-ms threshold is often used as a timer value for protocols that offer reliable transport of data. For example, many TCP implementations retransmit unacknowledged data after 100 ms by default. (Good TCP implementations also adjust the retransmit timer based on network conditions. TCP should keep track of the average amount of time to receive a response and dynamically adjust the retransmit timer based on the expected delay).

The 100-ms response time threshold applies to interactive applications. For bulk applications, such as transferring large files or graphical Web pages, users are willing to wait at least 10 to 20 seconds. Technically savvy users expect to wait even longer if they know the file is large and the transmission medium is slow. If your network users are not technically savvy, you should provide some guidelines on how long to wait, depending on the size of files and the technologies in use (modems, high-speed digital networks, geostationary satellites, and so on).

2.9 AVAILABILITY

Availability refers to the amount of time a network is available to users and is often a critical goal for network design customers. Availability can be expressed as a percent uptime per year, month, week, day, or hour, compared to the total time in that period. For example, in a network that offers 24-hour, seven-days-a-week service, if the network is up 165 hours in the 168-hour week, availability is 98.21 percent.

Network design customers don't use the word availability in everyday English and have a tendency to think it means more than it does. In general, availability means how much time the network is operational. Availability is linked to redundancy, but redundancy is not a network goal. Redundancy is a solution to the goal of availability. Redundancy means adding duplicate links or devices to a network to avoid downtime.

Availability is also linked to reliability, but has a more specific meaning (percent uptime) than reliability. Reliability refers to a variety of issues, including accuracy, error rates, stability, and the amount of time between failures. Some network users use the term recoverability to specify how easily and in what timeframe a network can recover from problems. Recoverability is an ingredient of availability.

Availability is also associated with resiliency, which is a word that is becoming more popular in networking magazines. Resiliency means how much stress a network can handle and how quickly the network can rebound from problems. A network that has good resiliency usually has good availability.

Sometimes network engineers classify capacity as part of availability. The thinking is that even if a network is available at Layer 1 (the physical layer), it is not available from a user's point of view if there is not enough capacity to send the user's traffic.

For example, Asynchronous Transfer Mode (ATM) has a connection admission control (CAC) function that regulates the number of cells allowed into an ATM network. If the capacity and quality of service requested for a connection are not available, cells for the connection are not allowed to enter the network. This problem could be considered an availability issue. However, this book classifies capacity with performance goals. Availability is considered simply a goal for percent uptime.

One other aspect of availability is disaster recovery. Most large institutions have a plan for recovering from natural disasters, such as floods, fires, hurricanes, and earthquakes. Also, some large enterprises (especially service providers) must plan how to recover from satellite outages. Satellite outages can be caused by meteorite storms, collisions with space debris, solar flares, or system failures. Unfortunately, some institutions have also found the need to specify a recovery plan for man-made disasters, such as bombs or hostage situations. A disaster recovery plan includes a process for keeping data backed up in a place that is unlikely to be hit by disaster, as well as a process for switching to backup technologies if the main technologies are affected by a disaster. The details of disaster-recovery planning are outside the scope of this book.

2.9.1 SPECIFYING AVAILABILITY REQUIREMENTS

You should encourage your customers to specify availability requirements with precision. Consider the difference between an uptime of 99.70 percent and an uptime of 99.95 percent. An uptime of 99.70 percent means the network is down 30 minutes per week, which is not acceptable to many customers. An uptime of 99.95 percent means the network is down five minutes per week, which probably is acceptable. Availability requirements should be specified with at least two digits following the decimal point.

It is also important to specify a timeframe with percent uptime requirements. Go back to the example of 99.70 percent uptime, which equated to 30 minutes of downtime per week. A downtime of 30 minutes in the middle of a working day is probably not acçeptable. But a downtime of 30 minutes every Saturday evening for regularly scheduled maintenance might be fine.

Not only should your customers specify a timeframe with percent uptime requirements, but they should also specify a time unit. Availability requirements should be specified as uptime per year, month, week, day, or hour. Consider an uptime of 99.70 percent again. This uptime means 30 minutes of downtime during a week. The downtime could be all at once, which would be a problem, or it could be spread out over the week. An uptime of 99.70 percent could mean that approximately every hour the network is down for 10.70 seconds. Will users notice a downtime of 10.70 seconds? Perhaps. For many applications, however, a downtime of 10.70 seconds every hour is tolerable.

Try doing the math yourself for a network goal of 99.80 percent uptime. How much downtime is permitted in hours per week? How much downtime is permitted in minutes per day and seconds per hour? Which values are acceptable?

2.9.2 THE COST OF DOWNTIME

In general, a customer's goal for availability is to keep mission-critical applications running smoothly, with little or no downtime. A method to help both you and your customer understand availability requirements is to specify a cost of downtime. For each critical application, document how much money the company loses per hour of downtime. (For some applications, such as order processing, specifying money lost per minute might have more impact.) If network operations will be outsourced to a third-party network management firm, explaining the cost of downtime can help the firm understand the criticality of applications to a business's mission.

Specifying the cost of downtime can also help clarify whether in-service upgrades must be supported. In-service upgrades refer to mechanisms for upgrading network equipment and services without disrupting operations. Most internetworking vendors sell high-end internetworking devices that include hot-swappable components for in-service upgrading.

2.9.3 MEAN TIME BETWEEN FAILURE AND MEAN TIME TO REPAIR

In addition to expressing availability as a percent uptime, you can define availability as a mean time between failure (MTBF) and mean time to repair (MTTR). You can use MTBF and MTTR to calculate availability goals when the customer wants to specify explicit periods of uptime and downtime, rather than a simple percent uptime value.

MTBF is a term that comes from the computer industry and is best suited to specifying how long a computer or computer component will last before it fails. When specifying availability requirements in the networking field, MTBF is sometimes designated with the more cumbersome phrase mean time between service outage (MTBSO), to account for the fact that a network is a service, not a component. Similarly, MTTR can be replaced with the phrase mean time to service repair (MTTSR). This book uses the simpler and better-known terms MTBF and MTTR.

A typical MTBF goal for a network that is highly relied upon is 4,000 hours. In other words, the network should not fail more often than once every 4,000 hours or 166.67 days. A typical MTTR goal is one hour In other words, the network failure should be fixed within one hour. In this case, the mean availability goal is

4,000 / 4,001 = 99.98 percent

A goal of 99.98 percent is typical for mission-critical operations.

When specifying availability using MTBF and MTTR, the equation to use is as follows:

Availability = MTBF / (MTBF + MTTR)

Using this availability equation allows a customer to clearly state the acceptable frequency and length of network outages.

Remember that what is calculated is the mean. The variation in failure and repair times can be high and must be considered as well. It is not enough to just consider mean rates, especially if you depend on external service agents (vendors or contractors) who are not under your tight control. Also, be aware that customers might need to specify different MTBF and MTTR goals for different parts of a network. For example, the goals for the core of the enterprise network are probably much more stringent than the goals for a switch port that only affects one user.

Although not all customers can specify detailed application requirements, it is a good idea to identify availability goals for specific applications, in addition to the network as a whole. Application availability goals can vary widely depending on the cost of downtime. For each application that has a high cost of downtime, you should document the acceptable MTBF and MTTR.

For MTBF values for specific networking components, you can generally use data supplied by the vendor of the component. Most router, switch, and hub manufacturers can provide MTBF and MTTR figures for their products. You should also investigate other sources of information, such as trade publications, to avoid any credibility problems with figures published by manufacturers. Search for variability figures as well as mean figures. Also, try to get written commitments for MTBF, MTTR, and variability values from the providers of equipment and services.

EXERCISES

1. Explain the concept of throughput calculations?
2. Explain the concept of packets/sec and bits/sec?
3. Explain the various examples of overhead in packets/sec and bits/sec?
4. Explain the concept of traffic characteristics and source models?
5. Explain the general source model parameters?
6. Explain the various traditional traffic engineering models?
7. Explain the concept of queued data and packet-switched traffic modeling?
8. Explain the various queuing systems models?
9. Explain the concept of delay or latency (designing for peaks)?
10. What do you mean b response time?
11. Explain the concept of availability?

Network Performance Modeling

3.1 NETWORK PERFORMANCE MODELING

Most users are concerned with modeling the performance of a network.

There are two basic modeling approaches:

1. Simulation: A simulation is usually much more accurate, but can become a formidable computational task when trying to simulate the performance of a large network. Analysis can be less computationally intensive, but is often inaccurate. Which is the best approach? The answer is similar to nodal modeling: It depends on how much information you have and how accurate an answer you require.

Simulation models are very useful in investigating the detailed operation of a system, which can lead to key insights into equipment, network, or application design. Detailed simulations generally take too long to execute to be used as an effective network design tool, and in many cases, the user does not know all the application traffic characteristics to simulate.

2. Analysis: A good way to bootstrap the analytical method is to simulate the network technology or switch performance under the expected mix of traffic inputs. Often an analytical approximation to the empirical simulation results can be developed as input to an analytical tool. An assumption often made in network modeling is that the nodes operate independently and that the traffic mixes and splits independently and randomly. If better information is not available, then this is a reasonable assumption, and simulation might be the only recourse. Analytical models become very complex without the assumption that nodes are independent of each other.

The inputs and outputs of a network model are similar for any packet/frame/cell-switched network design problem. The inputs are the topology, traffic, and routing. The network topology must be defined, usually as a graph with nodes and links. The characteristics of each node and link relevant to the simulation or analytical model must be described. Next, the pattern of traffic offered between the nodes must be defined. For point-to-point traffic this is commonly done via a traffic matrix. The routing, or set of links that traffic follows from source to destination, must be defined. Most applications work point to point and can be modeled in this fashion (for example, TCP/IP sessions between two IP addresses).

The principal outputs are measures of performance and cost. The principal performance measures of a model are loss and delay statistics. A model will often produce an economic cost to allow the network designer to select an effective price-performance tradeoff.

Now let's take a look at the first step in traffic modeling: The traffic matrix.

3.2 CREATING THE TRAFFIC MATRIX

A traffic matrix contains the information that who needs to talk with whom, and what traffic patterns need to go where. It is, in effect, a spreadsheet or table mapping traffic flows from origin to destination. We can then analyze the traffic matrix and start the capacity-planning cycle. At an even higher level, these traffic patterns are typically driven by the business traffic. Look at the way any company does business, and certain traffic patterns emerge: a centralized HQ communicating with remote offices (hub-and-spoke) or many distributed sales offices communicating in peer-to-peer arrangements (distributed or meshed topology). The application traffic patterns will generally follow these business topologies.

3.2.1 ASYMMETRIC VERSUS SYMMETRIC DISTRIBUTION

Asymmetrical traffic lacks directional symmetry through an imbalance of flows, speeds, or other characteristics. It originates from large sites to small, or vice versa, and does not follow a normal distribution. Access devices vary in quantity, design, engineering, and loading.

Symmetrical traffic often originates from communities of similar interest, such as specific geographic regions, and is uniformly spread across these sites within each region and the bidirectional quantity is similar. Most of access devices are similar in quantity, design, engineering, and loading.

Hierarchical networks, such as those using the SNA protocols, are often symmetrical in nature. Distributed networks often resemble asymmetrical rather than symmetrical traffic distributions. LAN traffic and WAN traffic made up of LAN traffic feeds tend to be asymmetrical and very hard to diagnose. In this instance, average and peak traffic patterns should be used in the traffic matrix. Figure 3.1 illustrates symmetrical and asymmetrical traffic distributions.

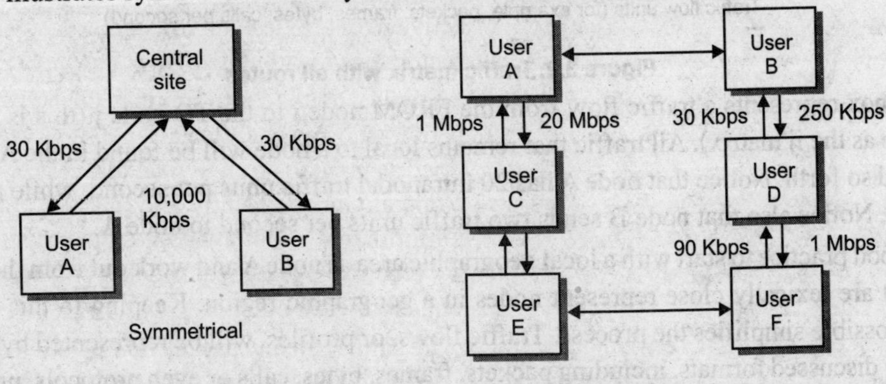

Figure 3.1: Symmetrical and asymmetrical traffic distributions

3.2.2 TRAFFIC MATRIX

The traffic matrix is an essential part of the access node design, and illustrates traffic flows not otherwise readily apparent. Traffic interfaces to the network through an access node or access point. Access nodes could take the form of a concentrator (for example, PAD or FRAD), DXC, access multiplexer, hub, bridge, switch, router, or any other device concentrating user inputs but not operating as a switching backbone. The traffic matrix helps define details about the access node requirements, such as location, size, operation, protocol support, performance characteristics, and device type. The traffic matrix is, effect, a spreadsheet or table mapping traffic flows from origin to destination. The FROM nodes are listed vertically down the left side of the matrix, and the TO nodes are listed horizontally across the top. Figure 3.2 shows a sample traffic matrix with simple data units (for example, bytes, calls, packets) per second for each site.

To location

From location (i) \ j	A	B	C	D	E	F
A	20	0	2	1	20	12
B	2	3	3	*	6	5
C	2	0	12	2	8	3
D	8	*	1	10	22!	5
E	12	4	0	31!	6	3
F	22	8	2	1	2	2

Traffic flow units (for example, packets, frames, bytes, calls per second)

Figure 3.2: Traffic matrix with all routes

Each box represents a traffic flow from the FROM node i to the TO node j (this is sometimes referred to as the ij matrix). All traffic that remains local to a node will be found in the A-A box, B-B box, and so forth. Notice that node A has 20 intranodal traffic units per second, while node B has only three. Notice also that node B sends two traffic units per second to node A.

It is good practice to start with a local geographic area as node A and work out from there, so that letters that are lexically close represent nodes in a geographic region. Keeping to this scheme as much as possible simplifies the process. Traffic flows, or profiles, will be represented by any of the previously discussed formats, including packets, frames, bytes, calls or even protocols, priorities, or other dependencies. Traffic measurements used should have a similar message (packet) length and should be measured in "mean busy hour" throughput (in bps) or in the peak-to-mean ratio. Traffic patterns are often provided in units per second (that is, packets, frames, cells) during average, peak, and maximum traffic patterns throughout a 24-hour period, and are designed for busy-hour traffic as previously discussed. Traffic measurements should be measured from either the network or the application point of view. Thus, a matrix can be built that shows specific application traffic flows (such as FTP or Telnet file transfer protocol traffic) or generic packet flows, such as Ethernet packets from a LAN interface. Rarely does an enterprise network know their traffic patterns to these levels, so gross approximations are often made. Also mark invalid and preferred routes. Figure 3.3 shows the same matrix, with the additional detail of invalid routed indicated with an asterisk, while preferred routes are indicated with an exclamation point.

To location (j) / From location (i)

i \ j	A	B	C	D	E	F
A	20	0	2	1	20	12
B	2	3	3	*	6	5
C	2	0	12	2	8	3
D	8	*	1	10	22!	5
E	12	4	0	31!	6	3
F	22	8	2	1	2	2

Traffic flow units (for example, packets, frames, bytes, calls per second)

Figure 3.3: Traffic matrix with invalid and preferred routes

3.2.3 INTERPRETING THE MATRIX

In its simplest use, the matrix shows the connectivity required between each site. Let M be the binary matrix, with a 1 indicating connectivity and a 0 indicating no connectivity. The following are then true:

- M = connectivity for one node (that is, direct connectivity)
- M X M = connectivity for a 2-hip path
- M X M X M = connectivity for a 3-hop path
- $M + M^2 + M^3$ = all paths up to path length of 3 hops

Note that this method can include "cycles", or loops (paths that traverse the same node more than once), which should be eliminated. For example, each level of connectivity between nodes might require a private line, PVC if FR, VC or VP if ATM, an IP routing protocol route, or tandem node. All traffic identified as remaining local to a given node would be placed into the same access node. Circles are then drawn around boxes that represent a small geographic area that could be served by a single concentrator. This is done by grouping nodal traffic distributions in a local geographical area together to form larger access nodes. This reduces the number of access devices required. Figure 3.3 shows the same matrix from the last example. Node A has 20 units of traffic (this could be 20 PPS, 20 frames per second, or 20 Kbps average traffic during busy hour), which remains local node B has only three units of traffic. Also note that node A sends no traffic to node B, and node B sends only two units of traffic to node A. Since in this example node A and node B are in the same geographic region, the traffic from both nodes is combined at node A, where a single access node is placed. The small amount of traffic originating at node B is "backhauled" to node A. Some amount of backhaul access is required in many public data services, where there are limited access points into the switched network, or where lower-cost regional hub-and-spoke subnetworks are required.

This also assumes that no other large amounts of traffic are generated or sent to node B from other nodes. This process continues until the number of access nodes required to begin the design is established. Ideally, one would like to place a separate concentrator node at each site, but often economics do not justify this, so the network design usually settles for smaller nodes at less concentrated regions and larger ones in more dense regions, or backhaul from less to more concentrated regions. Network designs for multimedia and multiprotocol networks are much more complicated. These complex designs often required many traffic matrices combined into a multidimensional matrix (for example, a x-axis forming a three-dimensional matrix to accommodate interdependencies such as priority of information, budget trade-offs, or protocols), or in large networks, design tools to perform these calculations. Ideally, this analysis would be performed by a design tool. Design tools are briefly covered next.

3.3 CAPACITY PLANNING AND NETWORK VISION

Capacity planning was once done on a five-to ten-year cycle. It is now a one-to three-year cycle, and many times even shorter. In fact, packet networks often demand a capacity review on a monthly basis. There are two elements to the plan, a short-term objective and task-oriented plan usually revised each year, and the long-term three- to five-year plan, which should also take into account the strategic vision of corporate communications for the next five to ten years.

As the cost of computing hardware decreases, the entropy of capacity requirements increases. This makes capacity planning for communications networks a challenging task. Short- and long-range capacity planning can provide the corporation with a competitive advantage, assuming that the plans fit in with the long-range strategic business plan. Each design must provide the flexibility to change technology as business needs change without major network restructuring. Both plans must take into account the business needs, customer needs, and the technologies available. One method is to migrate multiple network platforms to a consolidated network platform that conforms to industry standards. Decide early on whether to maintain the existing architecture and build upon it, or plan to build new integrated network architecture in the future. Better yet, look for migratory (evolutionary) versus forklift upgrades (revolutionary) strategies.

One for the best architectures is built in a hierarchical nature that caters to flexible peer-to-peer communications and can be replaced in layers over time. Plan for port expansion, CPU capacity, hardware storage requirements, memory storage requirements, growth in user application traffic, and many other critical growth areas discussed in this chapter. Many design tools have the capability to model future network changes and assist in both the short-term and long-range capacity planning process.

3.4 DESIGN TOOLS

Design tools provide an accurate method of modeling and designing networks. They are used to describe types of network tools and state which features belong to each tool, describe typical network design tasks; state standard requirements for a design took, and analyze and describe the features available on current commercial design tools. You can select a design tool that meets your specific requirements. Commercially available network design tools for packet, frame, and cell networks have been around since the late 1980s. The capabilities of these tools include analyzing existing networks, providing meshed and hierarchical network designs, modeling design change and failure scenarios, and modeling capacity planning scenarios. While these tools exist, few are actually used by most network designers and managers. This is in part due to the lack of tool flexibility and the inherent constraints of limited options, and also in part by the sheer difficulty of modeling distributed hybrid networks. The complexity of these tools greatly increases from circuit to packet switched networks. Some available tools are also well suited for modeling a specific vendor's networks, or specific protocols, but quickly break down in large routed and switched networks.

Design tools analyze two types of data networks: **circuit-switched and packet/frame/cell-switched networks.** When choosing a design tool, certain criteria should be present in the tool. At a minimum, it should support the basic user requirements defined in Chapter 1. Before a tool can be successful, the data fed into it must be accurate. Hence the importance of the detailed requirements analysis of chapters 5 and 6, so that good input will produce good outputs. Design tools use either mathematical modeling or packet-level simulation. Mathematical modeling uses statistics to predict user traffic flows and model their characteristics. Packet-level simulation is the most common method, however, where the tool inputs are a snapshot of the network at a single point in time. Since the traffic on packet networks is often bursty in nature, multiple snapshots are required. This type of modeling works well for small networks where the user traffic characteristics are well known, but processing times and the sheer computing power required to perform a large, dynamic network design often makes this process very time-consuming, resource insensitive, and difficult. Some design tools use neither of the above approaches. Instead, they model each user input as a single demand, based on their file-transfer protocol characteristics or "flows". The author has found that the best network-design tools focus on heuristic routing algorithms based on user-definable parameters and queuing theory, rather than any one form of mathematical simulation of theory.

3.4.1 TERMINOLOGY

There are two primary terms used throughput this section: transport and demand.

- **Transport:** It is used to define the bandwidth that is used to create user channels. Transport carriers user data from point A to point B. Transport comprises the bandwidth (private lines, FR, ATM, and so on) between switching devices (digital cross connects, switches, multiplexers, and so on). Transport is also referred to as backbone.

- **Demand:** It is the portion of the transport bandwidth that contains the user data. In private line networks, the demand traffic is the unit of circuit used such as 56 Kbps, 64 Kbps, fractional-T1 and T1 or packet/frame/cell flow into the network. No distinction is made between the amount of bandwidth required for a particular user, and the amount of bandwidth that is added due to overhead or routing inefficiencies. A session, file transfer, client-server application, or switched circuits are all types of demand. Demand is also referred to as the circuits that are carried by the backbone.

3.5 CATEGORIES OF TOOLS

Tools are mainly divided into three categories as follows:

1. Design Tools
2. Configuration-Management Tools
3. Event-Management Tools

3.5.1 DESIGN TOOLS

Design tools are used to describe a wide range of applications that are concerned with topics such as selection of the proper software and hardware, optimization of network topology, and failure analysis.

The services provided by a design tools include

1. **Cost model:** Calculates the cost of the transport, hardware, and software portions of the network.
2. **What-if analysis:** Recommends design changes based on failure or network configuration changes.
3. **Failure analysis:** Describes completely the effects on demand traffic of a failure of some portion of the transport network or devices (nodes) within the network.
4. **Visualize:** Shows network elements and connections on screen and on paper.
5. **Simulate:** Models the operation of the network devices with respect to physical, data link, network, layers and so forth, parameters.
6. **Characterize:** Calculates key performance indicators (KPIs) that describe design, efficiency, utilization, and so on.
7. **Optimize:** Changes the network design to achieve higher utilization or performance and models cost trade-offs.
8. **Design:** Produces transport from demand and demand from profiles.
9. **Report:** Produces utilization, link, equipment, site reports.

3.5.2 CONFIGURATION-MANAGEMENT TOOLS

Configuration-management tools are used to describe a wide range of applications that address topics such as storing software and hardware configurations, designing racks and cabling, and equipment placement.

The services provided by configuration-management tools include

- Keeps detailed records of the setting of network elements, including ports, cards, and devices. Settings include all software- and hardware-defined attributes of equipment. Other details such as serial numbers, revision levels, software options, and setup parameters can be stored by a configuration-management tool.

- Keeps detailed records of the layout of racks of equipment. This information will most likely be geographical in nature. The connections made by cables and routing information will also be stored.

3.5.3 EVENT-MANAGEMENT TOOLS

Event-management tools are used to describe a wide range of applications that are used for real-time network event monitoring, correlation, and notification.

The services provided by an alarm-and event-management tools include

- Storage of events, some of which will represent faults in the network (alarms)
- Correlation of events, which reduces multiple events related to a particular failure to a single event relaying the proximate cause of the multiple events
- Presentation of events
- Reporting and trending results

3.6 CLASSES OF DESIGN TOOLS

Design tools can be divided into three classes:

1. Physical-Design Tools
2. Logical-Design Tools
3. Statistical-Design Tools

These tools consider delay and throughput requirements of the applications. Their models are inherently statistical in nature, and cover all the previously mentioned connections.

3.6.1 PHYSICAL-DESIGN TOOLS

Physical-design tools are used to take into consideration attributes of equipment only to the physical level. Circuit switching is essentially the only type of network covered by physical-design tools. A physical-design tool has the capability to design networks that incorporate only physical entities. Transport facilities are always considered as physical when they are primary. Primary refers to a configuration where there is not a lower level of network providing the transport. Figure 3.4 shows a model for a physical design.

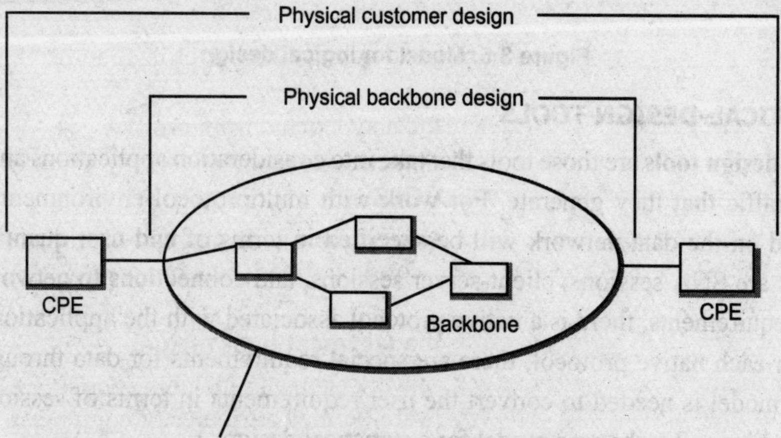

Figure 3.4 Model of physical design

3.6.2 LOGICAL-DESIGN TOOLS

Logical-design tools are used to take into consideration attributes of equipment beyond the physical level. Networks of this type frequently employ the concept of virtual circuits or datagram delivery. Logical-design tools cover packet-, frame- and cell-switched networks. A logical-design tool has the capability to design networks that incorporate logical entities such as permanent virtual circuits and switched virtual circuits. One example would be a FR switch that has multiple PVCs. Also included are networks that provide connectionless services such as IP. This type of tool converts a virtual circuit demand or packet flow into an optimized physical-transport network. Figure 3.5 shows a model for a logical design.

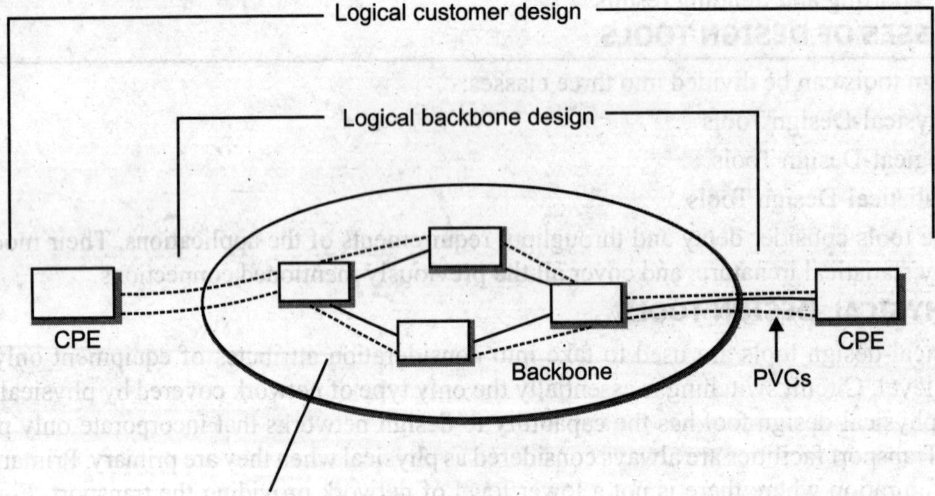

Figure 3.5: Model for logical design

3.6.3 STATISTICAL-DESIGN TOOLS

Statistical-design tools are those tools that take into consideration applications and the statistical nature of the traffic that they generate. For work with multiprotocol environments, the ultimate demands placed on the data network will be specified in terms of end-user quantifiable entities. Sample entities are SNA sessions, client-server sessions, and connections to network servers. For each of these requirements, there is a native protocol associated with the application that provides the service. For each native protocol, there are special requirements for data throughput, priority, and latency. A model is needed to convert the user requirements in terms of sessions into logical circuit demand. Figure 3.6 shows a model for a statistical design.

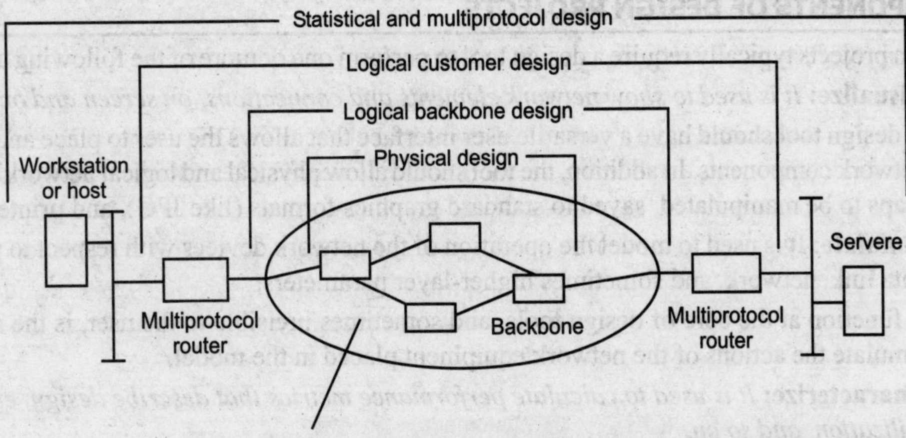

Figure 3.6: Model for statistical design

3.6.4 INTEGRATION OF THE PHYSICAL, LOGICAL AND STATISTICAL

To perform network design from the level of user demand to the level of physical transport, the three levels of design tool must be integrated, as shown in Figure 3.7. Ultimately, the three levels should exist in one tool.

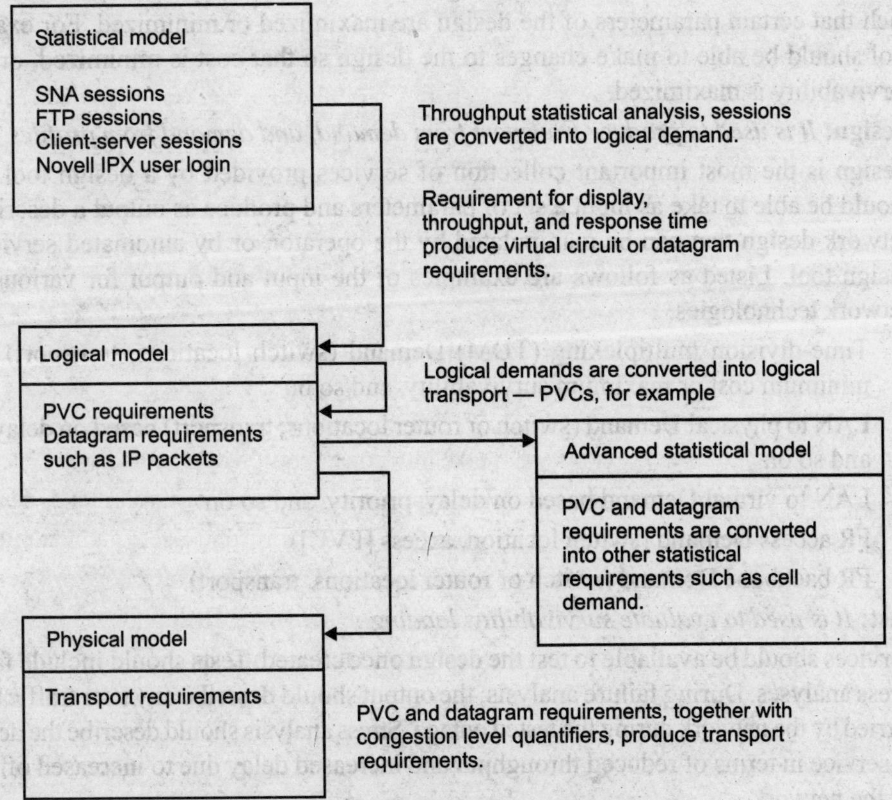

Figure 3.7: Integration of the three types of tools

3.7 COMPONENTS OF DESIGN PROJECTS

Design projects typically require a design tool to perform one or more of the following activities:

1. **Visualize:** *It is used to show network elements and connections, on screen and on paper.*

   A design tool should have a versatile user interface that allows the user to place and connect network components. In addition, the tool should allow physical and logical network topology maps to be manipulated, saved to standard graphics formats (like JPG), and printed.

2. **Simulate:** It is used to model the operation of the network devices with respect to physical, data link, network, and sometimes higher-layer parameters.

   A function at the core of design tools, and sometimes invisible to the user, is the ability to simulate the actions of the network equipment placed in the model.

3. **Characterize:** *It is used to calculate performance metrics that describe design, efficiency, utilization, and so on.*

   To quantify changes made during the design process, a number of performance metrics should be calculated by the design tool. These indicators could include utilization, efficiency, cost, survivability, throughput, and delay.

4. **Optimize:** *It is used to change the network design to increase performance metrics, us directives, strategies.*

   Services should be provided by the design tool to modify the design in an automated way such that certain parameters of the design are maximized or minimized. For example, the tool should be able to make changes to the design so that cost is minimized, or such that survivability is maximized.

5. **Design:** *It is used to produce transport from demand, and demand from profiles.*

   Design is the most important collection of services provided by a design tool. The tool should be able to take as input a set of parameters and produce as output a description of a network design that can be manipulated by the operator, or by automated services of the design tool. Listed as follows are examples of the input and output for various types of network technologies.

   - Time-division multiplexing (TDM) Demand (switch locations, transport) based on minimum cost or maximum survivability, and so on
   - LAN to physical Demand (switch or router locations, transport) based on delay, priority, and so on
   - LAN to virtual Demand based on delay, priority, and so on
   - FR access Demand (switch location, access [PVC])
   - FR backbone Demand (switch or router locations, transport)

6. **Test:** *It is used to evaluate survivability, loading.*

   Services should be available to test the design once created. Tests should include failure and stress analyses. During failure analysis, the output should describe any user traffic that is not carried by the network during the tested outage. Stress analysis should describe the degradation of service in terms of reduced throughput and increased delay due to increased offered load on the network.

7. **Report:** *It is used to produce utilization, link, equipment, site reports.*
   A versatile set of reports should be available to describe the components of the network that has been designed. In addition, performance metrics should be reported along with details of utilization, throughput, and efficiency of each component or circuit of the network.
8. **Performance Analysis:** *It is used to investigate performance parameters.*
   This area is particularly applicable to tools that address statistical networks. Ideally, a design tool should perform the design in stages. In the early stages, the placement of nodes and links, along with the determination of the size of links, are calculated based on aggregate parameters such as maximum packet-processing speed. At a later stage of the design, the simulation should switch to a more detailed level, and advanced statistical models should be employed to analyze packet throughput and delay and queue depth.

EXERCISES

1. Explain the concept of network performance modelling?
2. How can you create the traffic matrix?
3. Differentiate between asymmetric and symmetric distribution?
4. Explain the concept of traffic matrix with the help of example?
5. Explain the concept of capacity planning and network vision?
6. What do you mean by design tools?
7. Explain the basic terminology of design tools?
8. Explain the various categories of tools?
9. Explain the various classes of design tools?
10. Explain the various components of design projects?

Technology Comparisons

4.1 INTRODUCTION

In the last chapters we discuss about the traffic requirements, planning and choosing technologies. We also discuss about the traffic engineering basics and there characteristics using various source models.

Now in this chapter we draw the comparison of various technologies which are helpful for the designing process. We make comparison between protocols there interfaces and discuss about the detail of routing and the transport techniques. A good understanding of these technologies and there services are essential for network design engineer to make wise decision. Thus the access to network design can be accomplished using the comparison of technologies to meet user requirements and to meet the current and future capacity planning.

4.2 SWITCHING

Historically, most communications systems have started with point-to-point links which directly connect together the users wishing to communicate using a dedicated communications circuit. As the distance between user's increases beyond the length of the cable (e.g. the length of a telegraph wire), the connection between the users was formed by a number of sections which were connected end-to-end in series to form the circuit. The connection between the users (A and D) in the figure below (i.e. A and D) is represented by a series of links (AB, BC, and CD) each link connects two entities known as nodes. For a point-to-point circuit, (also known as a permanent circuit) the nodes are patch panels which provide a simple connection between the two links (i.e. the two transmission circuits).

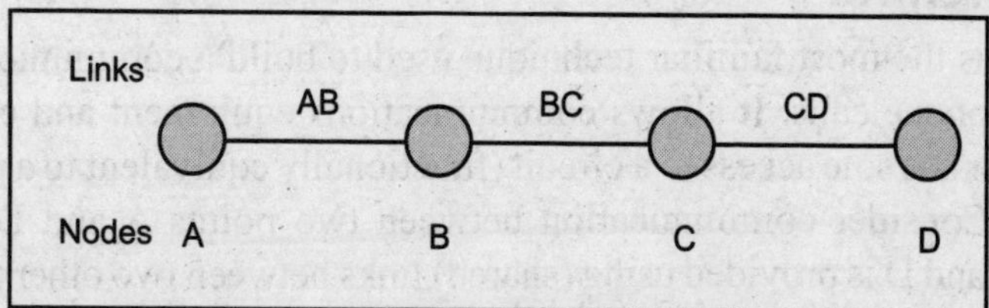

Figure 4.1: A connection between two systems A & D formed from 3 links

As the number of connected users increased, it has become infeasible to provide a circuit which connects every user to every other user, and some sharing of the transmission circuits (known as "switching") has become necessary. To accomplish this goal, the data communications network has evolved. A network is a set of nodes that are interconnected to permit the exchange of information.

Three switching techniques have been proposed for building networks:

- Circuit switching
- Message switching
- Packet switching (both virtual circuit and datagram)

Each allows sharing communication facilities among multiple users (end systems), and each uses equipment located at the nodes (intermediate systems) to replace the patch-panels used in a point-to-point connection. Packet switching is most often used for data communication. Most networks consist of many links (see the figure below) which allow more than one path through the network between nodes. A data communications network must be able to select an appropriate path for each required connection.

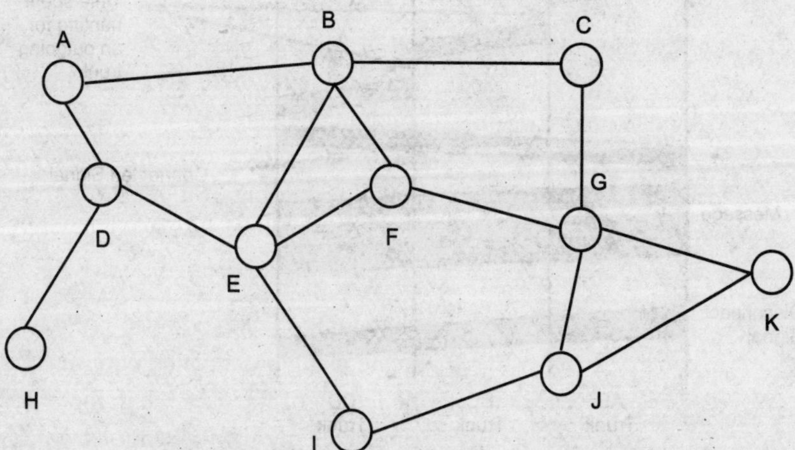

Figure 4.2: A mesh of network nodes (A-K) connected by links.

Any of the three approaches (circuit switching, message switching, and packet switching) could yield minimum delay in a particular situation, though situations where message switching yields minimum delay are rare. The relative performance of circuit switching and packet switching depends strongly on the speed and "cost" of establishing a connection.

4.2.1 CIRCUIT SWITCHING

Circuit switching is the most familiar technique used to build a communications network. It is used for ordinary telephone calls. It allows communications equipment and circuits, to be shared among users. Each user has sole access to a circuit (functionally equivalent to a pair of copper wires) during network use. Consider communication between two points A and D in a network. The connection between A and D is provided using (shared) links between two other pieces of equipment, B and C.

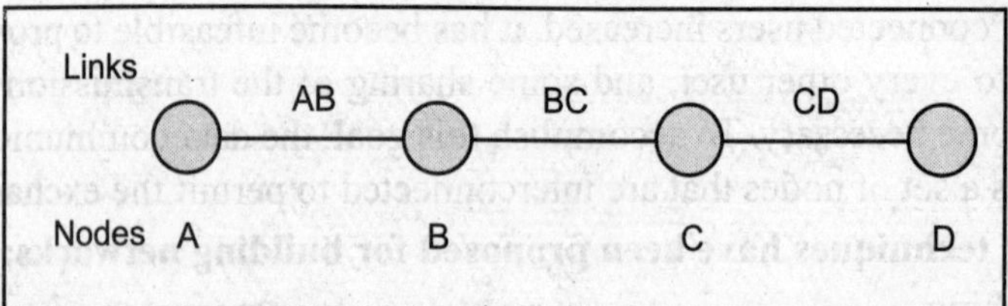

Figure 4.3: A connection between two systems A & D formed from 3 links

Network use is initiated by a connection phase, during which a circuit is set up between source and destination, and terminated by a disconnect phase. These phases, with associated timings, are illustrated in the figure below.

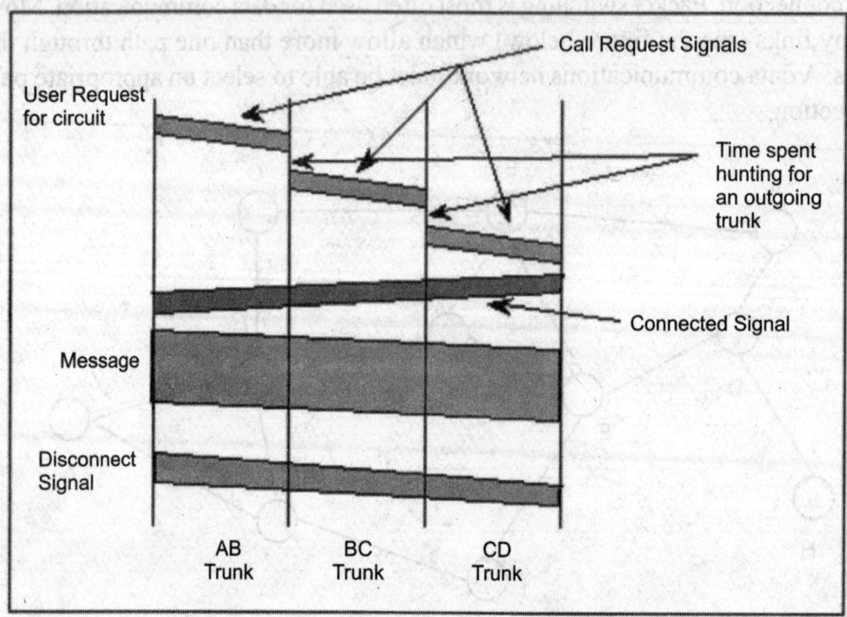

Figure 4.4: A circuit switched connection between A and D

(Information flows in two directions. Information sent from the calling end is shown in pink and information returned from the remote end is shown in blue)

After a user requests a circuit, the desired destination address must be communicated to the local switching node (B). In a telephony network, this is achieved by dialing the number.

Node B receives the connection request and identifies a path to the destination (D) via an intermediate node (C). This is followed by a circuit connection phase handled by the switching nodes and initiated by allocating a free circuit to C (link BC), followed by transmission of a call request signal from node B to node C. In turn, node C allocates a link (CD) and the request is then passed to node D after a similar delay.

The circuit is then established and may be used. While it is available for use, resources (i.e. in the intermediate equipment at B and C) and capacity on the links between the equipment are dedicated to the use of the circuit.

After completion of the connection, a signal confirming circuit establishment (a connect signal in the diagram) is returned; this flows directly back to node A with no search delays since the circuit has been established. Transfer of the data in the message then begins. After data transfer, the circuit is disconnected; a simple disconnect phase is included after the end of the data transmission.

Delays for setting up a circuit connection can be high, especially if ordinary telephone equipment is used. Call setup time with conventional equipment is typically on the order of 5 to 25 seconds after completion of dialing. New fast circuit switching techniques can reduce delays. Trade-offs between circuit switching and other types of switching depend strongly on switching times.

Examples of circuit switched networks

- Public Switched Telephone Network (PSTN)
- ISDN B-channel
- Circuit Switched Data (CSD) and High-Speed Circuit-Switched Data (HSCSD) service in cellular systems such as GSM
- Datakit
- X.21 (Used in the German DATEX-L and Scandinavian DATEX circuit switched data network)

The below table describes the example of circuit switched services.

Table 4.1: Examples of circuit-switched services

Type of service	Bandwidth	Features
POTS	<64 Kbps	Adequate for transmitting text and low quality video; it is a dial-up connection requiring modem; limited by 3 to 4 KHz bandwidth.
Switched 56	64 Kbps	Dial-up connection requiring DSU/CSU; sufficient for low-resolution video; also used as backup facilities.
Leased Lines	64 Kbps to 274 Mbps	Dedicated lines; expensive but dependable and offer high quality connection. Typically, they are provisioned within the circuit-switched infrastructure for the duration of a lease.
ISDN	144 Kbps to 2 Mbps	End-to-end digital connectivity with different interfaces offering various bandwidths.
SONET	N × 51.84 Mbps	Used with optical fibers; N = 1, 3, 12, 48, 192, 768

Advantages and Disadvantages

Circuit switching was the dominant switching technology for more than 100 years. With such a long technological history, circuit switching is well understood, extremely well developed, and widely deployed in the form of the world wide public telephone system. Furthermore, advances in solid-state technology and micro-processors have led to constant improvement of capabilities of circuit-switching technology and, consequently, its cost effectiveness. In addition, new switching techniques, including wavelength-division switching, as well as high speed signaling between switches, such as common channel signaling CCS) , have reduced average circuit setup delay and provided numerous new features.

In spite of emergence of newer switching technologies, namely packet switching, circuit-switching technology remains an appropriate and easily used technique with many unique advantages. One of the major advantages of circuit switching is that it is an essentially transparent service with no storage requirement. Once the connection is established, constant-rate data is provided to the connected stations. An important consequence of transparency is that no buffer overhead is required to accommodate data bursts that can be created by store and- forward packet switching. Furthermore, the analog or digital data is passed through as-is from source to destination. Clearly, upon establishing the switched path, the time delay in delivering the data is only that resulting from speed-of-light delays, which are typically small compared to buffer delays, allowing real-time interaction between stations.

Circuit-switching technology also has major drawbacks, which make it less desirable for certain applications. A major issue with circuit switching is that all resources must be available and dedicated through the network between terminals before the communication takes place. Otherwise, the communication request will be blocked. This can result in potential channel inefficiency. For example, consider a case in which channel capacity is dedicated for the entire duration of a connection, however, no data is actually being transferred. For voice communications, since the idle times are minimum,

high utilization can be expected. However, for data communications, since the capacity may be idle during most of the time of the connection (e.g., when we are only reading a downloaded Web page), circuit switching can result in relatively low utilization.

Another major issue with circuit switching is that in order to setup circuits between end-stations, circuit switching facilities must be capable of processing large signaling at high-speed. Hence, existing systems may not be efficient for busty traffic with short message durations and sporadic transmissions.

4.2.2 PACKET SWITCHING

Packet switching is similar to message switching using short messages. Any message exceeding a network-defined maximum length is broken up into shorter units, known as packets, for transmission; the packets, each with an associated header, are then transmitted individually through the network. The fundamental difference in packet communication is that the data is formed into packets with a pre-defined header format (i.e. PCI), and well-known "idle" patterns which are used to occupy the link when there is no data to be communicated.

Packet network equipment discards the "idle" patterns between packets and processes the entire packet as one piece of data. The equipment examines the packet header information (PCI) and then either removes the header (in an end system) or forwards the packet to another system. If the out-going link is not available, then the packet is placed in a queue until the link becomes free. A packet network is formed by links which connect packet network equipment.

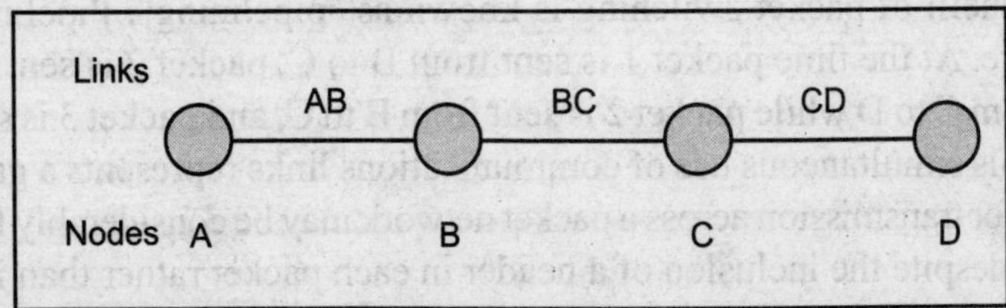

Figure 4.5: Communication between A and D using circuits which are shared using packet switching.

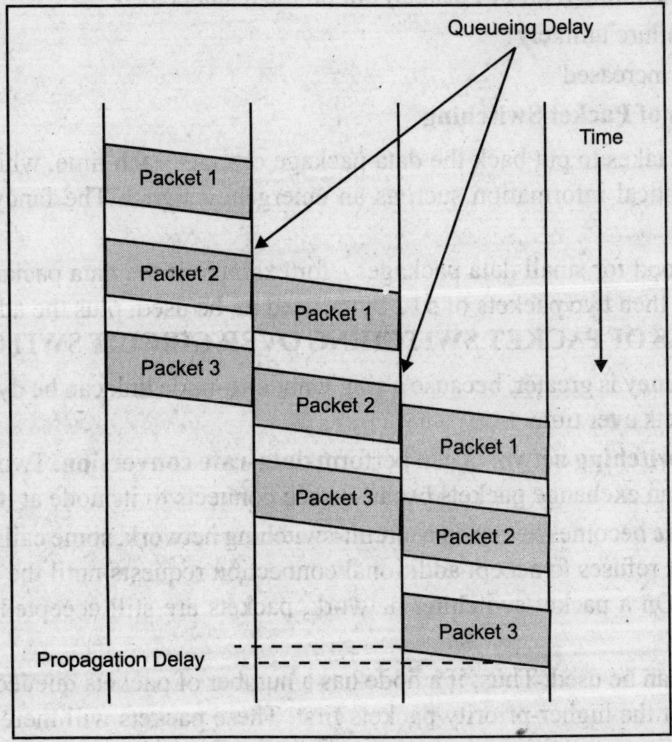

Figure 4.6: Packet-switched communication between systems A and D

(The message in this case has been broken into three parts labelled 1-3)

There are two important benefits from packet switching.

1. The first and most important benefit is that since packets are short, the communication links between the nodes are only allocated to transferring a single message for a short period of time while transmitting each packet. Longer messages require a series of packets to be sent, but do not require the link to be dedicated between the transmission of each packet. The implication is that packets belonging to other messages may be sent between the packets of the message being sent from A to D. This provides a much fairer sharing of the resources of each of the links.

2. Another benefit of packet switching is known as "pipelining". Pipelining is visible in the figure above. At the time packet 1 is sent from B to C, packet 2 is sent from A to B; packet 1 is sent from C to D while packet 2 is sent from B to C, and packet 3 is sent from A to B, and so forth. This simultaneous use of communications links represents a gain in efficiency; the total delay for transmission across a packet network may be considerably less than for message switching, despite the inclusion of a header in each packet rather than in each message.

Advantages of Packet Switching

- More efficient use of lines
- Cost based on time (No. of Packets) not on the distance.
- Network failure unlikely
- Security is increased

Disadvantages of Packet Switching

- The time it takes to put back the data package changes each time, which can be a problem for time-critical information such as an emergency signal. The fancy name is for this is 'latency'.
- Not very good for small data packages - for example if the data package itself is only 600 bytes long, then two packets of 512 bytes need to be used, plus the address information.

ADVANTAGES OF PACKET SWITCHING OVER CIRCUIT SWITCHING

1. **Line efficiency** is greater, because a single node-to-node link can be dynamically shared by many packets over time.
2. **A packet switching** networks can perform **data-rate conversion.** Two stations of different data rates can exchange packets because each connects to its node at its proper data rate.
3. When **traffic** becomes heavy on a circuit-switching network, some calls are blocked; that is, the network refuses to accept additional connection requests until the load on the network decreases. On a packet-switching network, packets are still accepted, but delivery delay increases.
4. **Priorities** can be used. Thus, if a node has a number of packets queued for transmission; it can transmit the higher-priority packets first. These packets will therefore experience less delay than lower-priority packets.

4.2.2.1 DATAGRAM NETWORKS

Two basic approaches to packet switching are common: The most common is datagram switching (also known as a "best-effort network" or a network supporting the connection-less network service).This is what is used in the network layer of the Internet.

1. Datagram Packet Networks

Datagram transmission uses a different scheme to determine the route through the network of links. Using datagram transmission, each packet is treated as a separate entity and contains a header with the full information about the intended recipient. The intermediate nodes examine the header of a packet and select an appropriate link to an intermediate node which is nearer the destination. In this system, the packets do not follow a pre-established route, and the intermediate nodes (usually known as "routers") do not require prior knowledge of the routes that will be used.

A datagram network is analogous to sending a message as a series of postcards through the postal system. Each card is independently sent to the final destination (using the postal system). To receive the whole message, the receiver must collect all the postcards and sort them into the original order. Not all postcards need be delivered by the postal system, and not all take the same length of time to arrive.

In a datagram network delivery is not guaranteed (although they are usually reliably sent). Enhancements, if required, to the basic service (e.g. reliable delivery) must be provided by the end systems (i.e. user's computers) using additional software. The most common datagram network is the Internet which uses the IP network protocol. Applications which do not require more than a best effort service can be supported by direct use of packets in a datagram network (using the User Datagram Protocol (UDP) transport protocol). Such applications include Internet Video, Voice Communication, messages notifying a user that she/he has received new email, etc.

One merit of the datagram approach is that not all packets need to follow the same path (route) through the network (although frequently packets do follow the same route). This removes the need to set-up and tear-down the path, reducing the processing overhead, and a need for Intermediate Systems to execute an additional protocol.

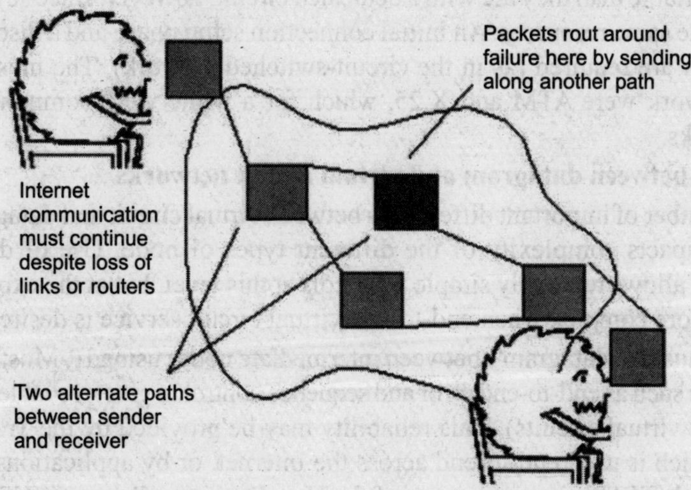

Figure 4.7: Datagram transmission

Packets may also be routed around busy parts of the network when alternate paths exist. This is useful when a particular intermediate system becomes busy or overloaded with excessive volumes of packets to send. It can also provide a high degree of fault tolerance, when an individual intermediate system or communication circuit fails. As long as a route exists through the network between two end systems, they are able to communicate. Only if there is no possible way to send the packets, will the packets be discarded and not delivered. The fate (success/failure) of an application therefore depends only on existence of an actual path between the two End Systems (ESs). This is known as "fate sharing" - since the application shares the "fate" of the network.

There is another type of network known as a virtual circuit network. This has some advantages in particular scenarios. Although it is **not** covered as a part of the course, there is a web page comparing the two approachès.

2. Datagram's Versus Virtual Circuits

Two basic approaches to packet switching are common: The most common is datagram switching (also known as a "best-effort network" or a network supporting the connection-less network service).This is what is used in the network layer of Internet.

3. Virtual Circuit Packet Networks

In virtual circuit packet switching, an initial setup phase is used to set up a fixed route between the intermediate nodes for all packets which are exchanged during a session between the end nodes (analogous to the circuit-switched telephony network). At each intermediate node, an entry is made in a table to indicate the route for the connection that has been set up. Packets can then use short headers, since only identification of the virtual circuit rather than complete destination address is needed. The intermediate nodes (B, C) process each packet according to the information which was stored in the node when the connection was established.

Enhancements to provide reliability may also be provided. Delivery of packets in proper sequence and with essentially no errors is guaranteed, and congestion control to minimise queuing is common. Delays are more variable than they are with a dedicated circuit, however, since several virtual circuits may compete for the same resources. An initial connection setup phase and a disconnect phase at the end of data transfer are required (as in the circuit-switched network). The most common form of virtual circuit network were ATM and X.25, which for a while were commonly used for public packet data networks.

4. Differences between datagram and virtual circuit networks

There are a number of important differences between virtual circuit and datagram networks. The choice strongly impacts complexity of the different types of node. Use of datagram's between intermediate nodes allows relatively simple protocols at this level, but at the expense of making the end (user) nodes more complex when end-to-end virtual circuit service is desired.

The Internet transmits datagram's between intermediate nodes using IP. Most Internet users need additional functions such as end-to-end error and sequence control to give a reliable service (equivalent to that provided by virtual circuits). This reliability may be provided by the Transmission Control Protocol (TCP) which is used end-to-end across the Internet, or by applications such as the trivial file transfer protocol (TFTP) running on top of the User Datagram Protocol (UDP).

4.2.2.2 COMPARISON OF CIRCUIT SWITCHING AND PACKET SWITCHING

We shall look at the important issue of performance.

Performance: To compare circuit switching with packet switching an important issue is performance. There are three types of delays that directly affect the performance. They are as follows.

Propagation delay: The time it takes a signal to propagate from one node to the next. This time is generally negligible. The speed of electromagnetic signals through a wire medium, for example, is typically 2 * 108 m/s.

Transmission time: The time it takes for a transmitter to send out a block of data. For example, it takes 1 s to transmit a 10,000-bit block of data onto a 10-kbps line.

Node delay: The time it takes for a node to perform the necessary processing as it switches data.

The following table illustrates the comparison of circuit switching and packet switching.

Circuit Switching	Datagram Packet Switching	Virtual Circuit Packet Switching
Dedicated transmission path	No Dedicated path	No Dedicated path
Continuous transmission of data	Transmission of packets	Transmission of packets
Interactive	Interactive	Interactive
Messages are not stored	Packets may be stored until delivered	Packets stored until delivered
A Path is established for entire conversation	A Route is established for each packet	Route established for entire conversation
Call setup delay negligible transmission delay	Packet transmission delay	Call setup delay, Packet transmission delay
Busy signal, if called party is busy	Sender may be notified if packet not delivered	Sender notified of connection denied
Overload may block call setup. No delay for established calls.	Overload increases packet delay	Overload may block call setup. Increases packet delay
Electromagnetic or computerized switching nodes	Small switching nodes	Small switching nodes
User responsible for message loss protection	Network responsible for individual packets	Network responsible for packet sequences
No speed or code conversion	Speed and code conversion	Speed and code conversion
Fixed bandwidth	Dynamic use of bandwidth	Dynamic use of bandwidth
No Overhead bits after call setup	Overhead bits in each packet	Overhead bits in each packet

4.2.3 MESSAGE SWITCHING

Sometimes there is no need for a circuit to be established all the way from the source to the destination. Consider a connection between the users (A and D) in the figure below (i.e. A and D) is represented by a series of links (AB, BC, and CD).

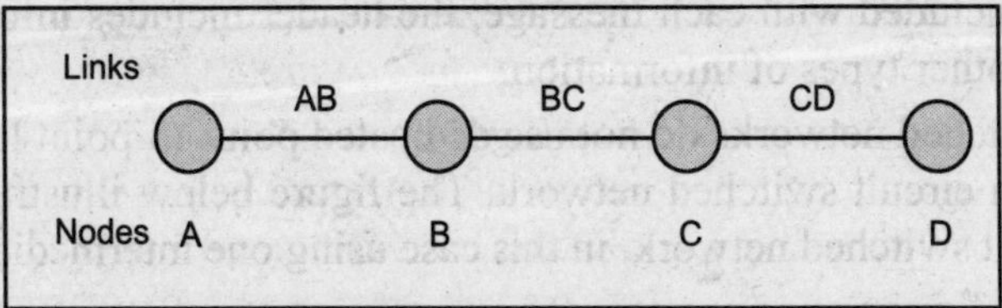

Figure 4.8: A connection between two systems A & D formed from 3 links

For instance, when a telex (or email) message is sent from A to D, it first passes over a local connection (AB). It is then passed at some later time to C (via link BC), and from there to the destination (via link CD). At each message switch, the received message is stored, and a connection is subsequently made to deliver the message to the neighbouring message switch. Message switching is also known as store-and-forward switching since the messages are stored at intermediate nodes en route to their destinations.

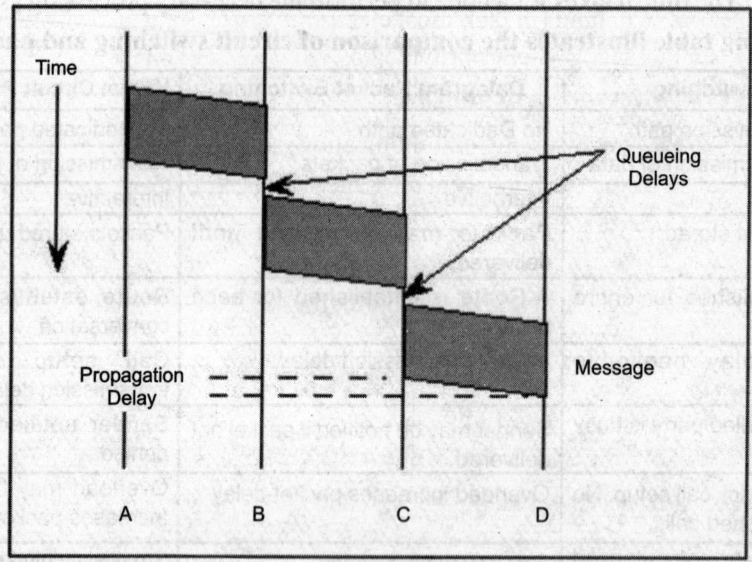

Figure 4.9: The use of message switching to communicate between A and D

The figure illustrates message switching; transmission of only one message is illustrated for simplicity. As the figure indicates, a complete message is sent from node A to node B when the link interconnecting them becomes available. Since the message may be competing with other messages for access to facilities, a queuing delay may be incurred while waiting for the link to become available. The message is stored at B until the next link becomes available, with another queuing delay before it can be forwarded. It repeats this process until it reaches its destination.

Circuit setup delays are replaced by queuing delays. Considerable extra delay may result from storage at individual nodes. A delay for putting the message on the communications link (message length in bits divided by link speed in bps) is also incurred at each node en route. Message lengths are slightly longer than they are in circuit switching, after establishment of the circuit, since header information must be included with each message; the header includes information identifying the destination as well as other types of information.

Most message switched networks do not use dedicated point-to-point links and therefore a call must be set-up using a circuit switched network. The figure below illustrates the use of message switching over a circuit switched network, in this case using one intermediate message switch.

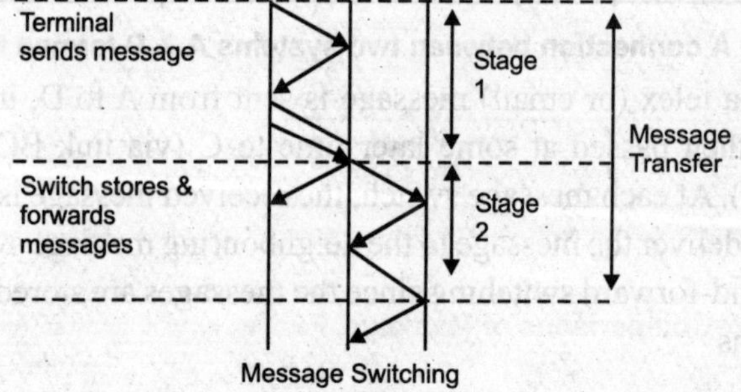

Figure 4.10: Message switching using circuit switched connections between message switches

Although message switching is still used for electronic mail and telex transmission, it has largely been replaced by packet switching (in fact, most electronic mail is carried using message switching with the links between message switches provided by packet or circuit-switched networks).

The advantages to Message Switching are:

- Data channels are shared among communication devices improving the use of bandwidth.
- Messages can be stored temporarily at message switches, when network congestion becomes a problem.
- Priorities may be used to manage network traffic.
- Broadcast addressing uses bandwidth more efficiently because messages are delivered to multiple destinations.

The only real disadvantage to Message Switching is it's not suitable for real time applications such as data communication, video or audio.

4.2.4 COMPARISON OF MESSAGE, PACKET, AND CIRCUIT SWITCHING

Table 4.2 - Comparisons of Message, Packet, and Circuit Switching (Stallings, 2004; Martin, 1985)

Circuit-Switched Networks	Message-Switched Networks	Packet-Switched Networks
Communication is performed through a dedicated path.	No dedicated path exists.	No dedicated path exists.
Provides real-time or continuous transmission of data.	Too slow for real-time or interactive data transmission.	Provides near real-time data transmission.
No data storing is required.	Messages are stored for later retrieval.	Packets are queued for delivery; they are not stored.
The switch path is established for the entire connection time.	The route is established for each message.	The route is established for each packet.
For small messages, the data transmission time is negligible compared to the time required to setup and tear-down the connection.	The message delivery time can be substantially long.	The packet delivery time is very short.
The connection is blocked if the end-user is busy or not available. Once the connection starts, no blocking may occur.	No message blocking can occur as long as the storage capacity is sufficiently large.	Packet blocking can occur, however, the blocked packets will be retrarnmitted to the end-user.
As the network load increases, more blocking can occur.	As the load increases, messages on average experience longer delivery delay.	As the load increases, packets on average experience longer queuing delay, although still very short compared to message switching.
The length of transmission is unlimited.	Messages have no theoretical maximum length and can be very long.	Packets have a maximum length.

Table 4.2: Comparisons of Message, Packet, and Circuit Switching

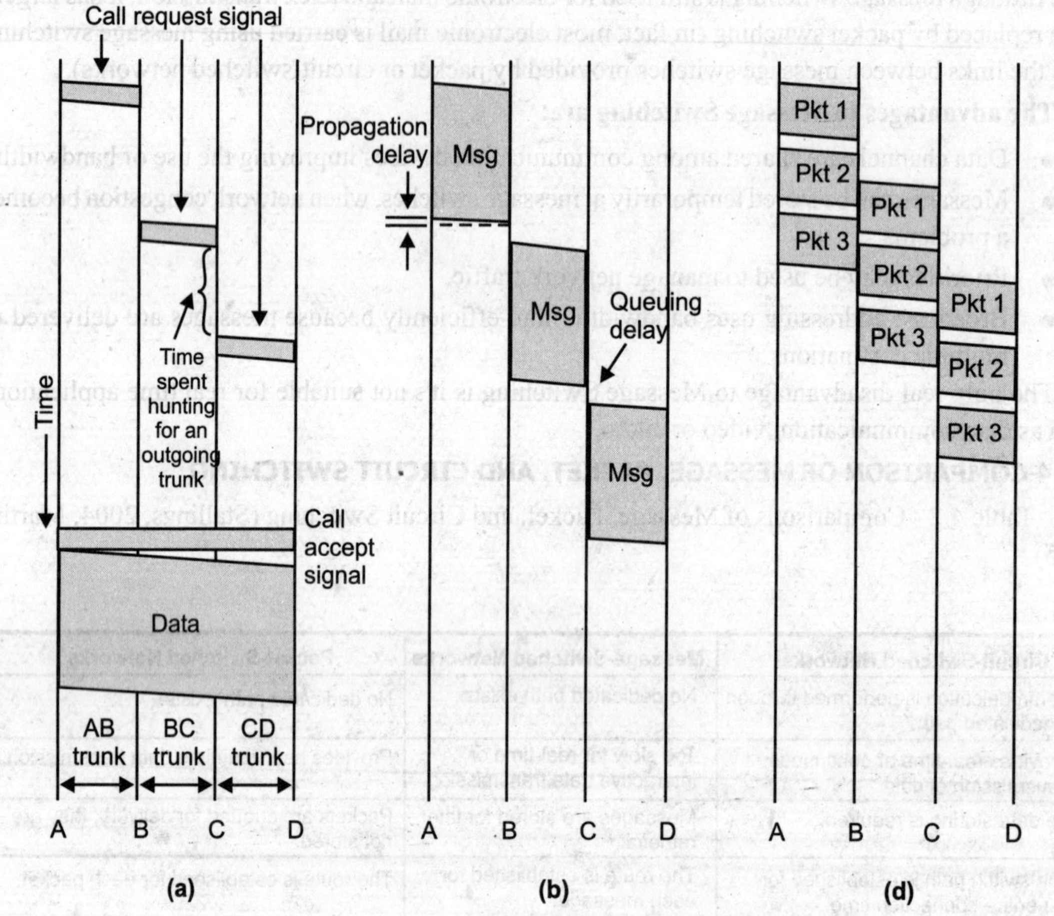

Figure 4.11: Event timing diagram in (a) a circuit-switched network and (b) a message-switched network; (c) packet switched network

4.3 CONNECTIONLESS AND CONNECTION ORIENTED SERVICES

Following are the Connectionless and connection oriented services:

4.3.1 CONNECTION-ORIENTED SERVICE

When an application uses the connection-oriented service, the client and the server (residing in different end systems) send control packets to each other before sending packets with real data (such as e-mail messages). This so-called handshaking procedure alerts the client and server, allowing them to prepare for an onslaught of packets.

Once the handshaking procedure is finished, a "connection" is said to be established between the two end systems. But the two end systems are connected in a very loose manner, hence the terminology "connection-oriented". In particular, only the end systems themselves are aware of this connection; the packet switches (i.e., routers) within the Internet are completely oblivious to the connection. This is because a TCP connection is nothing more than allocated resources (buffers) and state variables in the end systems. The packet switches do not maintain any connection state information.

The Internet's connection oriented service comes bundled with several other services, including reliable data transfer, flow control and congestion control. By **reliable data transfer,** we mean that an application can rely on the connection to deliver all of its data without error and in the proper order.

Reliability in the Internet is achieved through the use of acknowledgments and retransmissions. To get a preliminary idea about how the Internet implements the reliable transport service, consider an application that has established a connection between end systems A and B. When end system B receives a packet from A, it sends an acknowledgment; when end system A receives the acknowledgment, it knows that the corresponding packet has definitely been received. When end system A doesn't receive an acknowledgment, it assumes that the packet it sent was not received by B; it therefore retransmits the packet. Flow control makes sure that neither side of a connection overwhelms the other side by sending too many packets too fast. Indeed, the application at one one side of the connection may not be able to process information as quickly as it receives the information. Therefore, there is a risk of overwhelming either side of an application. The flow-control service forces the sending end system to reduce its rate whenever there is such a risk.

The Internet's congestion control service helps prevent the Internet from entering a state of grid lock. When a router becomes congested, its buffers can overflow and packet loss can occur. In such circumstances, if every pair of communicating end systems continues to pump packets into the network as fast as they can, gridlock sets in and few packets are delivered to their destinations. The Internet avoids this problem by forcing end systems to diminish the rate at which they send packets into the network during periods of congestion. End systems are alerted to the existence of several congestion when they stop receiving acknowledgments for the packets they have sent.

4.3.2 CONNECTIONLESS SERVICE

There is no handshaking with the Internet's connectionless service: When one side of an application wants to send packets to another side of an application, the sending application simply sends the packets. Since there is no handshaking procedure prior to the transmission of the packets, data can be delivered faster. But there are no acknowledgments either, so a source never knows for sure which packets arrive at the destination. Moreover, the service makes no provision for flow control or congestion control. The Internet's connectionless service is provided by UDP (User Datagram Protocol);

Most of the more familiar Internet applications use TCP, the Internet's connection-oriented service. These applications include Telnet (remote login), SMTP (for electronic mail), FTP (for file transfer), and HTTP (for the Web). Nevertheless, UDP, the Internet's connectionless service, is used by many applications, including many of the emerging multimedia applications, such as Internet phone, audio-on demand, and video conferencing.

4.4 GENERIC PACKET-SWITCHED NETWORK CHARACTERISTICS

Following are the various characteristics of generic packet-switched network:

4.4.1 DELAY

Delay is an important design and performance characteristic of a computer network or telecommunications network. The delay of a network specifies how long it takes for a bit of data to travel across the network from one node or endpoint to another. It is typically measured in multiples or fractions of seconds. Delay may differ slightly, depending on the location of the specific pair of communicating nodes. Although users only care about the total delay of a network, engineers need to perform precise measurements.

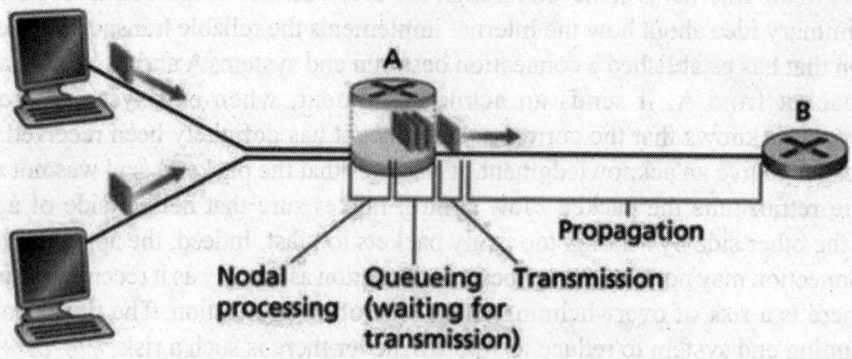

Figure 4.12: Packet transmission delay model

Nodal delay (one switch):

dnodal = dproc + dqueue + dtrans + dprop

Delay components:

1. **Processing delay:** integrity checking, routing, etc.
2. **Queuing delay:** Waiting in output buffer prior to transmission. Variable.
3. **Transmission delay:** Getting the entire packet "out the door." Let packet contain L bits and link transmission rate be R b/s. Transmission delay is then L/R.
4. **Propagation delay:** Time for one bit to traverse the medium between two switches.

End-to-end delay with n switches along the route:

$$\sum_{I=1}^{n} d \text{ nodal}$$

4.4.2 QUEUING DELAY AND PACKET LOSS

If packets arrive more quickly at the switch than we can send them, we have a couple problems:

1. Packets will begin to queue up in the switch's buffers - increasing queuing delay.
2. If the buffer fills completely, packets will be dropped - lost forever.

Traffic intensity is a metric used to describe queuing delay:

La/R, where a is the packet arrival rate, per second.

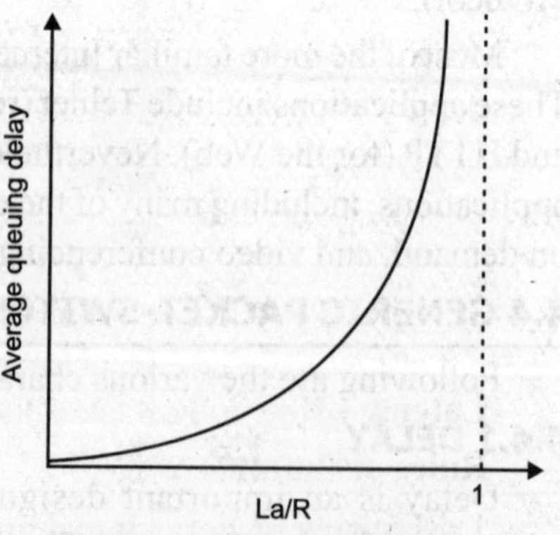

Figure 4.13: Queuing delay

4.4.3 THROUGHPUT AND LATENCY

Two throughput measures:

1. Instantaneous throughput - throughput at a particular instant.
2. Average throughput.

Transferred 5 MB MP3 file in 12 sec.: (5 *220* 8)/30 = 1.4 mb/s.

The "slowest" link determines the overall throughput - the bottleneck:

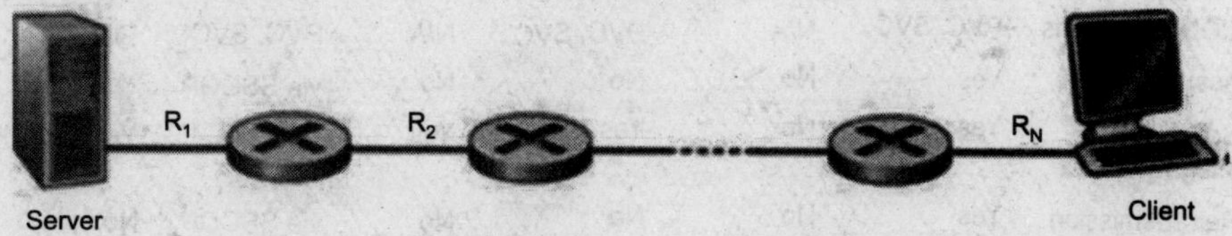

Figure 4.14: Average Throughput

4.4.4 INTERNET RESOURCES ARE SHARED

Following is the diagram of shared internet resources:

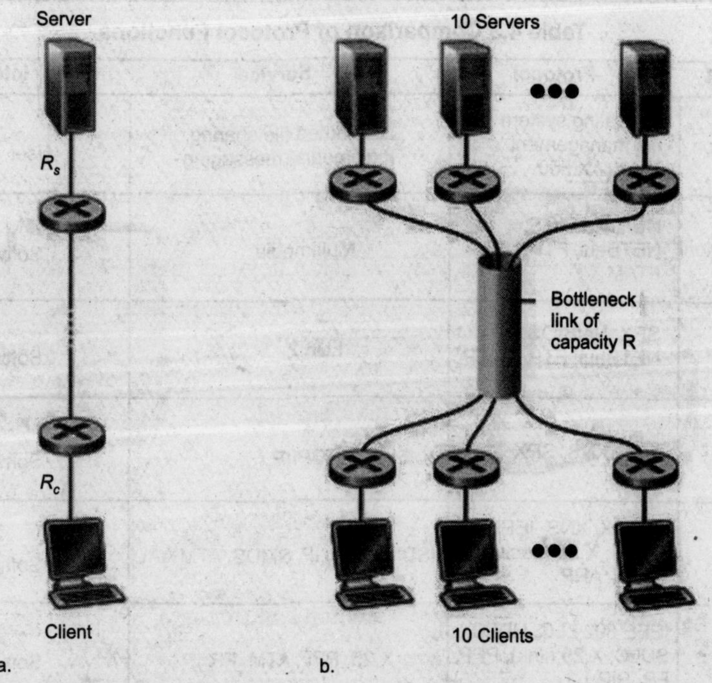

Figure 4.15: Internet resources are shared

Latency: How long it takes the first bit to make it from end-to-end.

Rules of thumb:

1. Latency matters for real time applications: gaming, telephony. Throughput may or may not matter - low-fi audio, no; video, yes.

2. Throughput usually matters for file transfer.
3. Neither particularly matter for email; maybe IM.

Function	X.25	IP	FR	SMDS	ATM	MPLS
Switching type	Packet	Packet	Frame	Cell	Cell	Packet/ Frame/Cell
Mode	CONS	CLNS		CLNS	CLNS w/CLNS	CLNS for CLNS
CONS elements	PVC, SVC	N/A	PVC, SVC	N/A	PVC, SVC	Flow
Assured mode	Yes	No	No	No	via SSCOP	Yes
Sequence integrity	Yes	No	Yes	Yes	Yes	Yes
Retransmission	Yes	No	No	No	via SSCOP	No
Traffic control	None	None	CIR, EIR	Access Class	PCR, SCR	FR ro ATM
Flo control	Yes	No	No	No	No	No
Congestion control	Transmit	No (but possible)	Transmit Receiver	No	Receiver	No

Table 4.3 Comparison of Protocol Functions

OSIRM	Protocol	Service	Interface
Application	Operating system file management X.400 / X.500	Distributed file sharing, multimedia, messaging	User, software
Presentation	NCP, NetBIOS, NETBeui, FTP, NFS FTAM	Multimedia	Software
Session	SPX, NetBIOS, NETBeui, FTP, SMTP	LU6.2	Software
Transport	TCP, XNS, SPX	TCP/IP	Software
Network	IP, IPX, XNS, IEEE, 802.1, X.25 (packet), ISDN, ARP	ISDN, X.25, IP, SMDS, ATM AAL	Software
LLC	IEEE 802 LLC, HDLC, SDLC, X.25 (link), PPP, FR, SIP, L2	X.25, PPP, ATM, FR	Software
MAC	IEED 802.X, SMDS SIP, FDDI	ATM, FDDI, High-speed-Ckt switching	Ethernet, Token Ring, FDDI X3.139
Physical	DS0, FT1, DS1, DS3	DS0, FT1, DS1, DS3, HSCS	Copper/coax/fiber media systems and interfaces

Figure 4.16: Mapping of services and protocols to the OSIRM

4.4.5 SUMMARY OF NETWORKING ASPECTS

Table 4.4 compares the networking aspects of public data communication services. The preceding sections defined the terms, concepts, and acronyms listed in this table.

Aspect	X.25	IP	FR	SMDS	ATM
Addressing Plan Layer 3	X.121	IPv4/IPv6	—	E.164	E.164, NSAP
Addressing Plan Layer 2	LCN	—	DLCI	MID	VPI/VCI
Maximum packet length	< 1024 octets	< 65,535 octets	< 8192 octets	< 9188 octets	< 65,535 octets[1]
IP encapsulation	RFC 877	Native	RFC 1490	RFC 1209	RFC 1483
Routing standard	None	RIP, OSPF, E-IGRP, BGP, MIPLS	None	ISSI	P-NNI
Access medium	Dedicated	Dedicated or shared	Dedicated	Shared or dedicated[2]	Dedicated
Access sharing	No	Yes	Yes	Yes	Yes
Point-to-point	Yes	Yes	Yes	Yes	Yes
Multicast	No	Yes	Yes[4]	Yes	No
Point-to-multipoint	No	No[3]	No	No	Yes

1. Depends on AAL
2. Multiple users share same access bus.
3. Multicast can be achieved by point-to-multipoint operations.
4. Can be achieved with MPLS and multipoint services

Table 4.4: Comparison of networking aspects

4.5 PRIVATE VERSUS PUBLIC NETWORKING

When implementing wide area networking, you need to decide whether to utilize a private or a public WAN. A private WAN consists of routers and links that the company (containing the system end users) owns and operates. This is the traditional approach to wide area networking. Private WANs often consist of leased T1 and 56Kbps digital circuits that provide connections between user-owned and user-maintained routers.

With public WANs, the company leases connections to a WAN architecture that supports multiple unrelated companies. Generally, these public networks utilize Frame Relay, SMDS, or ATM protocols.

In general, there are tradeoffs between the private and public approaches. The benefits and drawbacks of the private WAN are as follows:

- More suitable for WANs requiring a low degree of meshing (very few links, as in the case of a centralized topology)

- Service fees that are economically feasible for metropolitan areas
- Higher initial cost because of a greater number of hardware interfaces and circuit installations An MIS group of a company views a public WAN as a connection to a network "cloud," whereas it views a private WAN as a collection of routers and links (communications lines).
- Lease fees sensitive to the distance between sites
- In-house management required; therefore, potentially higher operating costs
- Fixed bandwidth

The benefits of the public WAN are as follows:

- More suitable for a WAN requiring a high degree of meshing (a large number of links, as in a distributed topology)
- Lower initial cost because of a fewer number of hardware interfaces and circuit installations
- Potentially lower operating cost because of less staffing requirements
- Lease fees not sensitive to the distance between sites
- Variable bandwidth offered (bandwidth on demand)
- Management provided by the carrier; therefore, potentially lower operating costs
- Service fees that are most economical for long-haul (outside the metropolitan area) distances
- Very little control, if any, over network restoration in the event of network failure

Traditionally, organizations have implemented private point-to-point WANs to support communications between remote terminals to centralized mainframe-based applications. T1 is a common communications circuit that companies lease to provide links between routers in a private network. Bell Labs originally developed the T1 standard to multiplex multiple phone calls into a composite signal, suitable for transmission through a digital communications circuit. A T1 signal consists of a serial transmission of T1 frames, with each frame carrying 8-bit samples of 24 separate channels. You can lease an entire T1 circuit (1.544Mbps) or only single fractional T1 channels (64Mbps each) from a telephone service carrier.

With the development of distributed client/server applications, most organizations now require technologies suitable for highly meshed topologies. There's a greater need to support communications among the remote sites, not just to a centralized data center. Thus, you should seriously consider leasing the use of a public packet-switching WAN to support today's demand for distributed computing. There are many technologies to choose from when implementing a WAN.

When do you require a specific technology? Here are a few guidelines based on. [Data Network Design by Darren L. spohn]

4.5.1 WHEN DO YOU NEED A PRIVATE LINE?

A private line, or dedicated circuit between two points, might be required when

- Point-to-point connectivity is required between only two locations.
- Average link utilization (traffic volume) between two points is very high (more than 30 percent average utilization during the busy hour of the busy day), such as with LAN extension.
- Building a star (hub-and-spoke) network configuration to a single hub site.
- Integrated access of voice, video, and data is required over a single circuit from an existing CPE device such as a PBX, channel bank, or multiplexer.

- Traffic characteristics are constant-bit-rate (CBR), as with video conferencing.
- A consistent QoS is required that can be provided only by a dedicated circuit (for example, less than 30 milliseconds delay).

4.5.2 WHEN DO YOU NEED X.25 SERVICE?

X.25 public service might be required when

- Traffic is bursty and delay-insensitive in nature.
- Reliable data transport is required at speeds from 150 bps to 56,000 bps.
- Facilities with poor-quality communications are prevalent.
- Error checking and flow control are required to be built into the protocol.
- International connectivity to countries and cities without fiber-optics is required.

4.5.3 WHEN DO YOU NEED FR SERVICE?

FR might be required when

- Consolidation of multiple protocols (that is, IP, IPX, and SNA) over a single network access circuit and technology is needed.
- A large amount of LAN-to-LAN traffic must be transported.
- Traffic is variable bit rate (VBR), very bursty, and non-delay-sensitive.
- Multiple locations (usually more than three) require interconnectivity (physical and/or logical meshing).
- Multiple traffic prioritizations down to the protocol or session level is required.
- In-band management capability such as SNMP is required.
- Flexibility for rapid network reconfiguration (at PVC level) is needed.
- Cost-effective alternatives over international PL are required.

4.5.4 WHEN DO YOU NEED ATM SERVICE?

ATM might be required when

- High-speed interconnectivity is required (DS1-DS3).
- Native LAN interconnect speeds of 100 Mbps (and higher) are required.
- Multiple QoS levels are required within a single physical circuit or path.
- Multiple-service interconnection (that is, FR to ATM, LAN to PSTN) is required.
- Integrated access or transport of multiple services, such as PL, FR, SMDS, voice, video and legacy service is required.

4.5.5 WHEN DO YOU NEED AN IP SERVICE?

There are three general types of IP services: remote IP network access (dial, xDSL, cable, private IP services, and public IP services such as the Internet), access to the public Internet (remote and dedicated), and dedicated site-to-site IP connectivity (IP VPN or over a public service like PL, FR, or ATM). These forms of IP services might be required when

- Traffic is bursty and delay-insensitive.
- Remote access such as dial, xDSL, or cable modem is required, but higher-speed dedicated services (PL, FR, and ATM) are not available.

- Facilities with poor-quality communications are prevalent.
- High and intermittent quantities of data retransmission are acceptable.
- International connectivity to countries and cities without fiber-optics is required.
- CoS vs. QoS is required.

4.5.6 WHEN DO YOU NEED A PUBLIC DATA SERVICE?

What criteria drive the decision to consider a public data service?

- Total cost of ownérship: lower cost to buy network services versus build private network
- Access to redundant/diverse facilities (no common facilities) in access and backbone
- Want to achieve the benefits of a public SONET/DWDM redundant, self-healing architecture
- Guarantees of availability, reliability, and performance as defined and guaranteed through SLAs with refund of predefined damages if not met
- Fixed, recurring price
- Multiprotocol and multiservice transport and interoperability
- Gateway services (Internet, PSTN)

Aspect	X.25	IP	FR	SMDS	ATM
Efficiency (1 best, 4 worst)	2nd	3rd	1st	4th	1st, 2nd, 3rd, and 4th
Multiple service support	Possible	Possible	Possible	Some	Best
CPE hardware use	Existing	Existing	Existing	Existing	New
CPE software use	Existing	Existing	New	New	New
Access ubiquity	Limited	Best	High	None	Medium
Market demand and geographic coverage	Low	High	High	Low	Moderate
Evolution potential	Low	Some	Some	None	High
Service	Low	Varies	Low	Varies	Medium
Technological obsolescence factor	High	Low	Low	High	Low

Table 4.5: Comparison of Business Aspects

4.6 BUSINESS ASPECTS OF PACKET-, FRAME-, AND CELL-SWITCHING SERVICES

Here we can compare several business aspects of data communication services. These include the trade-off between efficiency and features, impacts on user hardware and software, a quantification of the savings due to integration, an assessment of the market demand, and pricing comparisons of various data communications services.

4.6.1 EFFICIENCY VERSUS FEATURES

One thing that you might want to consider is the trade-off of efficiency versus features. Both might affect your higher-layer protocols and thus you're applications, as well as the cost of operating/managing your network. Increasing the number or quality of features often comes at the expense of decreased efficiency and increased support costs.

Here the efficiency and features of three major data protocols used in private or public networking are compared: FR, ATM (using AAL5), and IP.

FR supports variable-length packets, with an overhead of 5 to 7 bytes per packet (excluding zero insertion). This is the most efficient protocol with respect to overhead of the three protocols considered here. However, FR might not support multiple QoS classes, especially if some frames are very long. The longest standardized frame size required is 1600 bytes, while the protocol will support frames up to 8192 bytes long (but the CRC check is accurate only up to 4000 bytes). Its efficiency approaches 100 percent for very long user data packets (for example, IP packets).

ATM using AAL5 provides functions very similar to FR, and provides the additional flexibility of mixing very long packets with other delay-sensitive traffic. AAL5 also allows support for up to a 64-kbyte packet length which FR does not. The 8 bytes in the trailer combined with the 5 bytes of ATM cell header overhead reduce the achievable efficiency by 17 percent. Because the variable-length packet must be segmented into fixed-length cells, the resultant efficiency decreases markedly when this segmentation results in one or a few bytes of packet data in the last cell. Its efficiency approaches 90 percent for very large packets.

Figure 4.17 plots the resulting efficiency of each protocol versus user packet size. Note how very short packets are handled very inefficiently by ATM Adaptation Layers (AALs) 3, 4, and 5. In one more example, a study performed on current Internet traffic produced calculations showing that the efficiency of offering this traffic over ATM would be approximately 60 percent because of the large proportion of very short packets!

Now the question arises: Which protocol is best for your application?

Answer is depending on the following features:

- If you need a feature that only the less-efficiency protocols support, then the choice is clear; you can't use a more efficient protocol if it doesn't support a critical feature.
- If your network will require support for multiple QoS classes for different concurrent application, then ATM is probably a good choice.
- If you need to connect to other networks via a public service, access users on the public Internet, IP or FR are probably good choices, either as a stand-alone service or carried over an ATM-based service.
- If raw efficiency is key, and support for multimedia applications is not required, then FR is a good solid choice.

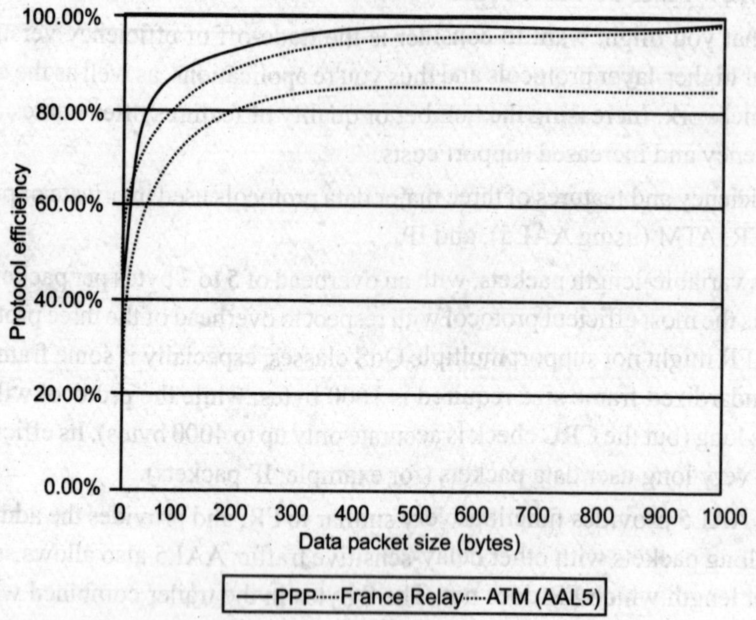

Figure 4.17: Protocol efficiency versus packet size

4.6.2 CPE HARDWARE AND SOFTWARE IMPACTS

Explain the hardware and software cost and changes made of adding a new protocol to, or changing the existing protocol of your WAN or LAN?

- IP already works on most existing hardware platforms, and therefore could require minimal upgrade, whereas upgrading from FR to ATM might require all new CPE.
- Hardware changes might include new interface cards, switches, hubs, routers, and potentially new CSU/DSUs.
- Software support for all three of these protocols is widely available, but might require new software load be applied to all CPE. Software changes might include operating systems, device drivers, and entirely new applications, or could have an impact on existing applications.

4.6.3 INTEGRATION SAVINGS

Services such as FR and ATM offer economies of integration as follows:

1. **Frame Relay:** An enterprise can purchase a public FR service and access the public Internet over the same FR access circuit. Access (though a gateway) to the PSTN is also available from a FR access circuit.
2. **ATM:** ATM supports integrated access and transport of voice, data, and video, and also allows Internet and PSTN access and termination from an originating ATM port. The need for multimedia and mixed services over a single integrated access line or shared switch port is a key advantage of ATM. Technologies that integrate multiple forms of traffic (voice, data, and video) and can prioritize between them can achieve and sustain higher bandwidth utilization patterns than single traffic pattern technologies.

This integration capability enables cost savings that must be measured against the additional cost of new hardware and network complexity.

4.6.4 UBIQUITY AND MARKET DEMAND

X.25 and IP services have been around for many years. They are widely available in Europe, Latin America, and Asia, and IP is extensively available in North America (most X.25 services have been decommissioned in North America, but remain active in other parts of the world). Part of the reason for this is the relatively expensive cost of a private line and the lack of fiber-optic transmission facilities in most areas of the world.

Furthermore, X.25 is slow and has high processing overhead and long delays. On the other hand, it has accuracy and guaranteed delivery, both of which are critical for low-quality transmission environments, and native IP provides a ubiquity of access better that any other public network service short of the PSTN.

IP network services continue to experience phenomenal growth, which indicates the pent-up demand for ubiquitous data communications access and cost-effective transport. Plus many IP services now offer the capability to purchase multiple CoS or reserve bandwidth. Most global IP service is provided over the public Internet, a good bit over private carrier IP infrastructures, and some is transported over transport-protocol service such as FR, ATM and MPLS where access is paid through an Internet service provider (ISP) in either a flat rate or usage-pricing configuration.

FR services continue to see strong growth. Most users are large corporations who use it for site-to-site corporate virtual private network connectivity. New MPSL deployments and consequently services such as IP-enabled FR and ATM have made virtual meshing of IP network communications routing over FR/ATM networks even more economical and flexible. And FR continues to be an excellent alternative to private lines.

The SMDS market has largely dissipated, especially in the United States, but some services are supported in Europe. Most SMDS users have converted to IP VPNs or ATM services.

ATM PVC and SVC services are being used by many corporate customers in a manner similar to FR to construct virtual private networks. In many cases, ATM is sued at the HQ or central site due to port speed requirements (FT1 or DS3) with FR at remote sites. Most providers offer ATM DS1 at the same cost as FR DS1 to make it attractive for the user to economically justify an upgrade from FR to ATM. Plus IP operates seamlessly over ATM.

4.6.5 GENERAL PRICING STRUCTURES

Services such as FR, SMDS, IP, and ATM can either be classified as enhanced services, and thus would not be offered under a structured tariff, or else would be offered under a tariff. Most are now nontariff public pricing. The pricing and billing policies of these enhanced data services are based on many factors, including

- Local Access Physical Circuit based on speed and distance to local serving PoP
- Physical Port access speed based on bandwidth available
- Total virtual connection bandwidth per port or per virtual channel/circuit based on defined traffic parameters
- CIR for FR

- Access class for SMDS
- PCR and SCR (or their PVC CIR equivalents) for ATM
- CoS for IP
- Other QoS class
- Fixed, Tiered, or Usage rates

Usage-based billing rates can be measured in packets, frames, cells, or just total bytes delivered over a time period and rounded off to some accuracy. For example, the charge can be based on millions of cells delivered per month. Fixed charges include a port charge, access charges (for the circuit from the customer premises to the service provider switch), installation charges, and other fees. A fixed-rate billing option might also include a charge based on the virtual connection bandwidth, priority, and QoS class. There are also many credits, bulk discounts, time-of-day discounts, and nonrecurring charges that for large accounts are typically waived. The excessive cost of dedicated access services often limit users to low-speed dial or shared circuits (xDSL or cable modems) for LAN-to-LAN traffic, creating a WAN bottleneck. If these circuits are analyzed, it is often seen that they are flooded during the busy hour but are not used much during off-peak, non-business hours. These applications are ideal candidates for virtual networking. For many users, the initial deployment of any virtual data service should be limited, allowing the users to learn their traffic patterns.

4.6.6 PRIVATE LINE PRICING

Various characteristics of Private line pricing include all of the following:

- Linear rate structure
- Fixed monthly recurring charge
- Mileage sensitivity
- Rate increases over longer distances (especially international)
- Significant rate increases with shorter terms

Common private line rates include DS0, FT1, T1, FT3, DS3, and OC-n.

4.6.7 FR PRICING

FR pricing is typically broken down into LEC and IXC components. Pricing characteristics usually include

- Flat rate monthly charge per FR port based on bandwidth selected
- Flat rate monthly charge per local loop (sometimes bundled with FR port)
- Flat rate charge per month per PVC typically based on CIR rate
- No mileage component (usually)
- Possibly a higher cost per MPLS (IP-FR) PVC, also called an enterprise PVC

Typically, the greater the PVC meshing of the network configuration, the more cost-effective the overall design compared with a private line meshed network. Some carriers also offer usage-based pricing at a few cents per megabyte of data received, but beware that the data received includes overhead plus the file being send (the amount depends on the protocols being used) and customers rarely buy usage pricing.

4.6.8 IP PRICING

IP pricing characteristics usually include

- **For dial:** A flat monthly fee up to a certain amount of hours, OR a monthly usage fee based on minutes used in given month
- **For Dedicated Access:** A flat monthly port connection fee that typically includes the local loop

IP pricing can vary widely; for example, IP VPN pricing can be fixed- or usage-based, while IP Internet access can be a flat monthly fee for a T1. xDSL and cable-modem IP Internet access range all across the board.

4.6.9 ATM Pricing

ATM pricing characteristics are broken down into the type of service required. VBR service is offered with a defined SCR (minimum peak BW) and PCR (maximum peak BW), but with only the SCR guaranteed. VBR can come in both connection-oriented (CO) and connectionless (CL) modes. A maximum burst duration and CDV rate is assigned for each VC. CBR service might be charged as a defined bandwidth similar to a traditional, dedicated private line. The primary elements of ATM service fees include a flat monthly fee per ATM access port (usually with the local loop bundled into the port price) (depending on speed) and a fee per PVC based on speed. There could also be usage- and mileage-sensitive cost components, and potentially enterprise PVC costs if using MPLSIP-ATM service. All services mentioned might include additional nonrecurring and bundling charges, many of which can be partially or fully waived for very large networks.

4.7 HIGH-SPEED LAN PROTOCOLS COMPARISON

Moving closer to the user, we inevitably come to the discussion of high-speed LAN technologies. The key contenders in 100 Mbps and higher-speed LAN technologies include FDDI, 100 Mbps Ethernet, ATM, and Gigabit Ethernet (GbE). Table 4.7 shows a comparison of these technologies.

Aspect	X.25	IP	FR	SMDS	ATM
Efficiency (1 best, 4 worst)	2nd	3rd	1st	4th	1st, 2nd, 3rd, and 4th
Multiple service support	Possible	Possible	Possible	Some	Best
CPE hardware use	Existing	Existing	Existing	Existing	New
CPE software use	Existing	Existing	New	New	New
Access ubiquity	Limited	Best	High	None	Medium
Market demand and geographic coverage	Low	High	High	Low	Moderate
Evolution potential	Low	Some	Some	None	High
Service	Low	Varies	Low	Varies	Medium
Technological obsolescence factor	High	Low	Low	High	Low

Table 4.6: Comparison of Business Aspects

Attribute	FDDI	100BASE-T (100 Mbps Ethernet)	ATM	Gigabit Ethernet (GbE)
Standard	ANSI X3T12	IEEE 802 3u	ATM Forum, ITU, IETF	IEEE 802.3ae
Throughput	100-Mbps simplex	100-Mbps Simplex	1-Mbps to 1.2-Gbps duplex	1-Gbps simplex
Packet or frame type	FDDI frame	Ethernet frame	Cell	Ethernet frame
Evolution potential	Fair	Excellent	Good	Excellent
Reserved bandwidth	No	No	Yes	No
Isochronous support	No	No	Yes	Nc
Multiple traffic classes	No	No	Yes	No
Cost to implement	High	Low	Medium	High
Uses existing wiring	Yes (CDDI)	Yes*	Yes*	Yes*
Scalable in speed	No	No	Yes	No
Scalable to MAN	No	Yes	Yes	Yes*
Scalable to WAN	No (MAN)	No	Yes	No

* Distance, category of wiring, and number of wire pairs required must be considered.

Table 4.7: Comparison of FDDI, 100 Mbps Ethernet, ATM, and GbE

4.8 COMPARISON OF HIGH-SPEED LAN PROTOCOLS AND OSI REFERENCE MODEL

LAN protocols function at the lowest two layers of the OSI reference model.

Figure: Popular LAN Protocols Mapped to the OSI Reference Model illustrates how several popular LAN protocols map to the OSI reference model.

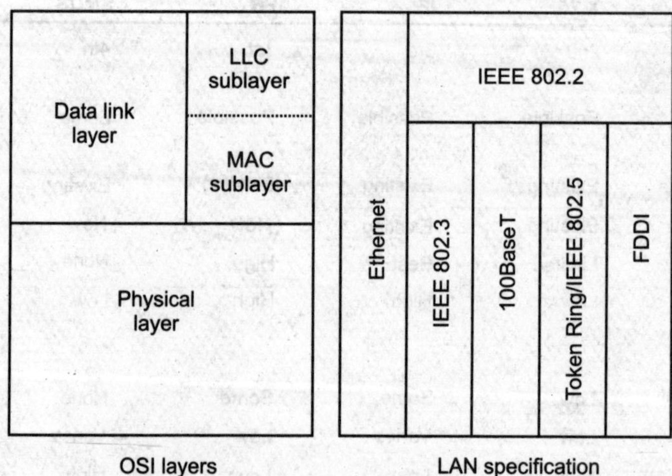

Figure 4.18: Popular LAN Protocols Mapped to the OSI Reference Model

4.9 APPLICATION PERFORMANCE NEEDS

In this topic, we can compare the various services to meet the performance needs of applications with their key characteristics. Following are the key characteristics:

1. The relative throughput of each service type and its underlying technology is summarized.
2. The trade-offs between burstiness, throughput, response time, and delay are examined.

This topic analyzes the attributed of user application needs for throughput, burstiness, and delay tolerance over a wide range of public data services.

4.9.1 THROUGHPUT

The maximum available throughput for commercially available data services are shown in figure 4.19. The time frame described the year in which the maximum data rate was offered and become cost effective. After analysis, there is a difference between in maximum throughput with ever-increasing maximum bandwidths on the horizon. However, throughput is not the only dimension of performance that must be considered.

4.9.2 BURSTINESS

In the figure 4.20 the characteristic of burstiness plotted, defined in Chapter 1 as the ratio of peak to average rate, on the vertical axis versus the supportable peak rate of the service, or throughput, on the horizontal axis.

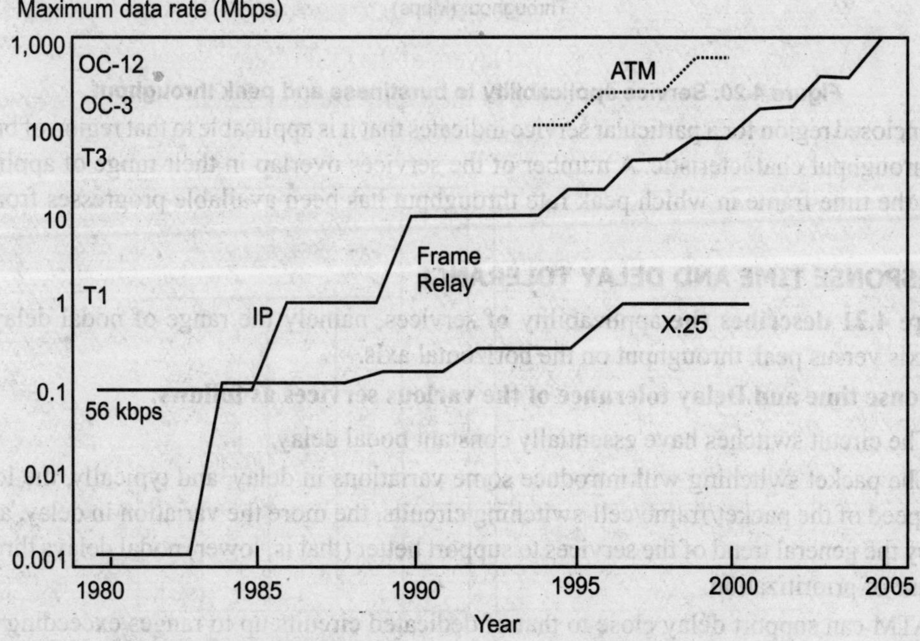

Figure 4.19: Comparison of maximum data-rate by service

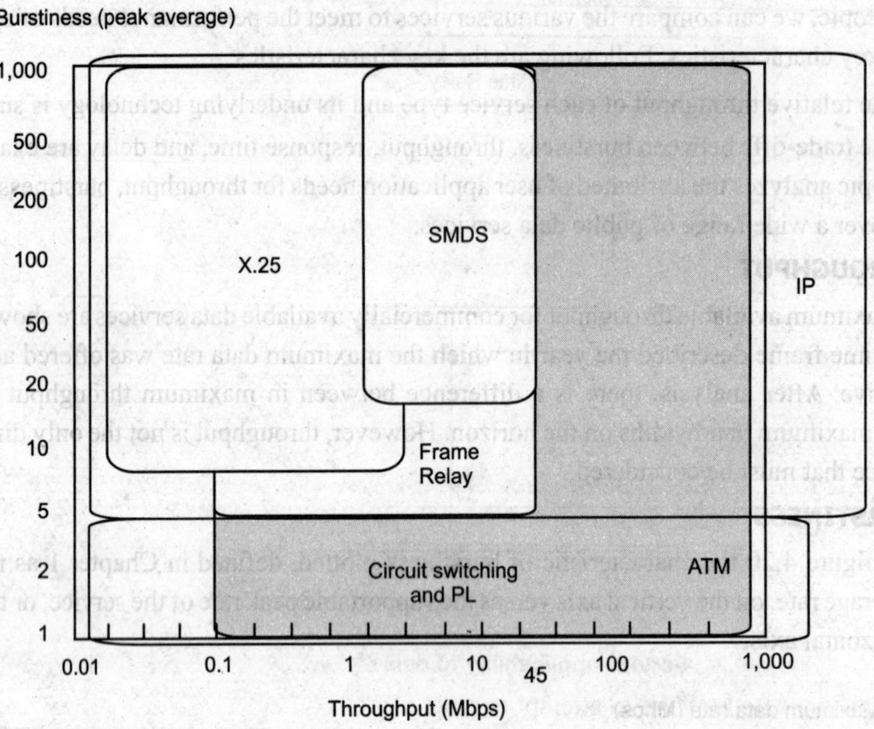

Figure 4.20: Service applicability to burstiness and peak throughput

The enclosed region for a particular service indicates that it is applicable to that region of burstiness and the throughput characteristic. A number of the services overlap in their range of applicability. Note that the time frame in which peak rate throughput has been available progresses from left to right.

4.9.3 RESPONSE TIME AND DELAY TOLERANCE

Figure 4.21 describes the applicability of services, namely the range of nodal delay on the vertical axis versus peak throughput on the horizontal axis.

Response time and Delay tolerance of the various services as follows:

1. The circuit switches have essentially constant nodal delay.
2. The packet switching will introduce some variations in delay, and typically, the lower the speed of the packet/frame/cell-switching circuits, the more the variation in delay, as shown by the general trend of the services to support better (that is, lower) nodal delays through the use of prioritization.
3. ATM can support delay close to that of dedicated circuits up to ranges exceeding those of the other services through the implementation of priority queuing in support of multiple QoS classes.

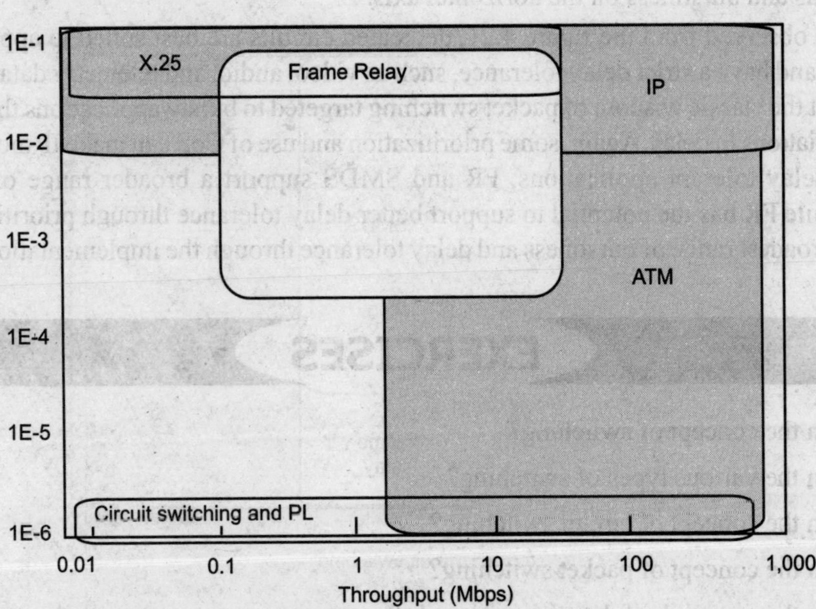

Figure 4.21: Service applicability to delay tolerance and peak throughput

4. IP is relegated to CoS to attempt to meet response time and delay tolerance requirements, but still predominantly remains a best-effort service.

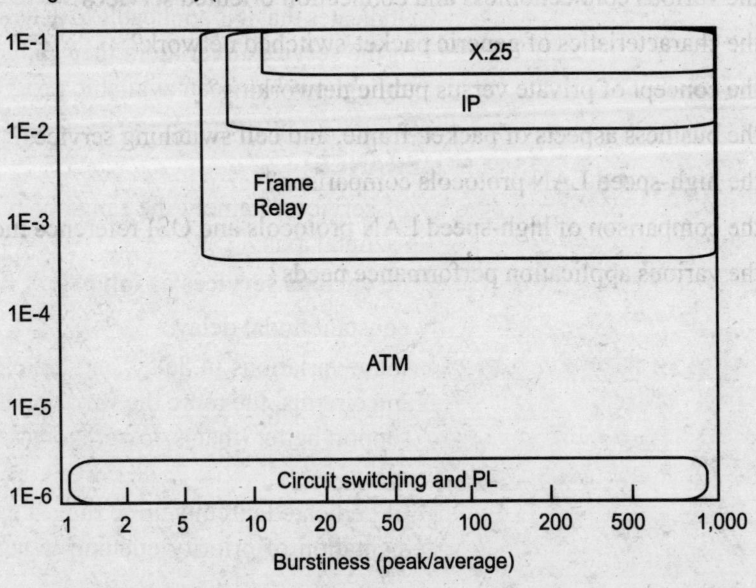

Figure 4.22: Service applicability to delay tolerance and burstiness

Figure 4.22 depicts the applicability of services in the dimensional of range of nodal delay on the vertical axis and burstiness on the horizontal axis.

As can be observed from the figure 4.21, dedicated circuits are best suited to applications that are not bursty and have a strict delay tolerance, such as video, audio, and telemetry data. X.25 and IP services depict the classic wisdom of packet switching targeted to bursty applications that can accept significant variations in delay. Again, some prioritization and use of CoS can make IP more conducive to transport delay tolerant applications. FR and SMDS support a broader range of application burstiness, while FR has the potential to support better delay tolerance through prioritization. ATM supports the broadest range of burstiness and delay tolerance through the implementation of multiple QoS classes.

EXERCISES

1. Explain the concept of switching?
2. Explain the various types of switching?
3. Explain the concept of circuit switching?
4. Explain the concept of packet switching?
5. Explain the approach of datagram networks?
6. Explain the comparison of circuit switching and packet switching?
7. Explain the concept of message switching?
8. Explain the comparison of message, packet, and circuit switching?
9. Explain the various connectionless and connection oriented services?
10. Explain the characteristics of generic packet-switched network?
11. Explain the concept of private versus public networking?
12. Explain the business aspects of packet, frame, and cell switching services?
13. Explain the high-speed LAN protocols comparison?
14. Explain the comparison of high-speed LAN protocols and OSI reference model?
15. Explain the various application performance needs?

Choosing Service Provider, Vendor and Service Levels

5.1 CHOOSING SERVICE PROVIDERS

Proposals for a relationship are extended through solicitations - requests for information (RFIs) and, later, proposals (RFPs) - providing a list of requirements by which to build a long-lasting relationship. The service provider (the user's future partner) responds to the RFI/RFP with a list of what it can provide, when it can provide it, and at what expense or expectations. The capabilities of each provider are examined carefully, and ultimately one is chosen (in some cultures, more than one) to build a network. A contract is written and the future (network) is committed to the service provider as the service provider commits its services to the user. Both find out how they must live with each other. Partnerships are expected to last for the life of the network, although the capability of "divorcing" the network from the service provider might become necessary if service becomes poor or the service provider's priorities change. The key is to never stop communicating. Vendors or service providers must be chosen sometime after the requirements have been defined; the technologies and services selected, and the high-level design process begun. Vendor selection should be done with care. The success of the network can affect the network manager's job, the users who rely on the network, and the business itself. All these rely directly or indirectly on vendor performance.

The RFP process is summarized. Conformance to standards, the business parameters of the company and the industry as a whole are critical. The RFP is the one chance to "get it all in writing." If a requirement or conformance is not included in the RFP, and subsequently is not in the contract, the vendor does not have to provide it. The watch watchword is being through in the selection and contract process. A method of choosing vendors based on weighted business and technical needs. Critical issues include what trade-offs to expect, how to derive various levels of support from the vendor, how to ensure industry standardization in the hardware and software purchased, and how to ensure vendors deliver on promises. The vendor-user relationship must benefit the strategic and technical direction of both parties to be a lasting relationship. In this chapter, the end user, network designer, network manager, partners, suppliers and so on, are all "users" when considering vendor relationships. Vendor responsiveness to user needs is critical. Vendor selection can affect the future business success of the company. This was especially true at the turn of the century when many telecommunications companies suddenly (some with days' notice) went out of business and caused customer outages.

The network is designed, the purchase orders are written, hardware and services are ordered, and the network sites are awaiting the equipment's arrival. Vendor ABC promised that the hardware would arrive in six weeks. It has now been more than three months, and still no equipment. The recent trade magazine shows that vendor ABC is having financial problems. A call is placed to the sales representative at vendor ABC. He or she tells you, "No problem, the stuff is on the way; it's only rumors." A week later the hardware arrives and the bill is paid. The next month, ABC goes out of business. When finally the equipment you bought is up and running, it does not work because the interfaces are proprietary. The network is eventually scrapped; the network designer loses his or her job. The same story could happen with network connectivity services (such as FR or IP connectivity services). This story, of course, is exaggerated to emphasize the point that a through vendor analysis must be completed prior to choosing a vendor.

5.2 RFI PROCESS

A request for information (RFI) is a standard business process whose purpose is to collect written information about the capabilities of various suppliers. Normally it follows a format that can be used for comparative purposes.

An RFI is primarily used to gather information to help make a decision on what steps to take next. RFIs are therefore seldom the final stage and are instead often used in combination with the following: request for proposal (RFP), request for tender (RFT), and request for quotation (RFQ). In addition to gathering basic information, an RFI is often used as a solicitation sent to a broad base of potential suppliers for the purpose of conditioning supplier's minds, developing strategy, building a database, and preparing for an RFP, RFT, or RFQ.

The RFI procedure is used in the construction industry in cases where it is necessary to confirm the interpretation of a detail, specification or note on the construction drawings or to secure a documented directive or clarification from the architect or client that is needed to continue work. An RFI raised by the general contractor that has been answered by the client or architect and distributed to all stakeholders is generally accepted as a change to the scope of work unless further approval is required for costs associated with the change. It is common and accepted practice for a subcontractor or supplier to use an RFI to state his/her concern related to the omission or misapplication of a product, and seek further clarification of the building owner's intended use or the building official acceptance of the specified product. It is also acceptable for the subcontractor to use an RFI to call attention to an inferior product that may not meet the building owner's needs, and use his/her expertise to recommend the better/correct product.

The user typically provides

- Rules of engagement during the RFI process
- Business and network performance objectives

- Existing applications and technologies to replace or integrate
- Traffic volumes and characteristics (as explained in this chapter)
- Future plans and requirements
- Evaluation criteria
- All information in electronic and hardcopy format

The user typically requests from the supplier respondents

- A specific response for each request or line item
- Specific vendor capabilities to meet each requirement by date
- Service and product delivery dates
- Complete supporting documentation
- General pricing

The user then uses the RFI responses to select a short list of vendors who will receive the RFP.

5.3 RFP PROCESS

A request for proposal (RFP) is an early stage in a procurement process, issuing an invitation for suppliers, often through a bidding process, to submit a proposal on a specific commodity or service. The RFP process brings structure to the procurement decision and allows the risks and benefits to be identified clearly upfront.

The RFP may dictate to varying degrees the exact structure and format of the supplier's response. Effective RFPs typically reflect the strategy and short/long-term business objectives, providing detailed insight upon which suppliers will be able to offer a matching perspective.

Similar requests include a request for quotation and a request for information.

RFPs are used

- To clarify buyer needs
- As a "soft" legal agreement of vendor provisions and capabilities
- To weed out competition
- To finalize the network design and direction
- To solve pricing discrepancies
- To give a true apples-to-apples comparison of the short-list vendors

RFPs are a mean of requesting multiple vendors to formally commit detailed solutions, propose the appropriate technology and service, and quote services to satisfy designated requirements.

Before issuing the RFP, the buyer must

- Understand the technology alternatives
- Properly define what is required from the vendor
- Clearly define the technology, business, and financial issues with priorities
- Clearly define support requirements

Make sure that user requirements are clearly articulated and define what you will and will not accept. All correspondence should be thoroughly documented. All answers to questions should be posted to all respondents as frequently asked questions (FAQs). This might seem harsh for two businesses that are trying to establish a lasting relationship, but it is necessary to build a professional relationship and to avoid finger-pointing later.

Key objectives

- Obtain correct information to enable sound business decisions.
- Decide correctly on strategic procurement.
- Leverage the company's purchasing power to obtain a favorable deal.
- Enable a broader and creative range of solutions to be considered.

Key benefits

- Informs suppliers that your company is looking to procure and encourages them to make their best effort.
- Requires the company to specify what it proposes to purchase. If the requirements analysis has been prepared properly, it can be incorporated quite easily into the Request document.
- Alerts suppliers that the selection process is competitive.
- Allows for wide distribution and response.
- Ensures that suppliers respond factually to the identified requirements.
- By following a structured evaluation and selection procedure an organization can demonstrate impartiality - a crucial factor in public sector procurements.

5.3.1 SPECIFICATIONS

An RFP typically involves more than a request for the price. Other requested information may include basic corporate information and history, financial information (can the company deliver without risk of bankruptcy), technical capability (used on major procurements of services, where the item has not previously been made or where the requirement could be met by varying technical means), product information such as stock availability and estimated completion period, and customer references that can be checked to determine a company's suitability.

In the military, an RFP is often raised to fulfill an Operational Requirement (OR), after which the military procurement authority will normally issue a detailed Technical Specification against which tenders (i.e., bids) will be made by potential contractors. In the civilian use, an RFP is usually part of a complex sales process, also known as enterprise sales.

RFPs often include specifications of the item, project or service for which a proposal is requested. The more detailed the specifications, the better the chances that the proposal provided will be accurate. Generally RFPs are sent to an approved supplier or vendor list.

The bidders return a proposal by a set date and time. Late proposals may or may not be considered, depending on the terms of the initial RFP. The proposals are used to evaluate the suitability as a supplier, vendor, or institutional partner. Discussions may be held on the proposals (often to clarify technical capabilities or to note errors in a proposal). In some instances, all or only selected bidders may be invited to participate in subsequent bids, or may be asked to submit their best technical and financial proposal, commonly referred to as a **Best and Final Offer (BAFO).** Subsequent changes can be referred to as the **Best and Revised Final Offer (BARFO).**

A general RFP format includes

- Synopsis or business objectives
- General contractual terms and conditions (explanations, interpretations, rules of engagement)
- Scope of work
- Timeline schedule with milestones and deliverables
- Qualifications of bidder
- Current systems, technologies, architectures, protocols, services, and applications
- Hardware and software technical specifications or proposed configurations with accepted substitutions
- Environmental requirements
- Vendor-required engineering and installation
- Implementation plan
- Performance objectives
- Services agreements (SLAs)
- arranty or availability requirements
- Summary of financial bid
- Payment options
- Statement of Work with specific responsibilities
- Proposal assumptions
- raining requirements
- Vendor credibility and reference requirements
- Legal or contractual considerations

5.4 OTHER REQUESTS

A request for quotation (RFQ) is used when discussions with bidders are not required (mainly when the specifications of a product or service are already known) and when price is the main or only factor in selecting the successful bidder. An RFQ may also be used as a step prior to going to a full-blown RFP to determine general price ranges. In this scenario, products, services or suppliers may be selected from the RFQ results to bring in to further research in order to write a more fully fleshed out RFP.

RFP is sometimes used for a **request for pricing.**

A request for information (RFI) is a proposal requested from a potential seller or a service provider to determine what products and services are potentially available in the marketplace to meet a buyer's needs and to know the capability of a seller in terms of offerings and strengths of the seller. RFIs are commonly used on major procurements, where a requirement could potentially be met through several alternate means. An RFI, however, is not an invitation to bid, is not binding on either the buyer or sellers, and may or may not lead to an RFP or RFQ.

A request for qualifications (RFQ) is a document often distributed before initiation of the RFP process. It is used to gather vendor information from multiple companies to generate a pool of prospects. This eases the RFP review process by preemptively short-listing candidates which meet the desired qualifications.

A request for tender (RFT) is more commonly used by government.

5.5 SAMPLE NETWORKS

In the case of sending out an RFP for a complete network, even though you have included the network application and transport requirements in the RFP, each vendor might come back with a different network solution, equipment vendor solutions, choice of WAN service, and "feeds and speeds" all might very widely. One of the best ways to ensure that all vendors provide similar responses is to provide a sample network design, or at least a minimum and maximum configuration. This design could take the form of a spreadsheet of equipment and circuit details, a topological map, or a written document. For example, if you are building a statewide FR network and want to connect ten cities, four of which are large cities and six, smaller (remote) cities, you might want to provide a design that requires specific port and PVC speeds per site. In this manner, the responses can be compared more closely to apples to apples in cost and configuration. Otherwise, you might get back five designs from five vendors, each with different port and PVC speeds, all at different prices, which would be difficult to compare.

5.6 SOLICITATION

Solicit the RFP to the vendors short-listed by the RFI process. Number all questions for response. Offer equal and fair guidance to all vendors. Set a maximum return date for all responses and stick to it. If vendors want your business, they will respond in time. Make sure you have given ample time for a comprehensive response. Keep in mind holidays. A time to respond that is too short will yield shoddy responses that can be vague or noncompliant. Set up a question-and-answer session with each respondent to clarify and amplify any areas that are not quite clear. A good rule of thumb is to allow two times the length of time it took to create the RFP for vendor questions, and at least two more weeks for a good response.

5.7 ANALYZING AND EVALUATING RFP RESPONSES

Each respondent to the RFP should respond paragraph by paragraph. Responses will be varied, but this seems to be the best format. Beware of terms such as "substantial compliance," "intend to comply," and "will be contained in future releases". Look for terms such as "full compliance" with an explanation of how they comply and to what extent. Vendors should clearly specify what they do not support.

Replies should contain the following:

- Product price
- Maintenance requirements
- Training and learning curve
- Ongoing expenses
- Tax financing
- Contract termination fees
- Warranties

- Documentation
- Purchase or lease decisions
- All nonrecurring and recurring costs

In the next section, each factor is examined for a determination of which vendor to choose.

5.8 HOW TO CHOOSE VENDORS

There are many reasons for choosing one vendor over another. The vendor is not chosen, only for meeting all the requirements of the RFI or RFP. There are some factors such as politics, business financial, and operational needs; future position or potential partnership with the vendor, balance of trade; goals of both business; and a variety of others might outweigh the technical abilities of the vendor to meet the requirements. This is particularly true for large corporations or users seeking large national or international vendors for multiple services.

Look into the vendor's part for not only the product or service you are purchasing, but financial history, payment history, billing accuracy, shipping and receiving procedures and politics, past and present customer base, and industry experience. Ask for references and, more importantly, check references.

Evaluation criteria f hardware and service providers include

- History of Vendor
- Product/service versatility and ability to provide a total solution
- Processor and packet/frame/cell-processing speeds and capabilities
- Interface and protocol support
- Local or remote support ability
- Standard versus proprietary protocol support and operation
- Performance characteristics
- Features and functions
- Network management
- Security
- Price to performance, or cost-effectiveness

Remember, price is often not be most important evaluation factor, because the labor and resources committed to making the network operate often exceed hardware costs. Do not allow the focus to become myopic on cost-technical decisions based strictly on cost constraints might place the design in jeopardy. Do not condone foolhardy or frivolous spending, but bargaining away technology and performance for low cost is foolhardy. There is often a point on all technology in which cost outweighs benefit. It is your job to find the balance point.

5.8.1 REQUIREMENTS MATRIX AND WEIGHTING METHODS

The next step is to build a requirements matrix, and assign a weight to each requirement based on its importance. More important criteria are given a greater weight, less important, a lower weight. Some requirements such as "total cost of solution" are often weighted more heavily than others, such as security. With the advent of Internet access and transport and the inherent security risks, security has lately taken a much higher priority.

Table 5.1 shows a sample weighting of ten typical requirements for an RFP, specifying a three-node router network. Each was provided a weight from 1 to 99 percent, with a total weight of all requirements of 100 percent. Each requirement was then assigned a rating from 1 to 10, with 10 being the highest score and 1 the lowest. In table 5.1, the vendor scored a total of 700 points out of a possible 1000.

Table 5.1 Requirements Matrix Weighting

Requirement	weight	score	total points
Total cost of solution	10	7	70
Pricing and billing options	5	8	40
Features and functions (protocols and interfaces)	10	10	100
Vendor and product reputation and philosophy	5	4	20
Architecture flexibility and technology migration path	5	6	30
System capacity and performance	15	8	120
Availability, reliability, and disaster recovery	15	4	60
Network management	25	8	200
CPE hardware support	5	8	40
Customer and field service and support aspects	5	4	20
Total	100		700

The weighting could be adjusted to provide an equal weighting for all requirements, or more requirements could be added. Either way, the vendor with the highest number of total points is probably the best choice for you. Another method of requirements analysis is the cost-benefit analysis, in which the costs of each requirement are weighted against the benefits realized by the requirement.

5.8.2 WHICH TRADE-OFFS IS CRITICAL?

The weighting method is an excellent way to determine which vendor to choose. But how can it be determined which trade-offs are critical and warrant higher weighting factors? This section presents a broad range of criteria to consider when choosing a data communications public services. This list is by no means comprehensive, but does represent the most commonly proposed options. These options can be converted to vendor questions for the RFI and RFP process. You should make your own detailed list, prioritize it, and use it to select the service or product that best meets your needs. There might be a large equipment base already existing in the corporation that will need integration and interoperability. If this is the case, integration must be factored into the requirements analysis.

Following are some of the areas to consider:

Pricing and Billing Options

- Order intervals
- Fixed or usage billing
- Minimums and maximums on usage billing
- Delivery options for bills (hardcopy, fax, e-mail, disk/tape)

- Frequency of billing
- Capacity to bundle all services (equipment, management, transport/circuit costs) in one bill

Hardware/Service Features and Functions (Protocols and Interfaces)

- Processor capability (PPS/FPS/CPS)
- Packet/frame/cell filtering/forwarding capability per protocol and in total
- Bus and data-transfer speeds
- Switching/routing protocols supported
- Physical interfaces required/supported
- Access classes and speeds (DS0 through STS-Nc)
- Multiple-service access supported
- Expansion capability
- Local- and remote-load software for operation
- Classes of service (CoSs) and quality of service (QoS0 offered and fully supported to standards
- Prioritization handling
- Traffic parameters supported (that is, CIR, SIR, PCR, SCR, MBS)
- Multiple, fully redundant, load-sharing options
- Portability of service
- Security features supported
- In-band or out-of-band network management

Vendor and Product Reputation and Philosophy

- Industry leader or follower
- References and recommendations-be sure to check them!
- Large range of internetworking products or single solution source
- Commonality of common logic across entire product line
- Service-level guarantee with refunds

Product Architecture Flexibility and Technology Migration Path

- Ability to migrate to future technologies (with minimal impact to CPE)
- Future product the line migration path (no disjointed software or hardware upgrades/revisions/ fixes and proven architecture)
- Standards-based for future investment protection
- Plug-and-play CPE-to-network compatibility
- Type of network architecture/equipment used

Architecture/System Capacity and Performance

- Fault tolerant robust network (1:N or 1:1 switch and component redundancy and availability)
- PPS/FPS/CPS transmission over lightly loaded and heavily loaded ports, cards, and nodes
- Minimal back-haul to closest switch (number of switches)
- Ease of expansion

- Amount of end-to-end network delay (latency) at normal- and peak-traffic conditions
- Minimal data loss rate
- Consistent and high throughput
- Type of equipment used by network
- Network architecture with high MTBF and low MTTR
- Minimal switching delay and buffer delay per switch

Availability, Reliability and Disaster Recovery

- Fault tolerance (no single physical or electronic point of future)
- Multiple processors per interface cart (look at processor MIPS, bus speed, PPS/FPS/CPS processing, memory, and so on) or live backup processors
- Symmetric multiprocessing
- Easy device configuration and customization (local and remote)
- Minimum/maximum network availability
- Redundancy in all components and systems
- Parallel back-plane/bus for reliability
- Independent load-sharing over data paths
- Redundant power supplies, common logic boards, local media
- Hot-swap functionality
- Dynamic reconfiguration while on line
- No single point of failure (1:N system redundancy)
- Automatic isolation of failed components, cards, and buses
- Disaster recovery options
- Number of switches, location and back-haul required
- Network-loadable firmware upgrades

Network Management

- SNMP-complaint at a minimum
- Network management system compatibility and portability with current systems
- Customer network management (CNM) features
- Reporting capabilities
- NMS costs and reporting costs
- Monitoring and real-time configuration capabilities
- Change management procedures
- Performance management and engineering provided
- Enhanced user interface, for example, web browser

Premises Hardware Support

- Flexible leasing/rental/purchase plans
- Software and firmware revision testing and implementation
- Meets all relevant industry standards

- Upgrade-capable equipment (software, hardware, new technologies)
- Free initial training provided
- Ongoing support

Total Cost Involved

- Total cost of the network for the configuration provided
- Price performance ratio-processing power and cost per unit (that is, packets/frames/cells per second and cost per packet/frame/cell per second)
- Modularity expansion or upgrade costs
- Price per port or trunk (DS1, DS3, OC-N)
- Lowest total cost of ownership (TCO)

Service Aspects: Operations and Support

- Defined and measurable quality of service levels
- 7x24x365 live customer support and troubleshooting expertise
- Same level of service regardless of customer size
- Large support staff with demonstrable talent
- Ease of software and hardware installation
- Online Documentation
- Customer intimacy and communications

5.8.3 PUBLIC SERVICE NETWORK OFFERINGS VERSUS PRIVATE NETWORKS

Users must at some decide whether to access a public network or to build their own private network. If the decision is made to use a public network service, the user must decide between global, national, local, or metro service providers. This decision will be based primarily on intra-LATA, inter-LATA, interstate, or international access as well as connectivity requirements, availability, and cost of similar services.

Public network service offerings have the following advantages over private networks:

- Lower capital investment required
- Higher network availability with large shared optical backbone
- Extensive points of presence (PoPs) and switches for less backhaul and higher network availability
- Broad choice of interface speeds
- Integrated access capabilities-support multiple service access over a single access circuit
- Sophisticated network management support and performance management capabilities
- Portfolio of services (X.25, FR, IP, ATM, IP-FR/ATM) that minimize technological obsolescence
- Smooth migration between services - minimal CPE changes required
- Usage-based and flat-rate billing structure flexibility
- Carrier-provider CPE offerings
- Outsourced solution packages available

- Highly skilled service- and equipment-support structures
- Inherent reliability, redundancy, and survivability of a virtual private shared backbone
- Access to public resources, for example, the Internet
- Ability to support simultaneous internetwork, intercompany, and internet connectivity and communications

Another very important deciding factor is the architecture that the service provider employs for the access and backbone network. Whereas the tariff or public pricing structure is key in the initial selection, the service provider's architecture is the long-term insurance that costs will remain stable, that service quality will be delivered per the SLAs, and that new features and technologies will be offered in a timely manner. International connectivity requirements often make public networking the only cost-effective option. Earlier chapters described additional benefits of public networks compared with private networks, such as value-added services, economy of scale, network redundancy, and network management.

5.8.4 ADHERENCE TO INDUSTRY STANDARDS

In today, age of data communications standardization and open system, it becomes increasingly important to choose vendors who adhere to de facto standards and justify this commitment to standards by continuing to develop products around them. Beware of vendors that are banking on a single-standard product (especially a proprietary-standard product), even though they might promise eventual standards compliance. These rules also apply to regulatory, protocol, and manufacturing compliance on both a national and international scale. Compliance to the standards previously listed leads to interoperability from the client-server level through the network access and into the network.

5.8.5 VENDOR PROMISES AND SUPPORT

Vendors will make many promises when courting a contract. Just make sure that all verbal commitments are fully explained in writing and included in the contract. If it is not in writing, it does not have to be honored. To verify information, research the vendor. Ask around. Talk to other customers of the vendor and even to their competitors (and weigh their responses accordingly). Ask the vendor for a few good references and then ask for one or two that had problems with their service. From them you might get a clearer picture of the vendor. Documentation of all vendor correspondence should be compiled and stored for future reference.

One of the major issues among vendors and buyers is support. When the vendor is first courting the user, look for vendors who both educate and consult your staff on the technologies and issues involved, and sell a solution rather than just a product.

The vendor promises and support include:

- Well-defined onsite or remote maintenance and customer services
- Support 24 hours a day, 7 days a week, 365 days a year (7x24x365) by trained staff who understand your network-test this support before you buy!
- How much assistance will be provided with the installation, test, and turn-up? After the sale with billing support and reconciliation?
- Percentage and size of staff assigned to support- does the vendor have a specific project manager assigned to its success?

- Ongoing training by the vendor for your staff (including features and functions, options, and fixing unforeseen problems.
- Automated tools available from vendor

5.8.6 VENDOR EXPERTISE

What type of expertise does the vendor hold in sales, marketing, product, design, security, networking, and system-level support? Have its account references been checked? Also check the manufacturer's position in the industry. A vendor might have to delay a product delivery because it has been short of power supplies from its overseas power-supply vendor (which has gone out of business), or might be trying to get that next round of funding to complete the fiber route it just sold you! Make sure the vendor's supply sources are easily accessible and that it has alternate sources for its parts or infrastructure.

5.8.7 VENDOR DELIVERY DATES AND REALITY

Again, check the vendor's references for its delivery track record.

- Does it often miss or postpone deliveries or installations?
- Does it build products at order levels or does it build at 80 percent of orders?

If the latter, the vendor might look good to the financial industry but shipments might be delayed.

- What have been some of its other customer's experiences with late deliveries or installations?
- How does the vendor ship and track these shipments?

In the United States, it is common to have two-week to two-month delivery cycles from the date the order is placed to the data the equipment ships from the vendor, and circuit installations sometimes exceed several months.

- Does the vendor have the required network capacity for when you order the service, or will it be build after your order is placed?

In Europe and Asia, the average delivery time is much longer, typically two to four months. This average is getting shorter, however, as many international vendors are now competing in U.S. markets, where project timelines and delivery dates are more competitive and much shorter.

5.8.8 PRODUCT ANNOUNCEMENTS AND PRODUCT FUTURES

Be aware of all product announcements and the future product direction of each vendor. Product announcements should be received free of charge through data sheets, advertisements, and electronic mail bulletins. If information is sensitive in nature and not yet public, a user-vendor mutual nondisclosure form can be used, which states that neither party will divulge information about the other without express written consent or until after a specific date. This contract is legally binding and strictly enforced. Nondisclosure agreements can be either selective or blanket agreements. Also ask for the future product direction of the company. What about the R&D activities, and what percentage of its profit goes toward research and new product development. Make sure that the vendor's spending direction for new products is the same as your product requirements direction.

5.8.9 THE PROPRIETY VENDOR AND FUTURES

While using the same vendor over time can provide backward compatibility, it can also lock the user into an obsolete product. The vendor could get off track from technological change, and take the user with it. Avoid proprietary vendor implementations, with the exception being cutting-edge pre-standards products. While proprietary implementations provide specialized solutions for the short term, they cause atrophy in the long term. Lastly, look at the overall future potential of the vendor. This includes market position, product futures, financial condition, strategic partnerships, existing and potential competition, and a myriad of other company "health" factors, which paint the true picture of whether the vendor is in for the short haul or the long haul. Many people disparage vendors that hold a predominant market share, but remember that they got there for a reason (a good product, strategy, large market, management team, and so on). A dominant player can also make some mistakes and recover, while a niche player might not. Brand name should be weighted heavily in the requirements matrix.

5.9 EVALUATION OF CHOOSING NETWORK VENDORS AND SERVICE PROVIDERS

As a value-added reseller (VAR) in the networking channel trying to grow a business, you need to work with the very best vendors, tools and network service providers. This tip presents a time-tested methodology for evaluating each.

The evaluation process presented here can be applied to vendors and service providers, their equipment and services. In general, this process consists of using products from network analysis and architecture to develop an initial set of options (termed seeding the evaluation process); conducting discussions to develop a complete set of candidate options, along with criteria to evaluate those options; gathering and developing data to apply to the evaluations; refining evaluation criteria and developing ratings; applying criteria and ratings to prioritize the candidate options; and modifying the set of candidate options, with the goal of selecting the optimal candidate. This process is shown in Figure 5.1.

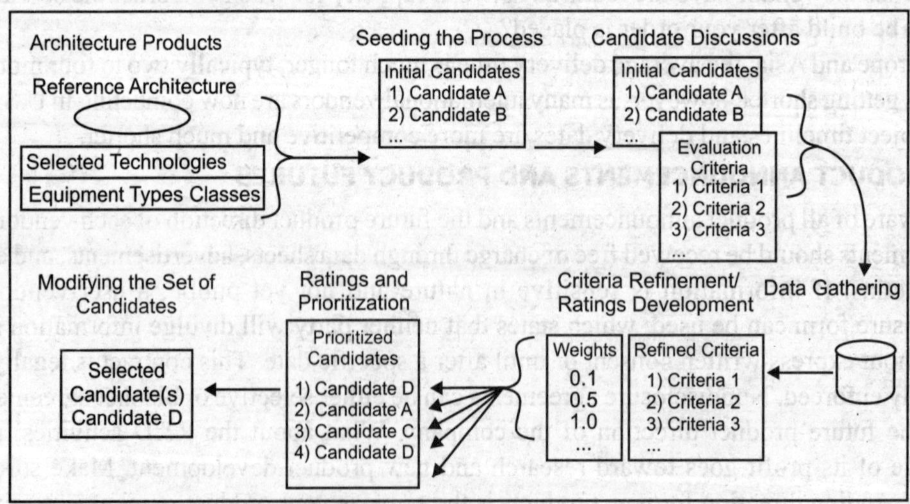

Figure 5.1: Vendor, equipment and service-provider evaluation process

This is an iterative process. There are times when an optimal candidate can be found with a single iteration of the process; at other times it may take two or three iterations to produce an optimal result. The number of iterations depends in part on the complexity of the evaluations, how well prepared you are, and how well you and your evaluation team perform the evaluation. As you get used to the process, you will be able to get results with fewer iterations.

Ideally, a template can be developed that can then be applied to each and every evaluation, making the process straightforward, predictable, and reproducible. That is what this section strives to provide. However, we also recognize that, depending on the project, some evaluations may have their own unique characteristics. In all cases I have found that this process can still provide excellent results.

Although this process can be applied to evaluate vendors, vendor equipment, and service providers, it is important to note that we do not want to combine these evaluations into one. Keep each evaluation separate-do not mix vendors, vendor equipment, and service providers-as this will confuse the evaluators and overly complicate the process. For example, some of the evaluation criteria for vendors will be different from those for service providers, and trying to apply criteria to both concurrently would be problematic.

An important part of this process is that you will develop a detailed set of information regarding how your evaluation decisions were made. This information can be used to help reduce or eliminate disagreements that may arise regarding your vendor, service provider, or equipment selections. Such disagreements tend to be more likely as the design budget increases.

Example 5.1

It has been my experience that a large part of the design process is often spent resolving protests brought by vendors, service providers, and even a subset of the evaluators, disagreeing with a selection (often a vendor selection). The evaluation process presented here will provide you with plenty of documentation with which you can resolve or even avoid such protests.

For example, I have participated in vendor evaluations where Vendor A is the popular choice, while Vendor B has the best technical solution. Without a process for evaluating and selecting vendors, Vendor A would have been chosen as the de facto choice, without regard to its inferior technical solution. I have used this process to help make it obvious that the technically superior vendor should be chosen.

5.10 EVALUATING NETWORKING VENDORS AND NETWORK SERVICE PROVIDERS

Once you've established the importance of evaluating networking vendors and network service providers as potential partners in your channel business, the first step is to seed the evaluation process by drawing up a list of prospective candidates.

The purpose of seeding an evaluation is to get the process started quickly. Seeding consists of generating an initial list of candidates for discussion. One person, such as the project manager, or a few select people can seed the evaluation process. Since the goal is to rapidly kick-start the evaluation process, we do not want to spend much time on this, but rather quickly put together a short list of candidates (vendors, service providers, or equipment, depending on the evaluation) for discussion. This list often consists of the most obvious candidates.

Why is this needed? I have found that it is much easier to generate discussion and develop options when some options are already on the table. This tends to focus the group and gives them something to work toward (or against).

Some or all of the analysis and architecture products shown in Section 10.3 should be directly applicable to start the evaluation process. We can use these products to determine an initial set of candidates. For example, the architecture process provides us with network technologies and network topology that were selected for the project. The selected network technologies may be available only from a subset of vendors (and their equipment) and may be supported by a subset of service providers. Similarly, the selected network topology may be supported only by a subset of service providers. In addition, only some service providers may be able to reach the strategic locations selected for the network architecture. For example, a strategic location may lie in a city that is not readily available to some providers, or it may be prohibitively expensive for them to provide service to those locations.

Architectural relationships, along with strategic locations, may have resulted in specific equipment types or classes being chosen. For example, strategic locations that require high-performance routing, security, and management indicate the need for larger-scale equipment (e.g., carrier-class equipment) where we can combine these functions, or the need for multiple instances and types of equipment to distribute these functions. The class or type of equipment chosen may indicate a particular set of vendors, maybe also particular pieces of equipment.

We also have the products of the network analysis-the requirements and flow specifications-which can be used to help determine initial candidates for evaluation.

The seeding of the evaluation process results in having some candidate vendors, vendor equipment options, or service providers to take into the next step in this process-discussions with project participants.

5.11 NETWORKING VENDORS, TOOLS AND SERVICE PROVIDERS

Choosing networking vendors, tools and service providers for your projects is not an easy task, which is why the second step in the evaluation process is getting a little help from your peers.

Having developed a short list (seed) of candidates, we want to use that list to generate a more complete list of candidates, as well as begin to develop a set of criteria that we can use for evaluation.

Whereas one or a few persons can develop the seed list, the complete list should involve a much larger group of participants, including the project team, select potential users of the network, technical staff, management, and/or stakeholders. Your evaluation team should represent the scale and scope of your project.

Using the seed as a starting point, discussions are held, often involving a whiteboard or Web equivalent, to expand this list. At this point in the process it is better to include all candidates, including obviously inferior ones, and reject them during the prioritization and selection, rather than rejecting them outright. Even if the list becomes unwieldy, it can be quickly pared down once your criteria and ratings have been developed. In this way you will be able to show that you considered a sizable number of options, along with reasons for rejecting them. This can be useful later if someone contests your selection with one that happens to be on your list of rejections. Additionally, you may find that one of your not-so-obvious choices turns out to be one of the better ones.

Along with the complete set of candidates you will need to develop your set of evaluation criteria. Common examples of evaluation criteria are shown in Figure 5.2. Your set will also likely contain evaluation criteria specific to your project, your network, and your organization.

At this point in the process you should not use these criteria to evaluate your candidates. We still need to refine the criteria, as well as develop weights for the criteria, before applying them. But even before that we need to perform some research and data gathering to support the evaluation.

Evaluation Criteria	
1	Costs
2	Technologies
3	Performance
4	Risks

Figure 5.2: An example set of initial evaluation criteria

5.12 SEEDING THE EVALUATION PROCESS AND ASKING PEERS FOR ADVICE

After taking the steps of seeding the evaluation process and asking peers for advice about choosing networking vendors and service providers to help with your projects, the third step is gathering data on top prospects.

Now that you have developed complete (or nearly complete) set of (vendor, vendor equipment, service provider) candidates, you need to gather and develop data that will be helpful to your evaluations.

Common sources and types of information are:

- Discussions with internal and external groups
- Discussions with vendors and/or service providers
- Independent (third-party) assessments of vendors, equipment, and/or service providers
- Modeling and simulation
- Information from risk assessments

Discussions with internal and external groups can provide information in addition to the candidate discussions. The intent of these discussions is to expand the amount of information by talking with more users and staff, and in greater detail. External groups may be able to relate their experiences with candidate vendors, vendor equipment, and service providers. This is especially useful when your design includes technologies or equipment that is new to you, but that others have experience with (e.g., implementation and operational experience with IPv6). External groups may be other organizations like yours, or groups with a common interest, such as user groups or technical forums.

Since we now have a list of candidates, discussions with vendors and/or service providers on that list are often useful to learn specific information about each vendor, service provider, or piece of equipment. Such discussions can also be helpful in learning what each is capable of doing for your project: providing value-added services, access to labs, testing and validation, and competitive pricing are some examples. However, vendors and service providers should not be allowed to get too close to the evaluation. They are motivated to represent their products and services in the best light and may try to steer the evaluation in their direction. Therefore, it is best to keep such discussions isolated from the evaluations (i.e., don't invite them to any meetings where the evaluations are being discussed).

Along with the above discussions, at times it is useful to get independent (third-party) assessments of vendors, equipment, and/or service providers. Independent assessments provide a prospective that is often different from what internal groups, vendors, and service providers will give. Like external groups, independent assessors may be able to provide you with implementation and operational experience with technologies and equipment that are new to you. For independent assessments I tend to choose small companies or individuals (consultants) instead of large consulting firms.

Modelling and simulation of all or part of the network architecture can provide valuable information for your evaluations. For example, you can use computer models to make comparisons of how your network will perform using different service providers, based on their services offered and on their infrastructures. You may already have some of this information if you have done modelling and simulation to refine your network analysis and/or architecture.

In addition to the above, any information from risk assessments that is applicable to vendors and/or service providers can be useful in evaluations. Your risk assessment, performed early in the analysis process, may reveal certain risks for your project. One or more of these risk factors may be applicable to your evaluation. For example, your project may be adverse to the risk of applying a new protocol, technology, or service. If vendors or service providers apply one of these, it can be used as a part of your evaluation.

All of this information is usually compiled as a document in support of the evaluations and is carried forward into criteria refinement and ratings development. In addition, this information can be very helpful in developing formal documents needed in the procurement and implementation of your design. One example of this is development of a request for purchase (RFP) for products and services.

For example, using the set of initial evaluation criteria from Figure 5.2, data gathering would probably allow us to expand that set based on input from various organizations. Vendors would probably be able to add technology and standards-specific information, while we may be able to learn about risks from other organizations that have already completed similar projects. We may be able to learn specifics regarding performance, from these same organizations or from groups that do equipment and system testing.

5.12.1 SEEDED THE EVALUATION PROCESS

Once you've seeded the evaluation process, had discussions with colleagues about finding top prospects for your networking projects, and gathered data on top prospects, the fourth step is refining your criteria to ensure that you make the best choices.

Now that you have additional information regarding your criteria (from the data gathering exercise), you can use this information to refine the criteria. Often, in gathering and developing data, we learn that there are some new criteria that should be added; that some existing criteria are not as appropriate as first thought and perhaps should be removed; or that some criteria should be modified according to the new information. The result is a refined and better set of evaluation criteria.

In order to apply these evaluation criteria to your list of candidates, you should have some way to compare and contrast the candidates. This is commonly done with a system of ratings. Ratings show how the candidates compare to one another. Ratings are applied with criteria (which you already have) and weights that show the relative importance of each criterion. In this section we are concerned with developing weights for our criteria. Although this is one of the more subjective parts of the process, it is necessary in order to make selections from your list.

In our example we had the following initial criteria: costs, technology, performance, and risks. From our data gathering we learned that costs should be separated into initial costs and recurring costs, and that other criteria should be added: standards compliance, available services, operations, and scalability. If our seed set of two candidates expanded into five design candidates, our evaluation chart would look something like Figure 5.3. Note that we have a column for relative weights, and a row to total the ratings for each candidate, both of which we have yet to complete.

In this figure we have nine criteria. Each criterion will be given a weight based on the importance of that criterion to the evaluation. This is determined through group discussion, which may include voting on suggested weights. The range of weights that you apply is not as important as maintaining consistency throughout your evaluation. One common range for weights across the set of criteria is 0-1, where 0 means that that criterion has no importance to your evaluation, 1 means that it has the highest importance to your evaluation, and any value in between indicates that criterion's degree of importance. (Note that you could decide that all criteria are equal, in which case you need not assign weights, or you could give each criterion a weight of 1.)

For our example we would take the data gathered so far, along with our refined sets of criteria and candidates, and conduct a discussion regarding how to weight each criterion. Using a range of 0-1, Figure 5.4 shows how the weights might be applied.

	Evaluation Criteria	Relative Weight	Candidates				
			Candidate 1	Candidate 2	Candidate 3	Candidate 4	Candidate 5
1	Initial Costs						
2	Recurring Costs						
3	Technologies						
4	Standards Compliance						
5	Risks						
6	Performance						
7	Available Services						
8	Operations						
9	Scalability						
	Candidate Totals						

Figure 5.3: A refined set of evaluation criteria

	Evaluation Criteria	Relative Weight (0–1)	Candidates				
			Candidate 1	Candidate 2	Candidate 3	Candidate 4	Candidate 5
1	Initial Costs	0.8					
2	Recurring Costs	1.0					
3	Technologies	0.5					
4	Standards Compliance	0.2					
5	Risks	0.9					
6	Performance	0.8					
7	Available Services	0.2					
8	Operations	0.5					
9	Scalability	0.1					
	Candidate Totals						

Figure 5.4: A set of evaluation criteria with relative weights added

In this figure recurring costs are weighted highest, followed by risks, initial costs, and performance. Operations and technology are weighted in the middle of the scale, while standards compliance, available services, and scalability are weighted the least. By looking at this comparison chart, you can see the importance the evaluation team places on each criterion.

It is useful to write down how you arrived at each weight and keep this as part of your documentation. If you are ever asked why certain criteria were weighted higher than others, you will be happy to have it documented. I have found that memory does not serve well here: There have been times when I was certain I would remember the reasons for a particular weight (it seemed obvious at the time), only to forget when asked later.

There are additional ways to develop weights for criteria. As discussed during the analysis process, some characteristics that we can apply to criteria are urgency, importance, and relevance. Urgency is a measure of how time-critical the criterion is; importance is a measure of how significant the criterion is to this project; and relevance is a measure of the appropriateness of this problem to the project. The default characteristic is importance.

Each criterion can be evaluated in terms of urgency, importance, and relevance and a weight assigned to the criterion that is based on all three characteristics. Then the candidates can be evaluated as in the previous example.

In the next section our weights are used with ratings based on how each candidate fares relative to one another for a given criterion.

5.13 DISCUSSING SELECTION CRITERIA FOR PROSPECTIVE NETWORKING CHANNEL PARTNERS WITH COLLEAGUES AND REFINED YOUR SELECTION CRITERIA

After you've performed steps such as discussing selection criteria for prospective networking channel partners with colleagues and refined your selection criteria, the fifth step in choosing networking partners for your project is establishing ratings for each prospect.

Armed with our criteria and the results of our data gathering exercise we now develop ratings for each candidate. As in developing the first set of weights, this should be a group effort that includes your best technical and executive decision makers. The size of such an evaluation group is important-you don't want such a large group that nothing gets accomplished, nor one so small that decisions made by the group will be protested by others in your organization.

Example 5.2

My experience is that a group size somewhere between six and twelve is optimal for making these types of decisions. Oddly enough, this works from small to very large designs.

One important requirement of the evaluation group is that there be no vendors or service providers present. This may seem obvious, but it is surprising how often they are able to get involved. Clearly, in order to develop fair and balanced decisions it is best to leave them out. You should have already gotten all relevant information from vendors and service providers during the data gathering process, before you develop and apply ratings.

To continue our exercise, we have our evaluation group together along with our evaluation chart. We then need to agree on a scale for our ratings. One common range is the same range previously used, 0–1, where 0 means that the candidate is least relevant for that criterion and 1 means that it is most relevant. Other common ranges are 1–5 or 1–10; where a weight of 1 means that that candidate is the worst or least relevant for that criterion, and 5 (or 10) means that that candidate is the best or most relevant for that criterion. You could use these ranges to rank the candidates, giving the best candidate (according to that criterion) a 1, the next best a 2, and so on.

Expanding the scale or reversing the numbers (so that 10 are the worst or least relevant) is entirely subjective. However, it is important that your evaluation group agrees on the scale. If you have problems with this, it indicates that you will have trouble during the evaluations.

Let's say that for this example we choose a scale of 1–5, 5 being the best and 1 the worst. We then take one of the evaluation criteria (e.g., costs) and discuss each design option based on this. This should be a democratic process, where each person gets a chance to express his or her opinion and vote on each candidate. The group leader or project manager would break ties if necessary.

For a discussion on costs we may have cost information (for each candidate design) that was provided to us by an independent assessment, from other organizations that are deploying a similar design, from our own past experience, or from the vendors and service providers themselves. You should be able to compile such cost information and use it to determine a relative rating for each design candidate. You would populate the evaluation chart with ratings for all of the candidates for the cost criterion and then do the same thing for the other criteria. Once you have given ratings to each of your candidates across all of the criteria, you can multiply the weight of each criterion with the rating given to each candidate. The result would look something like Figure 5.5.

In this example each candidate is rated from 1 (worst) to 5 (best) for each criterion. Those ratings are shown as the first number in each evaluation box. Then each rating is multiplied by that candidate's relative weight, resulting in a weighted rating. These weighted ratings are shown as the second number in each evaluation box. The ratings and weighted ratings for each candidate are added together, as reflected in the candidate totals at the bottom of the figure. Although totals for both weighted and unweighted ratings are shown (for illustration), only the weighted ratings would be totalled and applied to the evaluation. Having both weighted and unweighted ratings in an actual evaluation would be confusing.

	Evaluation Criteria	Relative Weight (0–1)	Candidates				
			Candidate 1	Candidate 2	Candidate 3	Candidate 4	Candidate 5
1	Initial Costs	0.8	3/2.4	5/4	4/3.2	2/1.6	1/0.8
2	Recurring Costs	1.0	4/4	5/5	3/3	1/1	2/2
3	Technologies	0.5	3/1.5	4/2.0	1/0.5	2/1.0	5/2.5
4	Standards Compliance	0.2	4/0.8	1/0.2	3/0.6	2/0.4	5/1.0
5	Risks	0.9	3/2.7	4/3.6	1/0.9	5/4.5	2/1.8
6	Performance	0.8	4/3.2	5/4.0	2/1.6	1/0.8	3/2.4
7	Available Services	0.2	5/1.0	1/0.2	3/0.6	2/0.4	4/0.8
8	Operations	0.5	3/1.5	5/2.5	4/2.0	2/1.0	1/0.5
9	Scalability	0.1	5/0.5	1/0.1	3/0.3	2/0.2	4/0.4
	Candidate Totals		34/1.76	31/21.6	24/12.7	10/10.0	27/12.2

Figure 5.5: A set of ratings for candidates

Notice from this figure that, if we follow the unweighted ratings (the first numbers), Candidate 1 has the highest score. However, using the weighted ratings, Candidate 2 receives the highest score. This is because Candidate 2 has the highest ratings for those criteria that have the highest weights. Thus, applying weights allows you to focus the evaluation on those areas of importance to your project.

Finally, it is helpful to have a way to determine when the overall (summary) ratings are so close that you should declare a tie, and what to do when that occurs. Best practice is to declare a tie when candidates are within a few percentage points of each other.

When ratings development and application to the candidates are done well, it helps to take the politics out of the evaluation process.

Having rated our candidates, it is now time to refine the set of candidates, with the objective of selecting the optimal vendor, equipment, or service provider for our project.

5.14 GATHERED DATA ON TOP PROSPECTS

Now that you've gathered data on top prospects that might help you with your networking projects, and established candidate ratings and prioritization, the sixth step is winnowing the list of candidates.

Evaluating networking vendors paves the way for the last step of deciding whether networking vendors, networking tools and network service providers for your project will be evaluated first.

You now have an evaluation chart that shows how each network design candidate performed against various criteria. Weights were developed for the set of criteria. Each candidate received a rating for each criterion, which were then multiplied by that criterion's weight to form weighted ratings. The weighted ratings were combined to form a total for each candidate. The result of the evaluation is a set of overall or summary ratings that combines the individual ratings for each candidate.

Rank	Candidate	Deltas	
		Relative	Total
1	Candidate 2	0	0
2	Candidate 1	– 4	– 4
3	Candidate 3	– 4.9	– 8.9
4	Candidate 5	– 0.5	– 9.4
5	Candidate 4	– 1.3	– 10.7

Figure 5.6: Rankings of the candidates after evaluation

Summary ratings are used to prioritize the set of candidates. For example, from our previous evaluation chart we would get the prioritization shown in Figure 5.6. This figure shows the ranking of each candidate, along with the relative difference in ratings between that candidate and the one next higher in rank (relative delta), and the difference in ratings between that candidate and the top candidate (total delta). Either delta can be used to determine whether a candidate should be dropped from the set, or whether a tie should be declared. If, for this example, we had decided that a candidate had to be within one point of the next higher-ranking candidate (about 5% of the summary rating for Candidate 2) in order to declare a tie, we could see from the relative deltas that no candidates are close enough to be tied, and that Candidate 2 is the clear winner.

With a prioritized set you can eliminate candidates with bad ratings, with the goal of achieving a single optimal candidate. Usually a single candidate is chosen when it is clearly superior, that is, when its ratings are significantly better than all other candidates. Typically, on a first run of the evaluation there will not be one clearly superior candidate; instead, there may be few or several, depending in part on how many candidates you start with.

When the evaluation process yields more than one superior candidate, another iteration of the evaluation process should be performed on this reduced set. Successive iterations of the evaluation process begin with candidate discussions and continue through data gathering, criteria refinement and ratings development, ratings and prioritization, and another modification of the candidate set.

An advantage of doing another iteration of the evaluation process is that you already have most of the work done: the data sets and evaluation criteria. The work done in each successive iteration improves upon that information and should result in clearer and better ratings and prioritizations. Eventually, the evaluations should result in a single superior candidate.

Example 5.3

Experience shows that often one or two iterations of the evaluation process will result in a single winner. If you do two evaluations and still have more than one candidate left (or worse, several candidates left), then you should reevaluate your evaluation data and how you are performing the evaluations.

5.15 EVALUATING VENDORS, TOOLS AND SERVICE PROVIDERS

The seventh and final step in evaluating vendors, tools and service providers for your networking projects is deciding which of them will be evaluated first.

Remember that this process can be used to select vendors, their equipment, and service providers for your design, and that you will apply this process to only one type of evaluation at a time. However, there may be information that you gathered for one evaluation that can also be used for the other evaluations. For example, vendor information, gathered for vendor evaluations, may also be useful to evaluate specific items of equipment from that vendor. Likewise, service providers may be using network equipment similar to those you are evaluating. This may be particularly important from compatibility and end-to-end service perspectives.

This implies that there may be an optimal order for evaluations. In fact, it can be to your advantage to sequence your evaluations so that you can reuse and build upon information. A common order to evaluations (as indicated by the title to this section) is vendor, vendor equipment, and service provider. The logic for doing this is as follows:

1. You may want to choose which vendors you want for your design before making specific selections for network equipment. Vendor choices can strongly influence equipment selection. Of course, there is a counter argument to this: that you should not let vendor selections influence your choice of equipment. However, typically your selections for vendors and for equipment are at the very least loosely coupled.
2. Understanding which network equipment you plan to acquire will help you to make better decisions regarding service providers.

An alternative to this is to evaluate vendors and service providers concurrently. This does not mean you would combine your evaluations, but rather perform them separately during the same time frame.

5.16 THE VENDOR-DESIGNER RELATIONSHIP

A user-vendor relationship can be a rewarding experience. As mentioned before, this is similar to a marriage, where both parties benefit under good conditions. Both must clearly understand each other's business needs, and maintain good communications channels to head off any misunderstandings. If you do not like or trust your salesperson, then a "divorce" might be eminent.

There are some rules to follow to achieve these goals. Don't let the vendor experiment with your network. This is especially true when you are trying to stabilize your network, and the vendor is experimenting with untried solutions such as new software revisions. All upgrades should be planned to eliminate these surprises, and strict change management procedures should be followed.

Maintain good interpersonal relationships. Make sure that what is expected of the vendor and the user is clearly understood. Speak honestly and cooperatively with the vendor, and work together to achieve your goals. Understand the levels of peer-to-peer relationships and the roles and responsibilities of the account team. Frequent presales and post sales support calls, as well as user visits to vendor facilities and labs are desirable. The vendor should make available a business and technical contract, such as a knowledgeable sale support person and network engineer, and provide some level of continuous on-site support for large accounts; but remember, true 7x24x365 maintenance support is left to maintenance contracts.

Make sure you are purchasing the products and services you want and need, not what the vendor wants you to purchase. When signing vendor development contracts, make sure you do not get locked in for long-term commitment with what you might pay in early cancellation penalties. Have the vendor product good documentation before project/product hand-off.

Look for vendors who are choosy about their business partners, and how the vendor relates the chosen customers to its long-term strategy. Does the vendor deal only with inter-exchange carriers, or does it also deal with local access providers? Do they focus on specific vertical markets, or sell to virtually anyone? The primary customer base of a vendor can tell much about how the vendor is positioning itself for the future.

The relationship between vendor and user will usually last a long time; therefore, the vendor will have a profound impact on the user's business. The two are ties together. If the primary vendor for a communications network suddenly goes out of business, it could mean substantial budgetary impacts on the user's business to either replace the existing product base or migrate to a new one.

5.17 STRATEGIC USER-VENDOR AGREEMENTS

Strategic agreements between users and vendors take many forms, depending on the level of commitment of each party. Flexibility is the most important aspects of the agreements listed below. Both user and vendor will learn through the process, and both will be required to adapt to each other's needs. Large users typically have enough buying clout to affect the R&D direction of the vendor. These agreements can offer many advantages, such as guaranteeing a revenue stream for both parties, providing the lowest prices, skipping the repetitive, resource-intensive, and expensive RFP process, and building on the strengths of both user and vendor. Often, the vendors achieve greater control, for without them there is no product.

The following are some common terms of agreement defined:

- **Affiliate:** No legal contract, but work together for business purpose
- **Alliance:** Nonexclusive contractual agreement; separate funding, but might lead to a joint product or service venture
- **Joint venture:** Central or pooled funds; often exclusive contract language or separate incorporation
- **Strategic partnership:** Work together to solve complex problems; might involve any level of those relationships listed earlier

5.18 SERVICE CHARACTERISTICS

One of the goals of network analysis is to be able to characterize services so that they can be designed into the network and purchased from vendors and service providers (e.g., via requests for information [RFI], quote [RFQ], or proposal [RFP], documents used in the procurement process). Service characteristics are individual network performance and functional parameters that are used to describe services. These services are offered by the network to the system (the service offering) or are requested from the network by users, applications, or devices (the service request). Characteristics of services that are requested from the network can also be considered requirements for that network.

Examples of service characteristics range from estimates of capacity requirements based on anecdotal or qualitative information about the network to elaborate listings of various capacity, delay, and RMA requirements, per user, application, and/or device, along with requirements for security, manageability, usability, flexibility, and others. Such requirements are useful in determining the need of the system for services, in providing input to the network architecture and design, and in configuring services in network devices (e.g., routers, switches, device operating systems).

Measurements of these characteristics in the network to monitor, verify, and manage services are called service metrics. In this book we focus on developing service requirements for the network and using those characteristics to configure, monitor, and verify services within the network.

For services to be useful and effective, they must be described and provisioned end-to-end at all network components between well-defined demarcation points. "End-to-end" does not necessarily mean only from one user's device to another user's device. It may be defined between networks, from users to servers, or between specialized devices (Figure 5.7). When services are not provisioned end-to-end, some components may not be capable of supporting them, and thus the services will fail. The demarcation points determine where end-to-end is in the network.

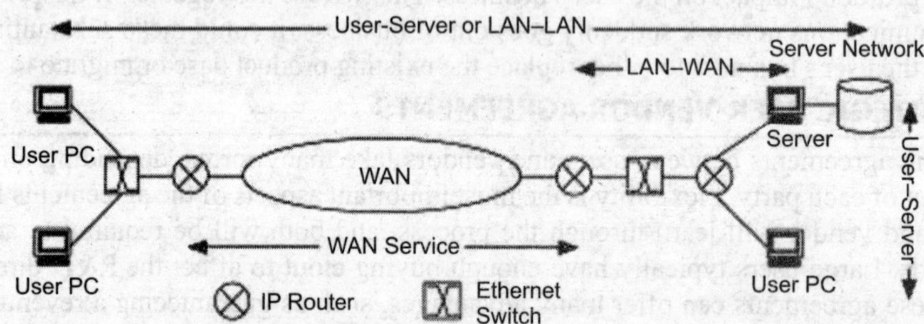

Figure 5.7: Example Demarcations Points to Describe End-to-End within a Network

Determining these demarcation points is an important part of describing a service. Services also need to be configurable, measurable, and verifiable within the system. This is necessary to ensure that end users, applications, and devices are getting the services they have requested (and possibly have been paying for), and this leads to accounting and billing for system (including network) resources. You will see how service metrics can be used to measure and verify services and their characteristics. Services are also likely to be hierarchical within the system, with different service types and mechanisms applied at each layer in the hierarchy. For example, Figure 5.8 shows a quality-of-service (QoS) hierarchy that focuses on bulk traffic transport in the core of the network while placing specific services at the access network close to the end users, applications, and devices.

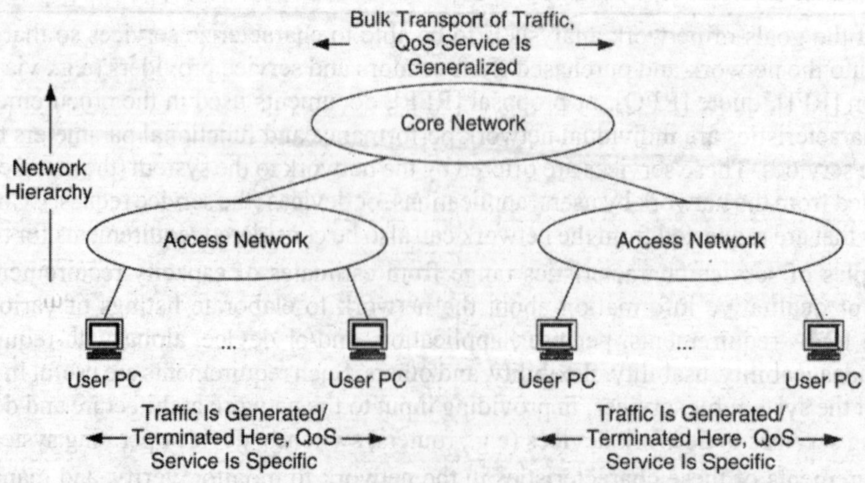

Figure 5.8: An example of service hierarchy within a network

5.18.1 SERVICE LEVELS

Service characteristics can be grouped together to form one or more service levels for the network. This is done to make service provisioning easier in that you can configure, manage, account, and bill for a group of service characteristics (service level) instead of a number of individual characteristics. For example, a service level (e.g., premium) may combine capacity (e.g., 1.5 Mb/s) and reliability (as 99.99% uptime). Service levels are also helpful in billing and accounting. This is a service provider view of the network, where services are offered to customers (users) for a fee. This view of networking is becoming more popular in enterprise networks, displacing the view of networks as purely the infrastructure of cost centers.

There are many ways to describe service levels, including frame relay committed information rates (CIRs), which are levels of capacity; classes of service (CoSs), which combine delay and capacity characteristics; and IP types of service (ToSs) and qualities of service (QoSs), which prioritize traffic for traffic conditioning functions. There can also be combinations of the aforementioned mechanisms, as well as custom service levels, based on groups of individual service characteristics. These combinations depend on which network technology, protocol, mechanism, or combination is providing the service.

In Figure 5.9 service offerings, requests, and metrics are shown applied to the system. In this example a demarcation of services is shown between the device and network components. Depending on the service requirement or characteristic, however, demarcation may also be between the device and application components.

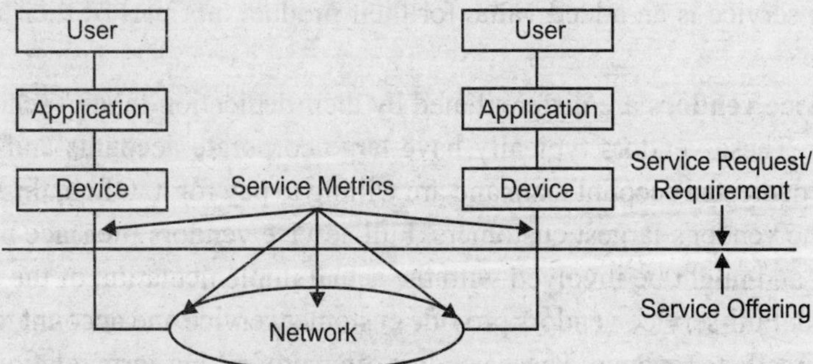

Figure 5.9: Service requests, offerings, and metrics

Services and service levels can be distinguished by their degrees of predictability or determinism. In the next section we discuss best-effort delivery, which is not predictable or deterministic, as well as predictable and guaranteed services. Services and service levels are also distinguished by their degrees of performance. You will see how the service performance characteristics capacity, delay, and RMA are used to describe services and service levels.

5.18.2 DIFFERENT TYPES OF SERVICE LEVELS

It is important to define the service expectations of the vendor. This includes the vendor's perspective-how service is defined, how that service is provided, and measurements for both. What are the categories of service provided, and what are its priorities? What priority is the user to the vendor - what size account - and how does the user compare to other users of that vendor? It is a fact of life that the customers that represent the largest amount of revenue typically are provided the greatest amount of vendor resources. What are the vendor's response and repair times, parts and sparing plan, software and hardware support hours? Are spares centrally located or dispersed to areas of dense customer-service areas? Are backup and fault tolerance inherent within the network service? These elements are critical to maintaining a highly available network.

Vendors provide many service levels to users. Four general levels of service can be provided, and the user must decide which best suits the business strategy and is most cost-effective. The four levels of service are nonparticipant, value-added, full-service and joint-development.

- **Nonparticipant vendors** deliver their products to their customers and do not provide continued service after receipt of delivery. These are typically off-the-shelf products not requiring vendor installation or maintenance. They are also often low-cost items with sales based on price, availability, and speed of delivery. An example is Black Box, a company that specializes in delivery of well-known low-end and midrange data communications products.
- **Value-added vendors** include some level of service and support with their products and services. These vendors are judged by factors other than price and availability, such as quality, feature function, and support staffs, and make it a part of their business to communicate with each customer. These vendors offer some long-term commitment to their products and services, as well as to the customers who purchase them. While value-added vendors provide customer support, they typically draw the line when it becomes a financial burden to do so; customer service is an added value for their product, not part of their revenue-generating business.
- **Full-service vendors** are differentiated by their dedication to, and relationship with, each customer. These vendors typically have large corporate accounts and support users who require a dedicated account team and are willing to pay for it. Often, this service is provided only to the vendor's largest customers. Full-service vendors interface much more with the end user, and might be involved with the actual implementation of the product or services purchased. Full-service vendors provide customer service and account teams and relate this service directly to revenue. These vendors often prefer long-term relationships with the user based on joint service offerings and future business potential. Service in this case is often measured and conforms to strict guidelines. Outsourcing and out-taking fit into this category.
- **Joint-development** vendor not only work with users, but also develop products in and around users. Vendors that can partner with large businesses can gain a strategic advantage in the marketplace. Small vendors can claim interoperability with major users and cut a niche into the marked at the expense of time spent on development work with the user.

Sometimes a vendor will not be able to provide all the service or product that is required. A good design will incorporate alternate sources and strategies for network support that will not leave you out in the cold. It is the network manager's job to find and implement these alternatives.

5.18.3 SERVICE-LEVEL AGREEMENT

A service-level agreement (SLA) is a contract between a network service provider and a customer that specifies, usually in measurable terms, what services the network service provider will furnish. Many Internet service providers (ISPs) provide their customers with an SLA. More recently, IS departments in major enterprises have adopted the idea of writing a service level agreement so that services for their customers (users in other departments within the enterprise) can be measured, justified, and perhaps compared with those of outsourcing network providers.

Some metrics that SLAs may specify includes:

- What percentage of the time services will be available
- The number of users that can be served simultaneously
- Specific performance benchmarks to which actual performance will be periodically compared
- The schedule for notification in advance of network changes that may affect users
- Help desk response time for various classes of problems
- Dial-in access availability
- Usage statistics that will be provided.

5.19 NETWORK AND SYSTEMS MANAGEMENT CAPABILITIES

Network and systems management should be one of the most important decisions in the vendor-analysis process. Networks can be managed via a single network management platform with distributed analysis and data and alarm collection from all equipment and elements compiled and correlated at a central location. Network management can span the WAN, LAN, down to the desktops and servers, and all three can be performed by one network management system. Thus, integrated network management needs to be incorporated into the RFP process. Some users might already have an existing hardware base that will be integrated with the new-mixing protocols, operating systems, billing, alarms, and operating platforms, making integrated network management all the more important. This creates a need for a network management platform that can do many things-provide proactive and reactive global fault detection, analysis, and correction; measure network performance; and help with proactive performance engineering, security control and accounting measures, alarm and event correlation, and local and remote configuration capability. Each of these capabilities should be available for every manageable device on the network.

There are two network-management protocols that provide the integrated capability needed in today's computing networks: all versions of TCP/IP's Simple Network Management Protocol (SNMP) and OSI's common Management Information Protocol/Common Management Information System (CMIP/CMIS). Both management protocol schemes enable integrated network management for network elements on a communications network and can be managed through hardware and software platforms such as HP Open View.

Much of the burden still lies with the user, who must both interpret the information provided by the network manager and develop interfaces for the translation of this data into a workable form. Just monitoring SNMP feeds on an HP Open View platform will not suffice.

Some important network-management requirements include

- Integration of all OSIRM layer of alarms
- Intelligent interpretation of alarm and management data
- Flexible alarm presentation and log structure
- Real-time geographical network status
- Real-time point-and-click graphics
- Statistical collection
- Remote and local downloads, nodal configuration, board diagnostics, and inventory management capabilities
- Local hard drive/floppy storage
- Multiple security levels other than system logon
- Data scope functions
- Accounting and billing collection (ASCII or binary)
- Integration of nonproprietary implementations

Of course a more cost-effective option might be to outsource the management of your network.

5.20 FUTURE BUSINESS OF YOUR COMPANY

It cannot be stressed enough that the future success or failure of a business (not to mention the designer's job) can ride on the success or failure of the vendor chosen for the data and computer communications networks. For this reason, a user will rarely give the entire business to a single vendor. Occasionally, a business relationship, partnership, or joint strategic direction will dictate a single vendor solution; however, a multivendor environment is a healthy and safe one. It creates a competitive environment so that the prime vendor works harder for the business and a secondary supplier is available in case the primary supplier falters. If all vendors meet the criteria presented in this chapter, especially standards compliance, there should be minimal difficulty in network integration and interoperability.

EXERCISES

1. How can you choose service providers?
2. Explain the RFI process in detail?
3. Explain the RFP process in detail?
4. What do you mean by sample networks and solicitation?
5. How can you analyze and evaluate RFP responses?
6. How can you choose vendors?

7. What are the various requirements matrix and weighting methods?
8. Which trade-offs is critical when choose vendors?
9. Explain the evaluation criteria of choosing network vendors and service providers?
10. How to evaluate networking vendors and network service providers?
11. Explain the networking vendors, tools and service providers?
12. How to seed the evaluation process and asking peers for advice?
13. Explain the discussion selection criteria for prospective networking channel partners with colleagues and refined your selection criteria?
14. How can you gather data on top prospects?
15. How to evaluate vendors, tools and service providers?
16. Explain the relationship between vendor-designer?
17. Explain the concept of strategic user-vendor agreements?
18. Explain the various service characteristics?
19. What do you mean by service levels?
20. Explain the different types of service levels?
21. What do you mean by service-level agreement?
22. Explain the various network and systems management capabilities?

CHAPTER

6

Access Network Design

6.1 HIERARCHICAL NETWORK DESIGN

To meet a customer's business and technical goals for a corporate network design, you might need to recommend a network topology consisting of many interrelated components. This task is made easier if you can "divide and conquer" the job and develop the design in layers.

Network design experts have developed the **hierarchical network design model** to help you develop a topology in discrete layers. Each layer can be focused on specific functions, allowing you to choose the right systems and features for the layer. For example, high-speed WAN routers can carry traffic across the enterprise WAN backbone, medium-speed routers can connect buildings at each campus, and switches can connect user devices and servers within buildings.

A typical hierarchical topology is

- **A core layer** of high-end routers and switches that are optimized for availability and performance.
- **A distribution layer** of routers and switches that implement policies.
- **An access layer** that connects users via lower-end switches and wireless access points.

6.2 WHY USE A HIERARCHICAL NETWORK DESIGN MODEL

Networks that grow unheeded without any plan in place tend to develop in an unstructured format. Dr. Peter Welcher, the author of network design and technology articles for Cisco World and other publications, refers to unplanned networks as fur-ball network.

Welcher explains the disadvantages of a fur-ball topology by pointing out the problems that too many CPU adjacencies cause. When network devices communicate with many other devices, the workload required of the CPUs on the devices can be burdensome. For example, in a large flat (switched) network, broadcast packets are burdensome. A broadcast packet interrupts the CPU on each device within the broadcast domain, and demands processing time on every device for which a protocol understanding for that broadcast is installed. This includes routers, workstations, and servers.

Another potential problem with nonhierarchical networks, besides broadcast packets, is the CPU workload required for routers to communicate with many other routers and process numerous route advertisements. A hierarchical network design methodology lets you design a modular topology that limits the number of communicating routers.

Using a hierarchical model can help you minimize costs. You can purchase the appropriate internetworking devices for each layer of the hierarchy, thus avoiding spending money on unnecessary features for a layer. Also, the modular nature of the hierarchical design model enables accurate capacity planning within each layer of the hierarchy, thus reducing wasted bandwidth. Network management responsibility and network management systems can be distributed to the different layers of modular network architecture to control management costs.

Modularity lets you keep each design element simple and easy to understand. Simplicity minimizes the need for extensive training for network operations personnel and expedites the implementation of a design. Testing a network design is made easy because there is clear functionality at each layer. Fault isolation is improved because network technicians can easily recognize the transition points in the network to help them isolate possible failure points.

Hierarchical design facilitates changes. As elements in a network require change, the cost of making an upgrade is contained to a small subset of the overall network. In large flat or meshed network architectures, changes tend to impact a large number of systems. Replacing one device can affect numerous networks because of the complex interconnections.

6.3 HOW CAN YOU TELL WHEN YOU HAVE A GOOD DESIGN

Here are some wise answers from Peter Welcher that are based on the tenets of hierarchical, modular network design:

- When you already know how to add a new building, floor, WAN link, remote site, e-commerce service, and so on.
- When new additions cause only local change, to the directly connected devices.
- When your network can double or triple in size without major design changes.
- When troubleshooting is easy because there are no complex protocol interactions to wrap your brain around.

When scalability is a major goal, a hierarchical topology is recommended because modularity in a design enables creating design elements that can be replicated as the network grows. Because each instance of a module is consistent, expansion is easy to plan and implement. For example, planning a campus network for a new site might simply be a matter of replicating an existing campus network design.

6.3.1 FLAT VERSUS HIERARCHICAL TOPOLOGIES

A flat network topology is adequate for very small networks. With a flat network design, there is no hierarchy. Each internetworking device has essentially the same job, and the network is not divided into layers or modules. A flat network topology is easy to design and implement, and it is easy to maintain, as long as the network stays small. When the network grows, however, a flat network is undesirable. The lack of hierarchy makes troubleshooting difficult. Rather than being able to concentrate troubleshooting efforts in just one area of the network, you may need to inspect the entire network.

6.3.2 FLAT WAN TOPOLOGIES

A wide-area network (WAN) for a small company can consist of a few sites connected in a loop. Each site has a WAN router that connects to two other adjacent sites via point-to-point links. As long as the WAN is small (a few sites), routing protocols can converge quickly, and communication with any other site can recover when a link fails. (As long as only one link fails, communication recovers. When more than one link fails, some sites are isolated from others.)

A flat loop topology is generally not recommended for networks with many sites, however. A loop topology can mean that there are many hops between routers on opposite sides of the loop, resulting in significant delay and a higher probability of failure. If your analysis of traffic flow indicates that routers on opposite sides of a loop topology exchange a lot of traffic, you should recommend a hierarchical topology instead of a loop. To avoid any single point of failure, redundant routers or switches can be placed at upper layers of the hierarchy.

6.3.3 FLAT LAN TOPOLOGIES

In the early and mid-1990s, a typical design for a LAN was PCs and servers attached to one or more hubs in a flat topology. The PCs and servers implemented a media-access control process, such as token passing or carrier sense multiple access with collision detection (CSMA/CD) to control access to the shared bandwidth. The devices were all part of the same bandwidth domain and had the ability to negatively affect delay and throughput for other devices.

These days, network designers usually recommend attaching the PCs and servers to data link layer (Layer 2) switches instead of hubs. In this case, the network is segmented into small bandwidth domains so that a limited number of devices compete for bandwidth at any one time. (However, the devices do compete for service by the switching hardware and software, so it is important to understand the performance characteristics of candidate switches.

6.3.4 MESH VERSUS HIERARCHICAL-MESH TOPOLOGIES

Network designers often recommend a mesh topology to meet availability requirements. In a full-mesh topology, every router or switch is connected to every other router or switch. A full-mesh network provides complete redundancy, and offers good performance because there is just a single-link delay between any two sites. A partial-mesh network has fewer connections. To reach another router or switch in a partial-mesh network might require traversing intermediate links.

6.4 THE CLASSIC THREE-LAYER HIERARCHICAL MODEL

Literature published by Cisco Systems, Inc. and other networking vendors talks about a classic three-layer hierarchical model for network design topologies. The three-layer model permits traffic aggregation and filtering at three successive routing or switching levels. This makes the three-layer hierarchical model scalable to large international internet works.

Although the model was developed at a time when routers delineated layers, the model can be used for switched networks as well as routed networks.

Each layer of the hierarchical model has a specific role. The core layer provides optimal transport between sites. The distribution layer connects network services to the access layer, and implements policies regarding security, traffic loading, and routing. In a WAN design, the access layer consists of the routers at the edge of the campus networks. In a campus network, the access layer provides switches or hubs for end-user access.

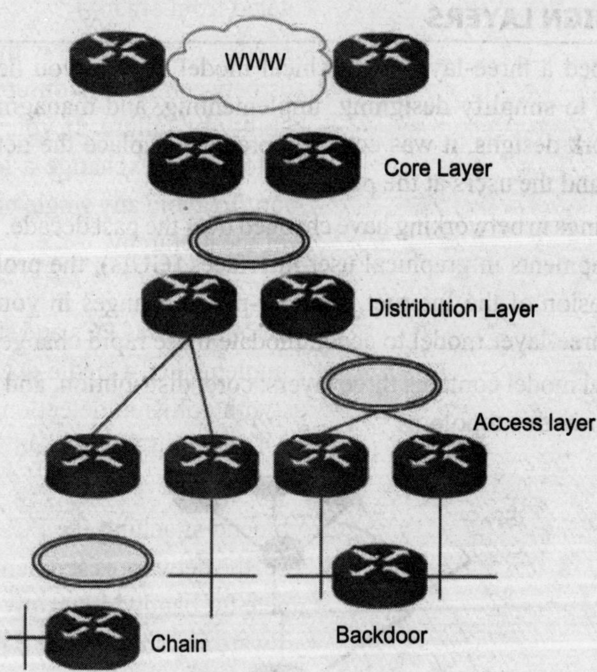

Figure 6.1: Three-Layer Hierarchical Model

6.4.1 GUIDELINES FOR HIERARCHICAL NETWORK DESIGN

This section briefly describes some guidelines for hierarchical network design. Following these simple guidelines will help you design networks that take advantage of the benefits of hierarchical design. The first guideline is that you should control the diameter of a hierarchical enterprise network topology.

In most cases, three major layers are sufficient:

1. The core layer
2. The distribution layer
3. The access layer

Controlling the network diameter provides low and predictable latency. It also helps you predict routing paths, traffic flows, and capacity requirements. A controlled network diameter also makes troubleshooting and network documentation easier.

Finally, one other guideline for hierarchical network design is that you should design the access layer first, followed by the distribution layer, and then finally the core layer. By starting with the access layer, you can more accurately perform capacity planning for the distribution and core layers. You can also recognize the optimization techniques you will need for the distribution and core layers.

6.5 NETWORK DESIGN LAYERS

Cisco has developed a three-layer hierarchical model to help you design campus networks. Cisco uses this model to simplify designing, implementing, and managing large-scale networks. With traditional network designs, it was common practice to place the networking services at the center of the network and the users at the periphery.

However, many things in networking have changed over the past decade, including advancements in applications, developments in graphical user interfaces (GUIs), the proliferation of multimedia applications, the explosion of the Internet, and fast-paced changes in your user's traffic patterns. Cisco developed the three-layer model to accommodate these rapid changes.

Cisco's hierarchical model contains three layers: core, distribution, and access. A well-designed network typically follows this topology.

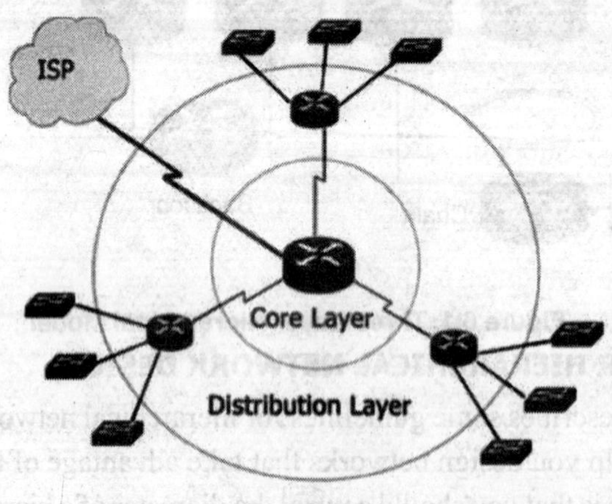

Figure 6.2: Network Design Layers

You can use the hierarchical model to design a modular topology using scalable "building blocks" that allow the network to meet evolving business needs. The modular design makes the network easy to scale, understand, and troubleshoot by promoting deterministic traffic patterns.

Cisco introduced the hierarchical design model, which uses a layered approach to network design in 1999 (see Figure 6.3). The building block components are the access layer, the distribution layer, and the core (backbone) layer. The principal advantages of this model are its hierarchical structure and its modularity.

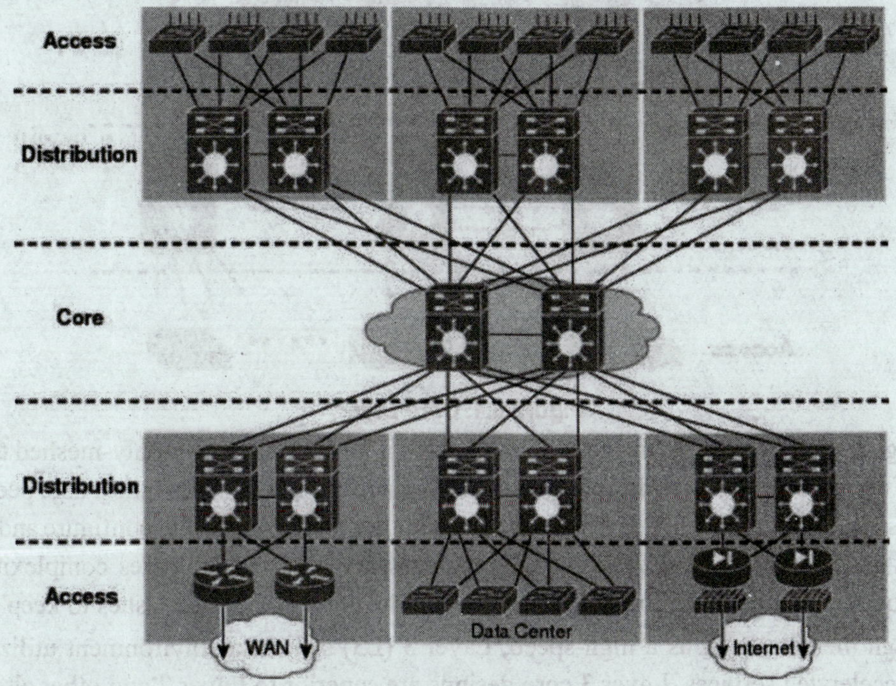

Figure 6.3: Hierarchical Campus Network Design

In a hierarchical design, the capacity, features, and functionality of a specific device are optimized for its position in the network and the role that it plays. This promotes scalability and stability. The number of flows and their associated bandwidth requirements increase as they traverse points of aggregation and move up the hierarchy from access to distribution to core. Functions are distributed at each layer. A hierarchical design avoids the need for a fully-meshed network in which all network nodes are interconnected.

The building blocks of modular networks are easy to replicate, redesign, and expand. There should be no need to redesign the whole network each time a module is added or removed. Distinct building blocks can be put in-service and taken out-of-service without impacting the rest of the network. This capability facilitates troubleshooting, problem isolation, and network management.

6.5.1 CORE LAYER

In a typical hierarchical model, the individual building blocks are interconnected using a core layer. The core serves as the backbone for the network, as shown in 6.4. The core needs to be fast and extremely resilient because every building block depends on it for connectivity. Current hardware accelerated systems have the potential to deliver complex services at wire speed. However, in the core of the network a "less is more" approach should be taken. A minimal configuration in the core reduces configuration complexity limiting the possibility for operational error.

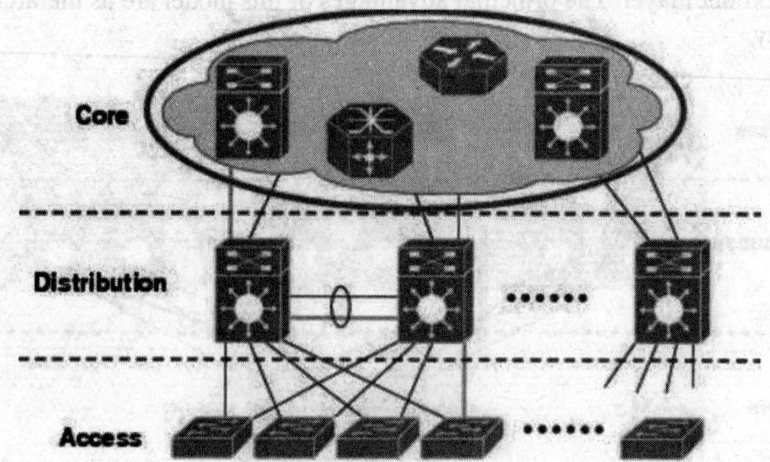

Figure 6.4: Core Layer

Although it is possible to achieve redundancy with a fully-meshed or highly-meshed topology, that type of design does not provide consistent convergence if a link or node fails. Also, peering and adjacency issues exist with a fully-meshed design, making routing complex to configure and difficult to scale. In addition, the high port count adds unnecessary cost and increases complexity as the network grows or changes. The following are some of the other key design issues to keep in mind:

1. Design the core layer as a high-speed, Layer 3 (L3) switching environment utilizing only hardware-accelerated services. Layer 3 core designs are superior to Layer 2 and other alternatives because they provide:

- Faster convergence around a link or node failure.
- Increased scalability because neighbor relationships and meshing are reduced.
- More efficient bandwidth utilization.

2. Use redundant point-to-point L3 interconnections in the core (triangles, not squares) wherever possible, because this design yields the fastest and most deterministic convergence results.

3. Avoid L2 loops and the complexity of L2 redundancy, such as Spanning Tree Protocol (STP) and indirect failure detection for L3 building block peers.

To summarize, the Core Layer should:

- Be used to provide high-speed switching.
- Provide reliability and fault tolerance.
- Grow by using faster, and not more, equipment.

Never implement performance-decreasing elements such as access lists.

6.5.2 DISTRIBUTION LAYER

The distribution layer aggregates nodes from the access layer, protecting the core from high-density peering (see Figure 6.5). Additionally, the distribution layer creates a fault boundary providing a logical isolation point in the event of a failure originating in the access layer. Typically deployed as a pair of L3 switches, the distribution layer uses L3 switching for its connectivity to the core of the network and L2 services for its connectivity to the access layer. Load balancing, Quality of Service (QoS), and ease of provisioning are key considerations for the distribution layer.

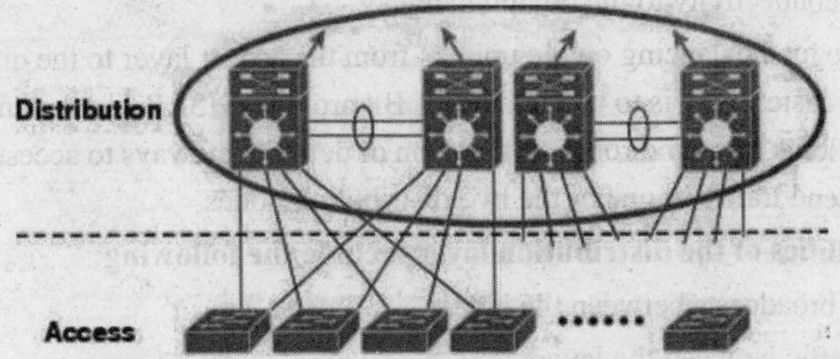

Figure 6.5: Distribution Layer

High availability in the distribution layer is provided through dual equal-cost paths from the distribution layer to the core and from the access layer to the distribution layer (see Figure 6.6). This results in fast, deterministic convergence in the event of a link or node failure. When redundant paths are present, failover depends primarily on hardware link failure detection instead of timer-based software failure detection. Convergence based on these functions, which are implemented in hardware, is the most deterministic.

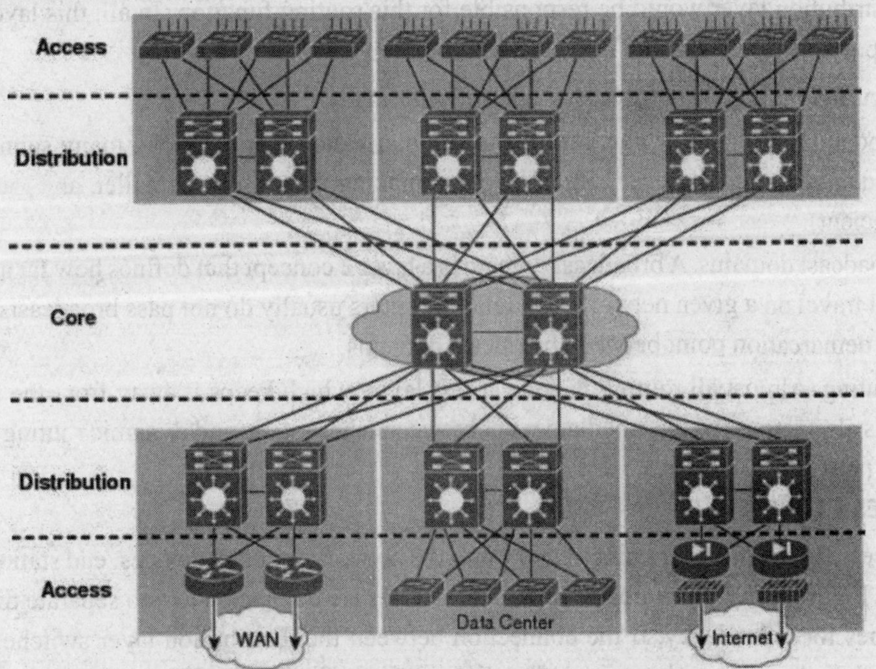

Figure 6.6: Distribution Layer-High Availability

L3 equal-cost load sharing allows both uplinks from the core to the distribution layer to be utilized. The distribution layer provides default gateway redundancy using the Gateway Load Balancing Protocol (GLBP), Hot Standby Router Protocol (HSRP), or Virtual Router Redundancy Protocol (VRRP). This allows for the failure or removal of one of the distribution nodes without affecting end point connectivity to the default gateway.

You can achieve load balancing on the uplinks from the access layer to the distribution layer in many ways, but the easiest way is to use GLBP. GLBP provides HSRP-like redundancy and failure protection. It also allows for round robin distribution of default gateways to access layer devices, so the end points can send traffic to one of the two distribution nodes.

The responsibilities of the distribution layer include the following:

- Containing broadcasts between the layers
- Securing traffic between the layers
- Providing a hierarchy through layer-3 logical addressing and route summarization
- Translating between different media types

As mentioned in the section (Network Layer), routers give you by far the most flexibility in enforcing your company's networking policies, since routers deal with logical addresses. And because routers are used at the distribution layer, the implementation of your policies, at least most of them, is done here.

The distribution layer would be responsible for this routing function. In all, this layer serves a number of purposes including the implementation of

- Security, in the form of Access Lists and filtering.
- A boundary for route aggregation and summarization (for example, many subnets can be hidden behind a single routing table entry, making these entries smaller, and routing more efficient).
- Broadcast domains. A broadcast domain is a layer 2 concept that defines how far a broadcast will travel on a given network. By default, routers usually do not pass broadcasts, acting as the demarcation point between broadcast domains.
- Routing. Almost all routing is done at this layer, which keeps it away from the backbone. This also acts as the intermediate point between where static and dynamic routing is used on the network.

6.5.3 ACCESS LAYER

The access layer is the first point of entry into the network for edge devices, end stations, and IP phones (see Figure 6.7). The switches in the access layer are connected to two separate distribution layer switches for redundancy. If the connection between the distribution layer switches is an L3 connection, then there are no loops and all uplinks actively forward traffic.

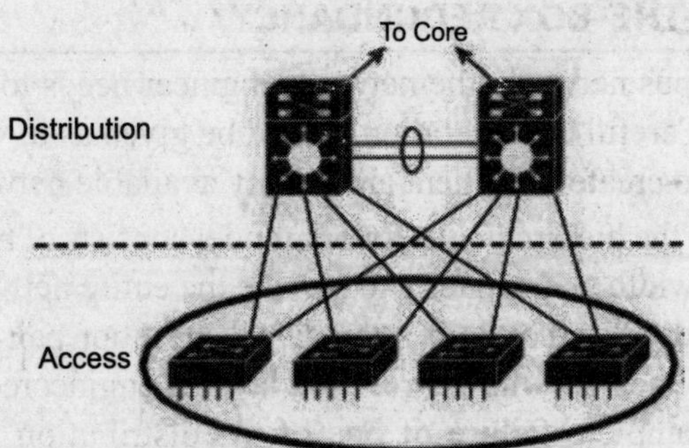

Figure 6.7: Access Layer

The bottom layer of the three-layer hierarchical model is the access layer. Actually, the access layer is at the periphery of your campus network, separated from the core layer by the distribution layer. The main function of the access layer is to provide the user's initial connection to your network.

Typically, this connection is provided by a switch, or sometimes, a hub. Sometimes if the user works at a small branch office or home office, this device can also be a router. But in most cases, the connection is provided by a switch.

A robust access layer provides the following key features:

- High availability (HA) supported by many hardware and software attributes.
- Inline power (POE) for IP telephony and wireless access points, allowing customers to converge voice onto their data network and providing roaming WLAN access for users.
- Foundation services.
- The hardware and software attributes of the access layer that support high availability include the following:
- System-level redundancy using redundant supervisor engines and redundant power supplies. This provides high-availability for critical user groups.
- Default gateway redundancy using dual connections to redundant systems (distribution layer switches) that use GLBP, HSRP, or VRRP. This provides fast failover from one switch to the backup switch at the distribution layer.
- Operating system high-availability features, such as Link Aggregation (EtherChannel or 802.3ad), which provide higher effective bandwidth while reducing complexity.
- Prioritization of mission-critical network traffic using QoS. This provides traffic classification and queuing as close to the ingress of the network as possible.
- Security services for additional security against unauthorized access to the network through the use of tools such as 802.1x, port security, DHCP snooping, Dynamic ARP Inspection, and IP Source Guard.
- Efficient network and bandwidth management using software features such as Internet Group Membership Protocol (IGMP) snooping. IGMP snooping helps control multicast packet flooding for multicast applications.

6.6 NETWORK AND IN-THE-BOX REDUNDANCY

When designing a campus network, the network engineer needs to plan the optimal use of the highly redundant devices. Careful consideration should be given as to when and where to make an investment in redundancy to create a resilient and highly available network.

As shown in Figure 6.8, the hierarchical network model consists of two actively forwarding core nodes, with sufficient bandwidth and capacity to service the entire network in the event of a failure of one of the nodes. This model also requires a redundant distribution pair supporting each distribution building block. Similarly to the core, the distribution layer is engineered with sufficient bandwidth and capacity so that the complete failure of one of the distribution nodes does not impact the performance of the network from a bandwidth or switching capacity perspective.

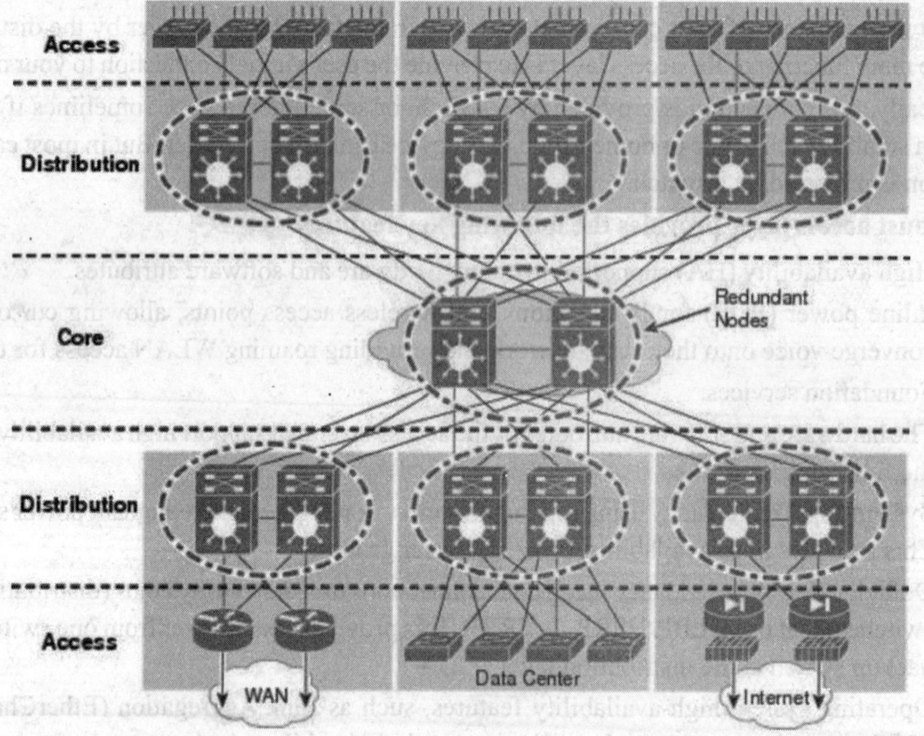

Figure 6.8: Redundant Network Nodes

Campus network devices can currently provide a high level of availability within the individual nodes. The Cisco Catalyst 6500 and 4500 switches can support redundant supervisor engines and provide L2 Stateful Switchover (SSO), which ensures that the standby supervisor engine is synchronized from an L2 perspective and can quickly assume L2 forwarding responsibilities in the event of a supervisor failure.

The Catalyst 6500 also provides L3 Non-Stop Forwarding (NSF), which allows the redundant supervisor to assume L3 forwarding responsibilities without resetting or re-establishing neighbor relationships with the surrounding L3 peers in the event of the failure of the primary supervisor.

When designing a network for optimum high availability, it is tempting to add redundant supervisors to the redundant topology in an attempt to achieve even higher availability. However, adding redundant supervisors to redundant core and distribution layers of the network can increase the convergence time in the event of a supervisor failure.

In the hierarchical model, the core and distribution nodes are connected by point-to-point L3 routed fiber optic links. This means that the primary method of convergence for core or distribution node failure is loss of link. If a supervisor fails on a non-redundant node, the links fail and the network converges around the outage through the second core or distribution node. This allows the network to converge in 60-200 milliseconds for EIGRP and OSPF.

When redundant supervisors are introduced, the links are not dropped during an SSO or NSF convergence event if a supervisor fails. Traffic is lost while SSO completes, or indirect detection of the failure occurs. SSO recovers in 1-3 seconds, depending on the physical configuration of device in question. L3 recovery using NSF happens after the SSO convergence event, minimizing L3 disruption and convergence. For the same events, where 60-200 milliseconds of packet loss occurred without redundant supervisors when dual supervisor nodes were used in the core or distribution, 1.8 seconds of loss was measured.

The access layer of the network is typically a single point of failure, as shown in Figure 6.9.

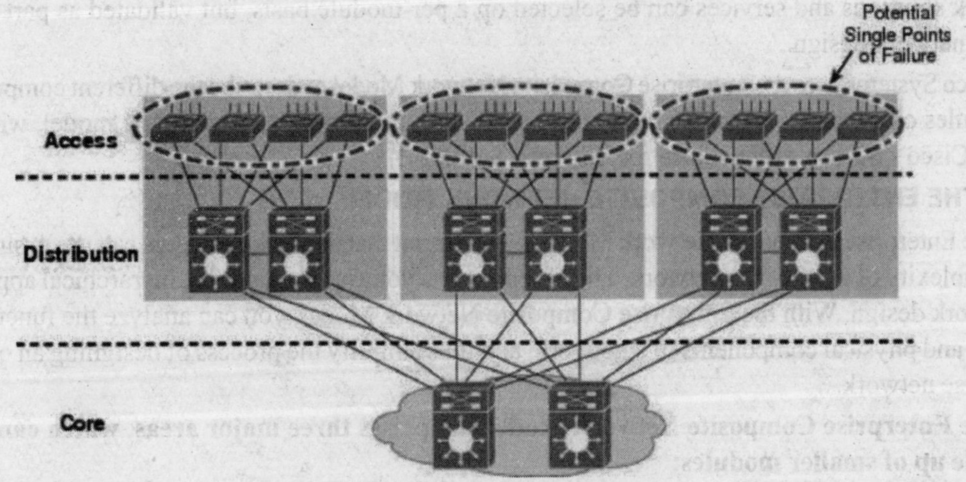

Figure 6.9: Potential Single Points of Failure

While the access nodes are dual connected to the distribution layer, it is not typical for endpoints on the network to be dual connected to redundant access layer switches (except in the data center). For this reason, SSO provides increased availability when redundant supervisors are used in the access layer and the L2/L3 boundary is in the distribution layer of the network. In this topology, SSO provides for protection against supervisor hardware or software failure with 1-3 seconds of packet loss and no network convergence. Without SSO and a single supervisor, devices serviced by this access switch would experience a total network outage until the supervisor was physically replaced or, in the case of a software failure, until the unit reloaded.

If the L2/L3 boundary is in the access layer of the network, a design in which a routing protocol is running in the access layer, then NSF with SSO provides an increased level of availability. Similarly to the L2/L3 distribution layer topology, NSF with SSO provides 1-3 seconds of packet loss without network convergence compared to total outage until a failed supervisor is physically replaced for the routed access topology.

Campus topologies with redundant network paths can converge faster than topologies that depend on redundant supervisors for convergence. NSF/SSO provides the most benefit in environments where single points of failure exist. In the campus topology, that is the access layer. If you have an L2 access layer design, redundant supervisors with SSO provide the most benefit. If you have a routed access layer design, redundant supervisors with NSF with SSO provide the most benefit.

6.7 MODULAR NETWORK DESIGN

Top-down network design lets you drill down to the components of the network design, and apply fundamental design principles to the components as well as the overall design. Hierarchy and redundancy, as mentioned in the previous sections, are fundamental network design concepts.

Another fundamental concept related to hierarchy is modularity. Large network design projects and large networks in general consist of different areas and modules. Each area should be designed using a systematic, top-down approach, applying hierarchy and redundancy where appropriate. Network solutions and services can be selected on a per-module basis, but validated as part of the overall network design.

Cisco Systems uses the Enterprise Composite Network Model to describe the different components or modules of a typical enterprise network. The next section briefly describes the model, which is part of Cisco's Secure Architecture for Enterprises (SAFE).

6.7.1 THE ENTERPRISE COMPOSITE NETWORK MODEL

The Enterprise Composite Network Model is a blueprint that network designers can use to simplify the complexity of a large internetwork. The blueprint lets you apply a modular, hierarchical approach to network design. With the Enterprise Composite Network Model, you can analyze the functional, logical, and physical components of a network, and thus simplify the process of designing an overall enterprise network.

The Enterprise Composite Network Model comprises three major areas, which can each be made up of smaller modules:

Enterprise campus: The enterprise campus includes the modules required to build a robust campus network that provides high availability, scalability, and flexibility. This area contains all the network elements for independent operation within one campus location. An enterprise can have more than one campus.

Enterprise edge: The enterprise edge aggregates the connectivity from the various elements at the edge of an enterprise network. The enterprise edge functional area filters traffic from the edge modules and routes it into the enterprise campus. The enterprise edge contains all the network elements for efficient and secure communication between the enterprise campus and remote locations, business partners, mobile users, and the Internet.

Service provider edge: The modules in this functional area are not implemented by the enterprise. The service provider edge modules are included to enable communication with other networks using different WAN technologies and Internet service providers (ISPs).

6.7.2 A HIERARCHICAL NETWORK IN A MEDIUM-SIZED BUSINESS

Let us look at the hierarchical network model applied to a business. In the figure, the access, distribution, and core layers are separated into a well-defined hierarchy. This logical representation makes it easy to see which switches perform which function. It is much harder to see these hierarchical layers when the network is installed in a business.

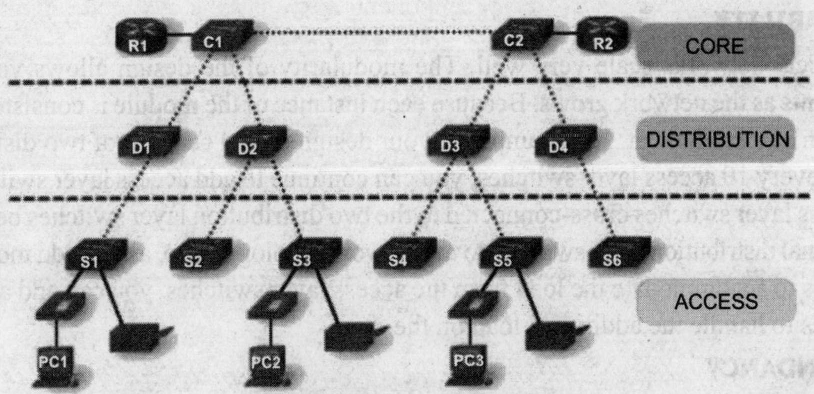

Figure 6.10: Logical layout

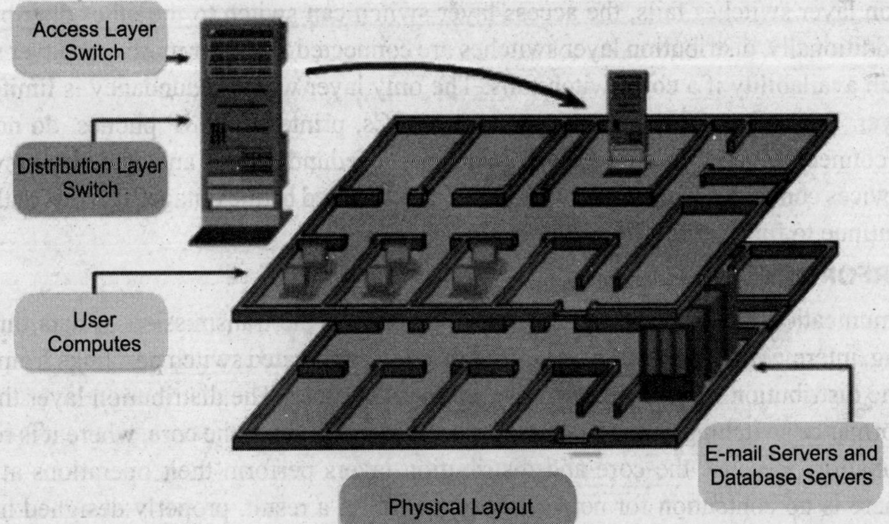

Figure 6.11: Physical layout

The figure shows two floors of a building. The user computers and network devices that need network access are on one floor. The resources, such as e-mail servers and database servers, are located on another floor. To ensure that each floor has access to the network, access layer and distribution switches are installed in the wiring closets of each floor and connected to each of the devices needing network access. The figure shows a small rack of switches. The access layer switch and distribution layer switch are stacked one on top of each other in the wiring closet.

Although the core and other distribution layer switches are not shown, you can see how the physical layout of a network differs from the logical layout of a network.

6.8 BENEFITS OF A HIERARCHICAL NETWORK

There are many benefits associated with hierarchical network designs.

6.8.1 SCALABILITY

Hierarchical networks scale very well. The modularity of the design allows you to replicate design elements as the network grows. Because each instance of the module is consistent, expansion is easy to plan and implement. For example, if your design model consists of two distribution layer switches for every 10 access layer switches, you can continue to add access layer switches until you have 10 access layer switches cross-connected to the two distribution layer switches before you need to add additional distribution layer switches to the network topology. Also, as you add more distribution layer switches to accommodate the load from the access layer switches, you can add additional core layer switches to handle the additional load on the core.

6.8.2 REDUNDANCY

As a network grows, availability becomes more important. You can dramatically increase availability through easy redundant implementations with hierarchical networks. Access layer switches are connected to two different distribution layer switches to ensure path redundancy. If one of the distribution layer switches fails, the access layer switch can switch to the other distribution layer switch. Additionally, distribution layer switches are connected to two or more core layer switches to ensure path availability if a core switch fails. The only layer where redundancy is limited is at the access layer. Typically, end node devices, such as PCs, printers, and IP phones, do not have the ability to connect to multiple access layer switches for redundancy. If an access layer switch fails, just the devices connected to that one switch would be affected by the outage. The rest of the network would continue to function unaffected.

6.8.3 PERFORMANCE

Communication performance is enhanced by avoiding the transmission of data through low-performing, intermediary switches. Data is sent through aggregated switch port links from the access layer to the distribution layer at near wire speed in most cases. The distribution layer then uses its high performance switching capabilities to forward the traffic up to the core, where it is routed to its final destination. Because the core and distribution layers perform their operations at very high speeds, there is no contention for network bandwidth. As a result, properly designed hierarchical networks can achieve near wire speed between all devices.

6.8.4 SECURITY

Security is improved and easier to manage. Access layer switches can be configured with various port security options that provide control over which devices are allowed to connect to the network. You also have the flexibility to use more advanced security policies at the distribution layer. You may apply access control policies that define which communication protocols are deployed on your network and where they are permitted to go. For example, if you want to limit the use of HTTP to a specific user community connected at the access layer, you could apply a policy that blocks HTTP traffic at the distribution layer. Restricting traffic based on higher layer protocols, such as IP and HTTP, requires that your switches are able to process policies at that layer. Some access layer switches support Layer 3 functionality, but it is usually the job of the distribution layer switches to process Layer 3 data, because they can process it much more efficiently.

6.8.5 MANAGEABILITY

Manageability is relatively simple on a hierarchical network. Each layer of the hierarchical design performs specific functions that are consistent throughout that layer. Therefore, if you need to change the functionality of an access layer switch, you could repeat that change across all access layer switches in the network because they presumably perform the same functions at their layer. Deployment of new switches is also simplified because switch configurations can be copied between devices with very few modifications. Consistency between the switches at each layer allows for rapid recovery and simplified troubleshooting. In some special situations, there could be configuration inconsistencies between devices, so you should ensure that configurations are well documented so that you can compare them before deployment.

6.8.6 MAINTAINABILITY

Because hierarchical networks are modular in nature and scale very easily, they are easy to maintain. With other network topology designs, manageability becomes increasingly complicated as the network grows. Also, in some network design models, there is a finite limit to how large the network can grow before it becomes too complicated and expensive to maintain. In the hierarchical design model, switch functions are defined at each layer, making the selection of the correct switch easier. Adding switches to one layer does not necessarily mean there will not be a bottleneck or other limitation at another layer. For a full mesh network topology to achieve maximum performance, all switches need to be high-performance switches, because each switch needs to be capable of performing all the functions on the network. In the hierarchical model, switch functions are different at each layer. You can save money by using less expensive access layer switches at the lowest layer, and spend more on the distribution and core layer switches to achieve high performance on the network.

6.9 HIERARCHICAL NETWORK DESIGN PRINCIPLES

Just because a network seems to have a hierarchical design does not mean that the network is well designed. These simple guidelines will help you differentiate between well-designed and poorly designed hierarchical networks. This section is not intended to provide you with all the skills and knowledge you need to design a hierarchical network, but it offers you an opportunity to begin to practice your skills by transforming a flat network topology into a hierarchical network topology.

6.9.1 NETWORK DIAMETER

When designing a hierarchical network topology, the first thing to consider is network diameter. Diameter is usually a measure of distance, but in this case, we are using the term to measure the number of devices. Network diameter is the number of devices that a packet has to cross before it reaches its destination. Keeping the network diameter low ensures low and predictable latency between devices.

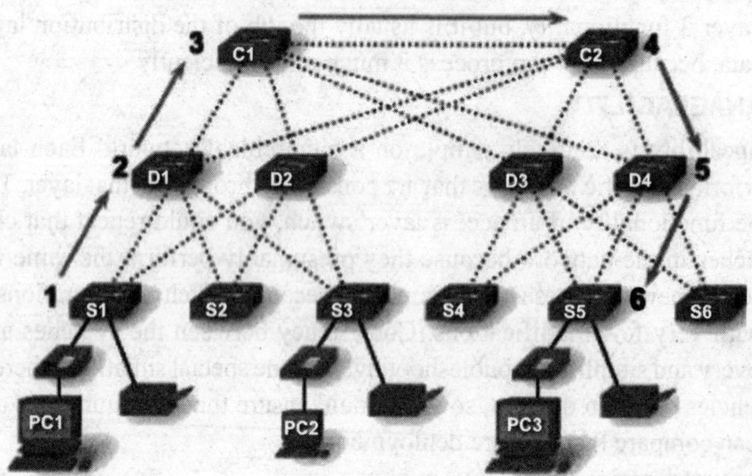

Figure 6.12: Network Diameter

In the figure, PC1 communicates with PC3. There could be up to six interconnected switches between PC1 and PC3. In this case, the network diameter is 6. Each switch in the path introduces some degree of latency. Network device latency is the time spent by a device as it processes a packet or frame. Each switch has to determine the destination MAC address of the frame, check its MAC address table, and forward the frame out the appropriate port. Even though that entire process happens in a fraction of a second, the time adds up when the frame has to cross many switches.

In the three-layer hierarchical model, Layer 2 segmentation at the distribution layer practically eliminates network diameter as an issue. In a hierarchical network, network diameter is always going to be a predictable number of hops between the source and destination devices.

6.9.2 BANDWIDTH AGGREGATION

Each layer in the hierarchical network model is a possible candidate for bandwidth aggregation. Bandwidth aggregation is the practice of considering the specific bandwidth requirements of each part of the hierarchy. After bandwidth requirements of the network are known, links between specific switches can be aggregated, which is called link aggregation. Link aggregation allows multiple switch port links to be combined so as to achieve higher throughput between switches. Cisco has a proprietary link aggregation technology called EtherChannel, which allows multiple Ethernet links to be consolidated. A discussion of EtherChannel is beyond the scope of this course.

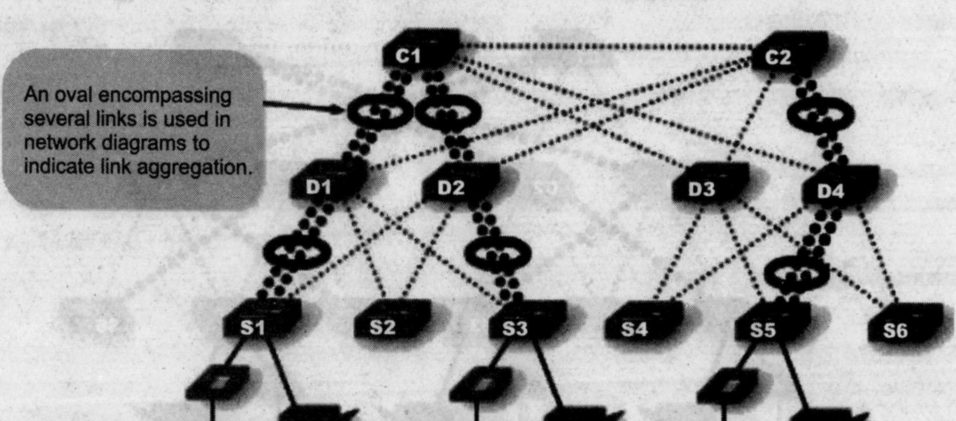

Figure 6.13: Bandwidth Aggregation

In figure, computers PC1 and PC3 require a significant amount of bandwidth because they are used for developing weather simulations. The network manager has determined that the access layer switches S1, S3, and S5 require increased bandwidth. Following up the hierarchy, these access layer switches connect to the distribution switches D1, D2, and D4. The distribution switches connect to core layer switches C1 and C2. Notice how specific links on specific ports in each switch are aggregated. In this way, increased bandwidth is provided for in a targeted, specific part of the network. Note that in this figure, aggregated links are indicated by two dotted lines with an oval tying them together. In other figures, aggregated links are represented by a single, dotted line with an oval.

6.9.3 REDUNDANCY

Redundancy is one part of creating a highly available network. Redundancy can be provided in a number of ways. For example, you can double up the network connections between devices, or you can double the devices themselves. This chapter explores how to employ redundant network paths between switches. A discussion on doubling up network devices and employing special network protocols to ensure high availability is beyond the scope of this course.

Implementing redundant links can be expensive. Imagine if every switch in each layer of the network hierarchy had a connection to every switch at the next layer. It is unlikely that you will be able to implement redundancy at the access layer because of the cost and limited features in the end devices, but you can build redundancy into the distribution and core layers of the network.

In the figure, redundant links are shown at the distribution layer and core layer. At the distribution layer, there are two distribution layer switches, the minimum required to support redundancy at this layer. The access layer switches, S1, S3, S4, and S6, are cross-connected to the distribution layer switches. This protects your network if one of the distribution switches fails. In case of a failure, the access layer switch adjusts its transmission path and forwards the traffic through the other distribution switch.

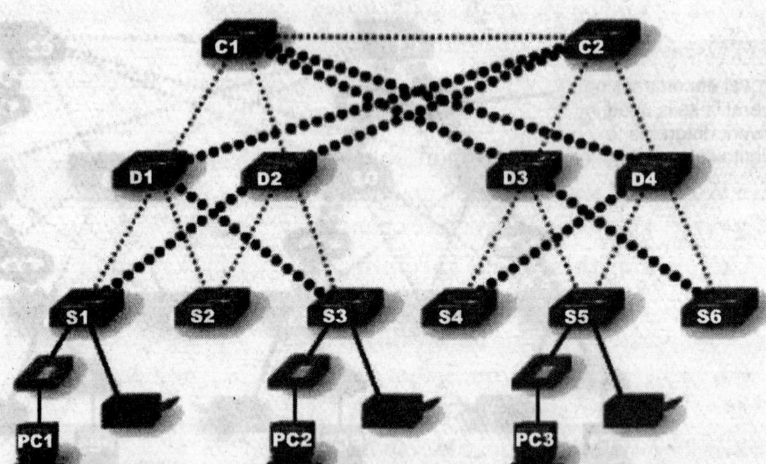

Figure 6.14: Redundancy

Some network failure scenarios can never be prevented, for example, if the power goes out in the entire city, or the entire building is demolished because of an earthquake. Redundancy does not attempt to address these types of disasters. Start at the Access Layer

Imagine that a new network design is required. Design requirements, such as the level of performance or redundancy necessary, are determined by the business goals of the organization. Once the design requirements are documented, the designer can begin selecting the equipment and infrastructure to implement the design.

When you start the equipment selection at the access layer, you can ensure that you accommodate all network devices needing access to the network. After you have all end devices accounted for, you have a better idea of how many access layer switches you need. The number of access layer switches, and the estimated traffic that each generates, helps you to determine how many distribution layer switches are required to achieve the performance and redundancy needed for the network. After you have determined the number of distribution layer switches, you can identify how many core switches are required to maintain the performance of the network.

6.10 GOALS FOR NETWORK DESIGN

Network users see the network as a bundle of applications, rather than as a bundle of wires, fiber connections, protocols, routers, and switches. What capabilities will a network need if it is going to carry traffic to support applications? What are some of the goals common to most network designs?

- The network should stay up all the time, in spite of what the world throws at it in terms of failed or dirty links, failing equipment, and overload conditions.
- The network should reliably deliver packets within reasonable delay and jitter characteristics from any host to any host.

- Troubleshooting should be fairly easy, because failures occasionally occur. Finding and fixing a problem should not take many hours, no matter how esoteric, or in what corner of the network the problem is found.
- The network should be secure. It should provide few places and opportunities for an attacker to disrupt it, consequently disrupting the traffic flow and applications that rely on it.
- The network should have some sort of monitoring facility to determine what is going on at any given time with devices, protocols, links, and traffic levels.
- The network should be easily modifiable to account for network growth or just changes in general. You do not want to deal with "flag days," or days when the network must be turned down to make a major infrastructure change.

If you look at each of these ideas carefully, you can find three underlying, fundamental goals:

- The network must be **reliable and resilient?** /span> Packets must be reliably delivered with fairly consistent travel times, and major changes in the topology, intentional or unintentional, should impact network performance as little as possible.
- The network must be **manageable?** /span> you need to be able to find and correct problems quickly within the network.
- The network must be **scalable?** /span> the network should be able to grow and change without requiring a forklift upgrade.

The following sections provide more detail for each of these three concepts. After providing an overview of reliability, manageability, and scaling, this chapter covers some common elements of network design, including redundancy and layering.

6.10.1 RELIABILITY

Reliability and resiliency often go hand in hand; a resilient network tends to provide a more reliable and stable platform for applications and a close examination of a reliable network tends to uncover a good amount of resiliency. Do not mistake resiliency for redundancy, however. Although redundancy is one good way to provide resiliency in some situations, simply adding redundancy to a network does not always increase resiliency.

The place to start is defining what a reliable network is. A reliable network provides a platform on which applications a business can rely on for day-to-day operations. What do applications rely on a network for? Applications rely on a network for reliable and timely data transmission. In other words, a reliable network delivers virtually every packet accepted by the network, to the right destination, within a reasonable amount of time. This definition has four important points:

- Not every packet that is transmitted by devices attached to the network will be accepted for delivery.
- Not every packet that is accepted by the network is going to be delivered.
- Accepted packets need to be delivered quickly.
- Accepted packets need to be delivered consistently.

Although diving deep into issues such as quality of service (QoS) is beyond the scope of this book, considering and keeping in mind packet delivery issues from a high level is important when designing a network.

6.10.1.1 PACKET DELIVERY RELIABILITY

If the job of a network is to reliably deliver data in the form of packets transmitted by devices that are attached to the network, why should a network reject traffic? It is because the aggregate traffic that is offered by the devices attached to the network will most likely always be higher than the total amount of traffic that the network can handle. For instance, the street in front of your house might generally have light traffic on it. If all your neighbours went out of their house at the same time one day, got into their cars, and tried to leave, all of them using the street simultaneously, however, there would be little chance that the road could handle the aggregate traffic. Some people would end up waiting a long time to traverse the road, whereas other people would give up and go home or simply stay home. The size of the road can be said to limit the amount of traffic offered from your area into the highway system.

Almost all networks limit the amount of traffic accepted into the network at some point, generally at or close to the edge of the network. For instance, a moderate speed serial link between a remote office and the distribution router in a network imposes a traffic acceptance policy near the edge of the network. The remote site cannot send more data than will fit onto the moderate size serial link that connects it to the main site.

QoS techniques, such as weighted fair queuing (WFQ), low latency queuing (LLQ), and others, are not technically packet admission policies. They can, however, determine which traffic is allowed into the network after the limiting impact of link bandwidth, for example, comes into play.

Generally, network engineers can determine how much legitimate traffic is offered to the network, at specific times and under specific conditions, and plan network capacities and policies accordingly. Tradeoffs always exist between the ability to carry more traffic and the cost of carrying extra offered traffic. The correct balance between cost and carrying capacity is going to depend on business factors primarily, rather than network design factors. You can take some steps to curb illegitimate use of the network, such as blocking certain protocols or blocking access to specific servers, but limiting traffic based on these sorts of techniques alone is rare.

After the network has accepted data, it must be able to deliver the accepted data reliably. Of course, "reliable delivery" can mean something different for every application. For instance, it is usually better to drop voice and video packets than to deliver them out of order or late. On the other hand, delivering a packet slowly in a File Transit Protocol (FTP) stream is better than dropping it.

This is because dropped packets in a Voice over IP (VoIP) stream, if the loss rate is low enough, are undetectable. Small numbers of dropped packets in an FTP stream can, however, make the transfer speed so slow as to make the network unusable. FTP runs over Transmission Control Protocol (TCP), and TCP regulates the speed of data transfer based on the number of dropped packets, among other things.

Therefore, one issue you need to consider when building a network is the types of applications that are using the network and the sorts of traffic those applications will offer to the network. You need to decide what sorts of edge admittance policies you are going to enforce for various types of traffic and other QoS issues. This book does not consider many of these sorts of questions. Instead, it focuses mostly on routing design. A network is a system, however, and considering all aspects of the network design, even while considering each component of the network design separately, is a good practice to follow.

1. Packet Delivery Times

Generally, the first thing that comes to mind when discussing timely delivery of packets is the total delay through the network-the amount of time it takes for a packet that is transmitted by one device to be received by a second device. This is not the only, or sometimes even the primary, issue when dealing with packet delivery times, however. In many cases, the delay through the network (the propagation delay) is not the only important thing; consistency of the delay (the jitter) also matters. Figure 6.15 illustrates the difference between delay and jitter through a network.

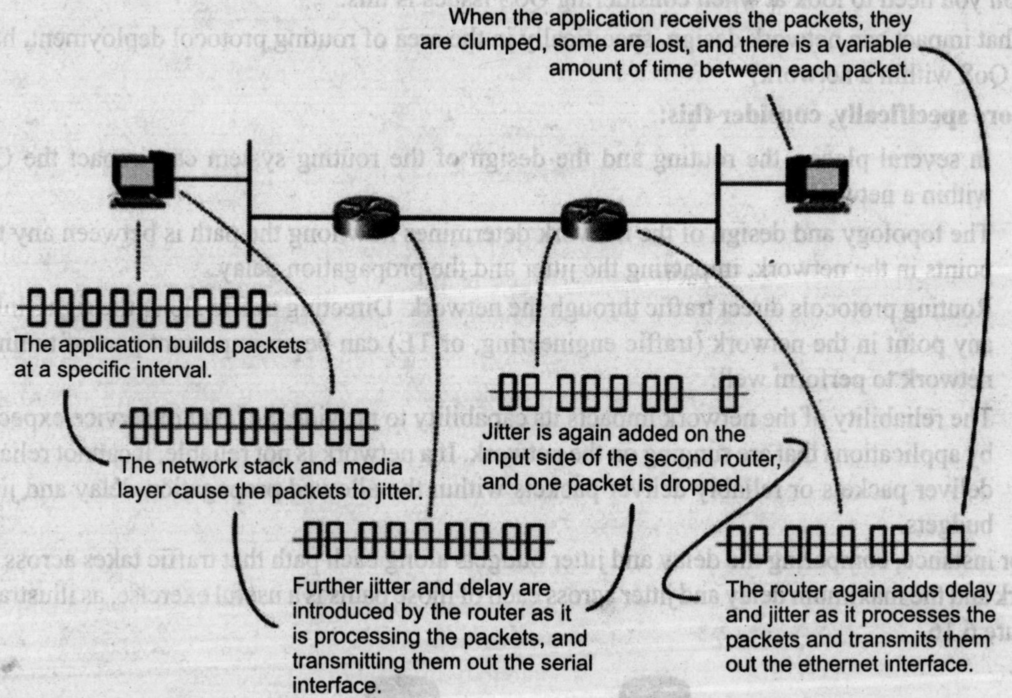

Figure 6.15: Increasing Jitter as a String of Packets Moves Through a Network

Of course, some applications are more sensitive to propagation delay than others:

- It is impossible for a user to know when a packet in a streaming audio connection is transmitted; therefore, propagation delay is not necessarily important. Jitter between streaming audio packets, however, can ruin the quality of the audio.
- Interaction with a remote host through a terminal program does not generally expose jitter between packets in the traffic stream, but long propagation delays can make the session feel sluggish or even unusable.
- VoIP generally works best in environments that have small to moderate amounts of propagation delay in the network, but jitter must be kept low enough to allow receiving devices to buffer and play back received packets at a constant pace.

6.10.1.2 DELAY AND JITTER BUDGETS

To determine how much propagation delay and jitter the network can be allowed to exhibit and still meet the requirements imposed by each of the applications running on it, you need to examine each type of traffic and determine delay and jitter budgets for each application s traffic. Because QoS is not the focus of this book, you will see little coverage on how to build these budgets. However, spending the time to build them is still important.

1. The Impact of Network Design on Delay and Jitter Budgets

Because this book focuses primarily on Layer 3 network design, including routing protocols, the question you need to look at when considering QoS issues is this:

What impact can network design, specifically in the area of routing protocol deployment, have on the QoS within a network?

More specifically, consider this:

- In several places, the routing and the design of the routing system can impact the QoS within a network.
- The topology and design of the network determines how long the path is between any two points in the network, impacting the jitter and the propagation delay.
- Routing protocols direct traffic through the network. Directing traffic along the right link at any point in the network (traffic engineering, or TE) can be an important part of tuning a network to perform well.
- The reliability of the network impacts its capability to provide the level of service expected by applications that are running on the network. If a network is not reliable, it cannot reliably deliver packets or reliably deliver packets within the allowed propagation delay and jitter budgets.

For instance, comparing the delay and jitter budgets along each path that traffic takes across the network and the maximum delay and jitter across each of those paths is a useful exercise, as illustrated in Figure 6.16.

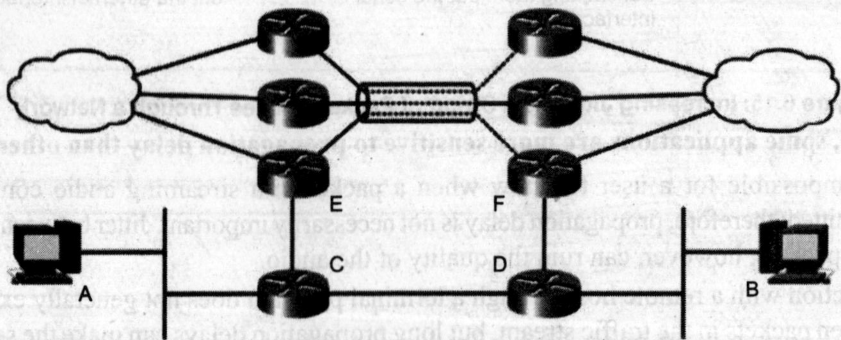

Figure 6.16: Understanding the Jitter and Delay Characteristics of Different Paths through a Network

In this network, the path from Host A to Host B through Router C and Router D is a lightly loaded moderate speed link. In contrast, the path through Router E and Router F is a high speed but heavily loaded trunk. Packets that are delivered along the path through Router E and Router F tend to have a lower delay; however, because the link is so heavily loaded, they also tend to have higher jitter or more variable delivery times. The path through Router C and Router D tends to have higher delay, but the link is lightly loaded, so the jitter that is introduced between packets tends to be lower.

After you understand these sorts of factors in the physical and topological design of the network, you can compare them to the application requirements for each application that is running on your network and build an effective plan for making the network deliver what the applications require, including various QoS techniques to ensure that those class of service (CoS) requirements are met.

6.10.2 RELIABILITY AND RESILIENCY

Applications cannot run if the network is not forwarding data between the attached devices. If the network is down, applications that are running across the network do not work. A network must be reliable if you are going to build applications that require connectivity to be available between attached devices. This might seem like an obvious statement, but as you investigate this concept a little further, you will find that it is more complicated than it appears on the surface.

Given the importance of reliability, how do you build a reliable network? The most obvious answer is to reduce the rate of change within the network. The less change that a network has, the more stable and reliable it is.

Changes in networks are a fact of life. The larger that a network becomes, the more likely at least some component of the network is changing or has failed on any given day. For instance, if any given device in your network fails or changes once in every five years (if every change or failure is one hour, this is an uptime rate of 99.99997 percent), and you have only five devices in your network, you are likely to have only one component change or failure every year. If you have 500 devices in your network, however, you are going to have 100 component changes or failures per year, at least one every three days. Figure 6.17 shows the compounding effect of multiple changes on multiple devices.

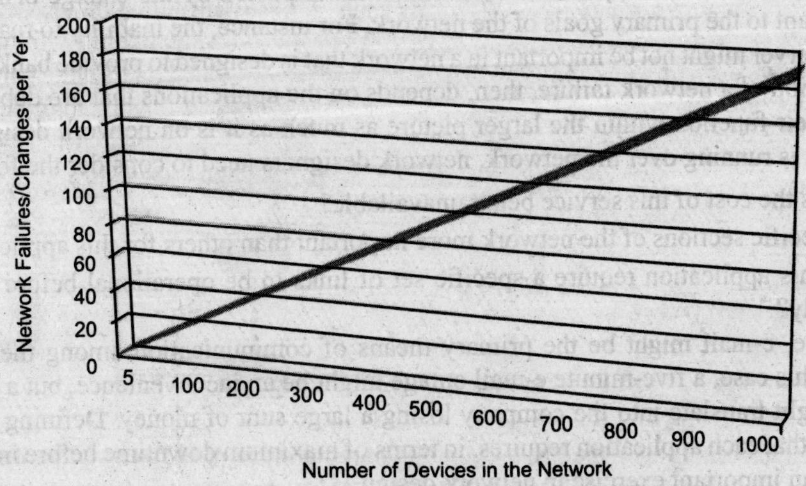

Figure 6.17: Network Changes versus Device Changes

Obviously, even with high rates of reliability, a network of any large size is going to be in a state of almost constant change, either because of component failures or modifications to the network.

Therefore, although you can gain some measure of reliability by reducing the rate of changes and failures in the network, you are not going to be able to prevent changes from occurring. Along with deploying higher reliability devices and employing methods to limit the amount of change occurring in the network within any given time window, you need to design the network around the changes you know are going to occur. This is what resiliency refers to.

Network resiliency is the capability of a network to adapt to changes (because of configuration changes or failure) without the network failing. You build reliable networks by determining how much change you want the network to be able to handle within specific timeframes and then building enough resiliencies into the network design to prevent the network from failing with the level of change you have decided the network must handle.

6.10.2.1 DEFINING NETWORK FAILURE

The chart in Figure 6.17 looks scary. As a network grows, no matter how reliable the devices in the network are, more component changes will occur because of changes in network equipment or failure of network equipment. However, does a change or failure in a network component equate to a network failure?

Go back to the original goal of building a reliable network. A network is working as long as it is delivering most of the packets offered at the edge in a timely manner. If a single link fails, can a network continue to deliver packets in a timely manner?

Even if a single link fails, the network will still be operational from the perspective of an application if the following points are true:

- The network can continue to deliver packets in a timely manner if an alternate way exists to carry the packets, such as a second path that is parallel to the failed path.
- The network could still be said to be delivering most of the packets offered at the edge in a timely manner if the application or set of users impacted by the change or failure is not important to the primary goals of the network. For instance, the inability to reach a specific game server might not be important in a network that is designed to provide banking services.

The definition of a network failure, then, depends on the applications that are deployed on the network and their function within the larger picture as much as it is on network design. For each application that is running over the network, network designers need to consider the following:

- What is the cost of this service being unavailable?
- Are specific sections of the network more important than others for this application?
- Does this application require a specific set of links to be operational before it can work correctly?

For instance, e-mail might be the primary means of communication among the company s employees. In this case, a five-minute e-mail outage might be an inconvenience, but a five-hour e-mail outage might translate into the company losing a large sum of money. Defining the specific level of service that each application requires, in terms of maximum downtime before impacting the bottom line, is an important exercise in network design.

Each application might also have specific servers or hosts requiring reliable connectivity. Again, using the e-mail example, every user who loses his connection to the network at the same time will have the same impact as the e-mail server becoming disconnected from the network: loss of e-mail service.

Some time-critical applications might actually fail on a wide scale even though the network does not fail in the traditional sense-even though no packets or just a few packets are actually dropped. For instance, a single link failure could cause widespread voice call resets if the network does not adjust to the change in topology quickly enough, causing just a small number of dropped or heavily delayed packets.

Other types of applications can be time sensitive, such as financial transactions that depend on quickly changing rates or prices. This could be especially true in high volume, high speed transactional models, such as large stock and financial instrument trading operations.

Beyond network failures in the traditional sense, you need to consider what impact a network failure is going to have on the timeliness of packet delivery for some applications. It is important to analyze each application and host (or host type) that is connected to your network and builds a definition of what a network failure means for each one. Without this definition of failure, the concept of five 9s reliability will have no meaning, because you won t be able to define which failures are "network failures," and you won t be able to accurately measure the uptime or downtime of your network (or the availability of the applications that are running over the network).

6.10.2.2 NETWORK RECOVERY TIME

Although the analysis of which applications require what types of network availability is outside the scope of this book, network recovery time after a component within the network is changed or fails is the primary topic of the remainder of this book. If a network fails once a year, but it takes three weeks to recover from the failure, the network is not going to have good uptime rates.

Network recovery has several levels, each with its own time:

- The time it takes for the network to recover from a failure. For instance, when a link fails, and the routing protocol routes around the link failure, the time it takes for the routing protocol to adjust the paths through the network to the failed link is the network recovery time. The remainder of this book deals with this issue in more depth.
- The time it takes to troubleshoot and correct a problem caused by a component failure or change when the network cannot automatically adjust to it. If a device or link fails, how long does it take to track down the problem and correct it? This time factors in the manageability of the network and several other issues.

6.10.3 MANAGEABILITY

Network geeks generally do not like to manage things–that is why they are network geeks, and not managers, right? Network designers still need to consider the manageability of the network when they are considering various design options, however. An intricate way of configuring something so that it works "just right" might have a large "cool factor," but it is not going to be so cool when it fails or makes the network hard to troubleshoot or modify as requirements change. An easily managed network always scales as the network grows and is easier to modify to adjust to changing business requirements.

This book will not berate you with the importance of network management, trying to convince you that network management is the best thing since sliced bread. You can use plenty of other books to discover the many intricacies of network management. Network management is not as hard as it looks, most of the time, and some basic network management can increase the resiliency of a network.

NOTE: You could compare a network without some sort of management to driving blindfolded. Although it can be done, it is not a good idea-you will eventually end up in an accident. Network management is a critical part of network design and scaling.

The following sections examine two specific areas where network manageability is important:

- Day-to-day operational maintenance
- Emergency management

6.10.3.1 DAY-TO-DAY OPERATIONAL MAINTENANCE

On small networks, it hardly seems worth the effort to monitor the day-to-day operation of the network, and on large networks, no one attempts to actually monitor the network, because it appears to be such an overwhelming challenge. In fact, day-to-day monitoring of networks is probably the least favorite job of every network engineer, right next to going to the company picnic and hobnobbing with the folks in accounting.

However, it is important to perform these types of maintenance to find and correct growing problems or required design and deployment problems before they result in a network failure. In addition, this type of monitoring and maintenance provides a base to work from when network failures do occur. What sorts of maintenance do you consider absolutely required, regardless of the network size? You should always do two essential tasks:

- Take a periodic network baseline.
- Document the network.

The following sections follow cover these activities in greater detail.

1. Taking a Network Baseline

Network baselines consist of normal traffic flow levels and device utilization taken periodically. Figure 6.18 illustrates a simple network baseline, taken four days of normal network operations.

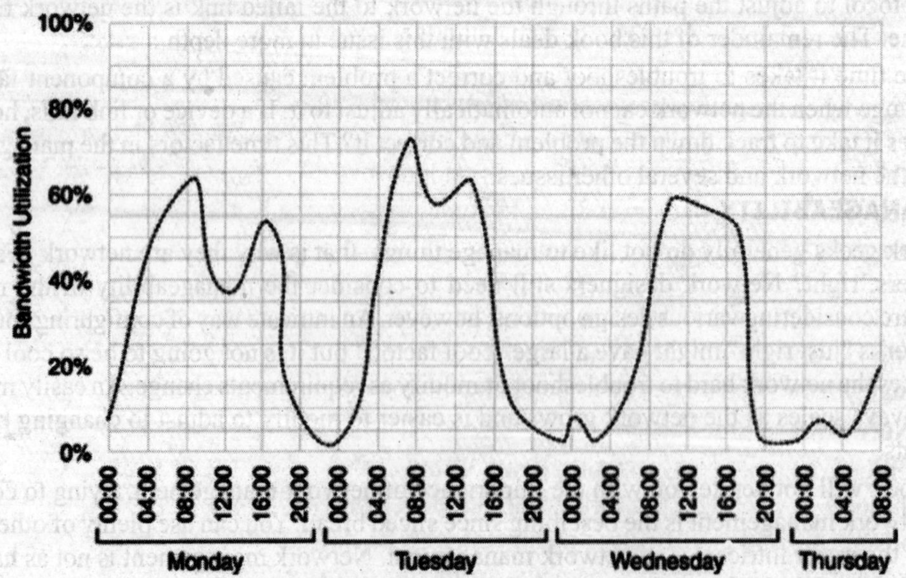

Figure 6.18: Sample Network Baseline

Figure 6.18 illustrates the utilization of a specific link in the network across four days, at different times of the day. This sort of baseline can be invaluable when you are determining network capacities and troubleshooting slow traffic flows and hard-to-find problems. It is also useful from a network design perspective to be able to determine when traffic shifts are occurring within the network, and to be able to see traffic shifts when a topology change occurs. This sort of information can help the network designer design routing for appropriate responses to equipment failures and changes.

For instance, network designers often plan backup paths for critical paths through a network, assuming that the backup path will be capable of meeting the bandwidth and delay requirements of the traffic offered. A baseline might expose areas in the network where the expected backup path simply will not work. In those cases, other backup paths must be chosen, or the backup path needs to be corrected to support the traffic it is expected to carry.

Numerous network management books discuss the tools and techniques you can use to monitor network parameters.

Following are some of the things you should be monitoring to aid in network design:

- Link utilization across primary and backup paths for those applications whose loss would severely cripple the business.
- Delay through primary and backup paths for those applications whose loss would severely cripple the business.
- Router and switch processor utilization, making certain to differentiate between processor utilization because of processes, and utilization because of packet switching.
- Router and switch memory utilization.
- Routing and switching table sizes.
- Routing table stability. An easy way to estimate routing table stability is by examining the timers in the routing table, but they do not really indicate what you might think they indicate, so you should be careful with them. Other good ways to determine the stability of the routing table might be to put a monitor router (or other device) on the network and log routing table changes, or monitor protocol event logs to determine how often routes change.

NOTE: Some are confused about what the timers in the routing table of a router that is running Cisco IOS Software really mean. When you first look at them, you might think they simply indicate when the route was installed or modified in some way, such as a change in the next hop, metric, or other parameter. In fact, however, this timer is changed every time the route is touched in any way-even if the route does not actually change when it is touched. For instance, if Enhanced Interior Gateway Routing Protocol (EIGRP) receives an update for a specific route, it recalculates the best path to the destination indicated and reinstalls the route in the routing table. Even if the route does not change, the timer is reset, and it looks like the route has changed.

2. Network Documentation

Everyone documents his network, right? Wrong. In fact, finding a well-documented network in the real world is rare. The network is too large to document properly because it is managed by numerous people and is difficult to document, or it is "too small to document." None of these are good excuses for not documenting a network, though.

What sorts of documentation do you need to manage and plan changes in a network? The primary documentation you keep should at least contain the following:

- A physical layer topology of the network
- A logical layer topology of the network
- An addressing and summarization plan

Device configurations, change logs, and other sorts of documentation can be useful, but these three pieces of documentation are critical to troubleshooting a network when it is failing and planning future network changes. Figure 6.19 illustrates a network that is documented at the physical and logical layers to show the difference between the two types of documentation.

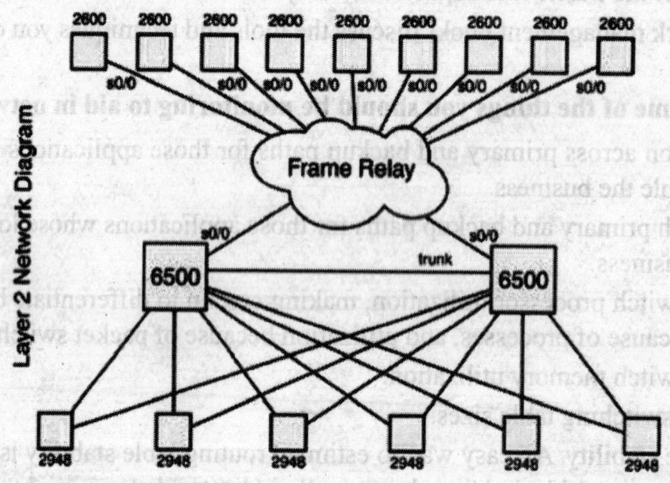

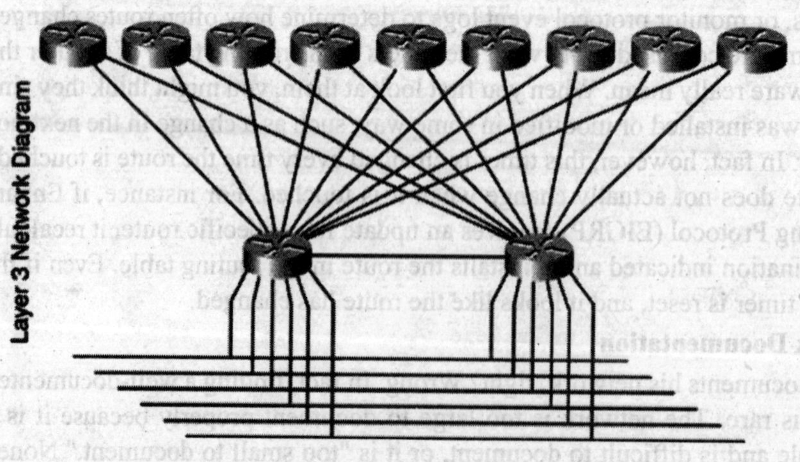

Figure 6.19: Layer 2 versus Layer 3 Network Diagrams

The addressing and summarization plan can be a spreadsheet or database indicating which addresses are allocated to each area of the network, preferably referring to topological areas illustrated on the Layer 3 network diagram and what summaries are advertised from each area of the network.

6.10.3.2 EMERGENCY MANAGEMENT

It is 2:00 a.m. and the network operations center has called you because the backups are failing- and it looks like a network problem. You crank up your laptop, open a Virtual Private Network (VPN) to the firewall, and log into the router to which the backup server is connected. You examine the configuration and notice that it does not look the same as the last time you looked at it. Why was it changed? Does the new configuration make sense? How does that prefix list interoperate with the route map it is being used in, and why are routing updates being tagged?

This is what is what is referred to in the industry as the "two in the morning test." Any time you configure a router or design a new solution to the problem, take the two in the morning test. Will you understand the configuration and be able to relate all the parts together correctly when you are half asleep at two in the morning?

Following are some basic rules for designing a network for manageability:

- If you can configure a specific capability or solve a certain problem in two different ways, and one way is simpler than the other but otherwise they are about equal, choose the simpler configuration.
- Apply controls at the point closest to where the control is being used, if possible. For instance, if you can configure packet filtering at the interface or globally, and the actual packets filtered are the same, configure the filtering at the interface level. Balance this rule with the first rule, because bringing the control to the point closest to where the control actually applies can complicate the configuration needlessly.
- If the configuration documentation is longer than a small book, the configuration is too complex. Most likely, the configuration should not require more than a few lines of documentation to be understood quickly by everyone on the engineering team or by technical support when a problem occurs that you need help with.

When considering how to handle a specific area of the network design and the configuration of actual devices within the network, always consider the maintainability of the design. Example 1-1 demonstrates two configurations accomplishing the same thing, but one is more complex than the other.

Example 6.1: Two Equivalent Configurations

```
! first configuration
!
hostname router-a
!
interface serial 0/0
ip address 10.1.1.2 255.255.255.254
!
interface serial 0/1
```

```
ip address 10.1.1.4 255.255.255.254
!
interface serial 0/2
ip address 10.1.1.6 255.255.255.254
!
interface serial 0/3
ip address 10.1.1.8 255.255.255.254
!
interface fastethernet 1/0
ip address 10.1.2.1 255.255.255.0
!
router ospf 100
network 10.1.2.0 0.0.0.255 area 0
redistribute connected route-map someserials subnets metric 10
!
access-list 10 permit 10.1.2.2 0.0.0.1
access-list 10 permit 10.1.2.4 0.0.0.1
!
route-map someserials permit 10
match ip address 10
```

```
! second configuration
!
hostname router-a
!
interface serial 0/0
ip address 10.1.1.2 255.255.255.254
!
interface serial 0/1
ip address 10.1.1.4 255.255.255.254
!
interface serial 0/2
ip address 10.1.1.6 255.255.255.254
!
interface serial 0/3
ip address 10.1.1.8 255.255.255.254
!
interface fastethernet 1/0
ip address 10.1.2.1 255.255.255.0
!
router ospf 100
network 0.0.0.0 0.0.0.0 area 0
passive-interface default
no passive-default fastethernet 1/0
```

The goal is to include the serial 0/2 and 0/3 interfaces in Open Shortest Path First (OSPF), but not serial interfaces 0/0 and 0/1. To include these addresses in OSPF in the first configuration, use the **redistribute static** command combined with the route map someserials. This route map relies on **access-list 10** to list the networks that should or should not be redistributed into OSPF. Thus, to understand the configuration, you need to examine **access-list 10.** Then examine the route map **someserials** and consider which interfaces on the router will be redistributed as externals into OSPF and which will not.

The second configuration configures **network** statements under the OSPF configuration directly, including serial interfaces 0/2 and 0/3. The configuration then marks the default interface state as passive, which means that OSPF will advertise the connected networks as OSPF internal routes, but it will not form neighbor adjacencies on those interfaces. The configuration marks FastEthernet 1/0 as active (by configuring no passive-interface fastethernet 1/0), allowing OSPF to form neighbor adjacencies on them. This configuration is simpler, because all the control over which networks are included as OSPF routes is entirely within the OSPF router configuration. Further, you have fewer lines of configuration to digest.

6.10.4 SCALABILITY

How many routers does a scalable network have? Perhaps when your network has 100 routers, it has become a large-scale network and you have proven your skills as a network designer. Or is it 1000 routers? Or does size really have anything to do with network scalability? Consider the following situations when you think about what a large-scale network means:

- Some networks are large, with thousands of routers, and are unstable, require major changes to add to or modify the network topology, and cannot be adapted to new applications without major work being done.
- Some networks are large, with thousands of routers, and are stable and can be adapted to changing conditions with minimal effort.
- Some networks are small, with tens of routers, and are unstable and difficult to change, fail with small modifications, and take a long time to troubleshoot when they fail.

These three observations imply that scalability has little to do with network size. Instead, a scalable network can adapt to its environment, can be resized as needed, and is manageable no matter what size it is. In short, a scalable network is built around a flexible design and easy management.

If a network technically can scale, but managing it would be incredibly difficult or even impossible to manage, it cannot scale in the real world.

It is important, then, to disconnect the idea of the size of a network from its scaling properties. Regardless of the size of the network you work on, making it scalable should be your goal. Set foundations and make changes so that the network can be more easily adapted to future needs.

This decreases network downtime by reducing the time required to troubleshoot and fix those inevitable component failures.

At this point, it should be clear to you what the fundamental network design goals are. The network should be reliable, manageable, and scalable. The rest of this chapter covers some of the techniques you can use to achieve these goals, beginning with redundancy.

6.10.4.1 REDUNDANCY

Most network engineers, when they think of network resiliency, automatically think of adding redundancy. Redundancy does not just impact the resilience of a network, however; it also impacts manageability and scalability.

The following sections contain ways of evaluating redundancy in relation to network resilience. You will find that a trade-offs exists, a point of diminishing returns where adding more redundancy does not improve but can actually harm network resilience, manageability, and scaling.

1. How Redundancy Increases Resiliency

In many cases, adding redundant hardware or redundant links to a section of the network can increase the resiliency of the network as a whole. For instance, in the network illustrated in Figure 6.20, adding some redundancy could increase the uptime of the network.

Figure 6.20: Increasing Redundancy to Increase Network Resilience

In the network illustrated in Figure 6.20, two hosts are connected through one pair of routers, Router A and Router B. These routers are connected via a single link. In the first change, an alternate link is added between Router A and Router B (shown with a dashed line in the illustration), so a single link failure will not result in the loss of connectivity between the two hosts. Although this prevents the single link failure from causing a network disruption, it leaves Router A and Router B as single points of failure. If either one of them fails, the entire network fails. To resolve this, you can add another pair of routers, Router C and Router D, as shown in Figure 6.21.

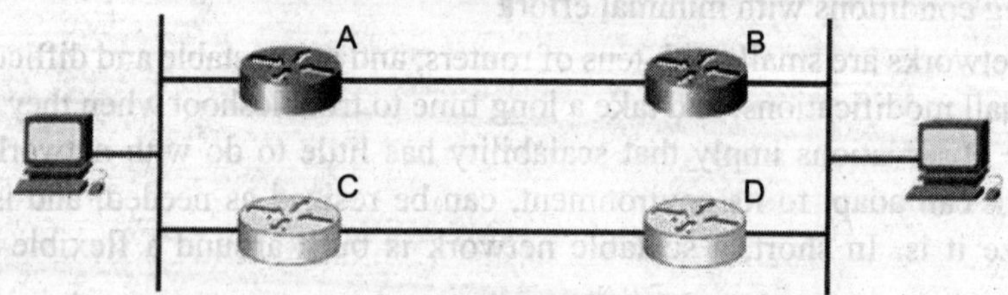

Figure 6.21: Adding a Second Pair of Routers for Redundancy

The additional routers increase network resiliency by providing a backup for Router A and Router B. In this network, a single link can fail with no impact, a single router can fail with no network impact, or a pair of routers, as long as they are both attached to the same link, can fail. However, if one router fails on each link, such as Router B and Router C, the network still fails. Therefore, although this network has no single points of failure, it has some double points of failure. Resolving all of the double points of failure would involve adding a third router at both sites, but you can resolve some of the failure points by adding another pair of links into the network, as illustrated in Figure 6.22.

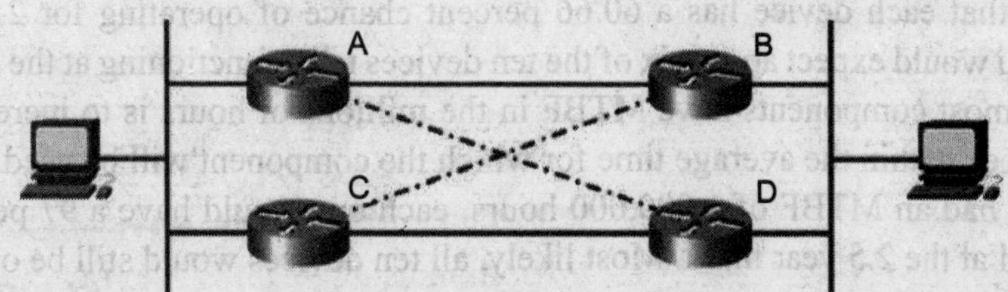

Figure 6.22: Removing Some Double Points of Failure by Adding Redundancy

After the links between Routers A and D and Routers B and C are added (illustrated as dashed lines), any pair of links between the routers can fail, or any one router and any one link or some pairs of routers can fail, and the network will still be capable of passing traffic.

How then, do you determine how much redundancy to build into a network to provide a given amount of resiliency? The method described thus far-analyzing the points of failure in the network and comparing this to the number of failures that the network should be able to resist at any point-is a common way of determining the amount of redundancy required at each point.

For instance, if you determine that a single equipment or link failure should not cause the network to fail, you need to eliminate all single points of failure in the network. If you decide that any two failures should not cause the network to fail, you need to examine the network for points where double points of failure exist and determine how to avoid them.

Statistical analysis

Is there any other way you can analyze redundancy in the network and compare it to the resiliency to determine how much redundancy should be installed at any point? Yes. For many years, the managers of road, power, and telephone networks have used statistical methods of determining network resiliency. These methods use the mean time between failures (MTBF) for each component of the network to determine the mean time between failures for the network as a whole. Combining the MTBF for the network to the amount of time required to bring the network back up after a failure, the mean time to repair (MTTR), you can predict the amount of downtime the network will experience each year.

The Mean Time between Failures

First, you need to consider the MTBF for each component within a system. Generally, this is expressed as the amount of time, in hours, that a particular component will run before it fails. This number is a bit trickier than it first appears. For instance, if you have ten identical components with a MTBF of 5 years, 43,800 hours, and you ran them for five years, how many would you expect to still be running after 2.5 years? To find out, you need to calculate the failure rate from the MTBF, which is done as follows:

$$R = e^{-T/MTBF}$$

e is approximately 2.718, a number used commonly when calculating natural logarithms. To find the percentage of devices with an MTBF of 43,800 hours that will fail in 21,900 hours, you would take the following:

$$2.718^{-21900/43800} = .60656$$

This means that each device has a 60.66 percent chance of operating for 2.5 years without failing. Thus, you would expect about six of the ten devices to be functioning at the end of 2.5 years. The reason that most components have MTBF in the millions of hours is to increase this ratio of operational devices within the average time for which the component will be used. For instance, if the devices each had an MTBF of 1,000,000 hours, each one would have a 97 percent chance of being operational at the 2.5 year mark. Most likely, all ten devices would still be operational at the 2.5 year mark.

Calculating the MTBF of a System

Suppose that you have a system built out of several components, each with its own MTBF. How can you calculate the MTBF of the system? You can use the following formula to compute the MTBF for a system using the MTBF of each component of the system.

$$\frac{1}{\frac{1}{MTBF_1}+\frac{1}{MTBF_2}+\frac{1}{MTBF_3}\cdots}$$

Therefore, calculating the MTBF of a system containing three components, one with an MTBF of 20,000 hours, a second with an MTBF of 25,000 hours, and a third with an MTBF of 35,000 hours, would result in the following:

$$\frac{1}{\frac{1}{20000}+\frac{1}{25000}+\frac{1}{35000}}=8433$$

Again, you can see the importance of the long MTBF that manufacturers place on their products. The MTBF of a system is much lower than the MTBF of any of its components.

MTTR

The MTBF, however, provides only one part of the equation that you need to determine regarding the percentage of time that a network will be available to users over a given time period. The second number you need is the MTTR, which is the average amount of time required to bring a system into an operational state after it has failed.

Suppose, for instance, that you have a device with the following requirements:

- Four hours to replace a card, and every fourth outage involves replacing a card
- One hour to load a new version of software, and every fourth outage involves replacing the software
- 15 minutes to reload, and every other outage requires a simple reload to return to an operational state

From these simple numbers, you can calculate an average outage for this device to be as follows:

$$\frac{4+1+(2*15)}{4}=1.375$$

Each time this device fails, it requires an average of 1.375 hours to restore it to service. If you combine this with the MTBF for the device, you can determine how much time the device should be unavailable in a given year. Assume that this device will fail an average of once every 3 years; this means that it will be unavailable:

$$\frac{1.375}{3} = .459$$

459 hours is about 30 minutes a year. To compute the uptime rate, take the number of minutes in a year and divide this into the 30 minutes of estimated downtime per year:

$$\frac{30}{365 * 24 * 60} = .00005$$

You know that the device will be down .00005 percent of the time, so it should be up for 99.99995 percent of the time. This would be considered six 9s of reliability, in common parlance. The same sort of reasoning applies to systems, but it is almost impossible to know the MTTR for a system, other than by working with the system and gaining experience with it. Again, that is why it is important to keep good records about your network, in this case the frequency and length of outages. These records allow you to build a good picture of the reliability of your network and project changes in reliability resulting from changes in the network design.

2. How Redundancy Can Increase Management Complexity

So far, you have learned how redundancy can improve the resilience of a network and several ways of evaluating the resilience provided through redundancy. Does redundancy have any downsides, though? Yes. For instance, increasing redundancy also increases management complexity.

Management complexity generally consists of three elements:

- The ability to configure the network, otherwise known as the "two o clock in the morning" test. If someone who is unfamiliar with your network works on it at two o clock in the morning, will that person be able to understand the configurations and why they are there?
- The ability to monitor the network.
- The ability to troubleshoot the network when a failure occurs.

As redundancy is increased, the difficulty of each of these management functions increases. For instance, when you are attempting to configure the network, a set of five or ten possible parallel paths through multiple intermediate devices can make it difficult to understand what the traffic flow should look like and to configure the devices to achieve the desired traffic flow.

Troubleshooting a highly complex redundancy scheme can also be difficult. Which direction should traffic be flowing? Is a transient loop across ten paths normal, or is it a symptom of the network failure you are working on?

One of the most useful tactics that an engineer has when beginning to work on a network failing to converge is to remove redundancy until the network converges. After the network stabilizes, perform a post mortem to determine what happened and how to prevent it from happening again.

Although management complexity is difficult to measure, experience indicates that two parallel paths is the optimum balance between management complexity and good resilience. This balance might vary from situation to situation-sometimes one path will be all the situation calls for, and sometimes three paths can be useful-but two parallel paths tends to be a good rule of thumb.

3. How Redundancy Can Reduce Scalability

Another tradeoffs that the network engineer makes when increasing redundancy in a network is between resilience and scaling. Each additional path added to a network can decrease the speed of convergence in the network. If you consider the job of a routing protocol and how routing protocols operate, this makes sense. The more paths that a routing protocol must examine before determining the best path to a destination, the longer it is going to take to determine the best path. Again, this is often difficult to quantify, but Figure 6.23 offers some guidance.

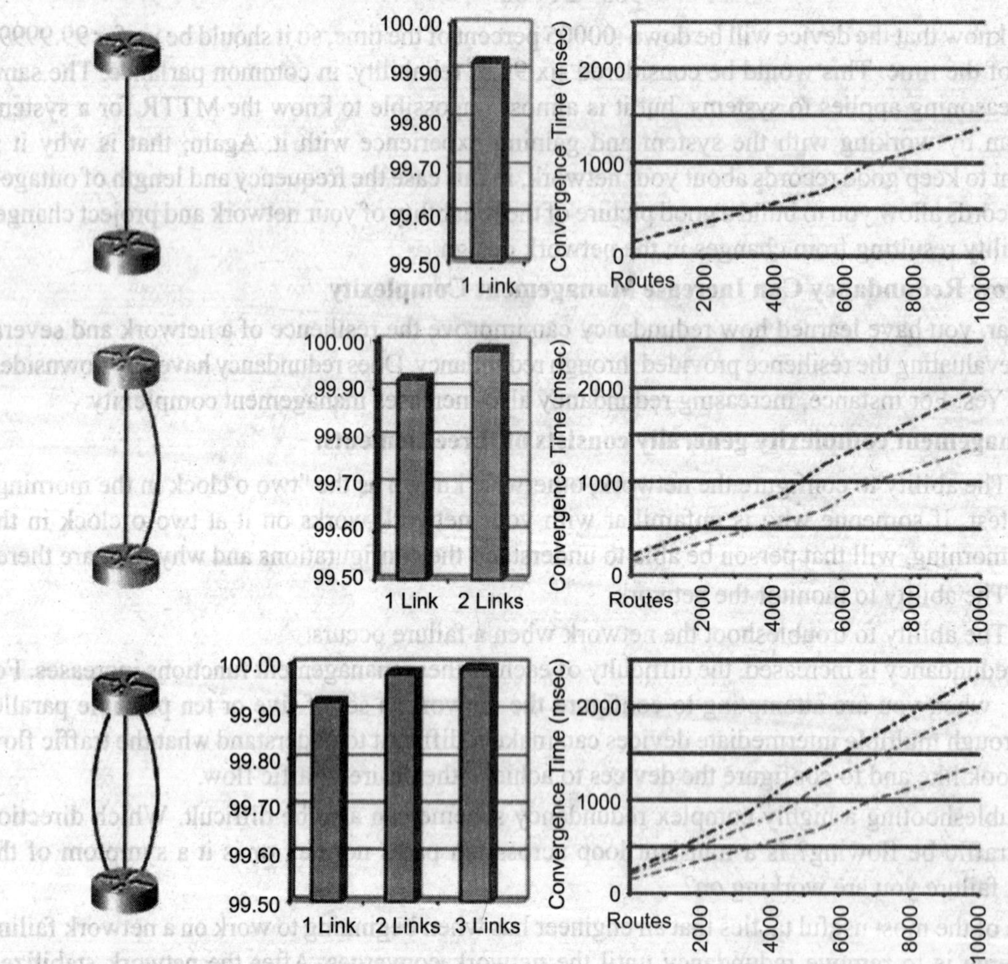

Figure 6.23: Redundancy versus Convergence Time

This figure is based on a small network, illustrated on the left side, running EIGRP. Several routes are injected at one router using a router emulator. The amount of time required to switch from one path to another path, when a single link is flapped, is measured, with the results shown on the far right graph.

From this illustration, you can see that the convergence times increase as the number of routes increases, as you would expect in all routing protocols. As the number of paths available increases, the convergence time also increases. The question is this: Will the network experience more total downtime because of increased convergence time with more parallel links, or will it experience less downtime because of the decreased downtimes involved with having more links?

The answer depends on the frequency of link failure, the amount of time required to restore a failed link, the number of routes in the network, the number of times the network converges on a given route, and other factors, so the answer is not straightforward. In most situations, however, adding a third parallel link tips the scales against higher resilience because of increased convergence times, with few gains in link uptime. To know for certain, you would need to calculate the uptime rates and the convergence time, and then compute total uptimes based on the number of convergence events versus the number of link failures.

NOTE: Another point to consider when adding a third link is the additional memory and processing requirements added with more links. With distance vector protocols, such as EIGRP and BGP, each link represents another entire copy of the information learned from a specific neighbor (or peer), which implies additional memory and processing requirements. For link-state protocols, the additional information exchanged is not greater, but the total size of the database and the time and processing required calculating the best paths through the network both increase with each path that is added.

6.10.5 LAYERING

Layering is a classic mechanism used in engineering and life in general to reduce the complexity of a problem. Layering allows you to work with one level of complexity at a time. For instance, when you drive a car, you are concentrating on driving, rather than how the engine works or any other system within the car. The car is a layered system, with one layer focused on operations, another focused on pushing the car forward, another on stopping the car, and so on.

A key characteristic of an elegant solution is the ability to examine the system in several abstract pieces, with minimal reference to other pieces of the system, for troubleshooting and design purposes. Networks are layered, too, using the familiar seven-layer Open System Interconnection (OSI) reference model (although Internet Protocol (IP) was designed around a less familiar four-layer model). When you are dealing with physical layer problems, you rarely consider IP addresses or TCP parameters; you focus on electrical or optical signaling, and so on. At the same time, a key characteristic of an inelegant design (commonly known as a hack) is the inability to divide the problem, or breaking layering boundaries. Most difficult problems in networking, if examined closely, involve some interlayer interaction or carrying information across layers.

These same concepts apply to network design and network technologies. A layered network allows different problems to be isolated from one another and resolved within a smaller set of parameters. This section discusses some of the concepts of layering within network design, including how layering hides information and separates functionality.

6.10.5.1 HIDING INFORMATION

Hiding information is critical to the success of any network design, because large, complex networks contain far too much information for any commonly available system to process and react to on a real-time basis. Two types of information can be hidden in a network:

- Topology information
- Reachability information

1. Hiding Topology Information

The topology of the network is its physical layout, or the interconnection graph. It is the set of connections and devices that provide physical paths across which traffic travels, or the paths available for traffic to travel along, if you want to examine the topology from the packet level.

Each of the three types of routing protocols (link-state, distance vector, and path vector) treat topology information differently:

- **Link-state protocols** calculate the best path to each reachable destination by examining the topology information directly. Each device advertises the state of each of its links; this information is used to build a directed graph to each destination. The directed graph is a subset of the physical topology, containing only those paths used to reach at least some destination.
- **Routers** that are running distance vector protocols advertise only reachability information to their peers, not topology information. The best path to any reachable destination is determined by comparing the cost of reaching a destination as advertised by each neighbor. The topology of the network is not considered when determining the best path.
- **Path vector protocols** advertise a set of "hops" through the network that the update has passed through. This does not represent a path to the destination necessarily, but rather a set of systems through which the path might pass; this path proves that the path advertised is loop free. Path vector protocols do not rely on cost to determine a loop-free path to the destination; thus, they can choose a suboptimal route in terms of cost to support or implement a policy.

Figure 6.24 illustrates the way that topology information is handled in each type of routing protocol.

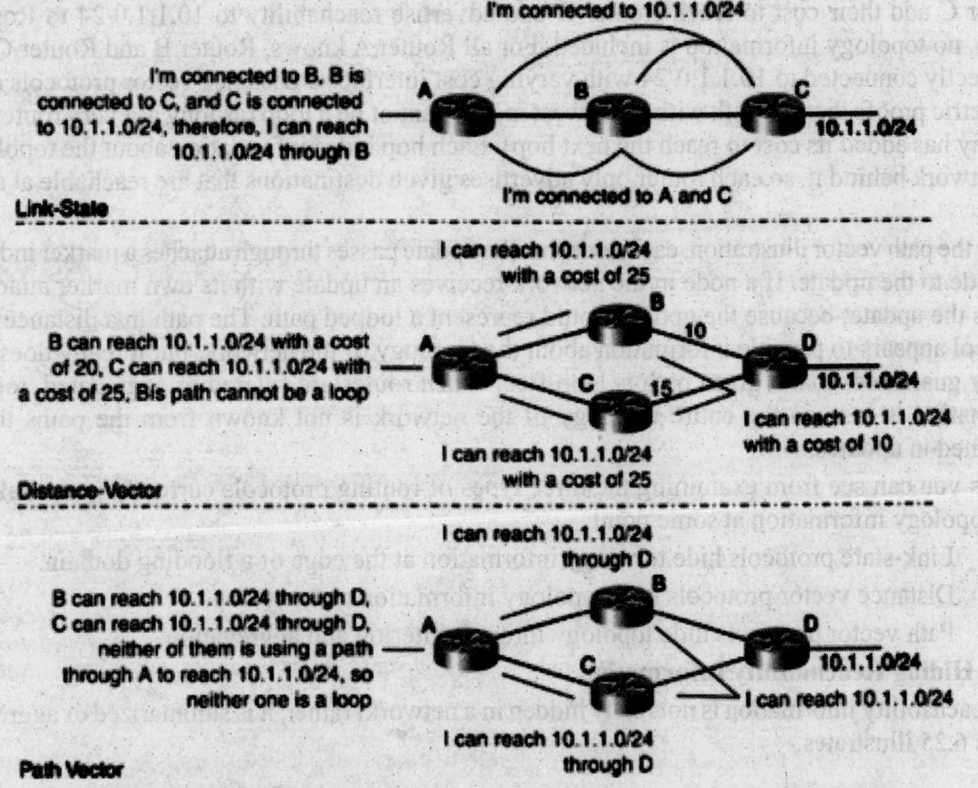

Figure 6.24: Routing Protocol Types and Distribution of Topology Information

In the link-state illustration, Router C floods the information about its connected links to Router B, which retransmits this information to Router A. Router B also floods information about its connected links to Router A and Router C. From this information, Router A can build a directed graph representing the topology of the network and choose the best loop-free path through the network. Router A knows that it is connected to Router B, and Router B likewise claims connectivity to Router A. Because both routers claim connectivity to each other, the link is entered into the tree. In the same way, the link between Router B and Router C is entered into the tree. Router C claims to be connected to a stub network, 10.1.1.0/24, which is also, entered into the directed graph, and Router A finds that it has a path to 10.1.1.0/24, with a next hop of Router B.

Every pair of routers receiving each other s flooded link states is said to be in the same flooding domain; every router in the same flooding domain must share the same view of the network topology for it to provide consistent, loop-free routing. Link-state networks almost never consist of a single flooding domain, however, but are broken into areas (OSPF) or domains (IS-IS). The router at the edge of a flooding domain adds the total cost to each reachable destination within the domain and advertises these destinations as though they were directly connected to the border router, with the cost computed. The border domain router, then, summarizes the information from the flooding domain by hiding information about the topology of the network within the flooding domain.

In the distance vector illustration, Router D advertises that it can reach 10.1.1.0/24 with a cost of 10. No topology information is supplied with this advertisement. Router B and Router C know only that Router D can reach this destination, not what path Router D uses to reach it. Router B and Router C add their cost to reach Router D and advertise reachability to 10.1.1.0/24 to Router A. Again, no topology information is included. For all Router A knows, Router B and Router C could be directly connected to 10.1.1.0/24 with varying cost interfaces. Distance vector protocols rely on geometric proofs that the path with the lowest metric cannot be a loop (as long as every router along the way has added its cost to reach the next hop). Each hop hides information about the topology of the network behind it, so each router only advertises given destinations that are reachable at a given cost.

In the path vector illustration, each node that the update passes through attaches a marker indicating the node to the update. If a node in the network receives an update with its own marker attached, it rejects the update, because the update would represent a looped path. The path in a distance vector protocol appears to provide information about the topology of the network, but it really does not; it simply guarantees that a given path is loop free. When routes are filtered or aggregated, topology information is lost, so the entire topology of the network is not known from the paths that are contained in updates.

As you can see from examining the three types of routing protocols currently in use, all three hide topology information at some point:

- Link-state protocols hide topology information at the edge of a flooding domain.
- Distance vector protocols hide topology information at every hop.
- Path vector protocols hide topology through filtering and aggregation.

2. Hiding Reachability Information

Reachability information is not really hidden in a network; rather, it is summarized or aggregated. Figure 6.25 illustrates.

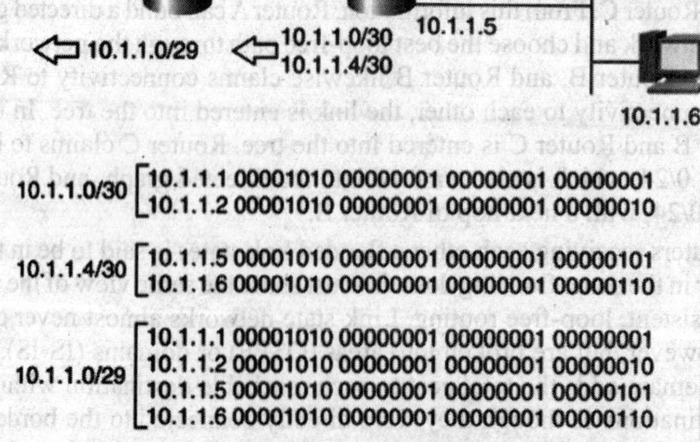

Figure 6.25: Aggregating Reachability Information

In this illustration, Router A is attached to hosts 10.1.1.2 and 10.1.1.6, and it is using IP addresses 10.1.1.1 and 10.1.1.5. When Router A advertises 10.1.1.0/30 to Router B, it is, in effect, stating the following:

"Any IP address between 10.1.1.0 and 10.1.1.3 is reachable through me."

Thus, Router A is summarizing the information about which IP addresses are connected to it. Router A also advertises 10.1.4.0/30, effectively stating this:

"Any IP address between 10.1.1.4 and 10.1.1.7 is reachable through me."

When Router B receives these two advertisements, it now has reachability information for IP addresses 10.1.1.0 through 10.1.1.7. Rather than building two routing updates to advertise reachability to these eight IP addresses, it can simply advertise 10.1.1.0/29, effectively stating the following:

"Any IP address between 10.1.1.0 and 10.1.1.7 is reachable through me."

Thus, Router B has aggregated, or summarized, the routing information that it received from Router A. This is how routing protocols hide reachability information.

Technically, this is not hiding reachability information; it is simply summarizing it. However, when you summarize, you are "hiding" more specific reachability information inside less specific reachability information. In other words, you are hiding the specific nature of the reachability information.

6.10.5.2 SEPARATE FUNCTIONALITY

One of the two primary purposes behind a layered network design is to separate functionality. **Networks typically need to do the following:**

- Provide a place for users and services to attach.
- Implement policy, including marking packets for quality of service, perform admission control, implement security measures, implement routing policy, and others.
- Aggregate traffic and network topology information.
- Forward traffic between major topological areas or sites within the network.
- Connect to outside networks, or internetworks.

If you attempted to solve all these problems in one place, the network would likely be hard to troubleshoot and manage. Instead, you can break up these goals and place each one in a different layer.

6.11 ACCESS N/W DESIGN LAYER

The access layer contains devices that allow workgroups and users to use the services provided by the distribution and core layers. In the access layer, you have the ability to expand or contract collision domains using a repeater, hub, or standard switch. In regards to the access layer, a switch is not a high-powered device, such as those found at the core layer.

Rather, a switch is an advanced version of a hub.

A collision domain describes a portion of an Ethernet network at layer 1 of the OSI model where any communication sent by a node can be sensed by any other node on the network. This is different from a broadcast domain which describes any part of a network at layer 2 or 3 of the OSI model where a node can broadcast to any node on the network.

At the access layer, you can:

- **Enable MAC address filtering:** It is possible to program a switch to allow only certain systems to access the connected LANs.
- **Create separate collision domains:** A switch can create separate collision domains for each connected node to improve performance.
- **Share bandwidth:** You can allow the same network connection to handle all data.
- **Handle switch bandwidth:** You can move data from one network to another to perform load balancing.

Here we can explain the following concepts:

- Physical addresses
- Ethernet frames
- LAN technologies

At the base of the TCP/IP protocol stack is the Network Access layer, the collection of services and specifications that provide and manage access to the network hardware. In this topic you'll learn about the duties of the Network Access layer and how the Network Access layer relates to the OSI model. This topic also looks at some common physical network technologies you'll find in the Network Access layer.

6.11.1 PROTOCOLS AND HARDWARE

The Network Access layer is the most mysterious and least uniform of TCP/IP's layers. The Network Access layer manages all the services and functions necessary to prepare the data for the physical network. These responsibilities include

- Interfacing with the computer's network adapter.
- Coordinating the data transmission with the conventions of the appropriate access method. You'll learn more about access methods later in this hour.
- Formatting the data into a unit called a frame and converting that frame into the stream of electric or analog pulses that passes across the transmission medium.
- Checking for errors in incoming frames.
- Adding error-checking information to outgoing frames so that the receiving computer can check the frame for errors.
- Acknowledging receipt of data frames and resending frames if acknowledgment is not received.

Of course, any formatting tasks performed on an outgoing frame must occur in reverse when the frame reaches its destination and is received by the computer to which it is addressed.

The Network Access layer defines the procedures for interfacing with the network hardware and accessing the transmission medium. Below the surface of TCP/IP's Network Access layer, you'll find an intricate interplay of hardware, software, and transmission-medium specifications. Unfortunately, at least for the purposes of a concise description, there are many different types of physical networks that all have their own conventions, and any one of these physical networks can form the basis for the Network Access layer.

A few examples include

- Ethernet
- Token ring
- FDDI
- PPP (Point-to-Point Protocol, through a modem)
- Wireless networks

Note: Not every networked computer is on a LAN. The network-access software might provide support for something other than a standard network adapter and a LAN cable. One of the most common alternatives is a modem connection to a remote network, such as the connection you establish when you dial in to an Internet service provider (ISP). Modem protocol standards such as Serial Line Internet Protocol (SLIP) and Point-to-Point Protocol (PPP) provide network access for the TCP/IP protocol stack through a modem connection.

The good news is that the Network Access layer is almost totally invisible to the everyday user. The network adapter driver, coupled with key low-level components of the operating system and protocol software, manages most of the tasks relegated to the Network Access layer, and a few short configuration steps are usually all that is required of a user. These steps are becoming simpler with the improved plug-and-play features of desktop operating systems.

As you read through this hour, remember that the logical, IP-style addressing discussed in Hours 1, 2, 4, and 5 exists entirely in the software. The protocol system requires additional services to deliver the data across a specific LAN system and up through the network adapter of a destination computer. These services are the purview of the Network Access layer.

Note: It is worth mentioning that the diversity, complexity, and invisibility of the Network Access layer has caused some authors to exclude it from discussions of TCP/IP completely, asserting instead that the stack rests on LAN drivers below the Internet layer. This viewpoint has some merit, but the Network Access layer really is part of TCP/IP, and no discussion of the network-communication process is complete without it.

6.11.2 THE NETWORK ACCESS LAYER AND THE OSI MODEL

TCP/IP is officially independent of the seven-layer OSI networking model, but the OSI model is often used as a general framework for understanding protocol systems. OSI terminology and concepts are particularly common in discussions of the Network Access layer because the OSI model provides additional subdivisions to the broad category of network access. These subdivisions reveal a bit more about the inner workings of this layer. The OSI model has been influential with computer networking vendors, and the recent trend toward multiprotocol standards such as NDIS and ODI (discussed later in this section) has accentuated the need for a common terminology that the OSI model provides.

As Figure 6.26 shows, the TCP/IP Network Access layer roughly corresponds to the OSI Physical and Data Link layers. The OSI Physical layer is responsible for turning the data frame into a stream of bits suitable for the transmission medium. In other words, the OSI Physical layer manages and synchronizes the electrical or analog pulses that form the actual transmission. On the receiving end, the Physical layer reassembles these pulses into a data frame.

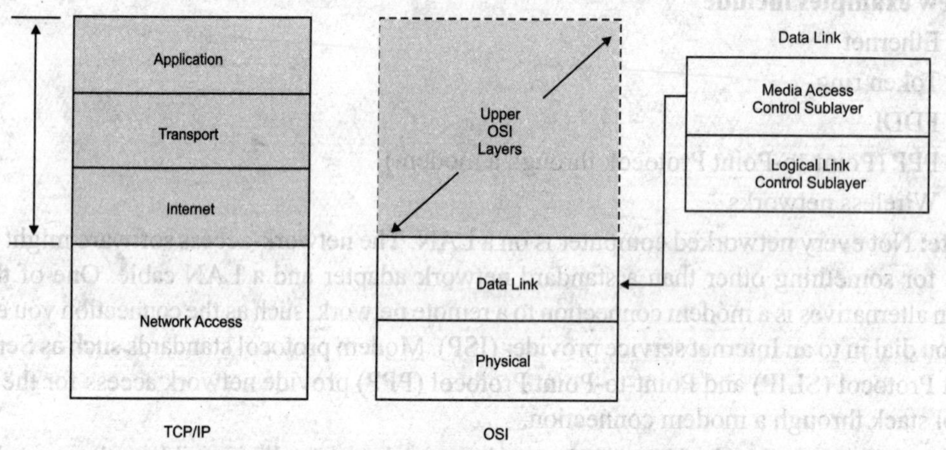

Figure 6.26: OSI and the Network Access layer.

The OSI Data Link layer performs two separate functions and is accordingly subdivided into the following two sublayers:

- **Media Access Control (MAC):** This sublayer provides an interface with the network adapter. The network adapter driver, in fact, is often called the MAC driver, and the hardware address burned into the card at the factory is often referred to as the MAC address.
- **Logical Link Control (LLC):** This sublayer performs error-checking functions for frames delivered over the subnet and manages links between devices communicating on the subnet.

Note: In real network protocol implementations, the distinction between the layers of TCP/IP and OSI systems has become further complicated by the development of the Network Driver Interface Specification (NDIS) and Open Data-Link Interface (ODI) specification. NDIS (developed by Microsoft and 3Com Corp.) and ODI (developed by Apple and Novell) are designed to let a single protocol stack (such as TCP/IP) use multiple network adapters and to let a single network adapter use multiple upper-layer protocols. This effectively enables the upper-layer protocols to float independently of the network access system, which adds great functionality to the network but also adds complexity and makes it even more difficult to provide a systematic discussion of how the software components interrelate at the lower layers.

6.11.3 NETWORK ARCHITECTURE

In practice, local area networks are not really thought of in terms of protocol layers but by what is called LAN architecture or network architecture. (Sometimes network architecture is referred to as a LAN type or a LAN topology.) Network architecture, such as ethernet, provides a bundle of specifications governing media access, physical addressing, and the interaction of the computers with the transmission medium. When you decide on network architecture, you are in effect deciding on a design for the Network Access layer.

Network architecture is a design for the physical network and a collection of specifications defining communications on that physical network. The communication details are dependent on the physical details, so the specifications usually come together as a complete package.

These specifications include considerations such as the following:

- **Access method:** An access method is a set of rules defining how the computers will share the transmission medium. To avoid data collisions, computers must follow these rules when they transmit data.
- **Data frame format:** The IP-level datagram from the Internet layer is encapsulated in a data frame with a predefined format. The data enclosed in the header must supply the information necessary to deliver data on the physical network. You'll learn more about data frames later in this hour.
- **Cabling type:** The type of cable used for a network has an effect on certain other design parameters, such as the electrical properties of the bitstream transmitted by the adapter.
- **Cabling rules:** The protocols, cable type, and electrical properties of the transmission have an effect on the maximum and minimum lengths for the cable and for the cable connector specifications.

Details such as cable type and connector type are not the direct responsibility of the Network Access layer, but to design the software components of the Network Access layer, developers must assume a specific set of characteristics for the physical network. Thus, the network access software must come with a specific hardware design.

6.11.3.1 PHYSICAL ADDRESSING

Network Access layer is necessary to relate the logical IP address, which is configured through the protocol software with the actual permanent physical address of the network adapter. The physical address is burned into the card at the factory. Data frames sent across the LAN must use this physical address to identify the source and destination adapters, but the lengthy physical address (48 bits in the case of ethernet) is so unfriendly that it is impractical for people to use. Also, encoding the physical address at higher protocol levels compromises the flexible modular architecture of TCP/IP, which requires that the upper layers remain independent of physical details. TCP/IP uses the Address Resolution Protocol (ARP) and Reverse Address Resolution Protocol (RARP) to relate IP addresses to the physical addresses of the network adapters on the local network. ARP and RARP provide a link between the logical IP addresses seen by the user and the (effectively invisible) hardware addresses used on the LAN.

6.11.3.2 ANATOMY OF A FRAME

The Network Access layer software accepts a datagram from the Internet layer and converts that data to a form that is consistent with the specifications of the physical network (see Figure 6.27). Because many forms of physical networks exist, there are many formats for data at the Network Access layer, and it would not be easy or useful to describe all these formats in detail.

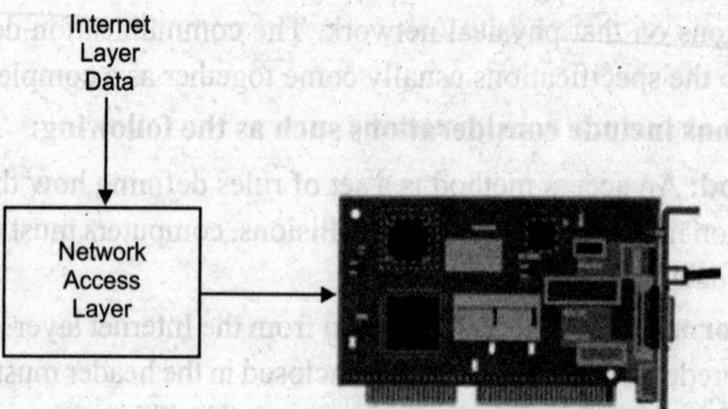

Figure 6.27: The Network Access layer formats data for the physical network.

As an example of what happens to the data at the Network Access layer, consider the case of ethernet, the most common of the LAN architectures. When the ethernet software receives a datagram from the Internet layer, it performs the following steps:

1. Breaks IP layer data into smaller chunks, if necessary, which will be sent in the data field of the ethernet frames. The total size of the ethernet frame must be between 64 bytes and 1,518 bytes (not including the preamble).
2. Packages the chunks of data into frames. Each frame includes data as well as other information that the network adapters on the ethernet need to process the frame. An IEEE 802.3 ethernet frame includes the following:

Preamble: A sequence of bits used to mark the beginning of the frame (8 bytes, the last of which is the 1-byte Start Frame Delimiter).

Recipient address: The 6-byte (48-bit) physical address of the network adapter that is to receive the frame.

Source address: The 6-byte (48-bit) physical address of the network adapter that is sending the frame.

Length: A 2-byte (16-bit) field indicating the size of the data field.

Data: The data that is transmitted with the frame.

Frame Check Sequence (FCS): A 4-byte (32-bit) checksum value for the frame. The FCS is a common means of verifying data transmissions. The sending computer calculates a Cyclical Redundancy Check (CRC) value for the frame and encodes the CRC value in the frame. The receiving computer then recalculates the CRC and checks the FCS field to see whether the values match. If the values don't match, some data was lost or changed during transmission, in which case the frame is retransmitted.

3. Passes the data frame to lower-level components corresponding to OSI's physical layer, which will convert the frame into a bitstream and send it over the transmission medium.

The other network adapters on the ethernet receive the frame and check the destination address. If the destination address matches the address of the network adapter, the adapter software processes the incoming frame and passes the data to higher layers of the protocol stack.

Note: IEEE 802.3 is not the only ethernet standard. The Ethernet II standard, used by some vendors, has a slightly different frame format.

6.11.4 LAN TECHNOLOGIES

The most common network architectures are the following:

- Ethernet
- Token ring

Note: The Institute of Electrical and Electronic Engineers (IEEE) has produced a set of standards for LAN architectures. Although token ring and ethernet were both created before the IEEE standards, the IEEE specifications for IEEE 802.3 (ethernet) and IEEE 802.5 (token ring) now provide vendor-neutral standards for these important LAN technologies.

The following sections will examine ethernet and token ring in greater detail, along with another LAN technology: FDDI.

6.11.4.1 ETHERNET

Ethernet and its newer sibling Fast Ethernet are the LAN technologies most commonly used today. Ethernet has become popular because of its modest price; Ethernet cable is inexpensive and easily installed. Ethernet network adapters and Ethernet hardware components are also relatively inexpensive.

On ethernet networks, all computers share a common transmission medium. Ethernet uses an access method called Carrier Sense Multiple Access with Collision Detect (CSMA/CD) for determining when a computer is free to transmit data on to the access medium. Using CSMA/CD, all computers monitor the transmission medium and wait until the line is available before transmitting. If two computers try to transmit at the same time, a collision occurs. The computers then stop, wait for a random time interval, and attempt to transmit again.

CSMA/CD can be compared to the protocol followed by a room full of polite people. Someone who wants to speak first listens to determine whether anybody else is currently speaking (this is the Carrier Sense). If two people start speaking at the same moment, both people will detect the problem, stop speaking, and wait before speaking again (this is Collision Detect).

Traditional ethernet works well under light-to-moderate use but suffers from high collision rates under heavy use. Some of the newer ethernet variants, which might include intelligent hubs or switches, support higher traffic levels.

Ethernet is capable of using a variety of media. Ethernet networks typically operate at baseband speeds of either 10Mbps or 100Mbps. 1000Mbps (Gigabit) Ethernet systems are now available and might soon be common. Table 6.1 lists terms used to identify cabling media, speeds, and maximum distances. Wireless ethernet is also becoming popular. 10BASE-2 and 10BASE-5 coaxial ethernet networks were once very common. Figure 6.28 show a coaxial 10BASE-2 network. Note that the computers are attached to a single cable that acts as the shared transmission medium. In recent years, hub-based ethernet variants such as 10BASE-T (see Figure 6.29) have become vastly more popular. On a 10BASE-T network, the computers are attached to a central hub. 10BASE-2 and 10BASE-T might appear to be dissimilar, but internally they are both still ethernet.

Table 6.1: Ethernet Media Technology			
Technology Name	**Media Type**	**Operating Speed**	**Maximum Distance**
10BASE-2	Thin coax	10 megabits	185 meters
10BASE-5	Thick coax	10 megabits	500 meters
10BASE-T	CAT3 or CAT5 UTP	10 megabits	100 meters
10BASE-F	Fiber optic	10 megabits	2,000 meters
100BASE-TX	CAT 5 UTP or STP	100 megabits	100 meters
100BASE-FX	Fiber optic	100 megabits	2,000 meters

The versatile ethernet architecture even lends itself to wireless networking. Wireless ethernet is becoming increasingly popular, and will become even more popular in the coming years as network hardware evolves to accommodate the wireless revolution. You might wonder how an architecture that is so focused on specifying the type, length, and configuration of its cable could get by with no cable at all. When you think about it, though, the broadcast nature of ethernet communication is quite compatible with the roving, free-flowing wireless paradigm.

Figure 6.28: A 10BASE-2 coaxial ethernet network.

Figure 6.29: A 10BASE-T hub-based ethernet network.

6.11.4.2 TOKEN RING

Token ring technology uses a completely different concept for allowing network adapters to transmit data on the media. This access method is known as token passing.

Under the token passing access method, the computers on the LAN are connected so that data is passed around the network in a logical ring (see Figure 6.30). The token ring configuration calls for the computers to be wired to a central hub called a MAU or MSAU. Figure 6.30 might not look like a ring, but the MSAU is wired so that the data passes from one computer to the next in a circular motion. The computers pass a packet of data called a token around the network. Only the computer that holds the token can transmit a message on to the ring.

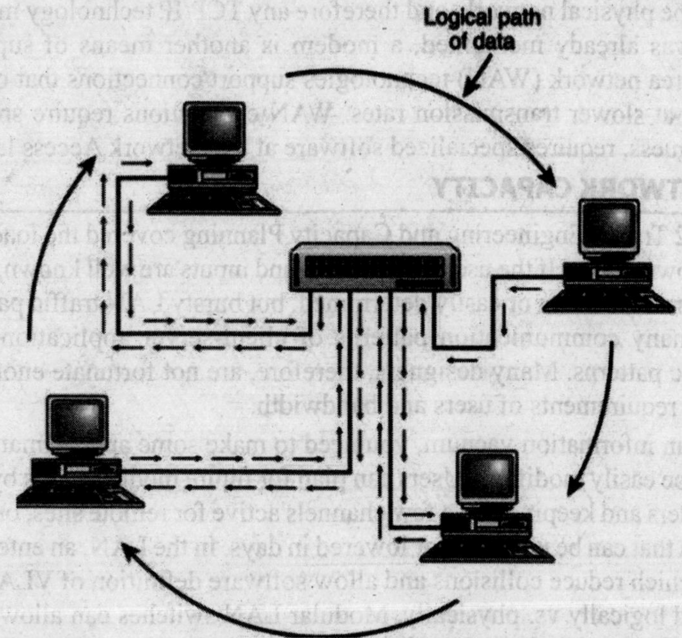

Figure 6.30: A token ring.

Token ring is technically more sophisticated than ethernet, and it includes a number of built-in diagnosis and correction mechanisms that can help troubleshoot network problems. Also, because data is transmitted in a more orderly fashion, token ring does not suffer as badly under heavy data traffic. Almost everything about token ring is more expensive than ethernet by comparison-the cable, the network adapter cards, and the other components as well.

Token ring typically operates at either 4Mbps or 16Mbps. It is also available at 100Mbps.

Token ring has declined in popularity in recent years, although the ring topology that evolved around Token Ring has found its way into other high-end technologies such as FDDI, which can be described in the next section.

6.11.4.3 FDDI

Fiber Distributed Data Interface (FDDI) is an expensive LAN technology that employs a pair of fiber-optic rings. One ring is considered primary and the second ring is there to replace the primary ring in the event of a breakdown. FDDI uses a token passing access method similar to token ring.

Like token ring, FDDI also has error-detection and correction capabilities. In a normally operating FDDI ring, the token passes by each machine every so often. If the token is not seen within the maximum amount of time that it takes to circulate the largest ring, it indicates a problem has occurred such as a broken cable.

Fiber-optic cable such as the cable used with FDDI can support very large volumes of data over large distances.

6.11.4.4 OTHER NETWORK ACCESS TECHNOLOGIES

LAN technologies such as ethernet are common throughout the mechanized world, but there are many other ways to connect computers. Any networking technology must have some means of preparing data for the physical network, and therefore any TCP/IP technology must have a Network Access layer. As was already mentioned, a modem is another means of supporting a network connection. Wide area network (WAN) technologies support connections that operate over greater distances but often at slower transmission rates. WAN connections require specialized hardware that, as you might guess, requires specialized software at the Network Access layer.

6.12 ACCESS NETWORK CAPACITY

In the Chapter 2 Traffic Engineering and Capacity Planning covered the loading on each access device based on known inputs. If the user applications and inputs are well known, the access network capacity is either already known or easily determined, but bursty LAN traffic patterns and the peer-to-peer, many-to-many communication patterns of client-server applications create extremely unpredictable traffic patterns. Many designers, therefore, are not fortunate enough to have current and future capacity requirements of users and bandwidth.

When there is an information vacuum, you need to make some approximations and make sure that the design can be easily modified. Users can plan for future modifications by using T1 facilities from service providers and keeping just a few channels active for remote sites, or for example, using FR with CIR values that can be upgraded or lowered in days. In the LAN, an enterprise can use layer 2 and 3 switches, which reduce collisions and allow software definition of VLANs, where network can be reconfigured logically vs. physically. Modular LAN switches can allow easy expansion by adding higher band width NICs for congestion points or switches that support QoS features that can prioritize different types of traffic.

Advances in switching and routing are changing the LAN landscape as they provide cost effective, high-bandwidth port switching and support VLANs, full-duplex ports, gigabit interfaces, 10/100 Mbps auto discovery, and network management capabilities.

EXERCISES

1. Explain the concept of hierarchical network design?
2. Why use a hierarchical network design model?
3. How can you tell when you have a good design?
4. Explain the three-layer hierarchical model?
5. Explain the various guidelines for hierarchical network design?
6. Explain the various network design layers?
7. Explain the core, distribution and access layer?
8. What are the redundant network nodes?
9. Explain the modular network design?
10. Explain the hierarchical network in a medium-sized business?
11. Explain the various benefits of a hierarchical network?
12. Explain the various principles of hierarchical network design?
13. Explain the various goals for network design?
14. Explain the concept of access N/W design layer in detail?
15. Explain the concept of access network capacity in detail?

Backbone Network Design

7.1 INTRODUCTION

In the previous chapter we have studied the layers of network design. The layer backbone is defined as the part of a network that handles the major traffic. It employees the highest speed transmission paths in the network and may also run the longest distance. Just like the human backbone carries signal to many smaller nerves in the body, a network backbone carries data to smaller lines of transmission. a local backbone refers to the main network lines that connect several local areas networks (LANS) together. The result is a wide area network (WAN) linked by a backbone connection.

7.2 REQUIREMENTS OF BACKBONE LAYER

The backbone network is a part of computer network infrastructure that interconnects various pieces of network. Backbone network can consist of virtual public networks services such as IP, FR, ATM, Private networks such as fiber optic connections. Virtual private networks enable organizations to connect geographically dispersed sites to one another across the packet switched network of a service provider. Softwires is an Internet Engineering Task Force (IETF) Working Group chartered to address the requirement of providing a generalized, network-based, multi-address family, IP routing and tunneling capability across native IP backbone networks.

7.2.1 REQUIREMENTS

Some of the efficient requirements of the backbone network are as follows.

- Traffic consolidation-elimination of multiple paths with different type of traffic.
- High-bandwidth switched-services platform
- Rerouting and redundancy
- Economies of scale
- Self-healing architecture

- Sharing of equipment and facilities by multiple locations
- Intelligent routing
- Dynamic bandwidth resource allocation
- Flexible topologies and styles of design
- Distributed or centralized network management
- Flexibility

7.3 BACKBONE NETWORKS PROTOCOL

Many of the user protocols will be transparent to the backbone, but the design of the backbone may still have an effect on them. The backbone design must be flexible enough to accommodate multiple protocols and operating systems, whether switching them transparently or actually becoming involved in the intelligent operations of the protocol.

Backbones must have the capability to interconnect diverse sites, switch or route all the protocols of the access network, and accommodate both in-band and out-of-band protocol Transmissions.

The most common backbone network and internetwork protocol are TCP/IP, FR.

From the previous studies of protocol IP are the often preferred protocol for WAN internetworking. The Internet Protocol (IP) is the principal communications protocol used for relaying datagram's (packets) across an internetwork using the Internet Protocol Suite. Responsible for routing packets across network boundaries, it is the primary protocol that establishes the backbone network. IP addressing scheme provides unique identification of computers, routers, and switch ports on TCP/IP networks and on the internet. Every computer requires a unique IP address to be a part of the internet and the IP address is provided by the internet service providers. Every IP address consists of the 32 bits and a binary system of 0s and 1s. The binary number system consist of only two types of digits 0 and 1. It is easier for us to remember the decimal numbers rather than the binary number system such as 011001101. On a same network segment, all the IP address share the same network address.

Frame relay and ATM is also one of the most popular publicly-used backbone Protocols.

Frame Relay is a protocol standard for LAN internetworking which provides a fast and efficient method of transmitting information from a user device to LAN bridges and routers.

7.4 VIRTUAL CIRCUITS

The Frame Relay frame is transmitted to its destination by way of virtual circuits (logical paths from an originating point in the network) to a destination point. Virtual circuits may be permanent (PVCs) or switched (SVCs). PVCs are set up administratively by the network manager for a dedicated point-to-point connection; SVCs are set up on a call-by-call basis.

7.4.1 ADVANTAGES OF FRAME RELAY

Frame Relay offers an attractive alternative to both dedicated lines and X.25 networks for connecting LANs to bridges and routers. The success of the Frame Relay protocol is based on the following two underlying factors:

- Because virtual circuits consume bandwidth only when they transport data, many virtual circuits can exist simultaneously across a given transmission line. In addition, each device can use more of the bandwidth as necessary, and thus operate at higher speeds.

- The improved reliability of communication lines and increased error-handling sophistication at end stations allows the Frame Relay protocol to discard erroneous frames and thus eliminate time-consuming error-handling processing.

ATM is a high-speed networking standard designed to support both voice and data communications. ATM is normally utilized by Internet service providers on their private long-distance networks. ATM technology is designed to improve utilization and quality of service (QoS) on high-traffic networks. Without routing and with fixed-size cells, networks can much more easily manage bandwidth under ATM than under Ethernet, for example. The high cost of ATM relative to Ethernet is one factor that has limited its adoption to "backbone" and other high-performance, specialized networks.

Note: Routable protocols such as TCP/IP are the preferred WAN protocols, while protocols such as LAT, IBM SRT, and NetBIOS (NetBEUI) can only be bridged. While designing the network backbone layer Determine whether the protocols are operating half or full duplex. Half-duplex protocols generate large amounts of overhead because the sender has to wait for acknowledgements from the receiving station before more information can be sent. Thus, over half of the available bandwidth is wasted with turn-arounds. Always minimize and localize the routing tables in each router. The backbone designs should always attempt to use standard protocols for wide area networking.

7.5 BACKBONE NETWORK CAPACITY

Chapter 2 helped you calculate the loading on each access device based on known inputs. If the user applications and inputs are well known, the access-node configurations are either already known or can easily be determined, and you can proceed directly to the topology section. If not, please read on.

When interfacing an access design to a large private or public data network, however, the user applications and transport specifies such as bandwidth use are usually not well defined. In fact, most network designers are faced with few facts on user application and traffic requirements. This is especially true when designing a network from scratch and the user inputs are estimations or, worse yet, speculations. In this case, some broad approximations of user traffic can be placed into a model to make a mathematical guess or educated assumption at the number of access and backbone ports required, their speeds, and use. This assumes that all user application and protocol characteristics are either the same or similar, and that a single technology and set of protocols is sued for internetworking these users, which in practice is rarely the case. These requirements must take into account service-specific aspects, such as the ACK/NACK overhead in SNA, TCP window sizes, IPX burst capability and CIR in FR, which provide logical constraints that might be and probably will be exceeded by the user at any time.

7.5.1 LINK USE

Now we look at calculating required backbone design capacity using only raw bandwidth numbers. These calculations are protocol- and technology-independent, and require modification for statistical multiplexing, queuing, or any other buffering or efficiency increases or decreases. These calculations are most applicable to calculating bandwidth and equipment requirements to access the backbone network such as FR, ATM, or IP. Obviously, since we have limited initial information, network tuning will be required.

A company will transmit a given number of bytes of information per day over the network M through a given number of access-node ports n. A model for the access network can be built with n user input ports and T backbone access trunks. A limit must be set on the size (in ports) of the access devices, as well as the access and trunk speeds available. Once this access model is done, modifications can be made to these variables by adding factors that model queuing delays, statistical multiplexing, and intermodal traffic.

Figure 7.1 shows an example where M = number of Mbytes/day/network = 950,000 and the number of access ports in the network n = 1000. For simplicity, we designated that all access ports speeds s = 1.544 Mbps (DS1). If we divide all transmitted traffic equally among all access ports, the average one-way utilization for each port (or link) would be calculated as 5.7 percent. The formula for average utilization per port is shown below. Naturally, some ports (such as the headquarters site in a star network) would have higher utilization than others, such as higher port-access speeds for headquarters and centralized processing sites and lower speeds for remote-access sites.

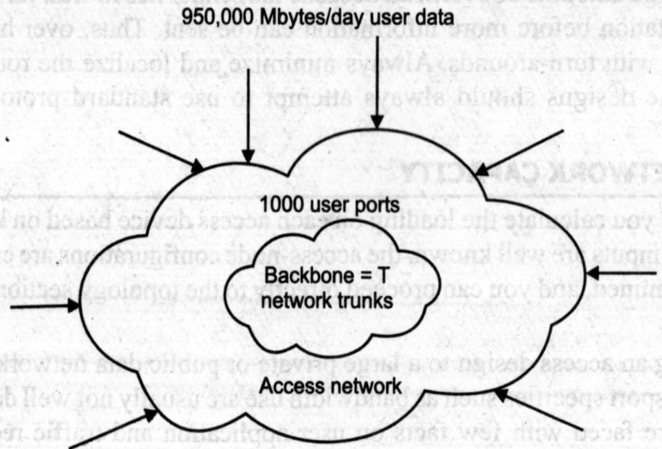

Figure 7.1: Port sizing

The utilization needs to be adjusted for protocol overhead but is acceptable for an estimate. These calculations should not take the place of protocol- and device-specific design modeling.

$$\frac{M}{n} \times \frac{1\,day}{24\,hours} \times \frac{1\,hour}{3600\,seconds} \times \frac{8\,bits}{1\,byte} \times \frac{1}{port\,speed} = \text{avg \% Utilization per port}$$

$$\frac{950{,}000}{1000} \times \frac{1\,day}{24\,hours} \times \frac{1\,hour}{3600\,seconds} \times \frac{8\,bits}{1\,byte} \times \frac{1}{1.544\,Mbps} = 5.7\%\ \text{Utilization}$$

Now add a busy-hour calculation where 20 percent of the total traffic occurs during the busy hour. The new calculation would include a factor of five hours per day to attain the 20 percent busy-hour peak (if 20 percent of total traffic is transferred during the busy hour, five hours represents all busy hours and 100 percent of the traffic).

$$\frac{950{,}000}{1000} \times \frac{1}{5} \times \frac{8}{1} \times \frac{1}{1.544} = 27.35\%\ \text{Utilization}$$

Notice that port utilization has increased from 5.7 to 27.35 percent during the busy-hour period (again assuming a flat traffic distribution; this utilization would be even greater in a star or hub-and-spoke network with a headquarters site). Remember, as the busy hours increased the utilization from 5.7 to 27.35 percent, the busy second are probably near or equal to 100 percent due to the "bursty" nature of data traffic. Data networks have buffers, which can keep packets from dropping during these spikes of traffic load. In addition to the buffers, queuing schemes can help your QoS-sensitive traffic make it through ahead of traffic that isn't QoS-sensitive.

7.5.2 BACKBONE CAPACITY

This section covers computing the backbone capacity. Backbone capacity relates to the total amount of bandwidth required to transport the input traffic to a remote destination (backbone ingress port to backbone egress port). Figure 7.2 shows a sample backbone node where the access ports go to remote sites and output trunks connect to other backbone nodes. To find the backbone node input-to-output utilization, a comparison is made concerning the number of ports, the speed of each port, and the port utilization to the output trunk utilization.

The following formula can be used to either compute number of trunks or trunk utilization based on number of access ports, their speeds, and their utilizations:

$$(T)(S)(\%UT) = \Sigma\,(p_i)(s)(\%Up_i)$$

where the

number of trunks required = T

number of ports of type i = p_i

speed of trunks = S

speed of port = s

percent utilization trunks = %UT

percent utilization of ports of type of i = $\%Up_i$

Example 7.1: There are three remote sites single-homed into a backbone node. Each remote site is connected via a T1 and each T1 has an average utilization of 27 percent. Your design objective is to have trunk ports designed for an average utilization of 50 percent. How many T1 trunk ports are required?

$$(T)\,(1.536)(.5) = (3)\,(1.536)(.27), \text{ then } T = 1.62, \text{ or } 2 \text{ T1 trunks}$$

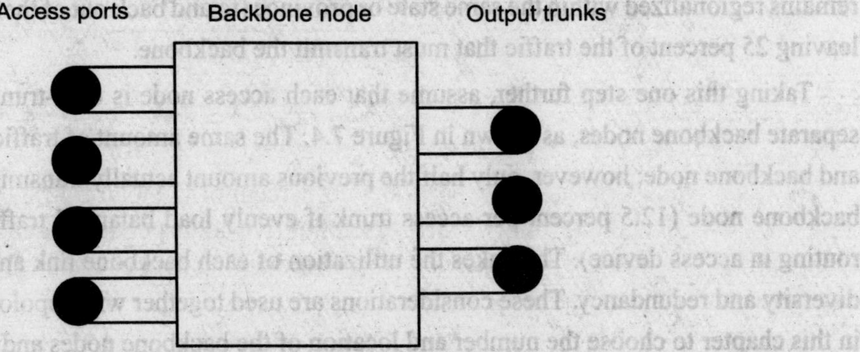

Figure 7.2: Simple backbone node

Note: The average utilization is 27 percent, but the peak might be 100 percent in the busy second.

Example 7.2: There are 27 remote sites. The ports speeds/utilizations for the remote sites are as follows: 5 T1s at 37 percent utilization, 10 FT1s (256 Kbps) at 57 percent utilization, and 12 DS0 (64 Kbps) at 75 percent utilization. Your design objective is to have trunk ports designed for an average utilization of 50 percent. How many T1 trunk ports are required?

(T)(1536 Kbps)(.5) = (5)(1536 Kbps)(.37) + (10)(256 Kbps)(.57)+(12)(64Kbps)(.75)

T = 6.35 or (7) T1 trunks

Note: You can bond multiple T1s together using inverse multiplexing algorithms in routers or an external hardware device. You also could use routing techniques to share the traffic across the T1s, but these schemes can be complicated and may not allow the design to scale affectively.

The numbers computed by this formula will vary based on statistical multiplexing efficiencies, time variances in utilization and busy-time periods, protocol overhead, and usage patterns, to name a few. It is important to note that you should not only design to the bandwidth required during normal transmission, but also design to the peak bandwidth during the busy utilization to be higher on average by allowing delay-sensitive traffic to go to the front of the line and quickly to its destination. If your backbone design doesn't have intelligent queuing options and you design it to run QoS-sensitive traffic such as voice/video, you will need to design the overall backbone to lower average utilizations.

The previous discussion assumed that all traffic, was destined to cross the backbone node, but in real networks some percent of the traffic is regionalized and thus goes "in and out" the same backbone node. Figure 7.3 shows an example of typical traffic patterns for a 12-node network with single-trunk access nodes. Notice that each access node is trucked to a single backbone node. Fifty percent of the user traffic remains local (to end back out of the same access node), 50 percent of the traffic remains regionalized within the same state or province (to and back out of the same backbone node), leaving 25 percent of the traffic that must transmit the backbone.

Taking this one step further, assume that each access node is dual-trunked: one trunk to two separate backbone nodes, as shown in Figure 7.4. The same amount of traffic accesses each access and backbone node; however, only half the previous amount actually transmits each access trunk to backbone node (12.5 percent per access trunk if evenly load balanced traffic pattern is based on routing in access device). This takes the utilization of each backbone link and affords even greater diversity and redundancy. These considerations are used together with topology styles defined later in this chapter to choose the number and location of the backbone nodes and trunks.

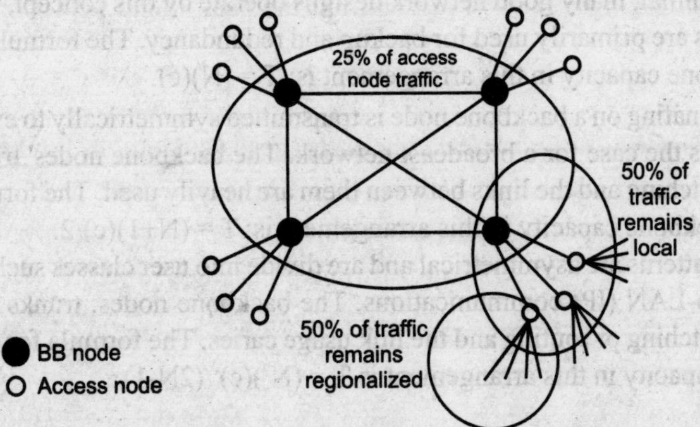

Figure 7.3: Typical traffic patterns: single-trunked access node example

Given the backbone-access traffic patterns, backbone capacity can be calculated in two ways.

- Determine capacity per node based on a chosen number of nodes. Number of nodes may be determined geographically or at central facilities.
- Determine number of nodes based on capacity restrains of node equipment.

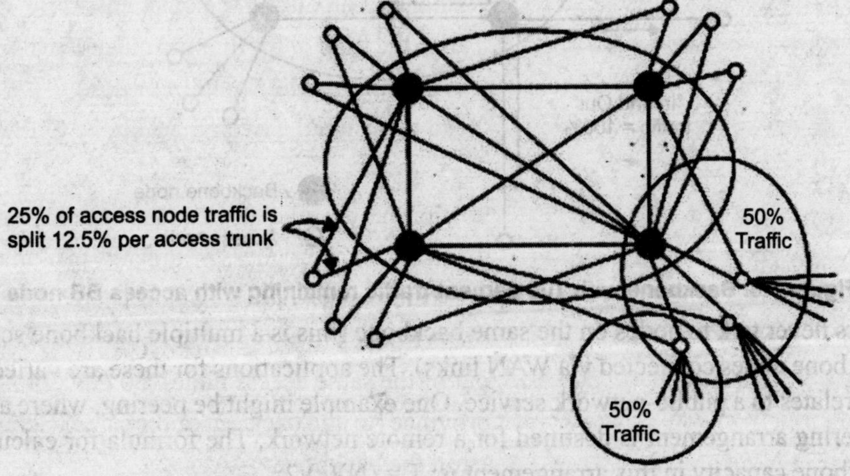

Figure 7.4: Typical traffic patterns: dual trunked

Take the case where users are single-trunked to a network backbone. Once a topology configuration is decide on, and if the number of nodes in the backbone N and capacity of each node c is known, the total capacity of the backbone T based on the type of traffic it will carry can be determined. There are four major types of traffic patterns.

- Most or all traffic that enters a node leaves the same node and does not transmit any other backbone node. There are time s when a majority of, or all, traffic that enters a node will leaves the same nodes, as shown in Figure 7.5. In the case where most of the traffic that enters leaves the same backbone node, the backbone trunking from this node to other backbone nodes is minimal; many good network designs operate by this concept, where the backbone nodal trunks are primarily used for backup and redundancy. The formula for calculating the total backbone capacity in this arrangement is: T = (N)(c).

- Traffic originating on a backbone node is transmitted symmetrically to every other backbone node. This is the case for a broadcast network. The backbone nodes' trunked are primarily used for switching and the links between them are heavily used. The formula for calculating the total backbone capacity in this arrangement is: T = (N+1)(c)/2.
- All traffic patterns are asymmetrical and are divide into user classes such as terminal to-host and LAN-to-LAN (IP) communications. The backbone nodes, trunks are again primarily used for switching or routing and the link usage caries. The formula for calculating the total backbone capacity in this arrangement is $T = (N^2)(c) / (2N-1)$.

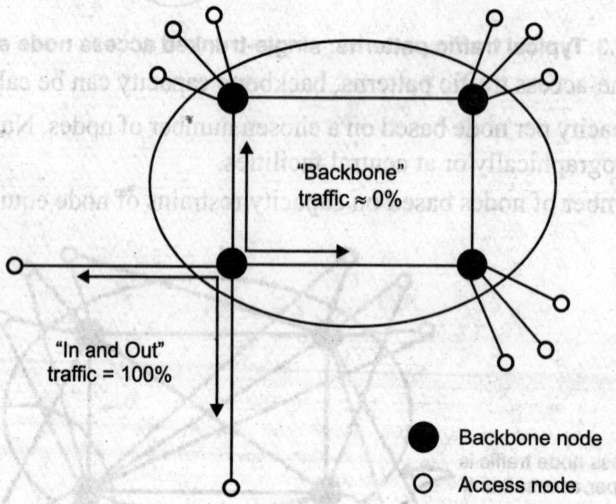

Figure 7.5: Backbone with 100 percent traffic remaining with access BB node

- Users never talk to nodes on the same backbone (this is a multiple backbone scenario with backbone nodes connected via WAN links). The applications for these are varied, but again this relates to a public-network service. One example might be peering, where all traffic on a peering arrangement is destined for a remote network. The formula for calculating total backbone capacity in this arrangement is: T = (N)(c)/2.

Say we select a Cisco 7206 with a NPE-400 process as our backbone node, which can process 400k packets per second (pps). The network configuration can be found in Figure 7.6.

- **Example 7.3:** If all the traffic stays local to the backbone node, what is the backbone capacity?

  T = (400 kpps)(4) = 1600 kpps

- **Example 7.4:** What if Figure 17-7 is changed from dual-homed to single-homed and the backbone is fully meshed? If all traffic crosses the backbone to another backbone node, what is the backbone capacity?

  T = (400 kpps)(4)/2 = 800 kpps

- **Example 7.5:** If traffic is distributed asymmetrically between the sites, what is the backbone capacity?

  T = (4 ^ 2)(400 kpps)/((2)(4) – 1 = 914.28 kpps

As the traffic patterns become more distributed, the network capacity decreases. This is because there is more options form traffic to use the limited bandwidth resources.

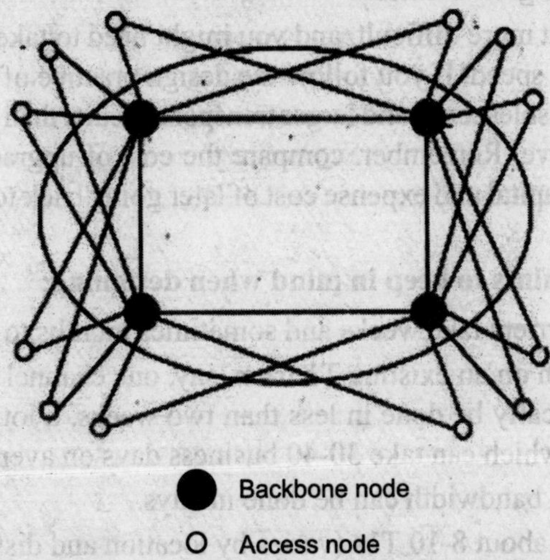

Figure 7.6 Dual-homed backbone network

This is a design challenge, particularly with the next-generation packet networks covered in this book. Many novice network designers are finding that the only way to add extra capacity to this type if network is to over-engineer from the beginning. Unfortunately, many networks were built over-engineered this way in the late 1990s. And now companies are going back and trying to recover the cost out of incorrectly designed networks. Remember that these calculations are approximations only, and should be confirmed through a good design and modeling tool.

7.5.3 ROUTE DETERMINATION

As reliability and availability are typically key user requirements, data networks need the intelligence to route around failures, thus increasing reliability and availability. FR, ATM, and IP networks provide an improvement to the customer over private lines because these packet networks can automatically route around network node and link failures.

In addition to network reliability, the designer can implement intelligence on the access device such as routing protocol (OSPF, E-IGRP, BGP) for IP traffic to select the best route and if that is down, select alternate routes. Route selection is typically based on a variety of variables (hop count, cost, bandwidth, priority, quality of line). In addition to dedicated facilities, critical data can be protected using dial-backup solutions from ISDN to dialup modem. Selecting the right routing protocol and an address scheme to work with the routing protocol can improve network reliability and overhead.

7.5.4 FUTURE CAPACITY

User requirements typically are always changing based on new application, growth, or seasonal trends of the business. So when designing, it is important think about the network should have the capability to quickly add capacity when and where required. Again, this means increased processing power, memory, and extra access and trunk bandwidth capacity at each backbone site. When turning up a new service, make sure that this extra capacity is available. For example, in FR, measure all the CIRs of each user input to the switch, calculate the total burst that might reach the backbone, and determine if the backbone can handle that burst or drop traffic. Then plan on providing more than what is required based on the growth rates.

IP traffic planning is a bit more difficult, and you might need to take a rough ratio of port speed to backbone transport circuit speed. If you follow the design practice of building a backbone with a lower factor of technology obsolescence and larger transport circuits than the access actually requires, the design will prove effective. Remember, compare the cost of upgrading equipment and access proactively now versus the capital and expense cost of later going back to a site and changing out the equipment or access circuits.

Some implementation hints to keep in mind when designing:

- Local loops from carriers take weeks and sometimes months to get installed.
- Increasing bandwidth on an existing T1 from, say, one channel (64 Kbps) to four channels (256 Kbps) can typically be done in less than two weeks, a lot faster than ordering a new DS1 access circuit, which can take 30-40 business days on average.
- Increasing PVC CIR bandwidth can be done in days.
- The cost of a DS3 is about 8-10 T1s (varies by location and distance).
- Using standard protocols allows vendor swapping, which might the important if your company merges with another company.
- Monitor the network thresholds on a regular basis to see trends or problems before they happen.

7.6 BACKBONE NETWORK TOPOLOGY

Backbone topologies come in two style Physical topologies and Logical topologies. The shape of the cabling layout used to link devices is called the physical topology of the network. This refers to the layout of wiring, cables, the locations of nodes, and the interconnections between the nodes and the cabling or wiring system.

The physical topology of a network is determined by the capabilities of the network access devices and media, the level of control or fault tolerance desired, and the cost associated with cabling or telecommunications circuits. Networks can be classified according to their physical span as follows:

- Local area networks
- Wide area networks
- Campus networks

The logical topology, in contrast to the "physical", is the way that the signals act on the network media, or the way that the data passes through the network from one device to the next without regard to the physical interconnection of the devices. A network's logical topology is not necessarily the same as its physical topology. For example, twisted pair Ethernet is a logical bus topology in a physical star topology layout. While Token Ring is a logical ring topology, it is physically set up in a star topology.

The logical classification of network topologies generally follows the same classifications as those in the physical classifications of network topologies but describes the path that the data takes between nodes being used as opposed to the actual physical connections between nodes. The logical topologies are generally determined by network protocols as opposed to being determined by the physical layout of cables, wires, and network devices or by the flow of the electrical signals, although in many cases the paths that the electrical signals take between nodes may closely match the logical flow of data, hence the convention of using the terms logical topology and signal topology interchangeably.

Logical topologies are often closely associated with Media Access Control methods and protocols. Logical topologies are able to be dynamically reconfigured by special types of equipment such as routers and switches.

All the public and the private data networks seem to fit in these two types. Private networks, especially LANs that grow into MANs and then into WANs, tend to take on very asymmetrical shapes, with definable communities of interest. On the other hand, public networks respond to user needs and applications. It is easier to plan a backbone design and then build the network than to try and modify an existing mesh of WAN connectivity. Either way, the backbone network topology should be a function of the user application traffic patterns, the access-network topology, traffic volume, and range and profile of connectivity (local to global).

7.7 NETWORK TOPOLOGIES

In networking, the term topology is the way of connecting computers or nodes on a network. There are many ways in which computers are connected together in a computer network. Therefore network topology is defined as: the schemes of joining a number of computers in the form of a network are called Network Topologies.

We know that two or more devices are connected to a link for data communication. Similarly, two or more links form a topology. The topology of a network is the geometric representation of the relationship of all the links and the nodes (communication devices) to one another.

There are three commonly used network topologies. These are:

1. Star topology
2. Ring topology
3. Bus topology

7.7.1 STAR TOPOLOGY

In a star network, each node (computer or other device) is directly connected to the central computer or Hub that provides connection points for nodes on the network. The star topology is the most common topology in use today. In star network, information or data is communicated from one computer to another through Hub. This form of network configuration looks like a star as shown in figure below.

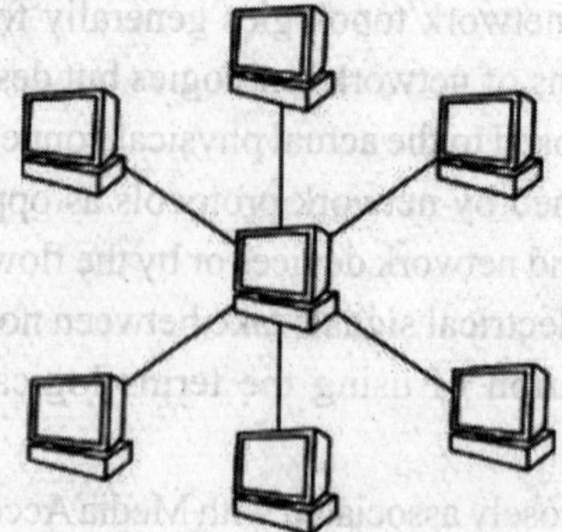

Figure 7.7: Star Topology

Advantages

The main advantages of star topology are:

- It is easy to install and to maintain.
- You can easily add and remove nodes to and from the network without affecting the network.
- If any node fails, other nodes are not affected.

Disadvantages

The main disadvantages of star topology are:

- This type of network depends upon the central Hub. If Hub fails the entire network is failed.
- Each computer is directly connected to the Hub through a cable, so it becomes more costly.

7.7.2 RING TOPOLOGY

In ring network, each node is connected to two adjacent nodes in the form a closed ring or loop. In ring topology, the last node connects to the first node to complete the ring. In ring topology, each node has a dedicated point-to-point connection only with the two devices on either side of it.

In this network, data is communicated in one direction from node to node around the entire ring. When a computer in ring network sends message to another computer on the network, the message travels to each node or computer until it reaches its destination. The ring network configuration is shown in figure below.

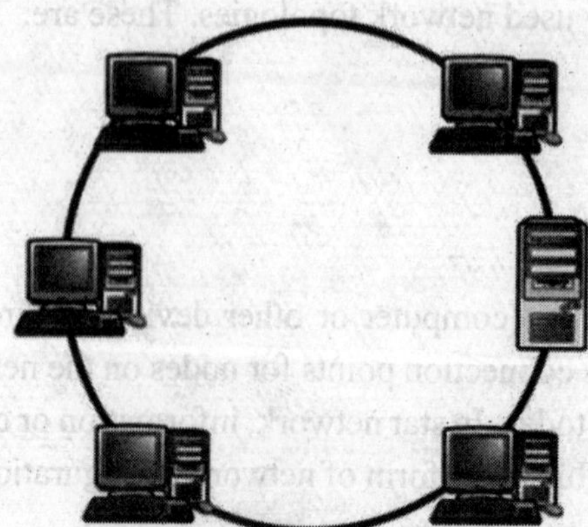

Figure 7.8: Ring Topology

Advantages

The main advantages of ring topology are:

- It is less expensive than star topology.
- Nodes can be easily added or removed.

Disadvantages

The main disadvantages of ring topology are:

- It is more difficult to install and maintain.
- If a node fails, it affects the entire network.

7.7.3 BUS TOPOLOGY

In bus network, all nodes are connected to a common communication medium or central cable. The central physical cable that connects the nodes is called Bus. The data is communicated between nodes in both directions through bus. A bus topology uses the multipoint connection. The central single cable (or bus) acts as backbone to link all the devices to the network.

In bus network, when a computer sends a message to another computer it also attaches the address of the destination computer. In bus topology, a special device called a terminator is attached at the cable's start and end points. A terminator stops the network signals.

In LAN, bus topology is mostly used. In this topology, each computer is assigned a unique address. The bus network configuration is given in figure image.

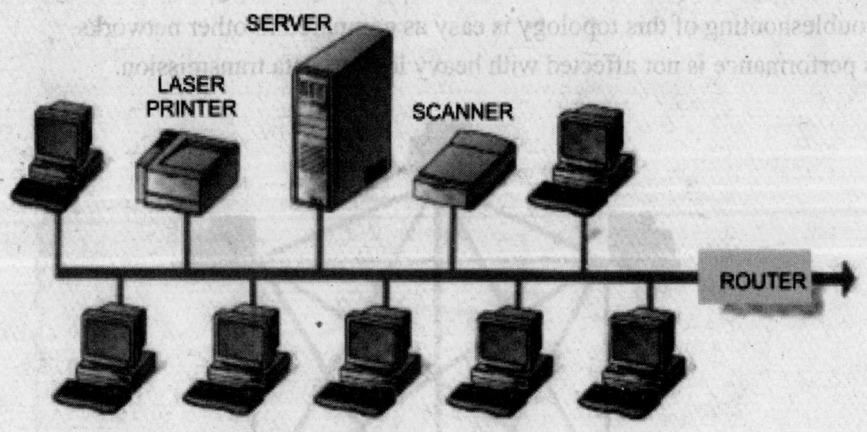

Figure 7.9: Bus Topology

Advantages

The main advantages of bus topology are:

- It is less expensive and easy to install and maintain.
- When nodes are added and removed to and from the network, the network is not affected.
- If one node fails other nodes are not affected.

Disadvantages

The main disadvantages of bus topology are:

- It supports only a small number of nodes.
- Entire network fails if there is any problem in the central cable.

Mesh Topology, Tree Topology and Hybrid Topology

7.7.4 MESH TOPOLOY

In this topology, every node has a dedicated point-to-point connection to every other node on the network. A fully connected mesh network has n(n-1)/2 channels to link 'n' devices. Therefore, every device on the network must have 'n-1? input/output (I/O) ports.

In mesh network, each node is directly connected to all nodes on the network. This type of network involves the concept of routes. In this type of network, each node may send message to destination through multiple paths. It means that each node of mesh network has several possible paths to send (or to receive) message, but in Bus, Star, Ring and Tree topologies each node has only one path.

Advantages

Mesh topology has the following advantages:

- It has multiple links, so if one route is blocked then other routes can be used for data communication.
- Each connection can have its own data load, so the traffic problem is eliminated.
- It ensures the data privacy or security, because every message travels along a dedicated link.
- Troubleshooting of this topology is easy as compared to other networks.
- Its performance is not affected with heavy load of data transmission.

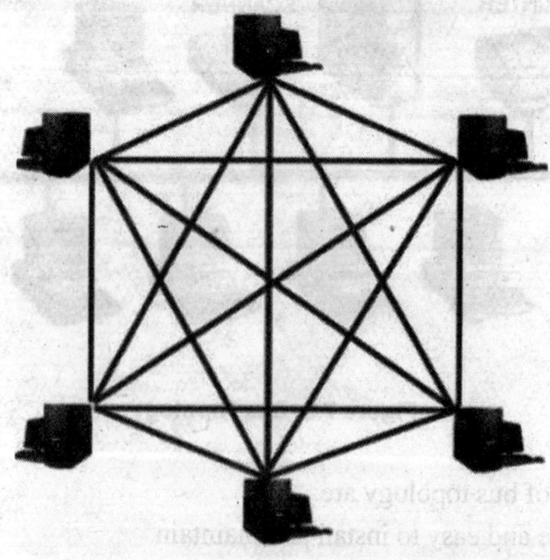

Figure 7.10: Mesh Topology

Disadvantages

Mesh topology has the following disadvantages:

- It becomes very expensive because a large number of cabling and 110 ports are required.
- It is difficult to install.

7.7.5 TREE TOPOLOGY

In tree network, the nodes are connected to each other in such a way that forms a tree like structure. Typically to form a tree network, multiple star topologies are combined together. This type of network has combined features of bus and star topology.

On tree topology the hubs of each star topology are connected to the central hub that controls the entire network. However, some nodes can be directly connected to the central hub. The tree topology configuration is shown in figure below.

The central Hub in the tree network is an active hub. It contains a repeater (a hardware device), which re-generates the received bit patterns. The secondary hubs usually are passive hubs. The passive hub controls the nodes directly connected to it and exchange data to other devices connected to the other secondary hubs (or same hub) through the central hub. The secondary hub may also be active hub if another secondary hub is directly connected to it. The cable TV network is an example of tree topology, where main cable is divided into, branches and each branch is further divided into smaller branches and so on. The hub is used when a branch is created.

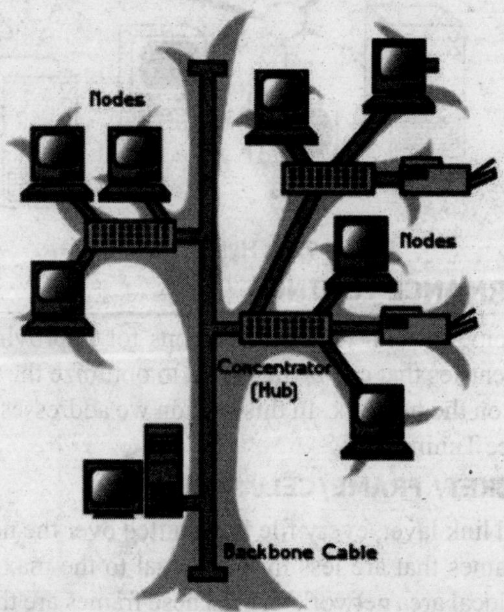

Figure 7.11: Tree Topology

Advantages

The tree topology has the same advantages as star topology but it has some additional advantages. These are.

- It allows more devices to be connected to the central Hub.

Disadvantages

The tree topology also has the same disadvantages as star topology built has some additional disadvantages such as:

- It because more expansive because more hubs are required to install the network.

7.7.6 HYBRID TOPOLOGY

Hybrid network is the combination of different topologies such as star, Ring, Mesh, Bus etc. For example, if a department uses a Bus network, second department uses the ring network, third department uses the Mesh network and fourth department uses the star network. All the networks of different types (of four departments) can be connected together through a central hub (in the form of star network) as shown in the figure below.

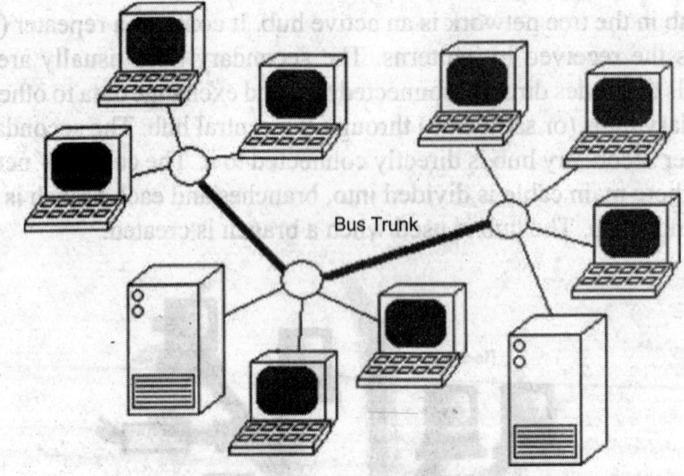

Figure 7.12: Hybrid Topology

7.8 NETWORK PERFORMANCE TUNING

This topic provides some general recommendations for improving network performance and describes several registry entries that can be modified to optimize the network stack to mitigate the occurrence of bottlenecks on the network. In this section we addresses five specific areas which are helpful for the performance Tuning.

7.8.1 OPTIMIZING PACKET/ FRAME/CELL SIZE

At the media level and link layer, every file transmitted over the network is broken down into a sequence of packets or frames that are less than or equal to the maximum frame (or packet) size defined for a given LAN (local area network) type. These frames are then shipped back-to-back in a bundle whose size is defined by the protocol window size. For Ethernet, the maximum frame size is 1514 bytes (or 1518 bytes at the media level, after the hardware adds a 4-byte CRC). Thus, the maximum frame size in fact offered/specified by the protocol stack for Ethernet is 1514 bytes. For Token Ring, it varies: for 4 Mbps, it is 4,550 bytes, while for 16 and 100 Mbps, it is 18,200 bytes. For ATM, every frame is further broken down into very small cells (53 bytes, with a 48 byte data payload). For LAN Emulation (LANE), these cells are then bundled into appropriate-sized frames, the maximum size of which is defined for the LAN being emulated and/or the LAN(s) encountered in the network path (see summary below). For Classical IP (CIP) over ATM, with no intervening traditional LANs between routers, the protocol MTU (maximum transfer unit) will usually define the final frame size. For TCP/IP, the typical default MTU size is 9180 bytes. This MTU includes the data portion being transmitted (called the MSS or maximum segment size), plus 40 bytes of TCP and IP headers. A fixed size MAC (medium access control) header is added to the MTU to create the physical frame or packet transmitted across the network media.

7.8.2 TRANSMISSION UNIT SIZE

As mentioned above, these data units are handled by the code executing in the adapter's workstation processor, where fixed per-data-unit overhead costs have their greatest impact. Therefore, overall performance can usually be improved by increasing the frame or packet size, up to a point. The impact of these data units on performance is demonstrated in using measured throughput curves, as well as the "bottleneck time" (in the main data path) curves that they generate. (Please note that ATM cells are only encountered by specialized hardware in the adapter, network switches, etc. They are never seen by the workstation software, and so they do not have the detrimental performance impact that the other data unit sizes can have if too small.)

However, there are instances in which a larger frame or packet size will not improve (and in some cases, even hurt) overall performance. In general, the transmitting workstation's maximum frame size should not exceed the smallest maximum frame size encountered in the network transmission path. For example, when transmitting between an Ethernet and a Token Ring LAN, this frame size should be set to the smaller maximum frame size allowed by the Ethernet LAN, i.e., 1514 bytes. Likewise, for a TCP/IP session, the maximum frame size should be no longer than the smallest IP MTU size encountered along the network path. Otherwise, frame fragmentation will occur when the smaller MTUs are encountered, with subsequent degradation in performance. For this reason,

Path MTU Discovery (RFC 1191) is typically used to determine the smallest MTU size defined along a network path (discussed shortly). Since some routers may have default IP MTU sizes of only 576 bytes (sometimes called the "Internet Standard"), it is often recommended that the MTU for dial-up or other Internet connections be appropriately reduced.

There are additional situations requiring a smaller than maximum frame size:

Because of data corruption caused by the Microsoft IP stack when ftp-ing large files (over 2 M bytes) using Token Ring LANE over ATM, the maximum frame size must be set to that for Ethernet LANE, i.e., 1516 bytes.

The family of IBM 827x Nways2 LAN switches (8270, 8271 models 108 and 216, and 8272) will only handle up to the default 4544 byte frame size for Token Ring LANE over ATM.

For some workstations with PCMCIA (Personal Computer Memory Card International Association) buses (e.g., laptops), it has been observed that very large frames (typically at or above 8K bytes) can cause a collapse in throughput performance. This effect appears to be asymmetric. For example, when a laptop transmits very large frames to a more powerful server, very large throughputs may be obtained; however, when very large frames are transmitted from the server to the laptop, throughput may drop dramatically. This phenomenon has also been observed for some ISA adapters. Optimal throughputs are often achieved at maximum frame sizes between 4K and 8K bytes.

In summary, the maximum frame or packet sizes for each adapter type are:

Ethernet: 1514 bytes (plus 4 byte CRC)

Token Ring: 4550 bytes for 4 Mbps; 18,200 bytes for 16 and 100 Mbps

ATM

LANE: four possible values - 1516, 4544 (default), 9234 and 18,190 bytes, with the last three possible only for Token Ring LANE

CIP: maximum frame/packet size is defined by the IP MTU

Please note that in some instances, e.g., when using Source Route Bridging, any changes to the maximum frame size may be ignored and/or undone automatically.

7.8.3 SEGMENTATION

Segmenting at its most basic level is the process of separating certain portions of network traffic, either for performance, security, or reliability reasons. You can use a bridge, a switch, or a router to separate your network's devices into segments.

Advantages

- **Reduced congestion:** Improved performance is achieved because on a segmented network there are fewer hosts per subnetwork, thus minimizing local traffic.
- **Improved security:** Broadcasts will be contained to local network. Internal network structure will not be visible from outside.
- **Containing network problems:** Limiting the effect of local failures on other parts of network.

Performance tuning is at once a science and an art. Knowing your options for grouping various devices to form a network is the science of network segmenting. However, successful networking requires you to choose your segmentation points wisely, considering all the devices on your network- this requirement is the art of network segmenting. To master this art, you must understand the types of traffic on your network and the path each type of traffic takes. Then, you must minimize the number of devices between the source and destination points of each packet.

7.8.4 WINDOW SIZE

In computer networking, RWIN (TCP Receive Window) is the amount of data that a computer can accept without acknowledging the sender. If the sender has not received acknowledgement for the first packet it sent, it will stop and wait and if this wait exceeds a certain limit, it may even retransmit. This is how TCP achieves reliable data transmission.

Even if there is no packet loss in the network, windowing can limit throughput. Because TCP transmits data up to the window size before waiting for the acknowledgements, the full bandwidth of the network may not always get used. The limitation caused by window size can be calculated as follows:

$$\text{Throughput} \leq \frac{\text{RWIN}}{\text{RTT}}$$

Where RWIN is the TCP Receive Window and RTT is the round-trip time for the path.

At any given time, the window advertised by the receive side of TCP corresponds to the amount of free receive memory it has allocated for this connection. Otherwise it would take the risk to have to drop received packets by lack of space.

Unrelated to the TCP receive window, the sending side should also allocate the same amount of memory as the receive side for good performance. That is because, even after data has been sent on the network, the sending side must hold it in memory until its has been acknowledged as successfully received, just in case it would have to be retransmitted. If the receiver is far away, acknowledgments will take a long time to arrive. If the send memory is small, it can saturate and block emission. A simple computation gives the same optimal send memory size as for the receive memory size given above.

7.8.5 PACKET LOSS

When packet loss occurs in the network, an additional limit is imposed on the connection. The limit can be calculated according to the formula (Mathis et al.):

$$\text{Throughput} \leq \frac{\text{MSS}}{\text{RTT}\sqrt{P_{\text{loss}}}}$$

where MSS is the maximum segment size and P_{loss} is the probability of packet loss.

7.8.6 BANDWIDTH

The amount of data that can be in transit in the network, termed Bandwidth Delay Product (BDP), is simply the product of the bottleneck link bandwidth and the Round Trip Time (RTT). BDP is a simple but important concept in a window based protocol such as TCP. Some of the issues discussed below arise because of the fact that the BDP of today's networks has increased way beyond what it was when the TCP/IP protocols were initially designed. In order to accommodate the large increases in BDP, some high performance extensions have been proposed and implemented in the TCP protocol. But these high performance options are sometimes not enabled by default and will have to be explicitly turned on by the system administrators.

The largest buffer the original TCP (without the high performance options) supports is limited to 64 bytes. If the BDP is small either because the link is slow or because the RTT is small (in a LAN, for example), the default configuration is usually adequate. But for a paths that have a large BDP, and hence require large buffers, it is necessary to have the high performance options discussed in the next sections be enabled.

To compute the BDP, we need to know the speed of the slowest link in the path and the Round Trip Time (RTT). The peak bandwidth of a link is typically expressed in Mbit/s. The RTT is a measure of the time it takes for a packet to travel from a computer, across a network to another computer, and back. The ping program can be used to retrieve the RTT.

The first step for tuning the network consists of retrieving the RTT. Execute the ping program on an IP address of the remote network. The RTT is displayed in milliseconds.

```
C:\>ping 192.168.28.100
Pinging 192.168.28.100 with 32 bytes of data:
Reply from 192.168.28.100: bytes=32 time=21ms TTL=125
Reply from 192.168.28.100: bytes=32 time=20ms TTL=125
Reply from 192.168.28.100: bytes=32 time=20ms TTL=125
Reply from 192.168.28.100: bytes=32 time=20ms TTL=125
Ping statistics for 192.168.28.100:
Packets: Sent = 4, Received = 4, Lost = 0 (0% loss),
Approximate round trip times in milli-seconds:
Minimum = 20ms, Maximum = 21ms, Average = 20ms
```

Knowing the bottleneck link speed and the RTT, the BDP can be calculated as follows:

BDP [kBytes] = (bandwidth [kBits/s] / 8 [bits]) * RTT [s]

Example:

Bandwidth = 100 Mbit/s, RTT = 20ms

BDP = (100000 [kBits/s] / 8 [bits]) * 0,02 [s] = 250 kBytes

Based on these calculations, it is easy to see why the typical default buffer size of 64 kBytes would be way inadequate for this connection.

7.9 QUEUING

Queuing schemes is an area that continues to be enhanced in networks due to the requirements of users to have special handling for multimedia traffic and other special needs traffic.

In the most basic queue of first in, first out (FIFO), there is still tuning of the depth of the buffer. If the traffic is really bursty (a big blast of traffic and then nothing followed by a big blast-defined as peak/average traffic), increasing the depth of the FIFO buffer will reduce drops and increase performance. But if you have a mix of traffic types, increasing buffer depth will increase end-to-end delay so modeling and trial and error may be required.

Priority queue schemes vary by vendors. The main purpose of priority queuing is to allow delay- and loss-sensitive traffic to cut to the front of the line. Many priority schemes allow multiple levels of queues and schemes to prevent queue starvation (when a queue isn't services). Understanding which applications require special handling and a method to notify network devices is critical to designing to application performance. Methods of notifying network devices could be TCP/UDP port, IP source or destination address, or IP Precedence bits, to name a few.

7.9.1 QUEUING MECHANISMS

In any QoS system, the role of the network devices is to ensure the packets get forwarded as efficiently as possible. That may be in order of priority or just as quickly as can be. Delays in this process start to occur when these devices cannot actually forward data at the desired rate and have to begin placing the data into queues for future forwarding. If these queues are not efficiently serviced, you begin to see some form of congestion as potential packet drops occur.

One way that network elements handle an overflow of arriving traffic is to use a queuing algorithm to sort the traffic, and then determine some method of prioritizing it onto an output link.

Cisco IOS Software includes the following queuing tools:

- First-in, first-out (FIFO) queuing
- Priority queuing (PQ)
- Custom queuing (CQ)
- Flow-based weighted fair queuing (WFQ)
- Class-based weighted fair queuing (CBWFQ)
- Low-latency queuing (LLQ)

Each queuing algorithm was designed to solve a specific network traffic problem and has a particular effect on network performance.

Queues and queue-servicing algorithms are critical elements of traffic handling in providing network QoS. Queuing happens only when the interface is busy. As long as the interface is idle, packets will be transmitted without special treatment. Regular queues invariably employ the FIFO principle: The packet that has been waiting the longest is transmitted first. When the queue is full, and additional packets come in, tail drops happen.

More sophisticated queuing mechanisms usually employ several queues. Packets are classified by user-configurable means and then placed in the appropriate queue. Then, when the interface is ready to transmit, a queue from which the next packet will be transmitted is selected as per the queuing algorithm. Note that special queuing mechanisms have effect only when it is not possible immediately to transmit a packet over the output interface. If the interface is idle and there are no queued packets, the new packet is transmitted immediately.

When evaluating the suitability of a queuing scheme, consider the following factors:

- **Type of scheme:** Should be appropriate for the task. Some schemes are designed to share available capacity optimally, whereas others are designed to control the impact of a particular type of traffic on the network.
- **Use of a dropping scheme:** This is a mechanism by which you can effectively control the length of a queue and in doing so can successfully define the latency.
- **Different mechanisms:** You are looking at a dynamic instance. Therefore, you may need to apply different mechanisms to different parts of the journey.

Queuing schemes provide QoS by controlling the forwarding capacity or bandwidth available to certain traffic flows.

This section separates queuing mechanisms into the following three broad categories related to serving general application characteristics requirements:

- FIFO
- Work-conserving
- Non-workconserving

Technically speaking, there are really only two categories, because FIFO is essentially classed as a work-conserving queuing discipline. For the purposes of this discussion, however, it is treated as a third category.

Work-conserving describes a queuing mechanism that saves the forwarding device work. When a device has packets in one of its queues, it wants to do as little work on it as possible. Holding it in a queue effectively means that the device must perform additional work on the packet. So a network device can be considered busy whenever the service queue contains queued requests. A work-conserving mechanism will always transmit one packet, provided there is at least one packet inside the queue.

A non-workconserving mechanism is one that expects the device to perform extra work, such as holding the transmission of packets on the output link even if some packets are waiting inside the router buffers. This is done to ensure delay and jitter can be guaranteed, which is imperative in delay-sensitive applications such as voice.

Based on this description, you can see that FIFO is in fact the simplest work-conserving queuing discipline. FIFO queuing is the most basic queuing strategy; packets are just transmitted in the same order they come in.

7.9.1.1 FIFO

In the context of QoS, you expect queuing mechanisms to enhance the delivery model by giving specific traffic priority over other traffic. Because FIFO queuing cannot alter the order in which the packets are forwarded, the service experienced by any particular flow is going to depend entirely on the order in which the packets arrive. FIFO also has the potential problem of delaying short frames behind longer frames. This is caused by the longer frame filling the queue.

Suppose we have three connections to a single router. Links A and B contain traffic coming from a priority application and site; however, the available link speeds are 128 kbps and 64 kbps, respectively. The less-important traffic is seen coming in on interface C and has been connected using a T1 (1.54-Mbps) circuit. The data arrives more frequently on this higher-bandwidth circuit than the data of higher-priority links A and C. The result is that the traffic arriving via link C will experience better service than the lower-bandwidth connections.

FIFO has been included for completeness, and does have a part to play in the overall delivery system. However, the FIFO queuing scheme is incapable of controlling the service allotted to a traffic flow and as such has limited use in supporting QoS.

7.9.1.2 WORK-CONSERVING QUEUING MECHANISMS

All the Cisco IOS queuing tools listed at the beginning of this section are work-conserving queuing mechanisms.

1. Priority Queuing

Priority queuing (PQ) ensures that important traffic gets the fastest handling at each point where it is used. It was designed to give strict priority to important traffic. PQ can flexibly prioritize according to network protocol (for example IP, IPX, or AppleTalk), incoming interface, packet size, source/destination address, and so on. In PQ, each packet is placed in one of four queues (high, medium, normal, or low) based on an assigned priority. Packets that are not classified by this priority list mechanism fall into the normal queue. During transmission, the algorithm gives higher-priority queues absolute preferential treatment over low-priority queues.

PQ can greatly improve latency for high-priority packets, but it does have FIFO-style problems of delaying short packets behind long ones. It also has issues of fairness within each queue. In addition, it may well starve some flows completely, preventing acknowledgment frames from returning in time, ultimately causing the entire VC to collapse. It also has the potential to increase jitter in lower-priority packets. Therefore, PQ is a relatively efficient method for prioritizing a few flows.

2. Custom Queuing

Custom queuing (CQ) was designed to allow various applications or organizations to share the network among applications with specific minimum bandwidth or latency requirements. In these environments, bandwidth must be shared proportionally among applications and users. CQ handles traffic by assigning a specified amount of queue space to each class of packets and then servicing the queues in a round-robin fashion. The queuing algorithm places the messages in 1 of 17 queues (queue 0 holds system messages such as keepalives, signaling, and so on) and is emptied with weighted priority. The router services queues 1 through 16 in round-robin order, de-queuing a configured byte count from each queue in each cycle. This feature improves fairness; a protocol stack that tries to push too many packets through will simply overflow its private queue instead of grabbing bandwidth from others when the line is under stress. The round-robin approach also avoids complete starvation of any flows. However, fairness still depends on packet size. Because one packet is taken on each cycle, flows using large packets can get much more bandwidth than flows with small packets.

7.9.1.3 FLOW-BASED WEIGHTED FAIR QUEUING

For situations in which it is desirable to provide consistent response time to heavy and light network users alike without adding excessive bandwidth, the solution is flow-based weighted fair queuing (commonly referred to as just WFQ). WFQ is a Cisco premier queuing technique. It is a flow-based queuing algorithm that creates bit-wise weighted fairness by allowing each queue to be serviced fairly in terms of byte count. For example, if queue 1 has 100-byte packets and queue 2 has 50-byte packets, the WFQ algorithm takes two packets from queue 2 for every one packet from queue 1. This makes service fair for each queue: 100 bytes each time the queue is serviced.

WFQ ensures that queues do not starve for bandwidth and that traffic gets predictable service. Low-volume traffic streams (which comprise the majority of traffic) receive increased service, transmitting the same number of bytes as high-volume streams. This behavior results in what appears to be preferential treatment for low-volume traffic, when in actuality it is creating fairness.

The weighted portion of WFQ comes from the use of IP precedence bits to provide greater service for certain queues. Using settings 0 to 5 (6 and 7 are reserved), WFQ uses its algorithm to determine how much more service to provide to a queue. In practical implementations, weights generally are not used on a per-conversation basis, but to bias certain aggregate flows.

WFQ is efficient in that it uses whatever bandwidth is available to forward traffic from lower-priority flows if no traffic from higher-priority flows is present. This is different from strict time-division multiplexing (TDM), which simply carves up the bandwidth and lets it go unused if no traffic is present for a particular traffic type. WFQ works with both IP precedence and RSVP (described later in this chapter) to help provide differentiated QoS as well as guaranteed services. WFQ is generally used for applications that need latency guarantees, such as real-time speech.

7.9.1.4 CLASS-BASED WEIGHTED FAIR QUEUING

Class-based weighted fair queuing (CBWFQ) extends the standard WFQ functionality to provide support for user-defined traffic classes. For CBWFQ, you define traffic classes based on match criteria including protocols, access control lists (ACLs), and input interfaces. CBWFQ enables a network administrator to create minimum guaranteed bandwidth classes. Instead of providing a queue for each individual flow, a class is defined that consists of one or more flows. Each class can be guaranteed a minimum amount of bandwidth.

7.9.1.5 LOW-LATENCY QUEUING

In addition, a low-latency queue (LLQ) may be designated, which essentially is a priority queue. Note that this feature is also referred to as priority queue class-based weighted fair queuing (PQCBWFQ). This mechanism provides a very fair and efficient distribution of bandwidth between classes, and it works well in high-speed circuits (such as T1 and above). It is normally used to allocate bandwidth on high-speed backbones.

Table 7.1 shows general application characteristics and QoS implementation guidelines.

Table 7.1: QoS Implementation Guidelines

Characteristi	Guideline
Application that is delay or loss sensitive (voice and real-time video)	Do not use WRED, traffic shaping, fragmentation (FRF-12), or policing. For this kind of traffic, implement LLQ and use a priority queue for the delay-sensitive traffic.
Application that is consistently bursty or is a bandwidth hog (FTP and HTTP)	Use WRED, policing, traffic shaping, or CBWFQ to guarantee bandwidth.
Application that is TCP based	Use WRED because lost packets will cause retransmissions. If the traffic is UDP based and does not retransmit, do not use WRED. Use policing if you need to rate-limit the application; otherwise let the packets tail drop.

7.9.1.6 NON-WORKCONSERVING QUEUING MECHANISMS

Non-workconserving queuing schemes are typically used to control the impact of traffic on the network by limiting the rate at which it is forwarded to the network. These mechanisms are often referred to as traffic-shaping mechanisms.

Traffic shaping attempts to adjust the transmission rate of packets that match a certain criteria. Holding packets in a buffer and releasing them at a preconfigured rate accomplishes this. Non-workconserving schemes or traffic-shaping schemes shape traffic according to a set of parameters. They are typically used to shape traffic either at the traffic source (as near to it as possible) or in network devices on the periphery of the network. This is because in the core the link speeds tend to be higher as is the number of flows that need to be shaped. This impact the amount of processing required in these devices.

In many environments, implementing a relatively simple LLQ or PQ scheme is sufficient. However, these queuing methods still pass traffic as fast as they can; their goal is to service some types of traffic before others. Sometimes you actually need to slow traffic down, which you can do with traffic shaping. This is most common in Frame Relay environments, where one access circuit is much faster than another, but it can be used on most other types of interfaces. Shaping can also help your Voice over IP (VoIP) network by regulating the speed of nonvoice traffic and normalizing the rate of flow for your voice traffic.

All traffic, real time or not, is bursty to some degree. Shaping is used to control the impact of bursts on the network. It is not used to completely eliminate bursts. To account for the bursty nature of traffic, the following two models are used:

- Leaky bucket
- Token bucket

The theory behind this shaping is to smooth out a traffic flow and reduce traffic clumping. This is essentially done by controlling the volume of traffic entering the network.

Both models operate in a similar way. In the leaky bucket method, the traffic arriving at the queuing stage is inserted into the bucket from the top. A hole in the bottom of the bucket allows traffic to leak out at a fixed rate. This is the rate at which the forwarding stage forwards the traffic.

In the token bucket method, the bucket is filled with tokens at a fixed rate. Each time the forwarder is ready to forward a packet from a queue, it must also remove a token from the bucket. When no tokens are available, the forwarder must either drop packets or delay them.

The rate at which the data is forwarded is controlled by a combination of the rate (at which the tokens are entered in token bucket and the rate at which packets leak in leaky bucket) and the depth of the bucket itself.

Figure 7.13 depicts a token bucket model with data being forwarded at a controlled (shaped) rate. The rate is controlled by the rate at which the tokens are placed in the bucket and the depth of the bucket. In this case, if the forwarder is unable to obtain a forwarding token it drops the packet to maintain the rate.

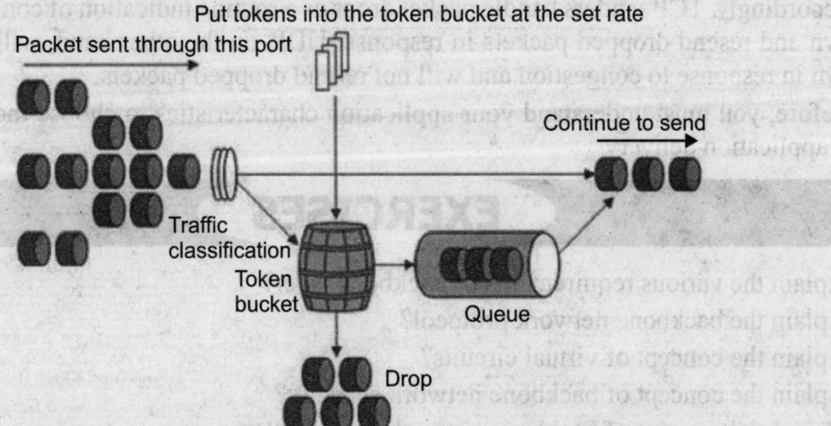

Figure 7.13: Traffic Shaping with a Token Bucket Model

So, in certain scenarios it may be necessary to drop packets to maintain the flow. By controlling the timing and selection of packet discard, packets can be dropped fairly.

In its simplest form, discards work on the last-in, first-out principle. That is, packets are dropped from the tail of the congested queue when there is no queue space left. This is known as tail drop, and it is not the fairest way. A bursty source flow can overflow a queue resulting in the dropping of a well-behaved flow. The other thing to note about tail drop is that it is a reaction to an already overloaded or congested device. In a perfect world, you would look to avoid that congestion by detecting the buildup early and taking corrective action before any bottlenecks occur.

Congestion-avoidance techniques monitor network traffic loads in an effort to anticipate and avoid congestion at common network and internetwork bottlenecks before it becomes a problem. These techniques are designed to provide preferential treatment for premium-class (priority) traffic under congestion situations while concurrently maximizing network throughput and capacity utilization and minimizing packet loss and delay. WRED and DWRED are the Cisco IOS QoS congestion-avoidance features.

Random early detection (RED) is a congestion-avoidance mechanism that takes advantage of TCP's congestion-control mechanism. The RED algorithms are designed to avoid congestion in networks before it becomes a problem. RED works by monitoring traffic load at points in the network and stochastically discarding packets if the congestion begins to increase. The result of the drop is that the source detects the dropped traffic and slows its transmission. RED is primarily designed to work with TCP in IP Internet work environments.

Weighted RED (WRED) generally drops packets selectively based on IP precedence. Packets with a higher IP precedence are less likely to be dropped than packets with a lower precedence.

Distributed weighted random early detection (DWRED) is a high-speed version of WRED that runs on VIP-distributed processors. The DWRED algorithm provides functionality beyond what WRED provides, such as minimum and maximum queue depth thresholds and drop capabilities for each class of service.

Flow-based WRED is a feature of WRED that forces WRED to afford greater fairness to all flows on an interface in regard to how packets are dropped.

Drop schemes are best suited to traffic types that understand the implication of a dropped packet and act accordingly. TCP senders handle packet drops as a routine indication of congestion, and will slow down and resend dropped packets in response. UDP, on the other hand, will not necessarily slow down in response to congestion and will not resend dropped packets.

Therefore, you must understand your application characteristics to choose the best method to optimize application delivery.

EXERCISES

1. Explain the various requirements of backbone layer?
2. Explain the backbone network protocol?
3. Explain the concept of virtual circuits?
4. Explain the concept of backbone network capacity?
5. Explain the concept of backbone network topology?
6. Explain the various network topologies?
7. Explain the advantages and disadvantages of network topologies?
8. Explain the concept of network performance tuning?
9. Explain the concept of queuing in detail?
10. Explain the concept of queuing mechanisms?

CHAPTER

8

Network Security

8.1 BACKGROUND

This chapter has been added to explain techniques and processes that are required to secure your network. In this chapter we provide only the elementary discussion on network security as it relates to network design.

8.2 INTRODUCTION

Network security has become more important to personal computer users, organizations, and the military. With the advent of the internet, security became a major concern and the history of security allows a better understanding of the emergence of security technology. The internet structure itself allowed for many security threats to occur. The architecture of the internet, when modified can reduce the possible attacks that can be sent across the network. Knowing the attack methods, allows for the appropriate security to emerge. Many businesses secure themselves from the internet by means of firewalls and encryption mechanisms. The businesses create an "intranet" to remain connected to the internet but secured from possible threats. The entire field of network security is vast and in an evolutionary stage. The range of study encompasses a brief history dating back to internet's beginnings and the current development in network security. In order to understand the research being performed today, background knowledge of the internet, its vulnerabilities, attack methods through the internet, and security technology is important and therefore they are reviewed.

8.3 HISTORY OF NETWORK SECURITY

Recent interest in security was fueled by the crime committed by Kevin Mitnick. Kevin Mitnick committed the largest computer related crime in U.S. history. The losses were eighty million dollars in U.S. intellectual property and source code from a variety of companies. Since then, information security came into the spotlight. Public networks are being relied upon to deliver financial and personal information. Due to the evolution of information that is made available through the internet, information security is also required to evolve. Due to Kevin Mitnick's offense, companies are emphasizing security for the intellectual property. Internet has been a driving force for data security improvement. Internet protocols in the past were not developed to secure themselves. Within the TCP/IP communication stack, security protocols are not implemented. This leaves the internet open to attacks. Modern developments in the internet architecture have made communication more secure.

The birth of the interne takes place in 1969 when Advanced Research Projects Agency Network (ARPANet) is commissioned by the department of defense (DOD) for research in networking. The ARPANET is a success from the very beginning. Although originally designed to allow scientists to share data and access remote computers, email quickly becomes the most popular application. The ARPANET becomes a high speed digital post office as people use it to collaborate on research projects and discuss topics of various interests. The Internetworking Working Group becomes the first of several standards setting entities to govern the growing network. Vinton Cerf is elected the first chairman of the INWG, and later becomes known as a "Father of the Internet." In the 1980s, Bob Kahn and Vinton Cerf are key members of a team that create TCP/IP, the common language of all Internet computers. For the first time the loose collection of networks which made up the ARPANET is seen as an "Internet", and the Internet as we know it today is born. The mid 80s marks a boom in the personal computer and super minicomputer industries. The combination of inexpensive desktop machines and powerful, network ready servers allows many companies to join the Internet for the first time. Corporations begin to use the Internet to communicate with each other and with their customers.

In the 1990s, the internet began to become available to the public. The World Wide Web was born. Netscape and Microsoft were both competing on developing a browser for the internet. Internet continues to grow and surfing the internet has become equivalent to TV viewing for many users.

8.4 SECURITY THREATS

Information is the key asset in most organizations. Companies gain a competitive advantage by knowing how to use that information. The threat comes from others who would like to acquire the information or limit business opportunities by interfering with normal business processes.

The object of security is to protect valuable or sensitive organizational information while making it readily available. Attackers trying to harm a system or disrupt normal business operations exploit vulnerabilities by using various techniques, methods, and tools. System administrators need to understand the various aspects of security to develop measures and policies to protect assets and limit their vulnerabilities.

Attackers generally have motives or goals-for example, to disrupt normal business operations or steal information. To achieve these motives or goals, they use various methods, tools, and techniques to exploit vulnerabilities in a computer system or security policy and controls.

8.4.1 TYPES OF SECURITY THREATS

Figure 8.1 introduces a layout that can be used to break up security threats into different areas.

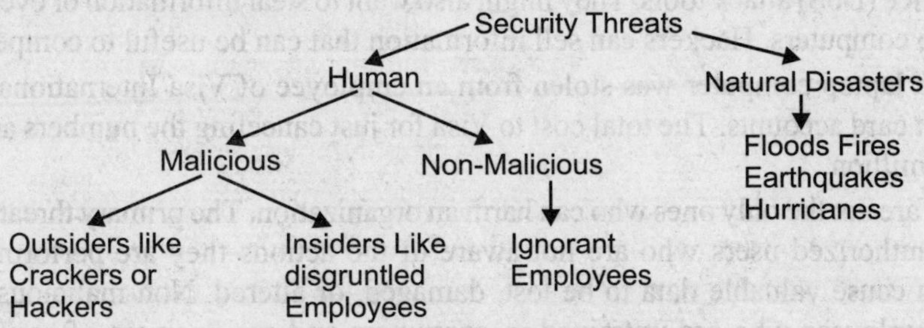

Figure 8.1: Types of security threats

1. Natural Disasters

Nobody can stop nature from taking its course. Earthquakes, hurricanes, floods, lightning, and fire can cause severe damage to computer systems. Information can be lost, downtime or loss of productivity can occur, and damage to hardware can disrupt other essential services. Few safeguards can be implemented against natural disasters. The best approach is to have disaster recovery plans and contingency plans in place. Other threats such as riots, wars, and terrorist attacks could be included here. Although they are human-caused threats, they are classified as disastrous.

2. Human Threats

Malicious threats consist of inside attacks by disgruntled or malicious employees and outside attacks by non-employees just looking to harm and disrupt an organization.

The most dangerous attackers are usually insiders (or former insiders), because they know many of the codes and security measures that are already in place. Insiders are likely to have specific goals and objectives, and have legitimate access to the system. Employees are the people most familiar with the organization's computers and applications, and they are most likely to know what actions might cause the most damage. Insiders can plant viruses, Trojan horses, or worms, and they can browse through the file system.

The insider attack can affect all components of computer security. By browsing through a system, confidential information could be revealed. Trojan horses are a threat to both the integrity and confidentiality of information in the system. Insider attacks can affect availability by overloading the system's processing or storage capacity, or by causing the system to crash.

People often refer to these individuals as "crackers" or "hackers." The definition of "hacker" has changed over the years. A hacker was once thought of as any individual who enjoyed getting the most out of the system he or she was using. A hacker would use a system extensively and study it until he or she became proficient in all its nuances. This individual was respected as a source of information for local computer users, someone referred to as a "guru" or "wizard."

Now, however, the term hacker refers to people who either break in to systems for which they have no authorization or intentionally overstep their bounds on systems for which they do not have legitimate access.

The correct term to use for someone who breaks in to systems is a "cracker." Common methods for gaining access to a system include password cracking, exploiting known security weaknesses, network spoofing, and social engineering.

Malicious attackers normally will have a specific goal, objective, or motive for an attack on a system. These goals could be to disrupt services and the continuity of business operations by using denial-of-service (DoS) attack tools. They might also want to steal information or even steal hardware such as laptop computers. Hackers can sell information that can be useful to competitors.

In 1996, a laptop computer was stolen from an employee of Visa International that contained 314,000 credit card accounts. The total cost to Visa for just canceling the numbers and replacing the cards was $6 million.

Attackers are not the only ones who can harm an organization. The primary threat to data integrity comes from authorized users who are not aware of the actions they are performing. Errors and omissions can cause valuable data to be lost, damaged, or altered. Non-malicious threats usually come from employees who are untrained in computers and are unaware of security threats and vulnerabilities. Users who open up Microsoft Word documents using Notepad, edit the documents, and then save them could cause serious damage to the information stored on the document.

Users, data entry clerks, system operators, and programmers frequently make unintentional errors that contribute to security problems, directly and indirectly. Sometimes the error is the threat, such as a data entry error or a programming error that crashes a system. In other cases, errors create vulnerabilities. Errors can occur in all phases of the system life cycle.

Below is the table that identifies the different types of threats.

Threat	Internal / External	Threat consequences
e-mail with virus	External origination, internal use	Could infect system reading email and subsequently spread throughout entire organization.
Network virus	External	Could enter through unprotected ports, compromise whole network.
Web based virus	Internal browsing to external site	Could cause compromise on system doing browsing and subsequently affect other internal systems.
Web server attack	External to web servers	If web server is compromised hacker could gain access to other systems internal to network
Denial of service attack	External	External services such as web, email and ftp could become unusable. If router is attacked, whole network could go down
Network User Attack (internal employee)	Internal to anywhere	Traditional border fire walls do nothing for this attack. Internal segmentation firewalls can help contain damage.

Table 8.1: Identify the threats

8.5 METHODS, TOOLS, AND TECHNIQUES FOR ATTACKS

Malicious attackers can gain access or deny services in numerous ways. Here are some of them:

- **Viruses:** Attackers can develop harmful code known as viruses. Using hacking techniques, they can break into systems and plant viruses. Viruses in general are a threat to any environment. They come in different forms and although not always malicious, they always take up time. Viruses can also be spread via e-mail and disks.

- **Trojan horses:** These are malicious programs or software code hidden inside what looks like a normal program. When a user runs the normal program, the hidden code runs as well. It can then start deleting files and causing other damage to the computer. Trojan horses are normally spread by e-mail attachments. The Melissa virus that caused denial-of-service attacks throughout the world in 1999 was a type of Trojan horse.
- **Worms:** These are programs that run independently and travel from computer to computer across network connections. Worms may have portions of themselves running on many different computers. Worms do not change other programs, although they may carry other code that does.
- **Password cracking:** This is a technique attacker's use to surreptitiously gain system access through another user's account. This is possible because users often select weak passwords. The two major problems with passwords is when they are easy to guess based on knowledge of the user (for example, wife's maiden name) and when they are susceptible to dictionary attacks (that is, using a dictionary as the source of guesses).
- **Denial-of-service attacks:** This attack exploits the need to have a service available. It is a growing trend on the Internet because Web sites in general are open doors ready for abuse. People can easily flood the Web server with communication in order to keep it busy. Therefore, companies connected to the Internet should prepare for (DoS) attacks. They also are difficult to trace and allow other types of attacks to be subdued.

Common Denial of Service Attacks

Name of DoS Attack	Vulnerability Exploited
TCP SYN attack	Memory is allocated for TCP connections such that not enough memory is left for other functions.
Ping of Death	Fragmentation implementation of IP whereby large packets are reassembled and can cause machines to crash.
Land.c attack	TCP connection establishment.
Teardrop.c attack	Fragmentation implementation of IP whereby reassembly problems can cause machines to crash.
Smurf attack	Flooding networks with broadcast traffic (ICMP echo requests) such that the network is congested.
Fraggle attack	Flooding networks with broadcast traffic (UDP echo requests) such that the network is congested.

- **E-mail hacking:** Electronic mail is one of the most popular features of the Internet. With access to Internet e-mail, someone can potentially correspond with any one of millions of people worldwide. Some of the threats associated with e-mail are:

- **Impersonation:** The sender address on Internet e-mail cannot be trusted because the sender can create a false return address. Someone could have modified the header in transit, or the sender could have connected directly to the Simple Mail Transfer Protocol (SMTP) port on the target computer to enter the e-mail.
- **Eavesdroppin:** E-mail headers and contents are transmitted in the clear text if no encryption is used. As a result, the contents of a message can be read or altered in transit. The header can be modified to hide or change the sender, or to redirect the message.
- **Packet replay:** This refers to the recording and retransmission of message packets in the network. Packet replay is a significant threat for programs that require authentication sequences, because an intruder could replay legitimate authentication sequence messages to gain access to a system. Packet replay is frequently undetectable, but can be prevented by using packet time stamping and packet sequence counting.
- **Packet modification:** This involves one system intercepting and modifying a packet destined for another system. Packet information may not only be modified, it could also be destroyed.
- **Eavesdropping:** This allows a cracker (hacker) to make a complete copy of network activity. As a result, a cracker can obtain sensitive information such as passwords, data, and procedures for performing functions. It is possible for a cracker to eavesdrop by wiretapping, using radio, or using auxiliary ports on terminals. It is also possible to eavesdrop using software that monitors packets sent over the network. In most cases, it is difficult to detect eavesdropping.
- **Social engineering:** This is a common form of cracking. It can be used by outsiders and by people within an organization. Social engineering is a hacker term for tricking people into revealing their password or some form of security information.
- **Intrusion attacks:** In these attacks, a hacker uses various hacking tools to gain access to systems. These can range from password-cracking tools to protocol hacking and manipulation tools. Intrusion detection tools often can help to detect changes and variants that take place within systems and networks.
- **Network spoofing:** In network spoofing, a system presents itself to the network as though it were a different system (computer A impersonates computer B by sending B's address instead of its own). The reason for doing this is that systems tend to operate within a group of other trusted systems. Trust is imparted in a one-to-one fashion; computer A trusts computer B (this does not imply that system B trusts system A). Implied with this trust is that the system administrator of the trusted system is performing the job properly and maintaining an appropriate level of security for the system. Network spoofing occurs in the following manner: if computer A trusts computer B and computer C spoofs (impersonates) computer B, then computer C can gain otherwise-denied access to computer A.

Common Unauthorized Access Scenarios

Ways of Obtaining Unauthorized Access	Ways to Use Unauthorized Access
Establishing false identity with false credentials	Sending e-mail that authorizes money transfers or terminating an employee
Physical access to network devices	Modifying records to establish a better credit rating
Eavesdropping on shared media networks	Retrieving confidential records, such as salary for all employees or medical histories
Reachability checks and port scanning to determine access to vulnerable hosts	Exploiting host vulnerabilities to perpetrate websites and modify the content
Using a wireless modem card and sitting in a car by a high office building to see whether there's a network to which it can connect	Using this "free access" to the Internet to misuse bandwidth or instigate malicious denial-of-service attacks

8.6 SECURITY SAFEGUARDS

Network safeguards are the first protection barrier of IT system resources against threats originating from outside the network (e.g., intruders, malicious code). The principle network security defenses are firewalls, intrusion detection and prevention systems (IPS/IDS), VPN protections and content inspection systems like anti-virus, anti-malware, anti-spam and URL filtering.

These hardware and software solutions complement and support the protection mechanisms associated with the operating systems, databases and applications. Deployment of an effective, scalable security system for medium to large scale networks requires careful, well thought out design based on the organization's risk analysis and sound security principles.

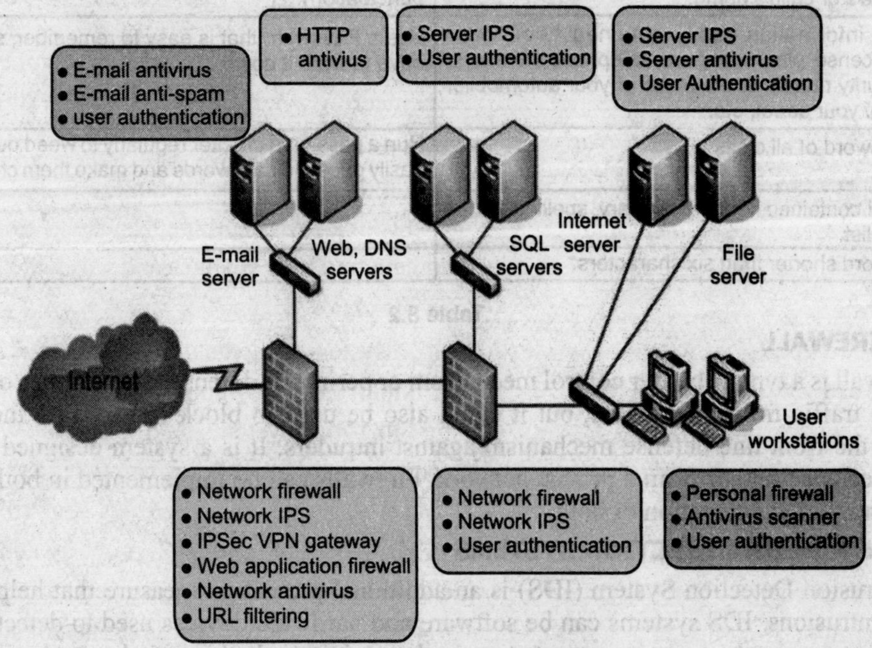

Figure 8.2: Security Safeguards

8.6.1 SECURITY PRINCIPLES

When designing the network security system, the following fundamental IT systems security principles should be taken into account:

8.6.1.1 DEFENSE-IN-DEPTH

Protection of IT system resources is based on many security layers as shown in Figure 1. Extensions of the defense-in-depth principle are the following rules:

1. **Layered protections:** Security layers complement one another: what one misses the other catches.
2. **Defense in multiple places:** Security defenses are located in different places of the IT system.
3. **Defense through diversification:** Safety of IT system resources should be based on the protection layers consisting of different types of safeguards. When two layers of the same type are being used (e.g., two network firewalls), they should come from different vendors. This rule should be used with caution as it increases the complexity of the security system and can make management and maintenance more difficult and costly.

8.6.1.2 PASSWORD PROCEDURE

Passwords are required to access almost any resource in a network environment, but poorly selected passwords can be determined easily. Software is available on the Internet to break poorly selected passwords, so implementing politics on passwords is an important step in security. Table 8.2 provides a list of Do's and don'ts on creating passwords.

Don,t	Do
Use your login name in any form.	Use a password of mixed-case alphabets.
Use your first, middle, or last name. In any form or use your spouse's or child's name.	Use a password with nonalphabetic characters (digits or punctuation).
Use other information easily obtained About you, including license plate numbers, telephone numbers, Social security numbers, the make of your automobile, the name of your street, etc.	Use a Password that is easy to remember, so you don't have to write it down.
Use a password of all digits	Run a password cracker regularly to weed out users with easily guessed passwords and make them change them.
Use a word contained in any dictionary, spelling list, or other word list.	
Use password shorter than six characters.	

Table 8.2

8.6.1.3 FIREWALL

A firewall is a typical border control mechanism or perimeter defense. The purpose of a firewall is to block traffic from the outside, but it could also be used to block traffic from the inside. A firewall is the front line defense mechanism against intruders. It is a system designed to prevent unauthorized access to or from a private network. Firewalls can be implemented in both hardware and software, or a combination of both.

8.6.1.4 INTRUSION DETECTION SYSTEMS

An Intrusion Detection System (IDS) is an additional protection measure that helps ward off computer intrusions. IDS systems can be software and hardware devices used to detect an attack. IDS products are used to monitor connection in determining whether attacks are been launched. Some IDS systems just monitor and alert of an attack, whereas others try to block the attack.

8.6.1.5 ANTIMALWARE SOFTWARE AND SCANNERS

Viruses, worms and Trojan horses are all examples of malicious software, or Malware for short. Special so called anti Malware tools are used to detect them and cure an infected system.

8.7 SECURITY IN DIFFERENT NETWORKS (VPN)

The businesses today use combinations of firewalls, encryption, and authentication mechanisms to create "intranets" that are connected to the internet but protected from it at the **same time.**

Intranet is a private computer network that uses internet protocols. Intranets differ from "Extranets" in that the former are generally restricted to employees of the organization while extranets can generally be accessed by customers, suppliers, or other approved parties. There does not necessarily have to be any access from the organization's internal network to the Internet itself. When such access is provided it is usually through a gateway with a firewall, along with user authentication, encryption of messages, and often makes use of virtual private networks (VPNs). Although intranets can be set up quickly to share data in a controlled environment, that data is still at risk unless there is tight security. The disadvantage of a closed intranet is that vital data might not get into the hands of those who need it. Intranets have a place within agencies. But for broader data sharing, it might be better to keep the networks open, with these safeguards:

1. Firewalls that detect and report intrusion attempts
2. Sophisticated virus checking at the firewall
3. Enforced rules for employee opening of email attachments
4. Encryption for all connections and data transfers
5. Authentication by synchronized, timed passwords or security certificates

It was mentioned that if the intranet wanted access to the internet, virtual private networks are often used. Intranets that exist across multiple locations generally run over separate leased lines or a newer approach of VPN can be utilized. VPN is a private network that uses a public network (usually the Internet) to connect remote sites or users together. Instead of using a dedicated, real world connection such as leased line, a VPN uses "virtual" connections routed through the Internet from the company's private network to the remote site or employee. Figure 8.3 is a graphical representation of an organization and VPN network.

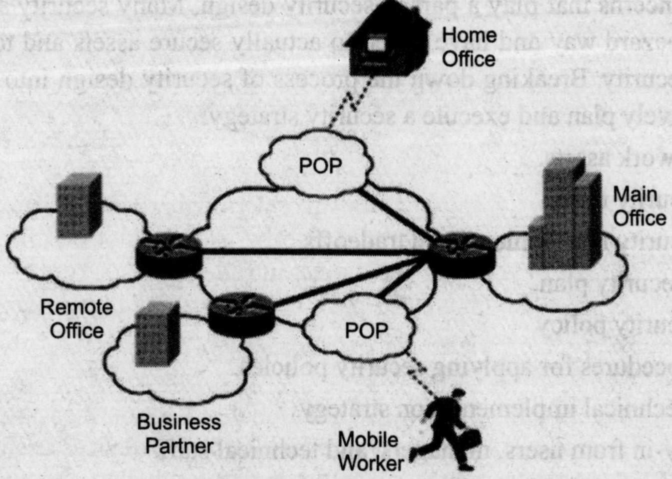

Figure 8.3: VPN network

8.8 DESIGNS FOR NETWORK SECURITY

Security on the Internet and on Local Area Networks is now at the forefront of computer network related issues the evolution of networking and the Internet, the threats to information and networks have risen dramatically. Many of these threats have become cleverly exercised attacks causing damage or committing theft. The Internet continues to grow exponentially. As personal, government and business-critical applications become more prevalent on the Internet, there are many immediate benefits. However, these network-based applications and services can pose security risks to individuals as well as to the information resources of companies and government. In many cases, the rush to get connected comes at the expense of adequate network security. Information is an asset that must be protected.

Without adequate protection or network security, many individuals, businesses, and governments are at risk of losing that asset. Network security is the process by which digital information assets are protected, the goals of security are to protect confidentiality, maintain integrity, and assure availability. With this in mind, it is imperative that all networks be protected from threats and vulnerabilities in order for a business to achieve its fullest potential. Typically, these threats are persistent due to vulnerabilities, which can arise from mis-configured hardware or software, poor network design, inherent technology weaknesses, or end-user carelessness. A router is similar to many computers in that it has many services enabled by default. Many of these services are unnecessary and may be used by an attacker for information gathering or for exploitation. All unnecessary services should be disabled in the router configuration to prevent the attacker from using it to damage the network or to stealing the important information, or network devices configuration. Routers and firewall are very critical parts of network operations and network security. Careful management and diligent audit of router and firewall operations, can reduce network downtime, improve security, prevent the attacks and hackers, network threats decrease, and aid in the analysis of suspected security breaches.

Following a structured set of steps which are helpful when developing and implementing network security concerns that play a part in security design. Many security strategies have been developed in a haphazard way and have failed to actually secure assets and to meet a customer's primary goals for security. Breaking down the process of security design into the following steps will help you effectively plan and execute a security strategy:

1. Identify network assets.
2. Analyze security risks.
3. Analyze security requirements and tradeoffs.
4. Develop a security plan.
5. Define a security policy.
6. Develop procedures for applying security policies.
7. Develop a technical implementation strategy.
8. Achieve buy-in from users, managers, and technical staff.
9. Train users, managers, and technical staff.

10. Implement the technical strategy and security procedures.
11. Test the security and update it if any problems are found.
12. Maintain security.

8.8.1 IDENTIFYING NETWORK ASSETS

Analyzing goals involves identifying network assets and the risk that those assets could be sabotaged or inappropriately accessed. It also involves analyzing the consequences of risks.

Network assets can include network hosts (including the hosts operating systems, applications, and data), internetworking devices (such as routers and switches), and network data that traverses the network. Less obvious, but still important, assets include intellectual property, trade secrets, and a company's reputation.

8.8.2 ANALYZING SECURITY RISKS

Risks can range from hostile intruders to untrained users who download Internet applications that have viruses. Hostile intruders can steal data, change data, and cause service to be denied to legitimate users. Denial-of-service (DoS) attacks have become increasingly common in the past few years.

8.8.3 ANALYZING SECURITY REQUIREMENTS AND TRADEOFFS

Although many customers have more specific goals, in general, security requirements boil down to the need to protect the following assets:

The confidentiality of data, so that only authorized users can view sensitive information The integrity of data, so that only authorized users can change sensitive information System and data availability, so that users have uninterrupted access to important computing resources.

According to RFC 2196, "Site Security Handbook:"

One old truism in security is that the cost of protecting yourself against a threat should be less than the cost of recovering if the threat were to strike you. Cost in this context should be remembered to include losses expressed in real currency, reputation, trustworthiness, and other less obvious measures.

As is the case with most technical design requirements, achieving security goals means making tradeoffs. Tradeoffs must be made between security goals and goals for affordability, usability, performance, and availability. Also, security adds to the amount of management work because user login IDs, passwords, and audit logs must be maintained.

Security also affects network performance. Security features such as packet filters and data encryption consume CPU power and memory on hosts, routers, and servers. Encryption can use upward of 15 percent of available CPU power on a router or server. Encryption can be implemented on dedicated appliances instead of on shared routers or servers, but there is still an effect on network performance because of the delay that packets experience while they are being encrypted or decrypted.

Another tradeoff is that security can reduce network redundancy. If all traffic must go through an encryption device, for example, the device becomes a single point of failure. This makes it hard to meet availability goals.

Security can also make it harder to offer load balancing. Some security mechanisms require traffic to always take the same path so that security mechanisms can be applied uniformly. For example, a mechanism that randomizes TCP sequence numbers (so that hackers can't guess the numbers) won't work if some TCP segments for a session take a path that bypasses the randomizing function due to load balancing.

8.8.4 DEVELOPING A SECURITY PLAN

One of the first steps in security design is developing a security plan. A security plan is a high-level document that proposes what an organization is going to do to meet security requirements. The plan specifies the time, people, and other resources that will be required to develop a security policy and achieve technical implementation of the policy. As the network designer, you can help your customer develop a plan that is practical and pertinent. The plan should be based on the customer's goals and the analysis of network assets and risks.

A security plan should reference the network topology and include a list of network services that will be provided (for example, FTP, web, email, and so on). This list should specify who provides the services, who has access to the services, how access is provided, and who administers the services.

As the network designer, you can help the customer evaluate which services are definitely needed, based on the customer's business and technical goals. Sometimes new services are added unnecessarily, simply because they are the latest trend. Adding services might require new packet filters on routers and firewalls to protect the services, or additional user-authentication processes to limit access to the services, adding complexity to the security strategy. Overly complex security strategies should be avoided because they can be self-defeating. Complicated security strategies are hard to implement correctly without introducing unexpected security holes.

One of the most important aspects of the security plan is a specification of the people who must be involved in implementing network security:

Will specialized security administrators be hired?

How will end users and their managers get involved?

How will end users, managers, and technical staff be trained on security policies and procedures?

For a security plan to be useful, it needs to have the support of all levels of employees within the organization. It is especially important that corporate management fully support the security plan. Technical staff at headquarters and remote sites should buy into the plan, as should end users.

8.8.5 DEVELOPING A SECURITY POLICY

According to RFC 2196, "Site Security Handbook:" A security policy is a formal statement of the rules by which people who are given access to an organization's technology and information assets must abide.

A security policy informs users, managers, and technical staff of their obligations for protecting technology and information assets. The policy should specify the mechanisms by which these obligations can be met. As was the case with the security plan, the security policy should have buy-in from employees, managers, executives, and technical personnel.

Developing a security policy is the job of senior management, with help from security and network administrators. The administrators get input from managers, users, network designers and engineers, and possibly legal counsel. As a network designer, you should work closely with the security administrators to understand how policies might affect the network design.

After a security policy has been developed, with the engagement of users, staff, and management, it should be explained to all by top management. Many enterprises require personnel to sign a statement indicating that they have read, understood, and agreed to abide by a policy.

A security policy is a living document. Because organizations constantly change, security policies should be regularly updated to reflect new business directions and technological shifts. Risks change over time also and affect the security policy.

8.8.6 COMPONENTS OF A SECURITY POLICY

In general, a policy should include at least the following items:

1. **An access policy that defines access rights and privileges.** The access policy should provide guidelines for connecting external networks, connecting devices to a network, and adding new software to systems. An access policy might also address how data is categorized (for example, confidential, internal, and top secret).
2. **An accountability policy that defines the responsibilities of users, operations staff, and management.** The accountability policy should specify an audit capability and provide incident-handling guidelines that specify what to do and whom to contact if a possible intrusion is detected.
3. **An authentication policy that establishes trust through an effective password policy and sets up guidelines for remote-location authentication.** A privacy policy that defines reasonable expectations of privacy regarding the monitoring of electronic mail, logging of keystrokes, and access to users' files. Computer-technology purchasing guidelines that specify the requirements for acquiring, configuring, and auditing computer systems and networks for compliance with the policy.

8.8.7 DEVELOPING SECURITY PROCEDURES

Security procedures implement security policies. Procedures define configuration, login, audit, and maintenance processes. Security procedures should be written for end users, network administrators, and security administrators. Security procedures should specify how to handle incidents (that is, what to do and who to contact if an intrusion is detected). Security procedures can be communicated to users and administrators in instructor-led and self-paced training classes.

8.8.8 MAINTAINING SECURITY

Security must be maintained by scheduling periodic independent audits, reading audit logs, responding to incidents, reading current literature and agency alerts, performing security testing, training security administrators, and updating the security plan and policy. Network security should be a perpetual process. Risks change over time, and so should security. Cisco security experts use the term security wheel to illustrate that implementing, monitoring, testing, and improving security is a never-ending process. Many overworked security engineers might relate to the wheel concept.

Continually updating security mechanisms to keep up with the latest attacks can sometimes make an administrator feel a bit like a hamster on a training wheel.

8.9 ROUTER AND FIREWALL SECURITY POLICY

Routers perform many different jobs in modern networks, forwards traffic between two or more local networks within an organization or enterprise routes. Interior routers may impose some restrictions on the traffic they forward between networks. Forwards traffic between different enterprises (sometimes called different 'autonomous systems'). The traffic between the different networks that make up the Internet is directed by backbone routers.

The level of trust between the networks connected by a backbone router is usually very low. Typically, backbone routers are designed and configured to forward traffic as quickly as possible, without imposing any restrictions on it. The primary security goals for a backbone router is to ensure that the management and operation of the router are conducted only by authorized parties, and to protect the integrity of the routing information it uses to forward traffic. Backbone routers typically employ Exterior Gateway Protocols to manage routes.

Configuring backbone routers is a very specialized task. The border router forwards traffic between an enterprise and exterior networks. The key aspect of a border router is that it forms part of the boundary between the trusted internal networks of an enterprise, and untrusted external networks (e.g. the Internet). It can help to secure the perimeter of an enterprise network by enforcing restrictions on the traffic that it controls. A border router may employ routing protocols, or it may depend entirely on static routes.

Security policy is the definition of security function against a network intrusion. Security engine provides security functions of a packet filtering, an authentication, an access control, an intrusion analysis and an audit trail in the kernel region of router. Router is a key component of the Internet, and an important part of networks that controls a data packet flow in a network and determines an optimal path to reach a destination, and their security is a vital part of the overall security for the networks they serve. An error of the router or an attack against the router can damage an entire network. Since the router is connected to at least two networks and manages network traffic, the security is necessary to control of an unauthorized router access and an illegal network intrusion. Secure router technology has security functions, such as intrusion detection, IPSec and access control, are applied to legacy router for secure networking. A router may be responsible for filtering traffic, allowing some packets to pass through and rejecting others . Filtering can be a very important function of routers; it allows them to help protect computers and other network components. It is also possible that at the destination end a router may have to break large packets up to accommodate the size limits of the destination LAN. Modern routers do not only perform relaying functions, but also filtering, separation, encryption and monitoring of data streams. Furthermore, they provide various management interfaces for configuration, (remote) maintenance, and monitoring. All these functions potentially affect the availability, integrity, and confidentiality of data connections, thus making routers highly security-critical network components. However, configuring a router is a difficult and error prone task.

A firewall can protect a network from external attacks by examining all packets of a message attempting to pass through the network and rejecting the packets that do not meet the security restrictions. However, it does not protect the data as it is transmitted from one network to another.

Data transmitted from one network to another via the Internet is susceptible to access at many points between the source and destination. The secure socket layer (SSL) is one means of providing secure communications between points connected via the Internet.

Routers and firewall support a large number of network services at layers 2, 3, 4, and 7 . Some of these services are application layer protocols that allow users and host processes to connect to the router, firewall and others network devices. Others are automatic processes and settings intended to support legacy or specialized configurations, which are detrimental to security. Some of these services can be restricted or disabled to improve security without degrading the operational use of the router and the network performance. Also attacks and hackers can utilize these services to find the weakness point in the network. General security practice for routers and firewall should be to support only traffic and protocols a network needs. The below figure describe the structure of router with firewall configuration for a network.

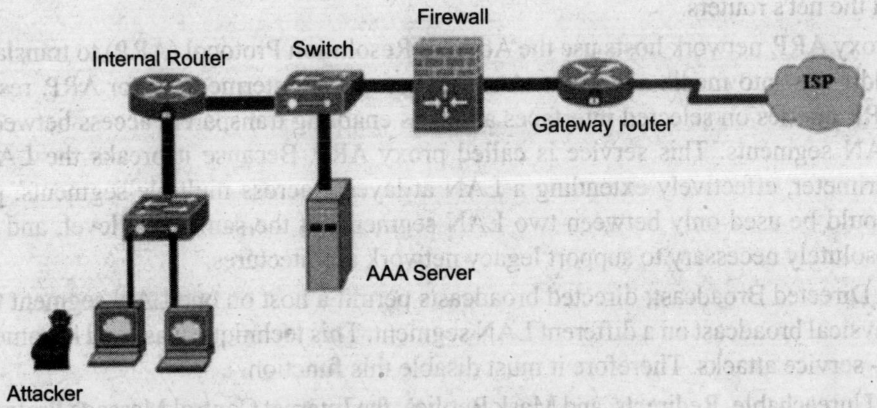

Figure 8.4: Firewall Protection

Examples for these services are:

1. CDP, the Cisco Discovery Protocol is a proprietary protocol that Cisco routers use to identify each other on a LAN segment. It is useful only in specialized situations, and is considered deleterious to security.
2. TCP and UDP Small Servers, the TCP and UDP protocol standards include a recommended list of simple services that hosts should provide. In virtually all cases, it is not necessary for routers to support these services, and they should be disabled.
3. Finger Server, the IOS finger server supports the Unix 'finger' protocol, which is used for querying a host about its logged in users.
4. HTTP Server, most router and firewall support web-based remote administration using the HTTP protocol. While the web access features are fairly rudimentary on most routers, they are a viable mechanism for monitoring, configuring, and attacking a router. If web-based remote administration is not needed, then it should be disabled as shown below. Web-based remote administration is useful primarily when intervening routers or firewalls prevent use of Telnet for that purpose. However, it is important to note that both Telnet and web-based remote administration reveal critical passwords in the clear. Therefore, web-based remote administration should be avoided.

5. Bootp Server, Bootp is a datagram protocol that is used by some hosts to load their operating system over the network. Cisco routers are capable of acting as bootp servers, primarily for other Cisco hardware. This facility is intended to support a deployment strategy where one Cisco router acts as the central repository of IOS software for a collection of such routers. In practice, bootp is very rarely used, and offers an attacker the ability to download a copy of a router's IOS software.
6. Configuration Auto-Loading, some routers such as Cisco routers and Linksys routers, are capable of loading their startup configuration from local memory or from the network. Loading from the network is not secure, and should be considered.
7. IP source routing, source routing is a feature of IP whereby individual packets can specify routes. This feature is used in several kinds of attacks. Cisco routers normally accept and process source routes. Unless a network depends on source routing, it should be disabled on all the net's routers.
8. Proxy ARP, network hosts use the Address Resolution Protocol (ARP) to translate network addresses into media addresses. A router can act as intermediary for ARP, responding to ARP queries on selected interfaces and thus enabling transparent access between multiple LAN segments. This service is called proxy ARP. Because it breaks the LAN security perimeter, effectively extending a LAN at layer 2 across multiple segments, proxy ARP should be used only between two LAN segments at the same trust level, and only when absolutely necessary to support legacy network architectures.
9. IP Directed Broadcast, directed broadcasts permit a host on one LAN segment to initiate a physical broadcast on a different LAN segment. This technique was used in some old denial of- service attacks. Therefore it must disable this function.
10. IP Unreachable, Redirects, and Mask Replies: the Internet Control Message Protocol (ICMP) supports IP traffic by relaying information about paths, routes, and network conditions. Cisco routers automatically send ICMP messages under a wide variety of conditions. Three ICMP messages are commonly used by attackers for network mapping and diagnosis: 'Host unreachable', 'Redirect', and 'Mask Reply'. Automatic generation of these messages it is important to be disabled on all interfaces, especially interfaces that are connected to untrusted networks.
11. SNMP Services, the Simple Network Management Protocol (SNMP) is the standard Internet protocol for automated remote monitoring and administration. There are several different versions of SNMP, with different security properties. If a network has a deployed SNMP infrastructure in place for administration, then all routers on that network should be configured to securely participate in it. As example a Cisco router can be configured to act as a client for SNMP. When SNMP service is enabled on a router, network management tools can use it to gather information about the router configuration, route table, traffic load, and more. In the absence of a deployed SNMP scheme, all SNMP facilities on all routers should be disabled using these steps:
    1. Erase all existing community strings.
    2. Disable SNMP system shutdown and trap features.
    3. Disable SNMP system processing.

After discussing the network design processes and the security policies the below table describes some of the weakness of the security policies.

Weakness	How the weakness is exploited
Lack of written security policy	An unwritten policy cannot be consistently or enforced.
Politics	Political battles and turf wars can make it difficult to implement a consistent security
Lack of continuity	Frequent replacement of personnel can lead to an erratic approach to security
Logic access controls not applied	Poorly chosen, easily cracked, or default passwords can allow unauthorized access to the network.
Software and hardware installation and changes do not follow policy	Unauthorized changes to the network topology or installation of unapproved application create security holes.
Disaster recovery plan is nonexistent	The lack of a disaster recovery plan allows chaos, panic, and confusion to occur when someone attacks the enterprise.

Table 8.3: Common security policy weaknesses

8.10 VIRTUAL PRIVATE NETWORK DESIGN

VPN - Virtual Private Networks Most businesses want remote locations to have full access to the company network, for seamless communication and increased productivity. Until recently, small and medium-sized businesses had only two options for creating this access: a leased-line-based wide area network (WAN), or dial-in service. Now there is a less expensive and more flexible option: Virtual Private Networks (VPNs). VPNs are affordable because they operate on a portion of the public telecommunications infrastructure rather than on leased lines. Because a VPN uses the Internet, real-time access to the network is available for the price of local Internet access. VPNs are flexible because new users can be added quickly and easily, without the configuration required to add users to a private network. As technology has evolved, VPN security has increased. VPNs use encryption and tunneling to protect confidential information as it travels over the Internet. Increasingly robust and easy-to-administer firewalls and other security measures keep hackers out of a business network. The increase in VPN popularity is good news for small and medium-sized business owners because it has increased competition among Internet Service Providers (ISPs). These companies now offer guaranteed 99% uptime, credits for outages, and other services that provide the same level of reliability as leased lines.

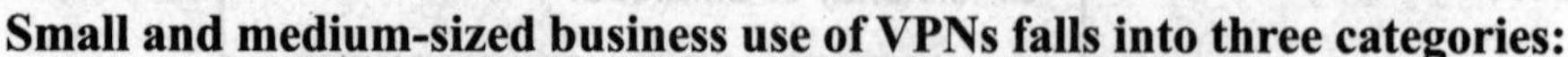

Small and medium-sized business use of VPNs falls into three categories:

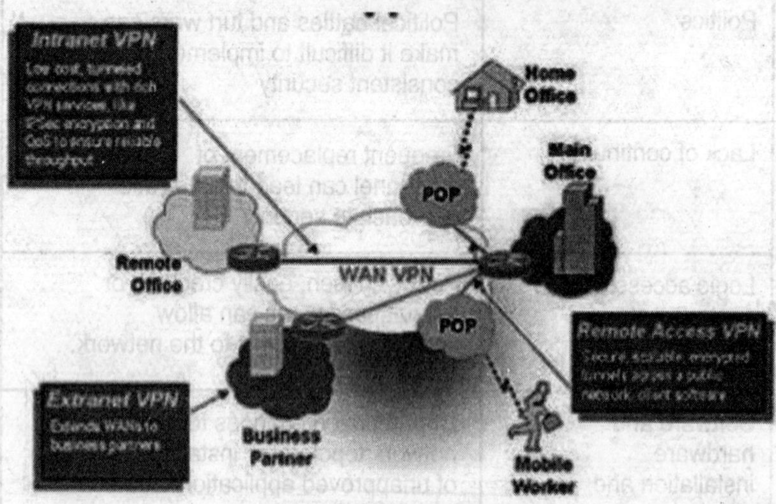

Figure 8.5: E-VPN Applications

1. Extended intranets: Use of a VPN for smaller branch offices, franchise sites, and remote workers provides nearly the same level of connectivity and reliability as a private network. Costs are lower, because Internet connections replace expensive leased lines. More desktops can gain access to the network, because a VPN allows new users to be added almost instantly. This extends the reach of the corporate intranet, so all employees can take advantage of its information and resources.

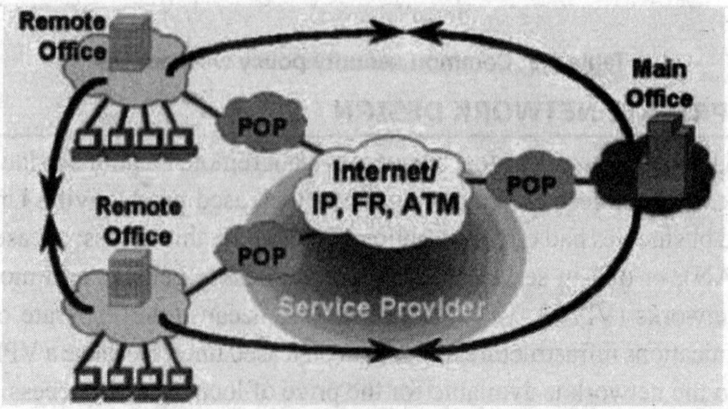

Figure 8.6: Extended intranets

2. Remote access: VPNs provide a cost-effective alternative to standard dial-in remote access to a company network. Users can connect to the network via the Internet, eliminating expensive long-distance or toll-free dial-in costs. An employee on the road can gain full network access simply by tapping into an Internet connection. Overseas offices can connect directly to the corporate database over local lines instead of a more expensive leased line.

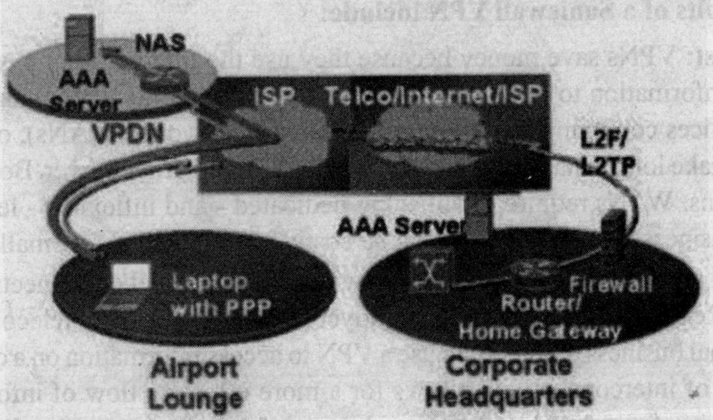

Figure 8.7: Remote Access

3. Extranets: Extending a corporate network to include customers, suppliers and other business partners enables workers to research products, place and fulfill orders, and collaborate via a secure Internet connection. By involving customers and suppliers, a VPN smoothes the transition to electronic commerce and other forms of online ordering and fulfillment. Because this business-to-business communication is done via the Internet, connection costs are low. It can enable productivity-boosting applications such as EDI, and streamline business processes such as ordering, shipping and billing. With a variety of SonicWALL's family of Internet security appliances which provide the first line of defense against Internet security threats. This includes a ICSA-certified, stateful packet inspection firewall, IPSec VPN for remote access, IP address management features, and support for SonicWALL value-added security services.

Figure 8.8: Extranets

8.11 HOW WILL A VPN BENEFIT YOUR BUSINESS?

VPN is a reliable way to maintain your company's privacy while streamlining operations, reducing costs and allowing for flexible network administration. Our VPNs are based on Sonicwall comprehensive portfolio of VPN products, from VPN-optimized routers and firewalls to dedicated VPN concentrators.

The key benefits of a Sonicwall VPN include:

1. **Lower cost:** VPNs save money because they use the Internet - not costly leased lines - to transmit information to and from authorized users. Prior to VPNs, many companies with remote offices communicated through Wide Area Networks (WANs), or by having remote workers make long distance calls to connect to the main office server. Both can be expensive propositions. WANs require establishing dedicated - and inflexible - leased lines between various business locations, which can be costly or impractical for smaller offices.
2. **Improved communications:** A VPN provides a robust level of connectivity comparable to a WAN. Remote offices, mobile employees, clients, vendors, telecommuters and even international business partners can use a VPN to access information on a company's network. This level of interconnectivity allows for a more effective flow of information between a large number of people. The VPN provides access to both extranets and wide-area intranets, which opens the door for improved client service, vendor support and company communications. Customers can order equipment over the VPN. Suppliers can check on orders electronically. Employees can collaborate on project documents.
3. **Increased flexibility:** With a VPN, customers, suppliers and remote users can be added to the network easily and quickly. Some VPN solutions simplify the process of administering the network by allowing the system's manager to implement changes from any desktop computer. Once the equipment is installed, the company simply signs up with a service provider that activates the network by giving the company a slice of its bandwidth. This is much easier than establishing a WAN, which must be designed, built and managed by the company that creates it. VPNs also easily adapt to a company's growth. These systems can connect 25 people as easily as 2,000.
4. **Security and Reliability:** VPNs maintain privacy through the use of tunneling protocols and standard security procedures. A secure VPN encrypts data before it travels through the public network and decrypts it at the receiving end. The encrypted information travels through a secure "tunnel" that connects to a company's gateway. The gateway then identifies the remote user and lets the user access only the information he or she is authorized to receive. A secure VPN can be used for the authorization of orders from suppliers, the forwarding of revised legal documents and many other confidential business processes. Recent improvements in VPN technology have also increased the system's reliability. Many service providers will guarantee 99% VPN uptime and will offer credits for unanticipated outages.
5. **Business Benefits:** Using the Network to Enable Secure Business Processes

Information security is a business concern for all organizations. With security threats increasing in number and sophistication, businesses want to gain protection, control, and visibility over their security systems, preventing incidents and threats that disrupt productivity, impact customer relationships, and erode profits. Government regulations concerning the protection of information also add to the growing emphasis on security.

The systems approach also provides greater visibility and control for overall network security, allowing organizations to operate according to security best practices and comply with government regulations.

The main benefits are:

- Minimize downtime
- Minimize data loss
- Optimum Utilization of Bandwidth
- Overcome the Geographical Barrier
- Enhancement of Human resources
- Extended Mobility
- High amount of Data Availability
- Downsize the Operational Cost

8.12 PERFORMANCE AND DESIGN CONSIDERATIONS

In designing security for your network, there are a number of tradeoffs that need to be considered, including

- **Availability:** Understand the reliability of your vendors, and if Internet access is critical to your business, redundant internet "pipes" and firewalls might be required.
- **Performance:** Separating firewall functions and selecting hardware-based vendors with better throughput or multiple firewalls might be required.
- **Security:** Dual firewall systems provide higher security but have a higher price point (benefits versus cost).
- If compromised, how will you recover?
- How will you monitor security? Regular checking of logs and automated notification of problems is a requirement.

In VPN designs, the key items to consider include

- If less than an 80-bit secret key is selected, you might be vulnerable.
- Will you use a stand-alone VPN server or integrate it into the firewall?
- Select Authentication method that meets the level of security required. (Simple UserName/ Password or MAC.)

8.13 FUTURE TRENDS IN SECURITY

What is going to drive the Internet security is the set of applications more than anything else. The Future will possibly be that the security is similar to an immune system. The immune system fights off attacks and builds itself to fight tougher enemies. Similarly, the network security will be able to function as an immune system. The trend towards biometrics could have taken place a while ago, but it seems that it isn't being actively pursued. Many security developments that are taking place are within the same set of security technology that is being used today with some minor adjustments Network security is an important field that is increasingly gaining attention as the internet expands. The security threats and internet protocol were analyzed to determine the necessary security technology. The security technology is mostly software based, but many common hardware devices are used. The current development in network security is not very impressive. Originally it was assumed that with the importance of the network security field, new approaches to security, both hardware and software, would be actively researched. It was a surprise to see most of the development taking place in the same technologies being currently used. The embedded security of the new internet protocol IPv6 may provide many benefits to internet users. Although some security issues were observed, the IPv6 internet protocol seems to evade many of the current popular attacks. Combined use of IPv6 and security tools such as firewalls, intrusion detection, and authentication mechanisms will prove effective in guarding intellectual property for the near future. The network security field may have to evolve more rapidly to deal with the threats further in the future.

EXERCISES

1. What do you mean by network security?
2. Explain the various types of security threats?
3. Explain the various methods, tools, and techniques for attacks?
4. Explain the concept of security safeguards?
5. Explain the security system in different networks?
6. Explain the various designs for network security?
7. Explain the various components of a security policy?
8. Explain the concept of router and firewall security policy?
9. Explain the concept of virtual private network design?
10. How will a VPN benefit your business?
11. Explain the concept of performance and design considerations?
12. Explain the various future trends in security?

Chapter 9

Documentation and Network Management

9.1 DOCUMENTATION AND NETWORK MANAGEMENT APPROACH

Documentation is the most important steps in any project development or network development it helps people to understand the design of the network in the past, allow them to remember and to keep record of updates and modifications to that design. So your design document should include the logical and physical components of the design, information on technologies and devices, and a proposal for implementing the design. The following sections describe the topics that should be included in a comprehensive design document.

In this section, we introduce the main functions that should be included in a network management system and give a brief introduction to popular and well-known network management and system management approaches including *Simple Network Management Protocol,* Remote Monitoring and new approaches *Policy-based Network Management and Web-based Enterprise Management* approaches.

9.2 EXECUTIVE SUMMARY

A comprehensive design document can be many pages in length. For this reason, it is essential that you include at the beginning of the document an Executive Summary that succinctly states the major points of the document. The Executive Summary should be no more than one page and should be targeted at the managers and key project participants who will decide whether to accept your design.

Although the Executive Summary can include some technical information, it should not provide technical details. The goal of the summary is to sell the decision-makers on the business benefits of your design. Technical information should be summarized and organized in order of the customer's highest-priority objectives for the design project.

9.3 PROJECT GOAL

This section should state the primary goal for the network design project. The goal should be business oriented and related to an overall objective that the organization has to become more successful in its core business. The Project Goal section should be no more than one paragraph; it often can be written as a single sentence. Writing it carefully will give you a chance to make it obvious to the decision-makers reading the document that you understand the primary purpose and importance of the network design project.

An example of a project goal that was written for an actual design customer follows:

The goal of this project is to develop a wide-area network (WAN) that will support new high-bandwidth and low-delay multimedia applications. The new applications are key to the successful implementation of new training programs for the sales force. The new WAN should facilitate the goal of increasing sales in the United States by 50 percent in the next fiscal year.

9.4 PROJECT SCOPE

The Project Scope section provides information on the extent of the project, including a summary of the departments and networks that will be affected by the project. The Project Scope section specifies whether the project is for a new network or modifications to an existing network. It indicates whether the design is for a single network segment, a set of LANs, a building or campus network, a set of WAN or remote-access networks, or possibly the whole enterprise network.

An example of a Project Scope section follows:

The scope of this project is to update the existing WAN that connects all major sales offices in the United States to corporate headquarters. The new WAN will be accessed by sales, marketing, and training employees. It is beyond the scope of this project to update any LANs that these employees use. It is also beyond the scope of this project to update the networks in satellite and telecommuter offices.

The scope of the project might intentionally not cover some matters. For example, fixing performance problems with a particular application might be intentionally beyond the scope of the project. By stating up front the assumptions you made about the scope of the project, you can avoid any perception that your solution inadvertently fails to address certain concerns.

9.5 DESIGN REQUIREMENTS

Whereas the Project Goal section is generally very short, the Design Requirements section is your opportunity to list all the major business and technical requirements for the network design. The Design Requirements section should list the goals in priority order. Critical goals should be marked as such.

9.5.1 BUSINESS GOALS

Business goals explain the role the network design will play in helping an organization provide better products and services to its customers. Executives who read the design document will be more likely to accept the network design if they recognize from the Business Goals section that the network designer understands the organization's business mission.

Many network designers have a hard time writing the Business Goals section because they are more interested in technical goals. However, it is critical that you focus your network design document on the ability of your design to help a customer solve real-world business problems.

As discussed most businesses embark on a network design project to help them increase revenue, reduce operational costs and inefficiencies, and improve corporate communications. Other typical goals include building partnerships with other companies and expanding into worldwide markets. At this point in the network design process, you should have a comprehensive understanding of your customer's business goals and be able to list them in the design document in priority order

9.5.2 TECHNICAL GOALS

The Technical Goals section documents the following goals "Analyzing Technical Goals and Tradeoffs:"

- **Scalability:** How much growth a network design must support.
- **Availability:** The amount of time a network is available to users, often expressed as a percent uptime, or as a mean time between failure (MTBF) and mean time to repair (MTTR). Availability documentation can also include any information gathered on the monetary cost associated with network downtime.
- **Network performance:** The customer's criteria for accepting the service level of a network, including its throughput, accuracy, efficiency, delay, delay variation (jitter), and response time. Specific throughput requirements for internetworking devices, in packets per second (PPS), can also be stated. Specific throughput requirements for applications should be included in the Applications section.
- **Security:** General and specific goals for protecting the organization's ability to conduct business without interference from intruders inappropriately accessing or damaging equipment, data, or operations. This section should also list the various security risks that the customer identified during the requirements-analysis phase of the design project.
- **Manageability:** General and specific goals for performance, fault, configuration, security, and accounting management.
- **Usability:** The ease with which network users can access the network and its services. This section can include information on goals for simplifying user tasks related to network addressing, naming, and resource discovery.
- **Adaptability:** The ease with which a network design and implementation can adapt to network faults, changing traffic patterns, additional business or technical requirements, new business practices, and other changes.
- **Affordability:** General information on the importance of containing the costs associated with purchasing and operating network equipment and services. Specific budget information should be included in the Project Budget section.

The Technical Goals section should also describe any tradeoffs the customer is willing to make. For example, some customers might indicate that affordability can be sacrificed to meet strict availability goals, or usability can be sacrificed to meet strict security goals.

9.6 NETWORK APPLICATIONS

The Network Applications section lists and characterizes the new and existing network applications. Information about applications can be summarized in the "Network Applications Technical Requirements" chart shown in Table 9.1, and in the "Network Applications Traffic Characteristics" chart shown in Table 9.2. If you want, you can merge these two tables so that there is just one row for each application

Table 9.1: Network Applications Technical Requirements

Name of Application	Type of Application	New Application? (Yes or No)	Criticality	Cost of Downtime	Acceptable MTBF

Table 9.2: Network Applications Traffic Characteristics

Name of Application	Type of Traffic Flow	Protocol (s) Used by Application	User Communities That Use the Application	Data Stores (Servers, Hosts, and So On)	Approximate Bandwidth for the Application	QoS Requirement

9.7 CURRENT STATE OF THE NETWORK

This section briefly describes the structure and performance of the existing network. It should include a high-level network map that identifies the location of major internetworking devices, data processing and storage systems, and network segments. The high-level map should document the names and addresses of major devices and segments and indicate the types and lengths of principal network segments. For very large internetworks, two or three high-level maps might be necessary. Detailed maps, however, should be placed in the Appendix rather than in this section.

The network maps should include logical as well as physical components (for example, the location and reach of any virtual private networks (VPNs), virtual LANs (VLANs), firewall segments, server clusters, and so on). The maps should also characterize the logical topology of the internetwork and the networks that make up the internetwork. Network drawings, or text associated with drawings, should indicate whether networks are hierarchical or flat, structured or unstructured, layered or not, and so on. They should also indicate network geometry (for example, star, ring, bus, hub and spoke, or mesh). The documentation of the current state of the network also briefly describes any strategies or standards your customer uses for network addressing and device naming. If the customer uses (or plans to use) address-summarization techniques, for example, this should be indicated in the design document.

A major portion of the Current State of the Network section of the network design document should be dedicated to an analysis of the health and performance of the present network.

Detailed reports (for example, 1-minute network-utilization charts) can be placed in the Appendix of the design document to avoid overwhelming the reader with too much information at this stage. It is important that the reader be able to quickly reach the Logical Design and Physical Design sections of the document, because those sections contain the essence of your design proposal.

9.7.1 LOGICAL DESIGN

The Logical Design section documents the following aspects of your network design:

- The network topology, including one or more drawings that illustrate the logical architecture of the new network.
- A model for addressing network segments and devices.
- A model for naming network devices.
- A list of the routing, bridging, and switching protocols that have been selected to implement the design and any specific implementation recommendations associated with those protocols.
- Recommended security mechanisms and products, including a summary of security policies and procedures. (If a detailed security plan was developed as part of the network design, it can be submitted as an addendum to the design document.)
- Recommended network-management architectures, processes, and products.
- Design rationale, outlining why various choices were made, in light of the customer's goals and the current state of the network.

Note: Not all designs include all these components. Based on your customer's requirements, you should recognize whether it is necessary to address all the issues included in the preceding list in your network design document.

9.7.2 PHYSICAL DESIGN

The Physical Design section describes the features and recommended uses for the technologies and devices you selected to implement the design. It can include information for campus networks and remote-access and wide-area networks. This section can also include information about any service providers selected.

If appropriate, the Physical Design section should include information on the pricing for network devices and services. Sometimes pricing is negotiable and is not appropriate to include in the design document. In most cases, however, customers expect to see product and service pricing in the design document.

The Physical Design section should also contain information on the availability of products. If your design recommends products that are not yet shipping, you should document a predicted ship date, as provided by the product vendor.

9.8 RESULTS OF NETWORK DESIGN TESTING

This section describes the results of the testing that you did to verify your network design. It is one of the most important portions of the design document because it gives you a chance to prove to your customer that your design will likely meet requirements for performance, security, usability, manageability, and so on. You can describe any prototype or pilot systems that you implemented and the following testing components:

- Test objectives
- Test acceptance criteria
- Testing tools
- Test scripts
- Results and observations

In the Results and Observations segment, be sure to include any optimization techniques you recommend be applied to the design to ensure that it meets requirements. Based on the results of your testing, you might recommend mechanisms for minimizing broadcast and multicast traffic, advanced features for meeting quality of service (QoS) requirements, and sophisticated router switching and queuing services.

9.9 IMPLEMENTATION PLAN

The Implementation Plan includes your recommendations for deploying the network design. The level of detail in this section varies from project to project, and depends on your relationship to your customer.

If you are a member of an Information Systems (IS) department that is responsible for the design and implementation of the new network, then this section should be quite detailed. If you are a sales engineer for a vendor of networking products, on the other hand, your role is probably to recommend solutions but not implement them, so this section should be short. (You should avoid appearing as if you are telling your customers how to do their jobs.)

The following topics are suitable for the Implementation Plan section:

- A project schedule.
- Plans with vendors or service providers for the installation of links, equipment, or services.
- Plans or recommendations for outsourcing the implementation or management of the network.
- A plan for communicating the design to end users, network administrators, and management. This section can also explain how implementation progress will be communicated (possibly via regularly scheduled status meetings or e-mail messages).
- A training plan for network administrators and end users.
- A plan for measuring the effectiveness of the design after it has been implemented.
- A list of known risks that could delay the project.

- A fallback plans if the network implementation fails.
- A plan for evolving the network design as new application requirements and goals arise.

9.9.1 PROJECT SCHEDULE

The Implementation Plan should include a project schedule or timeline. The level of detail you include in a schedule depends on your role on the project. In general, the schedule should at least include the dates and deliverables for major milestones. Table 9.3 shows an example of a high-level schedule that was developed by a sales engineer for an actual customer.

Table 9.3: High-level schedule developed for a network design customer.

Date of Completion	Milestone
June 1	Design completed and a beta version of the design document distributed to key executives, managers, network administrators, and end users
June 15	Comments on the design document due
June 22	Final design document distributed
June 25	Installation of leased lines between all buildings completed by WAN service provider
June 28-29	Network administrators trained on new system
June 30-July 1	End users trained on new system
July 6	Pilot implementation completed in Building 1
July 20	Feedback received on pilot from network administrators and end users
July 27	Implementation completed in Buildings 2-5
August 10	Feedback received on Buildings 2-5 implementation from network administrators and end users
August 17	Implementation completed in the rest of the buildings
Ongoing	New system monitored to verify that it meets goals

9.9.2 PROJECT BUDGET

The Project Budget section should document the funds the customer has available for equipment purchases, maintenance and support agreements, service contracts, software licenses, training, and staffing. The budget can also include consulting fees and outsourcing expenses.

9.9.3 RETURN ON INVESTMENT

In many cases the best way to sell a customer on a new network design is to convince the customer that the design will pay for itself in a reasonable time period. The network design document can include a return-on-investment (ROI) analysis that explains how quickly the design or new equipment will pay for itself.

Following is an example of an ROI that was completed for an actual customer, Customer ABC. The goal of this ROI analysis was to prove to the customer that the recommended WAN switching equipment will pay for itself very quickly because it will allow the customer to decrease the number of required T1 lines, and thus reduce the cost of leasing those lines from the local phone company.

ROI Analysis for Customer ABC

Customer ABC is considering spending $1 million on new WAN switching equipment.

If Customer ABC does not spend the $1 million on equipment and instead puts the money into other investments for 5 years, Company ABC can earn approximately 5 percent interest, and the original $1 million would be worth $1.05 million. This means that the investment in the equipment should actually be considered $1.05 million.

An assumption was made that the WAN switching equipment will have a 5-year life span before it is obsolete. So, the cost per year for owning the equipment was calculated as $1.05 million divided by 5, or $210,000. The cost per month for owning the equipment is $210,000 divided by 12, or $17,500.

The monthly cost must be compared to the cost of owning the existing time-division multiplexers (TDMs) that comprise the current design. That cost is 0 because the TDMs are old and fully paid for and depreciated.

However, the cost of operating the old network must be compared to the cost of operating the new network. The new design will make it possible for Customer ABC to use 8 T1 lines instead of the 20 T1 lines required in the old design. Each line costs Customer ABC $1500 per month. This means that 20 lines cost $30,000 per month, and 8 lines cost $12,000 per month.

The savings to Customer ABC with the new network design is $30,000 - $12,000, or $18,000 per month. Considering that the cost for the new equipment is approximately $17,500 per month, a conclusion can be drawn that the equipment will pay for itself.

9.9.4 DESIGN DOCUMENT APPENDIX

Most design documents include one or more appendixes that present supplemental information about the design and implementation. Supplemental information can include detailed topology maps, device configurations, network addressing and naming details, and comprehensive results from the testing of the network design.

You can also include business information such as a list of contacts at the customer's site and in your organization, including e-mail addresses, phone numbers, beeper numbers, and physical addresses. Information on where to ship equipment and any special shipping requirements or procedures is a useful addition in some cases.

If necessary, the Appendix can include exact information on pricing and payment options. Sometimes copies of purchase orders are included. The Appendix can also contain legal and contractual terms and conditions, and nondisclosure agreements.

Some design documents include information about the company presenting the design proposal, including pages from annual reports, product catalogs, or recent press releases favorable to the company. The goal of this type of information is to make sure the reader understands that the company is qualified to develop and implement the proposed network design. If appropriate, this section can include recommendations from other customers for whom the company has provided a solution.

9.10 NETWORK MANAGEMENT SYSTEM

At the earliest, the network is used to printer sharing, so the scale of network is not very large. The main work of network management is connection and configuration between hardware. But the evolution of computer network, network management not only being the monitoring facilities, it needs more efficient monitor and network status control methods to maintain system for daily operation and make a network have its maximum efficiency. For example, if a network is separate to several areas or sub networks, the operator must start up related link by configure routing table according to IP, sub network and subnet mask.

The goal of network management is detect potential problems. Network management must correct problems before system breakdown, reduce the complexity of network management and ensure the maximum rate of packet transmission.

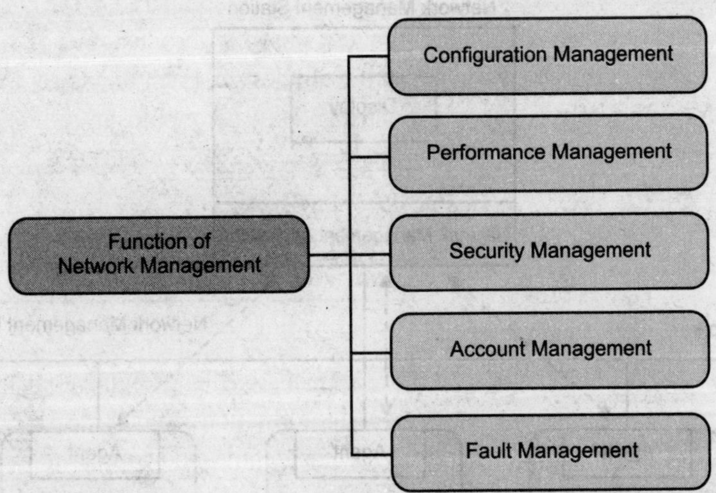

Figure 9.1: Typical Network Management System Functionality

There are five functions of network management were defined by the ISO (The International Organization for Standardization) in the document of ISO 7498-4, it shows in Figure 9.1:

- **Configuration Management:** Record and maintain network configuration, parameter updating for ensuring correct network operation.
- **Fault Management:** Finding problems or errors from network. Including detection and repair.
- **Security Management:** Control the process of message access in the network. Provide protection for network resources, services and data to avoid danger. It also provides user privacy.

- **Performance Management:** Including performance measurement of hardware, software and the media of transmission in the network. For example, Input, Output flow, error rate.
- **Accounting Management:** Handle users charging record by using personal network usage log, and provide necessary service for users when he on the network.

9.11 COMMON NETWORK MANAGEMENT ARCHITECTURE

In this session, we discuss a common architecture of network management. Figure 9.2 depicts the basic network management architecture. The management station is mainly consisted of display and network management application components. Display displays the information to the operators and gets control from operators, whereas the network management application communicates with the agent to get information from the managed devices. Agent serves as the broker between the management station and managed device, which implements a specific protocol for communication, for example, SNMP. This architecture simplifies the management application design by separating the design of "managed-device part" and the "managing part".

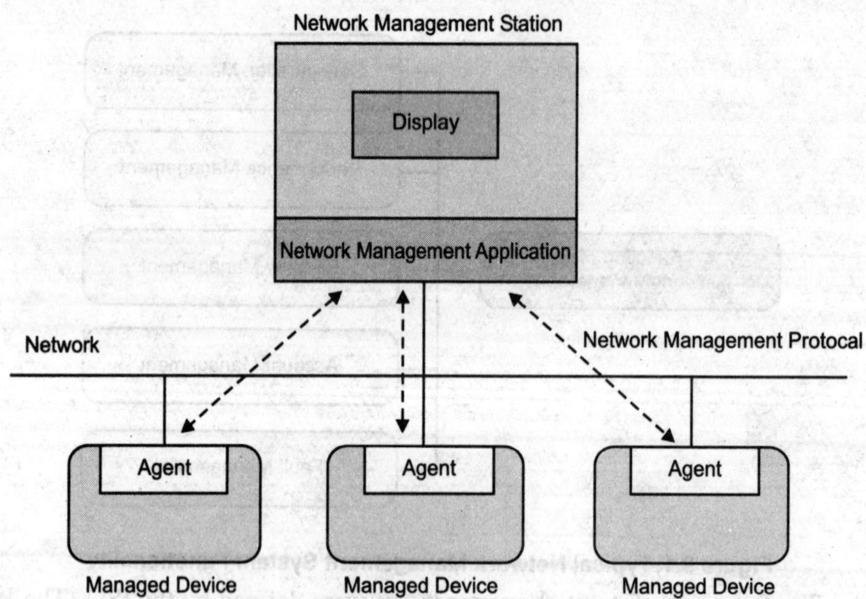

Figure 9.2: Typical two tier structure for network management

We can get specifically understand from Figure 9.3 to know a client-server model that provides stack of communication protocol and interface between networks. When the Network Management Program send a request, Network Management Protocol encapsulate the request and through encapsulation in each layer. The request will be arrived in managed device and unpacked in each layer and agent can know what data the Network Management Program wants to know. Agent encapsulates the data into a packet by the same method and sends the packet to the Network Management Program.

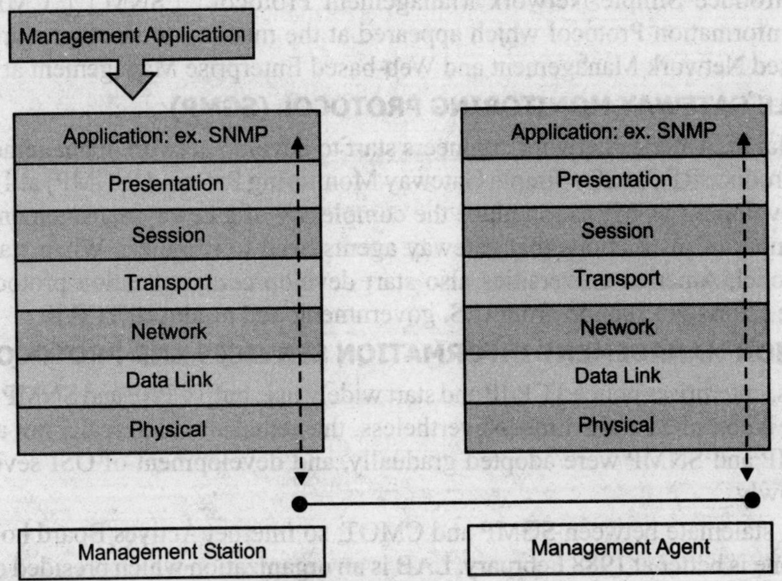

Figure 9.3: Relation to the stack of communication protocol and network

9.12 NETWORK MANAGEMENT APPROACHES

In this session, we introduce the histories of some network management protocols. We will put our focus on Simple Network Management Protocol, Policy-based Network Management and Web-Based Enterprise Management.

9.12.1 HISTORY NETWORK MANAGEMENT APPROACHES

Figure 9.4 illustrates the evolution of network management approaches.

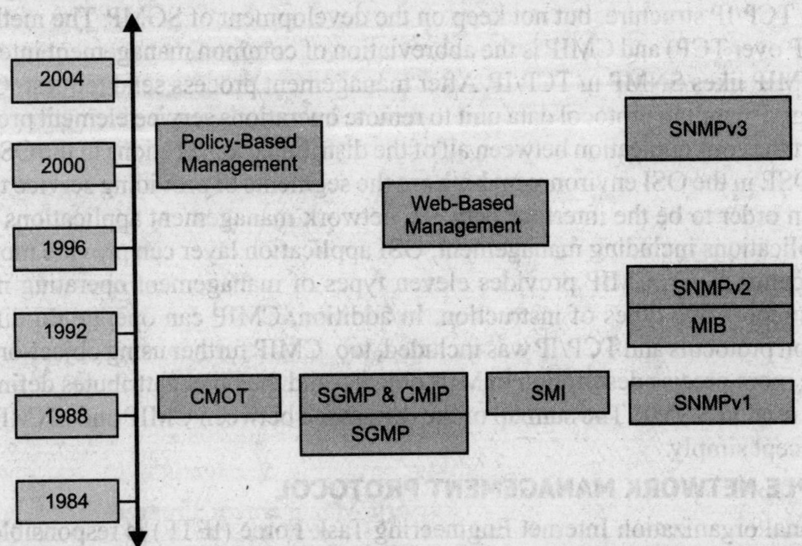

Figure 9.4: Relation to the stack of communication protocol and network

Mainly introduce Simple Network Management Protocol □ SNM □, CMIP □ Common Management Information Protocol which appeared at the medium term of network management, and Policy-based Network Management and Web-based Enterprise Management at nowadays.

9.12.2 SIMPLE GATEWAY MONITORING PROTOCOL (SGMP)

At 1987 March, America network engineers start to develop network management protocol for gateway, and produce RFC1028 - Simple Gateway Monitoring Protocol (SGMP) at 1987 November. The goal of developing SGMP is to reduce the complexity of gateway management software, and reduce the number of instructions that gateway agents need to response. When start develop OSI seven-layer model, America universities also start develop communication protocol at the same time, and these efforts got support from U.S. government, and produced TCP/IP.

9.12.3 COMMON MANAGEMENT INFORMATION SERVICES AND PROTOCOL (CMIP)

Afterwards, enterprises notice TCP/IP and start widely use; but TCP/IP and SNMP just a substitute for OSI before it complete at the time. Nevertheless, the actual situation really not accord with our thought. TCP/IP and SNMP were adopted gradually, and development of OSI seven-layer model was getting slowly.

It lead to a stalemate between SGMP and CMOT, so Internet Actives Board hold a meeting to decide which one is better at 1988 February. LAB is an organization which presided over all internet research and development in the America. And the conclusion of the session is that both of these two methods should keep on development. However, the consolidation version of SGMP, SNMP, is start developing. Many organizations invested in SNMP definition one after another. A network management organization was established for engaging in internet standards, and they chose SNMP.

Even though that TCP/IP and SNMP is the main of the communication protocol and the network management protocol, but OSI seven-layer model and CMIP are still in use. Common Management Information Services and Protocol, it defined in the ISO 7498.4 document. Because of appearance of OSI network structure, America research organizations think the long-term way out should be give first place to OSI network structure. Therefore, they thought OSI network management protocol should add to TCP/IP structure, but not keep on the development of SGMP. The method was called CMOT (CMIP over TCP) and CMIP is the abbreviation of common management interface protocol. The role of CMIP likes SNMP in TCP/IP. After management process send request, CMIP establish protocol unit and mapping protocol data unit to remotc operations service element protocol (ROSE). ROSE support the communication between all of the distributed applications in the OSI environment. CMIP and ROSE in the OSI environment both are the segments of providing service to management applications in order to be the interface between network management applications and protocols. For every applications including management, OSI application layer can provide more service than TCP/IP application layer. CMIP provides eleven types of management operating instruction, but SNMP only support five types of instruction. In addition, CMIP can operate on different kind of communication protocols and TCP/IP was included, too. CMIP further using object-oriented concept to provide the more precise description to MIB objects, and the object attributes defined in are more than the MIB used in SNMP. The sum up of the difference between CMIP and SNMP is that SNMP keeps the concept simply.

9.12.4 SIMPLE NETWORK MANAGEMENT PROTOCOL

The national organization Internet Engineering Task Force (IETF) is responsible to define the protocol for Internet traffic control which including SNMP. The IETF will issue RFCs (Request for

Comments) to standardize protocols which were used in IP region. The Structure of Management Information (SMI) was defined in RFC1155, and the data structure of SMI which called Management information base (MIB) was defined in RFC1156. And IETF defined the SNMP version one in RFC 1157; it has already been the standard of TCP/IP network management in practice.

9.12.4.1 MANAGER AND AGENT OF SNMP

As the structure presented in section 9.11, there are two entities in SNMP - Manager and Agent. A manager is a server which executes specific programs to manage networks. An agent is a tiny-software which works in the network device that we managed. We present the relation to Network Management System (NMS) and its agents in Figure 9.5

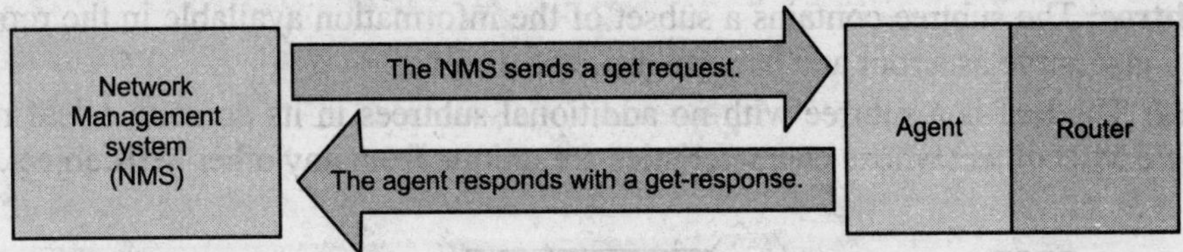

Figure 9.5: Network Management System (NMS) and its agents

1. AGENTS

Agents are any devices on the network that need to be managed and that have the SNMP protocol and the Management Information Base. Agents monitor the desired objects in their environment, package this information in the appropriate manner, and send it to the management station either immediately or upon request. Information is generated by the Agent, stored in its MIB, and made available to the Manager. Proxy Agents act on behalf of a device that has not implemented SNMP.

2. MANAGER

A manager program, which normally executes on a network server, exchanges messages with the agent to access the agent's MIB. The manager reads from, and writes to, objects in the MIB according to predefined access privileges that have been assigned to the MIB objects.

SNMP defines the protocols and message formats used to perform the read and write operations; these are called gets and sets, respectively.

9.13 THE MIB

The Management Information Base (MIB) contains data available to a network management program. MIBs are created by management agents so that each machine with an agent will have an associated MIB. The network manager will query these MIBs and may even have a management MIB of its own. The management MIB contains general information and the individual MIB contains machine-specific information. The MIB is the definition of the data, or objects, that are stored in the agent for the manager to access.

9.13.1 MIB OBJECTS

Agent MIB objects can include values that describe the status, statistics, and general operating parameters of the device. The agent contains the objects that are polled by the network manager and the objects contain data that the manager can collect and display such as:

- Interface Information
- IP datagrams
- UDP datagrams

Most networking devices that support SNMP support MIB II. As MIB II is a published set of data definitions, any SNMP Manager can access MIB II data. V vendors have also created their own sets of definitions, called custom MIBs, so that their own Managers can gather more product-specific information than is available from MIB II.

9.13.2 STRUCTURE OF THE MIB

The standard MIB's structure is represented by a tree. There are three components of the tree:

- **Root:** The unnamed root of the tree contains a set of characters common to all MIB objects located beneath that root. Objects beneath "unnamed" are said to be in that root's domain.
- **Subtree:** The subtree contains a subset of the information available in the root; a subtree may also serve as a root and have subtrees of its own.
- **Leaf:** The leaf is a subtree with no additional subtrees in its domain; a leaf represents a single MIB object whose characteristics are unique from any other MIB object.

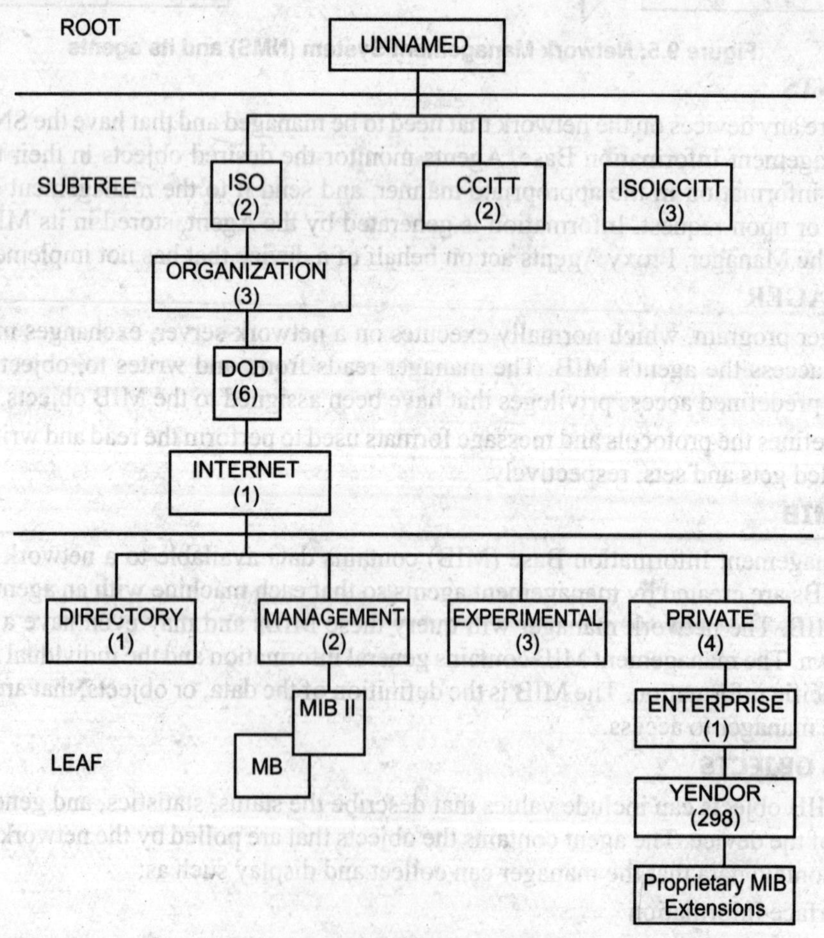

Figure 9.6: Structure of the MIB

Each MIB object can be located by following a path from "unnamed," through the subtrees, to the leaf. In order to simplify finding an individual MIB object, the paths are defined by a sequence of numbers.

9.13.3 SNMP PROTOCOL DATA UNITS

Information is passed between layers in the form of packets, known as protocol data units (PDUs). The packet size and definition depends on the protocol suite involved in the horizontal communications.

The SNMP PDUs are five commands, or operations, implemented by SNMP. They are used between the Agent and the Manager to pass information and make requests. They are:

- **GetRequest:** issued by the Manager to the Agent to request information about a particular object; fetches a value from a specific variable.
- **GetNextRequest:** issued by the Manager to the Agent to request information about the next object in the MIB; fetches a value without knowing the exact name.
- **GetResponse:** issued by the Agent to the Manager in response to a Get command; replies to a fetch operation; the agent returns the requested information to the Manager with this command.
- **SetRequest:** sets a variable in the MIB at the Agent.
- **Traps:** issued by an Agent to the Manager to report a significant network event.

9.13.4 TRAPS

A trap is issued by an Agent to the Manager to report a significant network event. These events are defined in RFC 1098.

The following are some generic traps:

- **ColdStart:** agent is initialising or re-initialising itself; objects may be altered.
- **WarmStart:** agent is re-initialising itself, but objects will not be altered.
- **LinkDown:** attached interface has changed from the up to the down state.
- **LinkUp:** attached interface has changed to the up state.
- **AuthenticationFailure:** wrong community string used.

Other traps include:

- **Enterprise:** value of the agent's sysObjectID.
- **Agent-addr:** value of the agent's NetworkAddress.
- **Specific-trap:** identifies the enterpriseSpecific trap.
- **Time-stamp:** value of the agent's sysUpTime MIB object.
- Variable-bindings: list of variables containing information about the trap.
- **Vendor-specific:** traps that are added by the device vendor.

9.14 SNMPV2

SNMP version 2 (SNMPv2) is an evolution of the SNMPv1. The Get, GetNext, and Set operations used in SNMPv1 are exactly the same as those used in SNMPv2. However, SNMPv2 adds and enhances some protocol operations. The SNMPv2 Trap operation, for example, serves the same function as that used in SNMPv1, but it uses a different message format and is designed to replace the SNMPv1 Trap.

SNMPv2 also defines two new operations: GetBulk and Inform. The GetBulk operation is used to efficiently retrieve large blocks of data. The Inform operation allows one NMS to send trap information to another NMS and to then receive a response. In SNMPv2, if the agent responding to GetBulk operations cannot provide values for all the variables in a list, it provides partial results

9.14.1 PROTOCOL STRUCTURE: SNMPV2 SIMPLE NETWORK MANAGEMENT PROTOCOL VERSION 2

The general formats for all SNMP versions are similar except the format of PDU (Protocol Data Unit). The format of the PDU for SNMPv2 is displayed as follows:

For SNMPv2, Get, GetNext, Inform, Response, Set, and Trap PDUs have the following format:

PDU type Request ID Error status Error index Object 1, value 1 Object 2, value 2 ...

- **PDU type:** Identifies the type of PDU transmitted (Get, GetNext, Inform, Response, Set, or Trap).
- **Request ID:** Associates SNMP requests with responses.
- **Error status:** Indicates one of a number of errors and error types. Only the response operation sets this field. Other operations set this field to zero.
- **Error index:** Associates an error with a particular object instance. Only the response operation sets this field. Other operations set this field to zero.
- **Variable bindings:** Serves as the data field (value 1, value 2¡) of the SNMPv2 PDU. Each variable binding associates a particular object instance with its current value (with the exception of Get and GetNext requests, for which the value is ignored).

SNMPv2 GetBulk PDU Format:

PDU type Request ID Non repeaters Max repetitions Obj 1,Val 1 Obj 1, Val 1 ...

- **PDU type:** Identifies the PDU as a GetBulk operation.
- **Request ID:** Associates SNMP requests with responses.
- **Non repeaters:** Specifies the number of object instances in the variable bindings field that should be retrieved no more than once from the beginning of the request. This field is used when some of the instances are scalar objects with only one variable.
- **Max repetitions:** Defines the maximum number of times that other variables beyond those specified by the Non repeaters field should be retrieved.
- **Variable bindings:** Serves as the data field (Obj 1, Obj 2 ¡) of the SNMPv2 PDU. Each variable binding associates a particular object instance with its current value (with the exception of Get and GetNext requests, for which the value is ignored).

9.15 SNMP V3

SNMP Version 3 (SNMPv3) adds security and remote configuration capabilities to the previous versions. The SNMPv3 architecture introduces the User-based Security Model (USM) for message security and the View-based Access Control Model (VACM) for access control. The architecture supports the concurrent use of different security, access control, and message processing models. More specifically:

- Security
- authentication and privacy
- authorization and access control
- Administrative Framework
- naming of entities
- people and policies
- usernames and key management
- notification destinations
- proxy relationships
- remotely configurable via SNMP operations

SNMPv3 also introduces the ability to dynamically configure the SNMP agent using SNMP SET commands against the MIB objects that represent the agent's configuration. This dynamic configuration support enables addition, deletion, and modification of configuration entries either locally or remotely.

9.15.1 PROTOCOL STRUCTURE: SNMPV3 SIMPLE NETWORK MANAGEMENT PROTOCOL VERSION 3

SNMPv3 message format:

Msg Processed by MPM (Msg Processing Model)					
Version	ID	Msg Size	Msg Flag	Security Model	
Msg Processed by USM (User Security Module)					
Authoritative Engin ID	Authoritative Boots	Authoritative Engine Time	User name	Authentication Parameter	Privacy parameters
Scoped PDU					
Context engine ID	Context name	PDU			

- **Version:** For SNMPv3 it is 3.
- **ID:** A unique identifier used between two SNMP entities to coordinate request and response messages
- **Msg Size:** Maximum size of a message in octets supported by the sender of the message
- **Msg Flags:** An octet string containing three flags in the least significant three bits: reportableFlag, privFlag, authFlag.
- **Security Model:** An identifier to indicate which security model was used by the sender and therefore which security model must be used by the receiver to process this message.

- **AuthoritativeEngineID:** The snmpEngineID of the authoritative SNMP engine involved in the exchange of this message. Thus, this value refers to the source for a Trap, Response, or Report, and to the destination for a Get, GetNext, GetBulk, Set, or Inform.
- **AuthoritativeEngineBoots:** The snmpEngineBoots value of the authoritative SNMP engine involved in the exchange of this message.
- **AuthoritativeEngineTime:** The snmpEngineTime value of the authoritative SNMP engine involved in the exchange of this message.
- **User Name:** The user (principal) on whose behalf the message is being exchanged.
- AuthenticationParameters: Null if authentication is not being used for this exchange. Otherwise, this is an authentication parameter.
- **PrivacyParameters:** Null if privacy is not being used for this exchange. Otherwise, this is a privacy parameter.
- **PDU (Protocol Data Unit):** The PDU types for SNMPv3 are the same as the SNMPv2.

9.16 RMON: REMOTE MONITORING MIBS (RMON1 AND RMON2)

Remote Monitoring (RMON) is a standard monitoring specification that enables various network monitors and console systems to exchange network-monitoring data. RMON provides network administrators with more freedom in selecting network-monitoring probes and consoles with features that meet their particular networking needs.

RMON was originally developed to address the problem of managing LAN segments and remote sites from a central location. The RMON specification, which is an extension of the SNMP MIB, is a standard monitoring specification. Within an RMON network monitoring data is defined by a set of statistics and functions and exchanged between various different monitors and console systems. Resultant data is used to monitor network utilization for network planning and performance-tuning, as well as assisting in network fault diagnosis.

There are 2 versions of RMON: RMON1 (RMONv1) and RMON2 (RMONv2). RMON1 defined 10 MIB groups for basic network monitoring, which can now be found on most modern network hardware. RMON2 (RMONv2) is an extension of RMON that focuses on higher layers of traffic above the medium access-control (MAC) layer. RMON2 has an emphasis on IP traffic and application-level traffic. RMON2 allows network management applications to monitor packets on all network layers. This is difference from RMON which only allows network monitoring at MAC layer or below.

RMON solutions are comprised of two components: a probe (or an agent or a monitor), and a client, usually a management station. Agents store network information within their RMON MIB and are normally found as embedded software on network hardware such as routers and switches although they can be a program running on a PC. Agents can only see the traffic that flows through them so they must be placed on each LAN segment or WAN link that is to be monitored. Clients, or management stations, communicate with the RMON agent or probe, using SNMP to obtain and correlate RMON data.

Now, there are a number of variations to the RMON MIB. For example, the Token Ring RMON MIB provides objects specific to managing Token Ring networks. The SMON MIB extends RMON by providing RMON analysis for switched networks.

9.16.1 PROTOCOL STRUCTURE - RMON: REMOTE MONITORING MIBS (RMON1 AND RMON2)

The RMON1 and RMON2 are focused at different network layers:

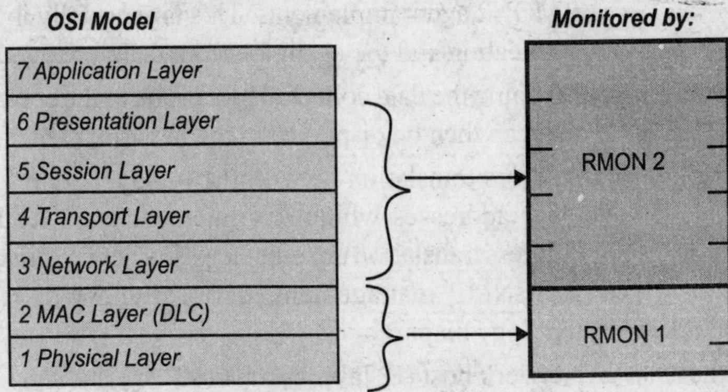

Figure 9.7: Protocol Structure

RMON 1 MIB Group	Function	Elements
Statistics	Contains statistics measured by the probe for each monitored interface on this device.	Packets dropped, packets sent, bytes sent (octets), broadcast packets, multicast packets, CRC errors, runts, giants, fragments, jabbers, collisions, and counters for packets ranging from 64 to 128, 128 to 256, 256 to 512, 512 to 1024, and 1024 to 1518 bytes.
History	Records periodic statistical samples from a network and stores for retrieval.	
Alarm	Periodically takes statistical samples and compares them with set thresholds for events generation.	Sample period, number of samples, items sampled.
Host	Contains statistics associated with each host discovered on the network.	Includes the alarm table and requires the implementation of the event group. Alarm type, interval, starting threshold, stop threshold.
HostTopN	Prepares tables that describe the top hosts.	Host address, packets, and bytes received and transmitted, as well as broadcast, multicast, and error packets.
Matrix	Stores and retrieves statistics for conversations between sets of two addresses.	Statistics, host(s), sample start and stop periods, rate base, and duration.
Filters	Enables packets to be matched by a filter equation for capturing or events.	Source and destination address pairs and packets, bytes, and errors for each pair.
Packet Capture	Enables packets to be captured after they flow through a channel.	Bit-filter type (mask or not mask), filter expression (bit level), conditional expression (and, or not) to other filters.
Events	Controls the generation and notification of events from this device.	Size of buffer for captured packets, full status (alarm), number of captured packets.
Token Ring	Support of Token Ring	Event type, description, last time event sent (not used often)

RMON 2 MIB Group	Functions
Protocol Directory	The Protocol Directory is a simple and interoperable way for an RMON2 application to establish which protocols a particular RMON2 agent implements. This is especially important when the application and the agent are from different vendors
Protocol Distribution	Mapping the data collected by a probe to the correct protocol name that can then be displayed to the network manager.
Address mapping	Address translation between MAC-layer addresses and network-layer addresses which are much easier to read and remember. Address translation not only helps the network manager, it supports the SNMP management platform and will lead to improved topology maps.
Network Layer host	Network host (IP layer) statistics
Network layer matrix	Stores and retrieves network layer (IP layer) statistics for conversations between sets of two addresses.
Application layer host	Application host statistic
Application layer matrix	Stores and retrieves application layer statistics for conversations between sets of two addresses.
User history	This feature enables the network manager to configure history studies of any counter in the system, such as a specific history on a particular file server or a router-to-router connection
Probe configuration	This RMON2, feature enable one vendor's RMON application to remotely configure another vendor's RMON probe.

9.17 POLICY-BASED NETWORK MANAGEMENT (PBNM)

Policy-based Network Management, the term policy was first used for the routing policies in the Internet, it is a concept. In 1996, IETF develops a protocol called Common Open Policy Service (COPS) that used to resource reservation (QoS). In 1998, Microsoft and Cisco propose the Directory Enabled Networks (DEN). At the end of 1998, the companies involved in DEN migrate the work to the DMTF (Distributed Management Task Force). The DMTF defines a common information model (CIM) that was originally intended to be used to describe the characteristics of a computer. Because the Policy-Based Network Management needs information model in order to decide policies,

PBNM is a condition action response mechanism and an abstraction and translation mechanism. It is used to provide an automatic response to condition in the network according to pre-defined policies. Define goals not device configurations. Changes in policy lead to changes in goals not implementations. Policy-based network management (PBNM) is the mechanism which cans response according to different situations and makes abstraction and translation. It generates responses according to the situation on the network that were already defined policies. The goal of policies definition is not the same as device configuration, because of the changes of policies is the changes of goal and is not influence to the device operation practically.

9.17.1 POLICY-BASED NETWORK MANAGEMENT ARCHITECTURE ELEMENTS

Figure 9.8 shows the four essential elements of PBNM structure defined by IETF/DMTF.

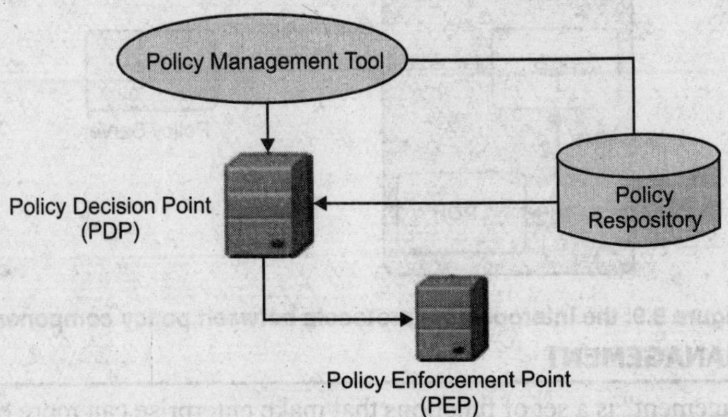

Figure 9.8: Four essential elements of PBNM architecture

PBNM' architecture has four components, it includes

- **Policy management tool:** Policy management tool is the interface that provides definition, update and monitoring to policy rules to system managers. System managers enter high level policy rules to policy management tools, after that policy management tool will translate the high level policy rules to low level configure files which can work by network devices.
- **Policy repository:** Policy repository is a place that store policy rules which handled by policy management tool. It can store high level policy rules and low level policy rules to be sure that the message which stored in policy repository can be accessed by different kind of devices. The policy messages stored in policy repository must use a standard message model.
- **Policy decision point:** Policy decision point (PDP) is a set of functions. Its responsibility is to develop and translate policy rules to the messages that policy enforcement point (PEP) can use.
- **Policy enforcement point:** Policy enforcement point is the entity. Its behaviors are all according to the policy rules send by PDP. In some devices, PDP and PEP can be the different functions at the same device. At some old devices, there is no idea to the concept about PBNM.

9.17.2 SOME APPROACHES TO PBNM

In actually implementation, there are some approaches to PBNM. It includes

- **Policy Specification:** IETF/DMTF Policy Core Information Model, Ponder, XACML, KeyNote, IBM Trust Policy Language can used to describe a policy.
- **Used Protocol:** As Figure 9.9, the interoperable protocols between policy components can be one of some protocols, such as Common Open Policy Services (COPS), Simple Network Management Protocol (SNMP), Lightweight Directory Access Protocol (LDAP), and Hypertext Transfer Protocol (HTTP).

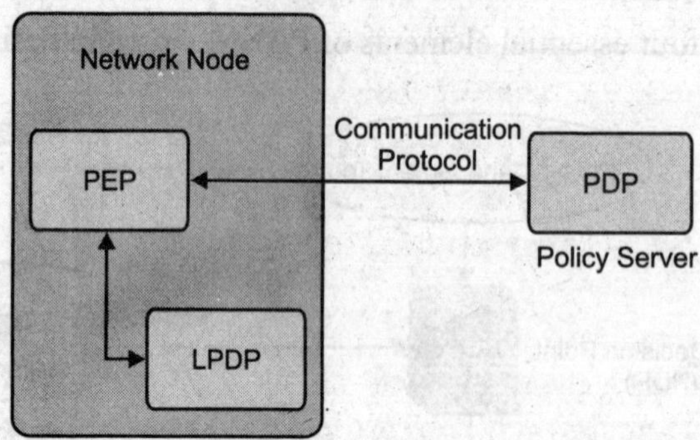

Figure 9.9: the interoperable protocols between policy components

9.18 SYSTEM MANAGEMENT

"System Management" is a set of functions that make enterprise can more easily to support the hardware and software of IT architectures in their life cycle. The goal of system management is that get much more efficiency and reduce system management and supporting cost. The key point to achieve this goal is that let the system manager install, setup and manage lots of computer problem on his/her desk. It will be the more efficiency way if system manager can operate systems in centralization and use on many systems. System management functions include: Software deploy and transplant, hardware configuration, system integrity, assets management, remote assist.

System manager will face the challenge of system configuration at the very start of new computer take off the seal. They should also consider that how to operate all systems. They hope that computer can send message when error occurred, and it is much better that can send error message before error will occur. It can help system managers solve problems as soon as possible. This complex work should complete in centralize as far as possible, so we can modify all system configurations in shortest time. So system managers should configure many systems on the same computer as possible, even the configuration come from different computer supplier.

9.18.1 DESKTOP MANAGEMENT INTERFACE (DMI)

Circa 1999, Microsoft required OEMs and BIOS vendors to support the Desktop Management Interface (DMI) interface/data set in order to have Microsoft certification. DMI was the first desktop management standard and has been developed by the Distributed Management Task Force (DMTF).

DMI is an industry framework for managing and keeping track of hardware and software components in a system of personal computers from a central location. Before talking about DMI, we should know what SMBIOS (System Management BIOS) is. It is an extension of the Basic Input Output System (BIOS) that formulates and delivers this information to the operating system. In other word, it is the specifications that define how to display product manage information on mother board and system manufacturer, or DMI is a layer of abstractization between system components and the software that manage them. But DMI information only can collect under SMBIOS specification.

DMI is hardware and operating system-independent, independent of specific management protocol, easy for vendors to adopt, mappable to existing management protocols such as the SNMP, and used on network and non-network computers. DMI consists of four components:

- **Management Information Format (MIF):** An MIF is a text file that contains specific information about the hardware and software being used on a computer. An MIF file consists of one or more groups containing attributes, which describe each component. By default, each MIF file contains the standard component ID group. This group contains the product name, version, serial number, and the time and date of the last installation. The ID number is assigned based on when the component was installed in relation to other components. Manufacturers can create their own MIFs specific to a component. For example, a manufacturer might write an MIF file for a fax/modem that contains two groups: a fax group and a modem group. Some group attributes include warranty information, support phone numbers, and any errors encountered. This information is then sent to an MIF database.
- **Service layer:** The service layer is memory-resident code that acts as a mediator for the management interface and the component interface and allows management and component software to access MIF files in the MIF database. The service layer is available as an operating system add-on and is a shared resource for all programs. Because the service layer must run all the time, it is designed not to use a lot of memory. The service layer also includes a common interface called the local agent, which is used to manage individual components.
- **Component interface (CI):** The CI is an application program interface (API) that sends status information to the appropriate MIF file via the service layer. Commands include the Get and Set command that modifies the MIF as needed and the Event command that notifies management software of critical events.
- **Management interface (MI):** The management software communicates with the service layer using the MI application program interface. The MI allows administrators to issue the Get and Set command and the List command that lists all the DMI-manageable devices.

Due to the rapid advancement of DMTF technologies, such as Common Information Model (CIM), the DMTF defined an "End of Life" process for its Desktop Management Interface (DMI), which ended March 31, 2005. Fully DMI-enabled PCs could also be monitored from a central management console in the network, but this depends on use uses of the protocols which allow this, e.g. SNMP. When queries are made to a memory-resident agent that resides in the background, it responds by sending data in MIFs (Management Information Files) or activating MIF routines. Static data in a MIF would contain items such as model ID, serial number, memory and port addresses. A MIF routine could read memory and report its contents.

9.19 WEB-BASED ENTERPRISE MANAGEMENT (WBEM)

Web-Based Enterprise Management (WBEM) is a set of systems management technologies developed to unify the management of distributed computing environments.

Web-Based Enterprise Management (WBEM) is a set of industry standards that an enterprise can use to manage its information operations in the distributed computing environment of the Internet. An important part of WBEM is the Common Information Model (CIM), a standard for defining device and application characteristics so that system and network administrators and management programs are able to control devices and applications from different manufacturers or sources in the same way. WBEM standards provide a Web-based approach for exchanging CIM data across different technologies and platforms. CIM data is encoded using Extensible Markup Language (XML) and usually transmitted between WBEM servers and clients using the Internet's Hypertext Transfer Protocol (HTTP).

WBEM is designed to be extensible, allowing new applications, devices, and operating systems to be specified in the future. Open-source implementations of WBEM are available from several vendors, including OpenPegasus, OpenWBEM, and WBEMsource. WBEM is said to be particularly appropriate for storage networking, grid computing, utility computing, and Web services.

WBEM was developed by the Distributed Management Task Force (DTMF), a collaboration of BMC Software, Cisco, Compaq, IBM, Intel, Microsoft, and other companies. A more limited approach to a network management standard, the Simple Network Management Protocol (SNMP) was developed earlier and is still in use.

Key features of WBEM technology include:

- remote management of applications
- management of several instances of an application as a single unit
- standard interface for remote application management across different applications
- decoupling of application management from the client
- "publishing" of key information about an application to other applications

9.19.1 HOW WEB-BASED ENTERPRISE MANAGEMENT (WBEM) WORKS

WBEM enables information such as the amount of RAM in a computer, the capacity of a hard disk, the type of process, and the version of the operating system or firmware to be extracted from computers, routers, switches, and other network devices. This information can be used for detection of potential problems before they occur, for remote management using products such as Microsoft Systems Management Server (SMS), and for planning and other decision-making purposes. WBEM is designed to work in heterogeneous enterprise networking environments to collect diagnostic and management data relating to hardware from multiple vendors, different operating systems, different network protocols, and distributed applications.

Currently, enterprise-level network management includes using Simple Network Management Protocol (SNMP) for managing routers and switches, Desktop Management Interface (DMI) for desktop systems management, proprietary management protocols and systems for managing vendor applications, and so on. WBEM simplifies management by providing a common model and data source that can be extended to function with existing protocols, networking components, and applications.

The framework for this standard is the Common Information Model (CIM), a set of schema for cross-platform network management also developed by the DMTF. Once information is collected, it can be shared across an enterprise and displayed using WBEM management systems.

Microsoft has built the WBEM architecture into Windows 98 and Windows 2000 and has made it available as an add-on for Windows NT 4. Windows Management Instrumentation (WMI) is Microsoft's implementation of WBEM for Microsoft Windows platforms.

9.19.2 WHY WE NEED A NEW MANAGEMENT SYSTEM

We know that TCP/IP network is the widely used network on enterprises and commonality. SNMP is the most popular and widely used network management in TCP/IP network. SNMP is the basis of much network management software, but it is getting less competence on requirement of equipments and high level abstract service management when network grow up. Let us see the problems that SNMP was met in several sides:

- **Communication Protocol:** SNMP is a application layer protocol and transmit data in TCIP/IP network by UDP. UDP is a connectionless communication protocol and can transmit large number of data very quickly, but it has the connatural unreliability and need program to support reliable mechanism. With the network transmission rate growing up, transmit large statistic data by UDP become unnecessary gradually. The more stable and accurate data transmission method is needed, and TCP can do. Data transmission in WBEM is that using HTTP or HTTPS. TCP is a connection-oriented communication protocol, so can transmit data steady.
- **Convenience:** In recent year, many enterprises provide variety of services, but maybe provide the variety of services is on the different platforms. It is not a easy thing that get manage data and system configuration from different platforms. WBEM provides a unitary interface which not only combines SNMP but also can add other application management interfaces, likes DMI, to achieve single operating environment.
- **Security:** SNMPv1 and SNMPv2 construct confidence relationship between manager and agent on Community. An agent can configure three kinds of community, named Read-Only, Read-Write and Trap. Community name is the password of that device. Otherwise, SNMP transmit community use as clear text, so it will be intercepted to use very easily. SNMPv3 using safe authentication and communication between devices to prevent this problem, but are not widely used. In the WBEM, it using HTTPS (HTTP with SSL) to achieve security.

9.19.3 WBEM ARCHITECTURE

The complexity of enterprise intranet and system management usually makes information manager in enterprise very agonizing. In 1996 July because of prevail on WWW, so that BMC Software, Cisco, Compaq, Intel, Microsoft and about fifty manufacturers think that WWW have possibility to become user interface standard. In order to let enterprise network and system management can use simple and easy browser interface, so they cooperated to define WBEM.

We can understand WBEM are integrated from many technologies in Figure 9.10. Likes SNMP can provide the ability of network device query; DMI can query system's peripheral status by ask system; and provide www user interface to manage network and system by HTTP.

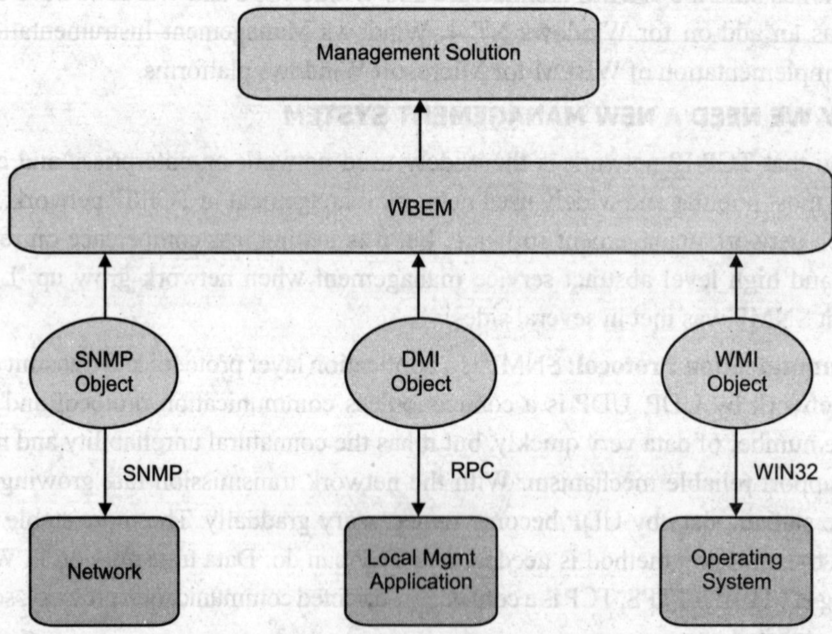

Figure 9.10: WBEM standards-based initiative for enterprise network management

Web Based Enterprise Management (WBEM) is systems management architecture initiative to unify the management of enterprise computing environments. WBEM allows the industry to deliver a set of standard-based management tools related to XML. The architecture has been standardized by the Distributed Management Task Force (DMTF). They have developed a core set of standards that make up WBEM, which includes a data model, the Common Information Model (CIM) standard. The architecture is independent of the device being managed and has been applied to devices as diverse as IP Routers, Electrical Power Distribution Systems, Private Branch Exchanges (PBXs), Desktop Computers, Printers, and Storage Servers.

To understand the WBEM architecture, consider the components which lie between the operator trying to manage a device (configure it, turn it off and on, collect alarms, etc.) and the actual hardware and software of the device:

- The operator will presumably be presented with some form of graphical user interface (GUI), browser user interface (BUI), or command-line interface (CLI). The WBEM standard really has nothing to say about this interface (although a CLI for specific applications is being defined): in fact it is one of the strengths of WBEM that it is independent of the human interface since human interfaces can be changed without the rest of the system needing to be aware of the changes.
- The GUI, BUI or CLI will interface with a WBEM client through a small set of Application Program Interfaces. This client will find the WBEM Server for the device being managed (typically on the device itself) and construct an XML message with the request.

- The client will use the HTTP (or HTTPS) protocol to pass the request, encoding in CIM-XML, to the WBEM client.
- For most operations, the WBEM server determines from the model that it needs to communicate with the actual hardware or software. This is handled by so-called "providers": small pieces of code which interface between the WBEM server (using a standardized interface known as CMPI) and the real hardware or software. Because the interface is well-defined and the number of types of call is small, it is normally easy to write providers. In particular, the provider writer knows nothing of the GUI, BUI, or CLI being used by the operator.

So, which pieces of this does a device manufacturer or service provider have to write?

- **Firstly the model:** This is normally done by extending as necessary one of the standard models published by the DMTF.
- **Then the BUI, GUI, or CLI:** The client and server usually do not need to be written because there are many open-source and commercial implementations available.
- **Then the providers:** In summary, the WBEM architecture allows the manufacturer of a device or developer of a service to provide a standards-compliant management interface to that device simply and cheaply.

While using the HTTPS WBEM connection, it is important to verify unknown WBEM certificates before accepting them as valid certificates. Accepting an attacker owned certificate as a valid certificate discloses any transmitted password. In a number of WBEM implementations, the providers run with elevated privileges. Unknown providers should not be loaded onto a system.

WBEM is a set of management and Internet standard technologies developed to unify the management of distributed computing environments, facilitating the exchange of data across otherwise disparate technologies and platforms. WBEM is extensible, facilitating the development of platform-neutral, reusable infrastructure, tools and applications. In addition to its use by vendors, end users and the open source community, you also can get open source implementations of WBEM are available from OpenPegasus, OpenWBEM, SBLIM, WBEM Services and WBEMsource, WBEM is enabling other industry organizations to build on its foundation in areas including Web services, security, storage, grid and utility computing.

EXERCISES

1. Explain the concept of documentation and network management?
2. Explain the concept of project goal and scope?
3. Explain the various design requirements?
4. Explain the various Network Applications?
5. What do you mean by current state of the network?
6. Explain the results of network design testing?
7. Explain the concept of implementation plan?

8. Explain the concept of network management system?
9. Explain the common network management architecture?
10. Explain the various approaches of network management?
11. Explain the concept of Simple Network Management Protocol?
12. Explain the concept of Management Information Base (MIB)?
13. What do you mean by SNMPV2?
14. What do you mean by SNMP V3?
15. Explain the concept of RMON: Remote Monitoring MIBS?
16. Explain the protocol structure of RMON?
17. Explain the concept of policy-based network management (PBNM)?
18. Explain the architecture elements of policy-based network management?
19. What do you mean by system management?
20. Explain the concept of web-based enterprise management (WBEM)?
21. How web-based enterprise management (WBEM) works? Why we need a new management system?
22. Explain the architecture of WBEM?

CHAPTER

10

Network Optimization

10.1 NETWORK OPTIMIZATION

Network optimization is a special type of linear programming model. Network models have three main advantages over linear programming:

1. They can be solved very **quickly.** Problems whose linear program would have 1000 rows and 30,000 columns can be solved in a matter of seconds. This allows network models to be used in many applications (such as real-time decision making) for which linear programming would be inappropriate.
2. They have naturally **integer solutions.** By recognizing that a problem can be formulated as a network program, it is possible to solve special types of integer programs without resorting to the ineffective and time consuming integer programming algorithms.
3. They are **intuitive.** Network models provide a language for talking about problems that is much more intuitive than the "variables, objective, and constraints"' language of linear and integer programming.

Of course these advantages come with a drawback: network models cannot formulate the wide range of models that linear and integer programs can. However, they occur often enough that they form an important tool for real decision making.

10.2 TERMINOLOGY

A network or graph consists of points, and lines connecting pairs of points. The points are called nodes or vertices. The lines are called arcs. The arcs may have a direction on them, in which case they are called directed arcs. If an arc has no direction, it is often called an edge. If all the arcs in a network are directed, the network is a directed network. If all the arcs are undirected, the network is an undirected network.

Two nodes may be connected by a series of arcs. A path is a sequence of distinct arcs (no nodes repeated) connecting the nodes. A directed path from node i to node *j* is a sequence of arcs, each of whose direction (if any) is towards *j*. An undirected path may have directed arcs pointed in either direction.

A path that begins and ends at the same node is a cycle and may be either directed or undirected.

A network is connected if there exists an undirected path between any pair of nodes. A connected network without any cycle is called a tree, mainly because it looks like one.

10.3 EXAMPLES

There are many examples of using network flows in practice. Here are a few:

10.3.1 SHORTEST PATHS

Consider a phone network. At any given time, a message may take a certain amount of time to traverse each line (due to congestion effects, switching delays, and so on). This time can vary greatly minute by minute and telecommunication companies spend a lot of time and money tracking these delays and communicating these delays throughout the system. Assuming a centralized switcher knows these delays, there remains the problem of routing a call so as to minimize the delays. So, in figure 10.1, what is the least delay path from LA to Boston? How can we find that path quickly?

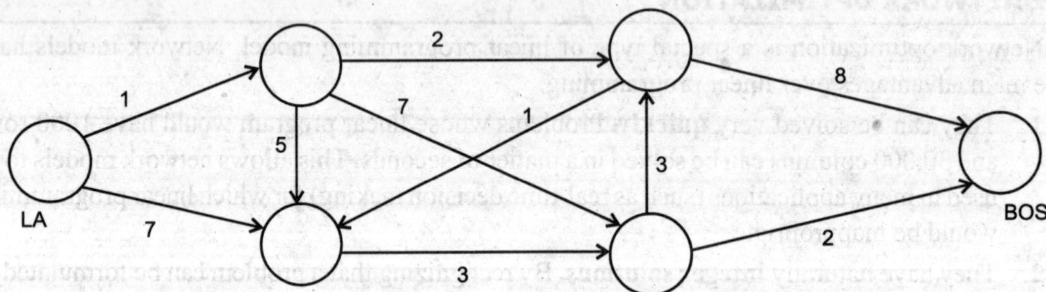

Figure 10.1: Phone Network

This is an example of a particular type of network model, called the shortest path problem. In such a problem, you have a network with costs on the edges and two special nodes: a start node and a finish node. The goal is to find a path from the start node to the finish node whose total weight is minimized.

Here is another problem that might not appear to be a shortest path problem, but really is:

At a small but growing airport, the local airline company is purchasing a new tractor for a tractor-trailer train to bring luggage to and from the airplanes. A new mechanized luggage system will be installed in 3 years, so the tractor will not be needed after that. However, because it will receive heavy use, and maintenance costs are high, it may still be more economical to replace the tractor after 1 or 2 years. The following table gives the total net discounted cost associated with purchasing a tractor in year *i* and trading it in year *j* (where year 0 is now):

	j		
	1	2	3
0	8	18	31
i 1	—	10	21
2	—	—	12

The problem is to determine at what times the tractor should be replaced (if ever) to minimize the total costs for tractors. How can this be formulated as a shortest path problem?

10.3.2 MAXIMUM FLOW

Another type of model again has a number on each arc, but now the number corresponds to a capacity. This limits the flow on the arc to be no more than that value. For instance, in a distribution system, the capacity might be the limit on the amount of material (in tons, say) that can go over a particular distribution channel. We would then be concerned with the capacity of the network: how much can be sent from a source node to the destination node? Using the same network as above, treating the numbers as capacities, how much can be sent from LA to Boston?

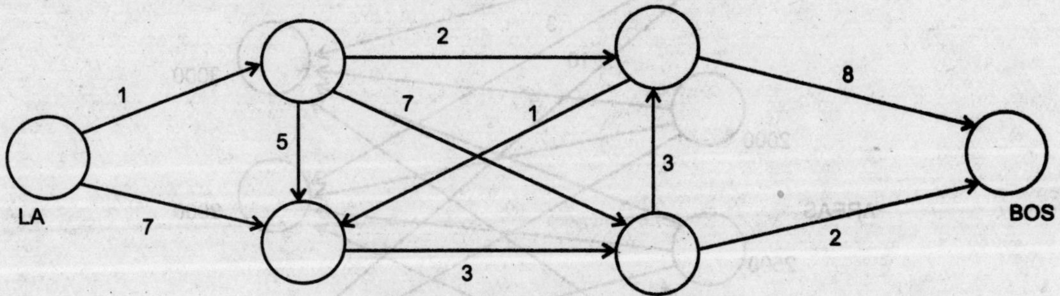

Figure 10.2: Distribution Network

Associated with the maximum flow is a bottleneck: a set of arcs whose total capacity equals the maximum flow, and whose removal leaves no path from source to destination in the network. It is actually a nontrivial result to show that the maximum flow equals the size of the minimum bottleneck. It is also an interesting task to find the bottleneck in the above example.

Maximum flow models occur in applications where cost is not an issue, and the goal is to maximize the number of items handled (in a broad sense). Here is a similar problem that can be formulated as a maximum flow problem (this was part of a conversation with a Chicago consulting firm on how to improve their internal operations):

Over the next three months, there are four projects to be completed. Project A requires 8 person-months of work, and must be done by the end of the second month. Project B requires 3 person-months and must be done by end of the first month. Project C can start at the beginning of the second month, and requires 7 man-months of work, no more than 2 of which are in the second month. Project D requires 6 man-months, no more than 3 of which occur in any month. There are 9 consultants available in the first and second month, and 6 in the third. Is it possible to meet the project deadlines? Surprisingly, this is a maximum flow problem. One nice (and surprising) aspect of the result is that this shows that no consultant need split a month's work between jobs.

10.3.3 TRANSPORTATION PROBLEM

Consider the following snow removal problem: there are a number of districts in a city. After a snowfall, the snow in each area must be moved out of the district into a convenient location. In Montreal (from where I am taking this example), these locations are large grates (leading to the sewer system), a couple large pits, and a couple entry points to the river. Each of these destinations has a capacity. The goal is to minimize the distance traveled to handle all of the snow.

This problem is an example of a transportation problem. In such a problem, there are a set of nodes called sources, and a set of nodes called destinations. All arcs go from a source to a destination. There is a per-unit cost on each arc. Each source has a supply of material, and each destination has a demand. We assume that the total supply equals the total demand (possibly adding a fake source or destination as needed). For the snow removal problem, the network might look like that in figure 10.3.

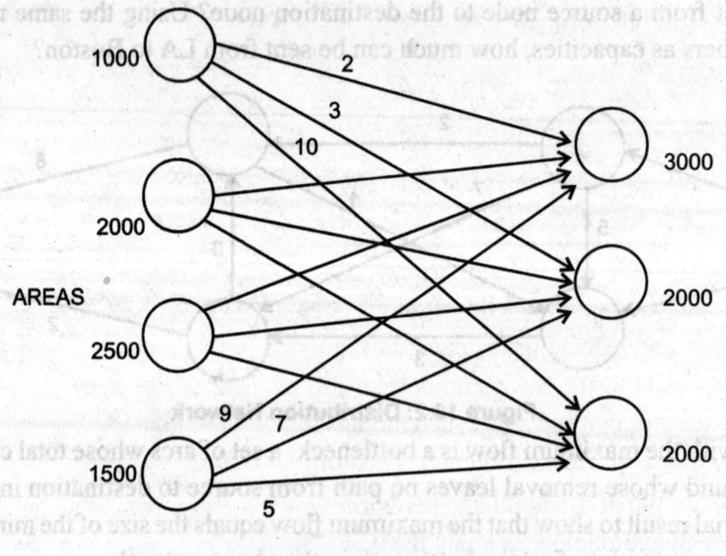

Figure 10.3: Snow Transportation Network

Transportation problems are often used in, surprise, transportation planning. For instance, in an application where goods are at a warehouse, one problem might be to assign customers to a warehouse so as to meet their demands. In such a case, the warehouses are the sources, the customers are the destinations, and the costs represent the per-unit transportation costs.

10.3.4 ASSIGNMENT PROBLEM

A special case of the transportation problem is the assignment problem which occurs when each supply is 1 and each demand is 1. In this case, the integrality implies that every supplier will be assigned one destination and every destination will have one supplier. The costs give the charge for assigning a supplier and destination to each other.

Example 10.1: A company has three new machines of different types. There are four different plants that could receive the machines. Each plant can only receive one machine, and each machine can only be given to one plant. The expected profit that can be made by each plant if assigned a machine is as follows:

	Plant 1	2	3	4
Machine 1	13	16	12	11
Machine 2	15	0	13	20
Machine 3	5	7	10	6

This is a transportation problem with all supplies and demands equal to 1, so it is an assignment problem.

Note that a balanced problem must have the same number of supplies and demands, so we must add a dummy machine (corresponding to receiving no machine) and assign a zero cost for assigning the dummy machine to a plant.

10.4 GENERALIZED NETWORKS

The final model I would like to familiarize you with is called the generalized network model. In this model, there may be gains or loses as flow goes along an arc. Each arc has a multiplier to represent these gains and loses. For instance, if 3 units of flow enter an arc with a multiplier of .5, then 1.5 unit of flow exit the arc. Such a model can still be represented as a linear program, and there are specialized techniques that can solve such models much faster than linear programming (but a bit slower than regular network flow problems). The optimal solution need not be integer however.

The standard example of a generalized network is in power generation: as electricity moves over wires, there is some unavoidable loss along the way. This loss is represented as a multiplier. Here is another example on how generalized networks might be used:

Consider the world's currency market. Given two currencies, say the Yen and the USDollar, there is an exchange rate between them (currently about 110 Yen to the Dollar). It is axiomatic of a arbitrage-free market that there is no method of converting, say, a Dollar to Yen then to Deutsch Marks, to Francs, the Pounds, and to Dollars so that you end up with more than a dollar. How would you recognize when there is an arbitrage possibility?

For this model, we use a node to represent each currency. An arc between currency *i* and *j* gives the exchange rate from *i* to *j*. We begin with a single dollar and which to send flow through the network and maximize the amount we generate back at the USDollar node. This can be drawn as in figure 10.4.

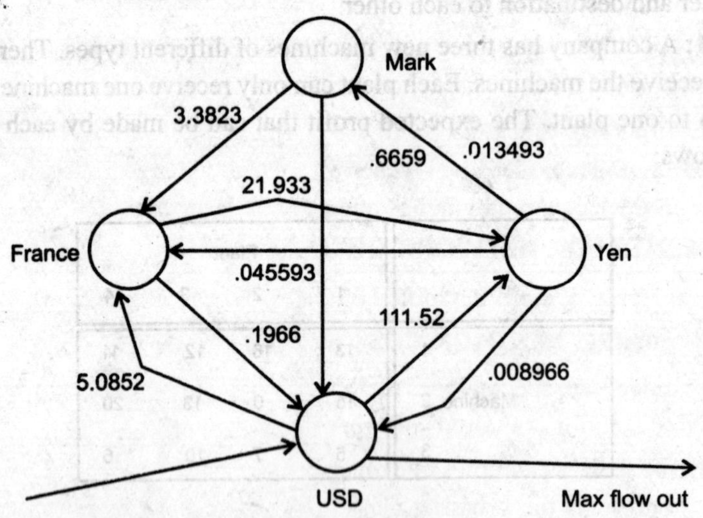

Figure 10.4: Financial Exchange Network

These are actual trades made on November 10, 1996. It is not obvious, but the Dollar-Yen-Mark-Dollar conversion actually makes \$0.002. How would you formulate a linear program to recognize this? We will discuss this matter in next section 10.6.

10.5 GOALS OF NETWORK OPTIMIZATION

Most companies who have a production and distribution network in India use optimization at some level. In fact, a very well known color and paint company in India had created their own network optimization tool much before the practice caught on here and commercial solutions started becoming available. Significant numbers of Indian supply chain planners depend on custom build spreadsheet or script based solutions developed in-house or provided by niche vendors. Depending on the organization these decisions are sometimes also taken locally based on empirical observation and experiential learning.

The scenario is changing though and larger technology solution companies are showing greater interest in the Indian market. According to supply chain planners in pharmaceuticals, food and consumer goods industry, commercial Network Optimization tool availability and usage is on the rise. Adoption is being driven by multinationals that having taken world-wide licenses for these tools in other geographies are extending them to their Indian businesses. We also need to understand that most of these solutions sit atop the ERP system installed and by and large installation of optimization tools is dependent on the wave of ERP installation. Most companies choose to go for an additional solution in average only after 5 years of taking the decision of commissioning an ERP application. However, the movement towards commercially available solutions is gaining traction because of the following advantages:

- well designed graphical user interface
- built in grids and validation logic to simplify data accumulation
- customizable interfaces to link with ERP solutions that a company may already be using
- integrated maps and other visual representation of the network
- ability to incorporate scale and complexity that cant be modelled easily
- better algorithms developed over years of specialized research which reduce run time, incorporate more decision parameters and provide mature results.

10.6 MEASUREMENTS FOR NETWORK OPTIMIZATION

Here we are explaining the unifying model of minimum cost network flows:

10.6.1 UNIFYING MODEL: MINIMUM COST NETWORK FLOWS

All of the above models are special types of network flow problems: they each have a specialized algorithm that can find solutions hundreds of times faster than plain linear programming.

They can all also be seen as examples of a much broader model, the minimum cost network flow model. This model represents the broadest class of problem that can be solved much faster than linear programming while still retaining such nice properties as integrality of solution and appeal of concept.

Like the maximum flow problem, it considers flows in networks with capacities. Like the shortest path problem, it considers a cost for flow through an arc. Like the transportation problem, it allows multiple sources and destinations. In fact, all of these problems can be seen as special cases of the minimum cost flow problem.

Consider a directed network with *n* nodes. The decision variables are x_{ij}, the flow through arc (i,j). The given information includes:

- c_{ij}: cost per unit of flow from *i* to *j* (may be negative),
- u_{ij}: capacity (or upper bound) on flow from *i* to *j*,
- b_i: net flow generated at *i*.

This last value has a sign convention:

- $b_i > 0$if i is a supply node,
- $b_i < 0$if i is a demand node,
- $b_i = 0$if i is a transshipment node.

The objective is to minimize the total cost of sending the supply through the network to satisfy the demand.

Note that for this model, it is not necessary that every arc exists. We will use the convention that summations are only taken over arcs that exist. The linear programming formulation for this problem is:

$$\begin{aligned} &\textbf{Minimize} && \sum_i \sum_j c_{ij} x_{ij} \\ &\textbf{Subject to} && \sum_j x_{ij} - \sum_j x_{ji} = b_i \text{ for all nodes } i, \\ & && 0 \le x_{ij} \le u_{ij} \text{ for all arcs } (i,j). \end{aligned}$$

Again, we will assume that the network is balanced, so $\Sigma_i b_i = 0$, since dummies can be added as needed. We also still have a nice integrality property. If all the b_i and u_{ij} are integral, then the resulting solution to the linear program is also integral.

Minimum cost network flows are solved by a variation of the simplex algorithm and can be solved more than 100 times faster than equivalently sized linear programs. From a modeling point of view, it is most important to know the sort of things that can and cannot be modeled in a single network flow problem:

Can do

1. Lower bounds on arcs. If a variable x_{ij} has a lower bound of l_{ij}, upper bound of u_{ij}, and cost of c_{ij}, change the problem as follows:
   - Replace the upper bound with $u_{ij} - l_{ij}$
   - Replace the supply at i with $b_i - l_{ij}$
   - Replace the supply at j with $b_i + l_{ij}$,

Now you have a minimum cost flow problem. Add $c_{ij} l_{ij}$ to the objective after solving and l_{ij} to the flow on arc (i,j) to obtain a solution of the original problem.

2. Upper bounds on flow through a node. Replace the node i with nodes i' and i''. Create an arc from i' to i'' with the appropriate capacity, and cost 0. Replace every arc (j,i) with one from j to i' and every arc (i,j) with one from i'' to j. Lower bounds can also be handled this way.
3. Convex, piecewise linear costs on arc flows (for minimization). This is handled by introducing multiple arcs between the nodes, one for each portion of the piecewise linear function. The convexity will assure that costs are handled correctly in an optimal solution.

Can't do

1. Fixed cost to use a node.
2. Fixed cost to use an arc.
3. ``Proportionality of flow." That is, if one unit enters node i, then you insist that .5 units go to node j and .5 to node k.
4. Gains and losses of flow along arcs, as in power distribution.

Note that although these cannot be done in a single network, it may be possible to use the solutions to multiple networks to give you an answer. For instance, if there is only one arc with a fixed cost, you can solve both with and without the arc to see if it is advantageous to pay the fixed cost.

Here is an example of a problem that doesn't look like a network flow problem, but it really is:

A company must meet the following demands for cash at the beginning of each of the next six months:

Month	1	2	3	4	5	6
Needs	$200	$100	$50	$80	$160	$140

At the beginning of month 1, the company has $150 in cash and $200 worth of bond 1, $100 worth of bond 2 and $400 worth of bond 3. Of course, the company will have to sell some bonds to meet demands, but a penalty will be charged for any bonds sold before the end of month 6. The penalties for selling $1 worth of each bond are shown in the table below.

		Month of sale					
		1	2	3	4	5	6
	1	$0.07	$0.06	$0.06	$0.04	$0.03	$0.03
Bond	2	$0.17	$0.17	$0.17	$0.11	$0	$0
	3	$0.33	$0.33	$0.33	$0.33	$0.33	$0

(a) Assuming that all bills must be paid on time, formulate a balanced transportation problem that can be used to minimize the cost of meeting the cash demands for the next six months.

(b) Assume that payment of bills can be made after they are due, but a penalty of $0.02 per month is assessed for each dollar of cash demands that is postponed for one month. Assuming all bills must be paid by the end of month 6, develop a transshipment model that can be used to minimize the cost of paying the next six months' bills.

[Hint: Transshipment points are needed, in the form C_t = cash available at beginning of month t after bonds for month t have been sold, but before month t demand is met. Shipments into Ct occur from bond sales and C_{t-1}. Shipments out of C_t occur toC_{t+1} and demands for months 1, 2,...., t.]

10.7 NETWORK OPTIMIZATION TOOLS

Following are the various network optimization tools:

10.7.1 TEST MS

Test MS is a daily must for engineers to perform network test. The test MS can display the service cell of a mobile telecommunication network and the six neighbor cells. It can also be used to test network parameters. The test MS can be connected to a computer, so it can collect and analyze data with the help of drive test software.

The functions of a SAGEM test MS are listed below:

- View the IMSI of the SIM card
- Scan BCCH

The SAGEM test MS can scan the BCCH, and it will provides the Rxlev and BSIC of the scanned BCCH in each cell.

- View network parameters

The SAGEM test MS can display network parameters of the service cell of and the six neighbor cells when it is idle or in conversation state.

- Forced cell selection

The test MS can be forced to reselect the designated cell for dialing test and handover test.

- Forced handover

The test MS can be forced to hand over to the designated cell to analyze whether the handover is normal during conversation.

- Frequency selection
- GPRS function test (The MSs of SAGEM OT96 support this function)

10.7.2 DRIVE TEST SOFTWARE

ANT, TEMS, and SAFCO are the GSM drive test software in common use. Generally, the drive test software consists of two parts: foreground data collection software and background data analysis software.

10.7.2.1 FOREGROUND DATA COLLECTION SOFTWARE

The foreground data collection software is mainly responsible for collecting the uplink and downlink data at the Um interface of the GSM mobile network. If the BTSs and the landform map of the test areas are imported, the track of the drive test, the radio parameters of each test point, and the main information of the service cell, neighbor cell, and the Um interface can be observed.

The functions of foreground data collection software are listed below:

- **Test functions**

Test functions include call test, scan test, call interference test, double-network synchronization test, dialing record test, dual-band comparison test, and MS selection test.

- **Topical test**

Topical test is responsible for forced handover and frequency locking (call) test, BCCH frequency locking (standby) test, forced location update test, and band locking test.

- **Interference test**

Interference aims to locate the BCCH same-frequency and neighbor frequency interference and TCH neighbor frequency interference within the same network in time.

- **Parameter collection**

The field strength of the service cell and the neighbor cells, bit error ratio, frame error rate, and various radio parameters of the cell need to be collected.

- **Geographic navigation**

The foreground data collection software can be used to display the geographic navigation through combing the digital map and BTS resources.

- **SQI (Speech Quality Index) test**

SQI test aims to evaluate the speech quality experienced by mobile users.

- **Traffic statistics**

The foreground data collection software can be used for CQT traffic statistics. It enables the call setup, call duration, and call release to be recorded respectively. In addition, it is also responsible for recording call drop rate and congestion rate.

- **Data record**

The foreground data collection software can record and store the test data of the test MS synchronously, and can record and store the scanned data of the 900MHz and 1800MHz synchronously.

- **Scanning test**

Scanning test aims to test and record the field strength of the channels of the GSM 900MHz network and GSM1800MHz network.

- **Competitive test**

The comparison between real-time field strength and speech quality is available. In addition, real-time check of cell parameters is allowed.

10.7.2.2 BACKGROUND DATA ANALYSIS SOFTWARE

The background data analysis software can geographically present the radio network test data and reflect the distribution of network parameters on the electronic map visually. It can locate the problem cell by fully considering the drive test data, network resource data, digital frequency sweep receiver data, and GSM signaling characteristics, thus guiding engineers to evaluate and optimize the network rationally and effectively.

The functions of background data analysis software are listed below:

- Radio coverage evaluation and analysis
- Interference analysis
- Neighbor cell analysis
- Handover analysis
- Signaling analysis
- Speech record and analysis

10.7.3 SPECTRUM ANALYZER

A spectrum analyzer is a laboratory instrument that displays signal amplitude (strength) as it varies by signal frequency. The frequency appears on the horizontal axis, and the amplitude is displayed on the vertical axis. To the casual observer, a spectrum analyzer looks like an oscilloscope and, in fact, some lab instruments can function either as oscilloscopes or spectrum analyzers.

A spectrum analyzer can be used to determine whether or not a wireless transmitter is working according to federally defined standards for purity of emissions. Output signals at frequencies other than the intended communications frequency appear as vertical lines (pips) on the display. A spectrum analyzer can also be used to determine, by direct observation, the bandwidth of a digital or analog signal.

A spectrum analyzer interface is a device that can be connected to a wireless receiver or a personal computer to allow visual detection and analysis of electromagnetic signals over a defined band of frequencies. This is called panoramic reception and it can be used to determine the frequencies of sources of interference to wireless networking equipment, such as Wi-Fi and wireless routers.

10.7.4 SIGNALING ANALYZER

MA-10 and K1205 are the GSM signaling analyzer in common use. This section introduces the functions of the signaling analyzer.

MA-10 signaling analyzer can test the Abis interface signaling messages, the A-G interface signaling messages, and the SS#7 interface signaling messages of ISUP, TUP, and INAP when it is on line. In addition, it can perform PCM BERT (bit error rate test) and GSM BERT. Furthermore, it can enable the signaling message files saved during on-line monitoring when it is off-line.

The MA-10 signaling analyzer has five sub-applications. They are listed below:

- MA-10 control (It is used to test Abis interface signaling messages, A-G interface signaling messages, and bit errors when it is on line.)
- MONITOR ABIS offline (It is used to analyze the Abis interface signaling messages when it is off line.)
- MONITOR MSC offline (It is used to analyze the A-G interface signaling messages when it is off line.)
- GSM-BERT offline (It is used to analyze GSM BERT when it is off line.)
- PCM-BERT offline (It is used to analyze PCH BERT when it is off line.)

With the help of MA-10 signaling analyzer, network optimization engineers can collect and analyze Abis interface data and A-interface data, view the whole signaling procedure, and obtain the measurement report, and then compare the information with the downlink signals obtained from drive test. These means can help network optimization engineers have an overall understanding of the operation of the network. In this case, the causes and places for the problems, such as call drop, handover failure, and congestion can be located.

10.7.5 NETWORK OPTIMIZATION SOFTWARE

Good network optimization software can work as a platform for radio projects and maintenance personnel. NASTAR, Huawei network planning and optimization tool, can deeply analyze GSM network by integrating OMCR traffic statistics, configuration data, alarm data, engineering data, and so on. In addition, it also provides the interfaces for network planning, performance analysis, alarm analysis, and geography conditions.

The functions of NASTAR are listed below:

- Import static traffic statistics data (import the traffic statistics files of the maintenance console into database)
- Import static traffic statistics data according to time
- Import dynamic Huawei traffic statistics
- Import BSC data configuration
- Display the geographic view of BTSs
- Cancel, add, and move the cells based on the geographic view of BTSs
- Record spectrum utilization and analyze idle channel number
- Check same-frequency BSIC
- Analyze neighbor cells
- Measure distance and azimuth angle
- Display navigation window and legend
- Query performance analysis tasks in common use
- Make performance analysis task
- Query network optimization tasks in common use
- Make network optimization tasks
- Perform tasks and alarms automatically
- Import and export tasks
- Display task result and site view
- Query traffic statistics inversely from the cell set selected by site view
- Display the traffic tasks in direct views, including linear figure, column, pie (support the display of double y-axis and the simultaneous display of multiple indexes; support 2D and 3D.)
- Export electronic table (Excel) for query results.

10.8 NETWORK OPTIMIZATION TECHNIQUES

When performing a network baseline study, specific techniques enable an analyst to troubleshoot network issues. Some of these techniques involve processes discussed earlier in this book, such as utilization and quantitative measurement analysis. Unique methods exist to isolate specific traffic flow events, which can be very helpful during isolation and statistical baselining.

First, an analyst must engage the standard methodology as presented in the preceding chapter. Next, the analyst should apply techniques that provide a more focused review of dataflow from each specific baseline session. Some of these techniques can be applied to cause isolation; others can be used to optimize a network's performance (see Figure 10.5).

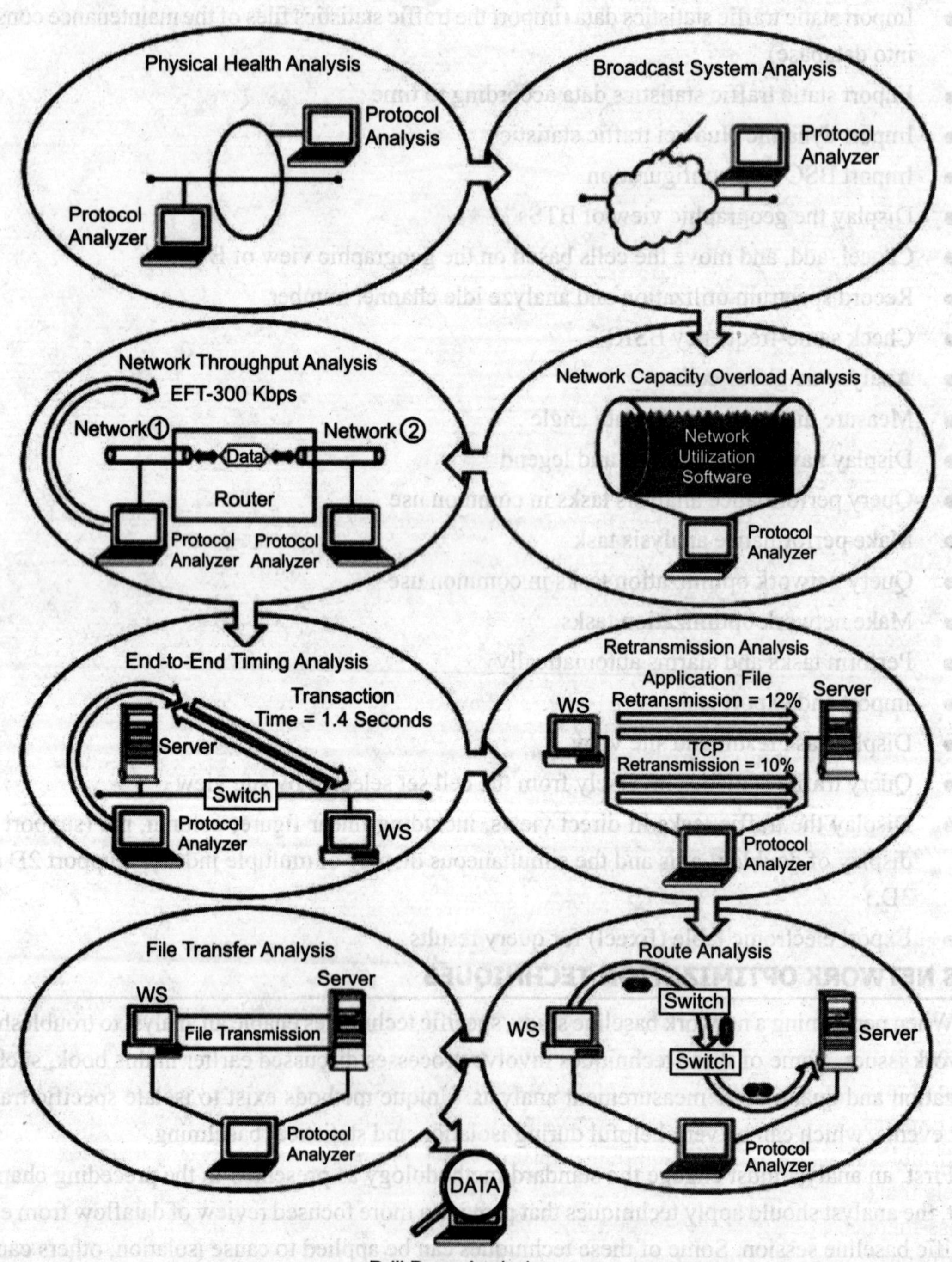
Physical Health Analysis
Protocol Analysis
Protocol Analyzer
Broadcast System Analysis
Protocol Analyzer
Network Throughput Analysis
EFT-300 Kbps
Network ①
Network ②
Data
Router
Protocol Analyzer
Protocol Analyzer
Network Capacity Overload Analysis
Network Utilization Software
Protocol Analyzer
End-to-End Timing Analysis
Transaction Time = 1.4 Seconds
Server
Switch
Protocol Analyzer
WS
Retransmission Analysis
Application File Retransmission = 12%
WS
Server
TCP Retransmission = 10%
Protocol Analyzer
File Transfer Analysis
WS
Server
File Transmission
Protocol Analyzer
Route Analysis
Switch
WS
Switch
Server
Protocol Analyzer
DATA
Drill Down Analysis

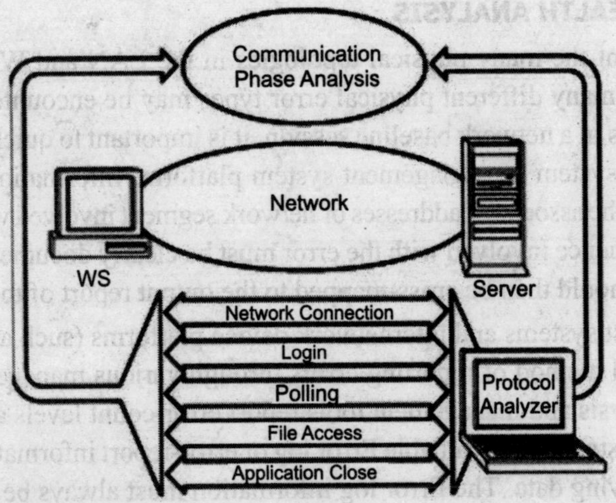

Figure 10.5: The main network optimization techniques.

Among the techniques involved are the following:

- Physical health analysis
- Broadcast storm analysis
- Network capacity overload analysis
- Network throughput analysis
- Network end-to-end interpacket timing analysis
- Transport and file retransmission analysis
- Packet route and path cost analysis
- End-to-end file transfer analysis
- Drill-down data-decoding steps and specific techniques

The techniques listed above will yield a palette of data information that will be extremely valuable in problematic and network baseline data profiling situations.

When reviewing a data trace during a network baseline session, an analyzer's Expert system output information or the internal indications in the data trace may immediately point to a specific type of problem, such as excessive physical errors. Rather than quickly taking the information from the Expert system and immediately attempting to troubleshoot the specific area of the network flagged as troublesome, the analyst should also further examine the internal data-trace results. It is highly likely that the data-trace internal view holds additional information that should also be reviewed and cross-mapped to a higher-level report information-extraction engine or Expert system screen results. Further examination of the data trace will most probably result in a more exact cause analysis mapping of the problem, yielding a more exact technical synopsis and applied recommendation.

This chapter describes each analysis technique. These techniques should be applied when performing a network baseline study. This is important so that you can isolate issues to their exact cause and profile data for optimization reasons.

10.8.1 PHYSICAL HEALTH ANALYSIS

Taking into account the many physical topologies in the LAN and WAN environments, it is natural to assume that many different physical error types may be encountered. When performing physical health analysis in a network baseline session, it is important to quickly note all information gathered in an Expert system or management system platform. Information related to error type, time of the error event, the associated addresses or network segment involved with the area in question, and protocol event sequence involved with the error must be clearly documented. The internal data-trace analysis results should then be cross-mapped to the output report of the error.

Many different host systems and internetwork device platforms (such as routers and switches) have their own internal method of reporting errors through various management platforms. Many different protocol analysis and management tools report error-count levels and time-of-occurrence conditions. All these systems yield valuable Error log or error-report information, which is a primary focus area when reviewing data. The Error log information must always be carefully gathered and documented.

For the purposes of illustrating error-report gathering, the following discussion describes how to apply this approach using a protocol analyzer tool.

Using a Protocol Analyzer for Error-Report Gathering

A protocol analyzer used during a network baseline session enables an analyst to quickly assess the types of errors encountered, the error count, and the time of occurrence. This relevant information proves extremely valuable because it assists in identifying the error event and the possible impact of the error on a network. In a reactive analysis session, this information is crucial and relevant to a rapid troubleshooting process. In a proactive network baselining session, this information is also important; however, the information can be quickly noted and documented for later review through the baseline process. This is especially important during a large internetwork study involving many different network areas, because certain physical errors may repeat and show a pattern of events that might be related to a center networking device, such as a main computer room hub, switch, or router. Within the protocol analysis capture, the error event is contained within a frame or a packet sequence, depending on the LAN or WAN topology.

It is important to cross-map the statistical Error log or output report from a specific management system (if one is present). It is important to map the Expert results with the internals of the protocol analysis dataflow events. The protocol analyzer error-reporting screens should be carefully examined for the key error event. After the error event information has been noted, the protocol analyzer should be paused or stopped. The capture should then be immediately saved to disk to ensure that the error frame or error frame occurrence is stored properly within the protocol analyzer platform. The data trace should then be opened and reviewed carefully, following a "page through the trace" process. The process of paging through the trace just involves slowly moving through the internal data gathered by the protocol analyzer to locate any unique anomalies. Some protocol analyzer Expert-based systems have a hotkey filtering system to quickly filter to the error event inside the data-trace results.

A protocol analysis trace taken during a network baseline session, may contain a large number of packets and frames. Some data traces could contain 50,000 or 100,000 frames or even more within one single capture. It can be quite cumbersome to page through the complete data trace after the trace has been opened for review. An Expert system feature provides a hotkey filtering system can facilitate an immediate extraction filter based on the error occurrence in the particular analyzer Expert system screen. The approach in this case is to highlight the error on the analyzer Expert system or statistical monitoring screen. After the error has been highlighted, a an analyst can use this feature to quickly filter to the area within the set of packets within the overall data trace to the exact area of the error occurrence. After the error event has been found, other relevant information in packets surrounding the error occurrence frame may also be identified; these may point to the actual cause of the error.

An inexperienced analyst may too quickly map the cause of a problem to an Expert system error-output report or a management system Error log. By using the actual data-trace error event and packet-sequence review process to access packet data around the error, it is possible to be more defined and accurate as to the cause analysis. In summary, a thorough review of the error frames within the trace may uncover packets or frames surrounding the error occurrence that may pinpoint the cause of a problem.

Consider, for example, 16Mbps Token Ring network that is operating abnormally from an upper-layer application standpoint. Users are complaining significantly about performance. In this case, the analyst should immediately deploy a protocol analyzer, because this is a rapid baseline situation (or a reactive analysis event).

As stated earlier, certain quantitative baseline measurements must be taken prior to topology error analysis, such as utilization, protocol percentages, and other statistical measurements. If the analyst moves through the initial steps in the quantitative baseline measurement process and notices a high number of error reports from the protocol analyzer indicating a high ring purge error MAC occurrence, this is a relevant event.

Assume, for example, that through an analysis session a high number of ring purge MAC frames are found within a Token Ring environment. The protocol analyzer could then just stop the capture, save the information, and filter on the ring purge events via a hotkey filtering system. The analyst could identify the ring purge MAC frames within the Token Ring trace analysis session. If, prior to the ring purge MAC frames, it is noted that excessive ring insertion failures are associated with a specific device, or excessive Soft Error Report MAC frames, this might indicate the cause of the ring purge error noted in the Expert system or Error log. This is just one example of how internal data-trace analysis, as associated with Expert system mapping, facilitates a cross-review process that yields a more accurate analysis.

Another illustration is an Ethernet internetwork that is showing a high number of corrupted CRC frames within the analyzer Expert system analysis screen. If the protocol analyzer filters on the artificial intelligent Expert screen displaying the CRC corrupt Ethernet errors, the analyst should then move directly to the internal area of the trace that shows the CRC-corrupted error frames involved.

By doing so, the analyst can determine that prior to the CRC frames, and possibly after the frames, certain frames indicate a high number of communication events on the Ethernet medium. Because the Ethernet medium engages a carrier sense multiple access/collision detection (CSMA/CD) sequence that is an ongoing process and is part of the Ethernet architecture, the cause analysis can be somewhat complex. Certain Ethernet frames, when including errors such as a CRC type, may be shorter than normal and may have physical addresses that cannot be interpreted. Because of this, sometimes the source and destination addresses may not be able to be read related to the CRC error cause. If prior to the CRC error frames, the trace shows that a certain set of devices are communicating, it is quite possible (based on the operation of CSMA/CD within Ethernet) that these devices are involved in conversations when a high number of CRC errors are occurring.

If retransmissions of frames at the Ethernet level are occurring, it is very possible that the CRC errors that are not readable are related to the frames that communicated most recently prior to the CRC error. This is another example of how a cross-mapping of the internal data-trace results as related to the analyzer Expert system are invaluable to protocol analysis and network baselining.

Later in this book, specific topology techniques such as analysis of Token Ring errors, Ethernet errors, and WAN errors are discussed in detail. In the context of this discussion, however, the point is that more is involved in isolating errors via network baselining other than just a simple review of protocol analyzer Expert screens or management system Error logs. All error reports encountered in these types of systems should be backed up by a close review of the internal data-trace results. The information should be cross-mapped between the management or Error log systems and the internal data-trace results. This method allows for a more accurate physical health analysis technique (see Figure 10.6).

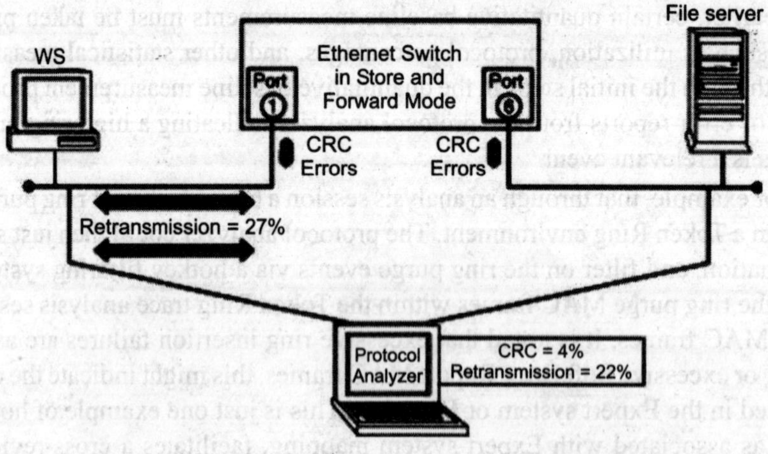

Figure 10.6: Approach of physical health analysis.

10.8.2 BROADCAST STORM ANALYSIS

When encountering a broadcast storm in a network baseline session, analyst can apply a specific technique to isolate the cause of the storm and the possible effect of the broadcast event on the internetwork.

A broadcast storm is a sequence of broadcast operations from a specific device or group of devices that occurs at a rapid frame-per-second rate that could cause network problems.

Network architecture, topology design, and layout configurations determine the network's tolerance level as it relates to frame-per-second broadcasts.

Consider, for example, a frame-per-second rate related to a broadcast storm generation of a specific protocol (Address Resolution Protocol [ARP], for example). Such generation, at more than 500 frames per second and on a continuing basis, is considered an abnormal protocol-sequencing event and can be extremely problematic.

The key here is to understand the difference between a normal broadcast event and an actual broadcast storm. When a normal broadcast event occurs, the broadcast is engaged from a specific physical device on a network for the express purpose of achieving a network communication cycle. There are conditions when a device, such as a router, broadcasts information to update other routers on the network to ensure that routing tables are maintained as consecutive and consistent related to internal route table information. Another standard broadcast event is when a device attempts to locate another device and requires the physical address or IP address of another device.

When a specific workstation device has a default gateway assigned, a "normal" broadcast event can occur. The device knows, for example, the target IP address of a device on the internetwork. It is common for this device to broadcast an ARP sequence to attempt to locate the target hardware address. ARP broadcasting is discussed in detail later in this book.

A workstation that broadcasts an ARP sequence to locate a target server but doesn't establish a broadcast resolve and doesn't receive a target hardware address for the server provides an example of an "abnormal" broadcast event. If the target device fails or the source broadcast operation mechanism or protocol-sequencing mechanism of the device fails, the source workstation device could start performing a loop ARP sequence that could be interpreted as a broadcast storm. Such an event in itself could cause a broadcast storm.

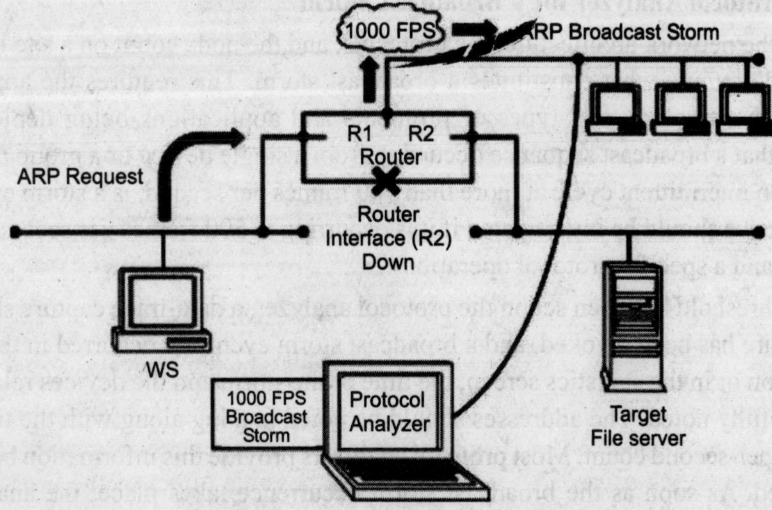

Figure 10.7: Broadcast storm analysis.

The point to be made here is that the frame-per-second rate of the broadcast sequence and the frequency of the broadcast sequence event occurrence can constitute an abnormal event.

Another example can be found in a Novell environment, when the Service Advertising Protocol (SAP) sequencing is engaged by specific servers. If the servers are broadcasting an SAP on standard NetWare sequence timing, the occurrence may take place on 60-second intervals. If there are hundreds or thousands of servers, the SAP sequence packets generated may become highly cumulative and affect areas of the enterprise internetwork that are not utilizing Novell processes.

In large internetworks, many of these concerns are addressed through protocol filtering within routers and switches in the network Layer 3 routing design. When a problem does occur because of an anomaly or possible misconfiguration of an internetwork, it is important to capture the information upon occurrence.

By applying an exact technique with a protocol analyzer, an analyst can very quickly capture a broadcast storm and identify the cause of the broadcast storm and develop a method to resolve the storm. Many different tools enable an analyst to achieve this. Almost all management systems for internetwork hubs, routers, and switches facilitate broadcast storm identification. The threshold that determines what is an actual broadcast occurrence versus an actual broadcast storm is usually set by the network manager or the configuring analyst of the network management platform.

The following discussion details the use of a protocol analyzer for broadcast storm analysis. When performing a data-analysis capture, a protocol analyzer is a useful tool for capturing a broadcast storm. Many protocol analyzers have thresholds that allow for an artificial intelligent-based Expert system to identify a broadcast storm. A storm can be identified by preconfiguring and studying a trigger or threshold for determining what would constitute a storm occurrence. When performing a network baseline, an analyst should always engage the threshold setting on the protocol analyzer prior to a baseline session.

Using a Protocol Analyzer for a Broadcast Storm

Based on the network architecture, the protocols, and the node count on a site being studied, an analyst must determine what constitutes a broadcast storm. This requires the analyst to be quite familiar with the topology and types of protocols and applications being deployed. A general benchmark is that a broadcast sequence occurring from a single device or a group of devices, either rapidly or on an intermittent cycle at more than 500 frames per second, is a storm event. At the very least, the sequence should be investigated if it is occurring at 500 frames per second (relative to just a few devices and a specific protocol operation).

After the threshold has been set on the protocol analyzer, a data-trace capture should be started. After the capture has been invoked, and a broadcast storm event has occurred in the Expert system with notification or in the statistics screen, the time of the storm and the devices related to the storm should be carefully noted. The addresses should be noted in a log along with the time of the storm and the frame-per-second count. Most protocol analyzers provide this information before the capture is even stopped. As soon as the broadcast storm occurrence takes place, the analyzer should be immediately stopped to ensure that the internal data-trace information is still within the memory buffer of the protocol analyzer. The data trace should then be saved to a disk drive or printed to a file to ensure that the information can be reviewed. The data-trace capture should then be opened and the actual absolute storm time noted from the Expert system or the statistical screen. Based on the absolute time, it may be possible on the protocol analyzer to turn on an absolute time feature. When turned on in the data trace, the absolute time feature enables an analyst to search on the actual storm for the absolute time event. This may immediately isolate and identify the cause of the broadcast storm.

Certain protocol analyzers offer hotkey filtering to move directly within the data-trace analysis results of the storm event. Either way, by using absolute time or hotkey filtering, the broadcast storm should be located within the data-trace capture.

Other metrics can be turned on in a protocol analysis display view when examining a broadcast storm, such as relative time and packet size. After the start of the storm has been located, the key devices starting and invoking the storm should be logged. Sometimes only one or two devices cause a cyclical broadcast storm occurrence throughout an internetwork, resulting in a broadcast storm event across many different network areas. The devices communicating at the time closest to the start of the storm inside the data-trace analysis results may be the devices causing the event.

After the storm has been located, the Relative Time field should be zeroed out and the storm should be closely reviewed by examining all packets or frames involved in the storm. If 500 or 1,000 frames are involved, all frames should be closely examined by paging through the trace. After the end of the storm has been located, the time between the start of the storm and the end of the storm should be measured by using a relative time process. This is achieved by just zeroing out the relative time at the beginning of the storm occurrence and examining the cumulative relative time at the end of the sequence. This provides a clear picture of the storm device participation and processes, the packet-size generation during the storm, and the source of the storm location. The initial several packets located for the broadcast storm should be investigated for the physical, network, and transport layer addressing schemes that may relate to the storm occurrence. This helps an analyst to understand the sequence of the storm event.

This is an extremely important process in network baselining and should be engaged in proactive and reactive analysis. In proactive baselining, an analyst must configure the proper broadcast storm thresholds on the protocol analyzer. This way, the storm events will show during the network baseline session. In a troubleshooting (reactive) event, it is important to know whether certain failure occurrences or site network failures are also being reported by the users; these may relate to the time of the storm occurrence. If this is the case, just isolating and identifying the broadcast storm may make it possible to isolate the devices causing the storm or the protocol operations involved. It may then be possible to stop the storm occurrence. This will increase performance levels and optimize the network.

10.8.3 NETWORK CAPACITY OVERLOAD ANALYSIS

When examining utilization, it is important to understand both the available capacity on any network medium and actual achieved utilization levels from an average, peak, and historical perspective. Every network LAN or WAN topology has an available capacity. Determining the utilization levels of a topology is important, but equally important is identifying any problematic utilization levels or saturation utilization levels. As discussed earlier, saturation of any main network medium can cause outages on a network related to an end-to-end session. Peak utilization and time measurement methods must be used to identify any outages.

Other conditions exist when the capacity, even if available, may be in an overload condition in certain topologies.

Consider, for example, a 10Mbps shared media Ethernet topology operating at 60+% utilization levels. The Ethernet topology in a shared configuration normally allows for a specific maximum capacity of 10Mbps or 100Mbps. Can the shared Ethernet medium sustain the applied utilization levels and continue to operate in a positive manner? Although capacity levels may only be operating at a peak transition of 60% or 70%, and approximately 30% to 40% of medium may appear available, the CSMA/CD mechanism of shared Ethernet could trigger an excessive collision problem at this level. As noted later in this book, in shared Ethernet media the collision-detection mechanism can increase to a level that causes problematic events at the physical level when utilization exceeds 30% of available capacity. In this example, a level as high as 60% of the available capacity can constitute a network overload condition.

With most network analyzers and management systems, an analyst can set a threshold that will immediately identify whether a specific LAN or WAN is in overload. The thresholds of certain internetwork management systems are specific to switches, hubs, and routers, and usually facilitate this process.

For the purposes of this discussion, a protocol analysis approach is followed. When performing a network baseline, the protocol analyzer should be preset for a network overload threshold setting (if an available option). This feature is usually found in an artificial intelligent Expert system threshold setting mode. An analyst should determine whether a network overload threshold setup feature is available prior to a baseline session. The next focus is the exact type of topology and protocol sequencing being examined. A 16Mbps Token Ring network requires a different overload threshold setting than a 10Mbps Ethernet environment requires.

Another consideration factor is the type of application traffic and NOS environments that are deploying various protocols across the architecture. The combined topologies and protocols create a specific architecture that must be considered when assessing an overload condition during the network baseline process. In a network continually sustaining a 50% utilization level, for example, setting an alarm below this level will trigger abnormal error occurrences or will cause already well-known information to be continuously logged. Presetting the threshold setting is somewhat of an intuitive process on the part of the analyst. The message here is that the analyst must understand the type of topology and protocol environment deployed and determine what type of a condition will cause a utilization overload of the available capacity. Figure 10.8 illustrates the concept of analyzing a network overload event.

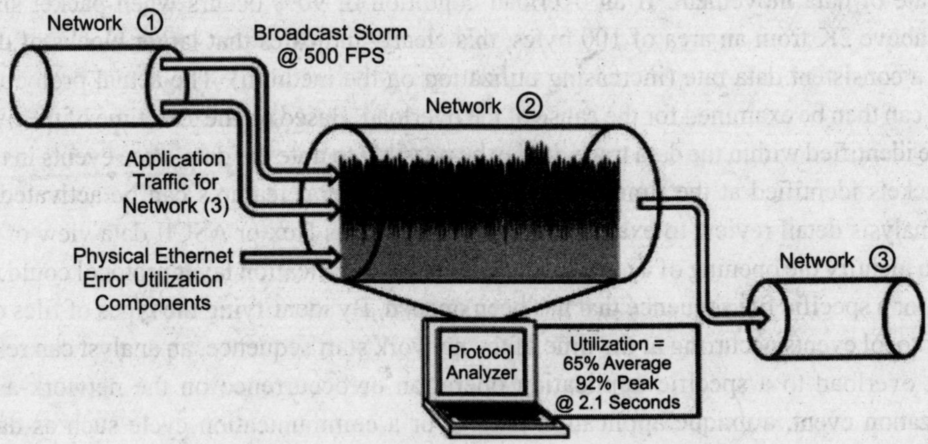

Figure 10.8: Analyzing a network overload event.

A dedicated-circuit WAN with a fractional T1 link engaging a 256K circuit provides another example. You should not continue to run data across the circuit at 80% to 90% capacity. This type of level could cause excessive retransmissions and overflow of some of the buffers in the end-to-end router platforms between two specific wide area sites. If more than 80% to 90% utilization is being achieved, even though there is still 10% available capacity, it would be better to upgrade the circuit to increase performance levels. The other factors involved in making this decision would be the type of router technology, the type of protocols, and the consistency of this traffic level. There are many factors related to this occurrence.

A protocol analyzer example illustrates this technique. A protocol analyzer can be deployed across a certain network topology. When the network baseline session is initially configured, a threshold can be set for the proper overload condition. This is the alarm that occurs when the overload event happens. If the network baseline process is active, and the analyst encounters a network overload alarm, the protocol analyzer should then be stopped and the capture should be saved. The analyst should note the network overload event as to the time of occurrence and the type of devices involved. The data-trace capture should then be reviewed by isolating high-utilization occurrences within the trace. Some, but not all, network analyzers enable an analyst to turn on network utilization as a metric within the data-trace view results. The key is to properly mark the absolute time of the occurrence from the analyzer Expert system or the management system. The Absolute Time field should be turned on within the data-trace capture results.

Whether the network overload is located through a hotkey filtering system or absolute time, the overload occurrence should be closely examined. Most likely, a set of devices is involved in communication when the network overload occurrence takes place.

The network utilization column in the data trace should be examined and noted. The internal trace results should also be closely examined for the type of packet size used during the data movement when the utilization overload condition occurred. As noted earlier, utilization is a component of data size and rate of data movement. If an overload condition of 90% occurs when packet sizes are increased above 2K from an area of 100 bytes, this clearly indicates that larger blocks of data are present at a consistent data rate (increasing utilization on the medium). The actual protocol event sequences can then be examined for the cause of the overload. Based on the start time of the overload occurrence identified within the data trace, it may be possible to note the data-trace events in the first several packets identified at the time of the occurrence. Several features can be activated in the protocol analysis detail review to examine information such as Hex or ASCII data view of packet internals to identify the opening of a certain type of file. The application layer protocol could also be examined for a specific file sequence that has been opened. By identifying the types of files opened and the protocol events occurring at the time of the network start sequence, an analyst can relate the utilization overload to a specific application operation or occurrence on the network-a server synchronization event, a unique application launch, or a communication cycle such as database transfer, for example.

Figure 10.9 shows how changing the size of data movement affects network utilization.

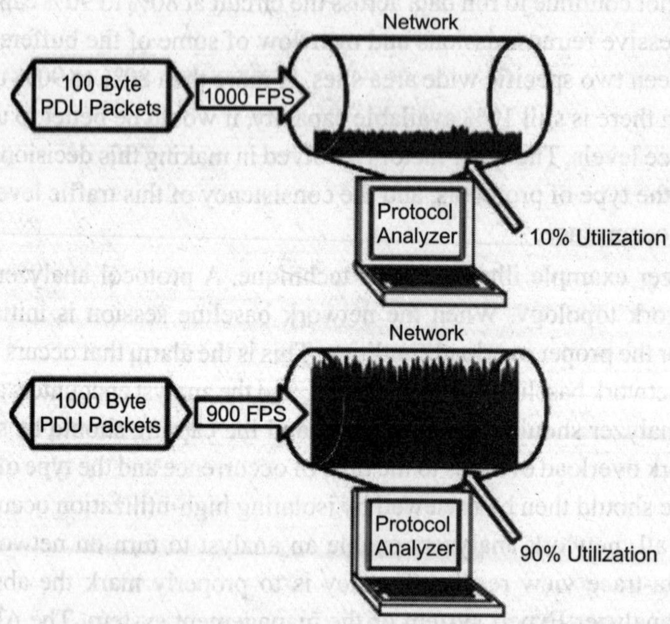

Figure 10.9: Changing the size of data movement.

It is critical to perform network capacity overload analysis during network baselining. An analyst can use this technique in both a reactive analysis for emergency troubleshooting, as well as in a proactive way to examine capacity overloads.

10.8.4 NETWORK THROUGHPUT ANALYSIS

When performing a network baseline, effective throughput should always be considered a standard measurement. The most accurate way to perform effective file throughput (EFT) analysis is to measure

EFT against exact file transfer. General throughput measurements can also be taken against a specific network LAN or WAN area.

A specific technique applies to performing throughput analysis consistent with protocol analysis methodology in a network baselining session. This technique involves cross-mapping throughput measurements obtained from a protocol analyzer statistical or Expert screen with the throughput within the actual data-trace results.

When performing throughput analysis, it is very important to mark the beginning of a file open and a file close sequence. This is because after a file transfer begins, the transfer of data units in packets between two specific devices is usually a consecutive process and data movement can be consecutive and rapid.

Marking the file open and close sequences helps the analyst to determine the throughput across the internetwork channel in a LAN or WAN area. The following discussion focuses on measuring EFT with a protocol analyzer.

Prior to the study, the protocol analyzer deployed on the network should be set up for a network baseline study, and any Expert system threshold in an artificial intelligence-based protocol analysis or statistical screen threshold should be set. Several effective throughput levels are standard. During the network baseline study, the analyst should be familiar with the internetwork architecture and aware of the throughput typically achieved in the particular internetwork architecture. After the standard throughput levels for the specific network have been determined, they should be entered into the Expert system.

If the required achieved level of effective throughput for a network baseline study is 500Kbps, for example, this threshold level should be set in the protocol analyzer prior to a capture session. After the 500Kbps threshold has been set, the protocol analyzer alarm triggers or a statistical screen is identified while a capture is active when a file transfer drops below the 500Kbps mark. The analyst should mark the time of the effective throughput drop and note any devices involved in transfer during the low effective throughput drop. It is next important to identify the timing event of the actual low effective throughput alarm occurrence. Most analyzers include an absolute time mark in the statistical output screen or the Expert analysis screen. With these items being noted, a low EFT event could then be cross-mapped to the internal area of the trace by using the effective throughput measurements discussed earlier in this book.

After the trace analysis data has been saved and the detail trace opened, it is then possible to view the data and locate the low EFT occurrence within the data by cross-mapping the statistical absolute time or hotkey filtering to a low effective throughput event.

When a low effective throughput occurrence is found within the trace, it should be verified by setting relative and cumulative bytes and adding the relative-time metric against data movement that is cumulative to determine the effective throughput achieved for the dataflow operation.

Figure 10.10 displays the technique of measuring EFT.

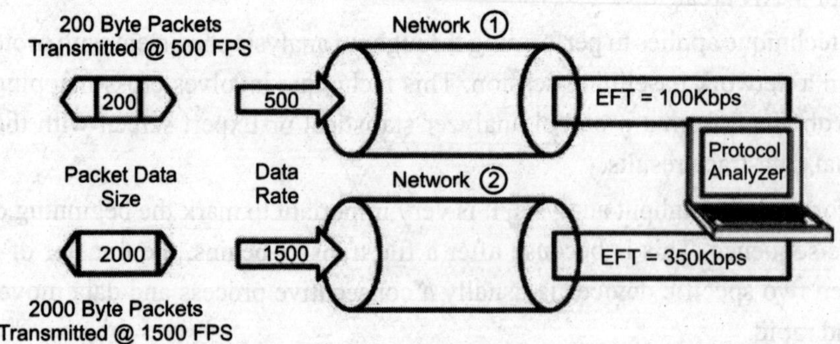

Figure 10.10: Measuring EFT.

It is also possible to trace throughput on a consistent basis by setting several protocol analyzers or management systems at specific threshold levels. This is another unique technique, because it enables the analyst to consistently capture the throughput levels of various devices communicating across an internetwork. Most protocol analyzers can develop multiple sets of views against certain devices communicating with application- or connection-based protocols within a LAN or WAN topology. When specific devices are being tracked in a statistical or Expert screen of a network analyzer, it is possible to monitor the ongoing effective throughput by examining statistical screens.

Measuring effective throughput is not only valuable for low effective throughput occurrences, but also for ongoing tracking of file transfers. The technique for this process is to set up the thresholds correctly and to consistently view the specific devices being reviewed for throughput during the baseline.

An example is to monitor the client stations related to the most critical servers at the site. Specific applications could be launched and the throughput could be compared for different applications. This enables an analyst to determine the data movement and the data-rate for standard throughput; it also enables an analyst to compare application PDU inputs within different application profiles. This identifies throughput differences in certain areas of the internetwork and also the throughput differences related to certain application sequencing.

This is a critical technique that should be followed in proactive baseline studies. This process can also be used in reactive analysis for low throughput or performance problems.

10.8.5 NETWORK END-TO END INTERPACKET TIMING ANALYSIS

Network communication involves at least two devices communicating with each other: a workstation and a server; or a server communicating with another server (at a minimum).

Specifically, any two devices communicating across an internetwork identifies an end-to-end communication channel. A data communication sequence occurs across a network channel and data is processed and a data transfer is achieved.

It is possible to use protocol analyzers and network management systems to examine the network end-to-end timing between two specific devices. As discussed under the timing section in the last chapter of this book, several different timing metrics or statistics can be activated in a protocol analyzer when measuring this process. Some of these metrics or statistics include absolute, delta, and relative time.

A specific technique applies, however, when examining how workstations and servers are communicating as to timing in a network baseline session. This is accomplished by determining the time difference between Request and Response sequences.

A workstation and server across any topology usually invoke a specific protocol sequence to transfer information, and may engage another protocol sequence to call on a specific server file and so forth. Later in this book, there are extensive discussions on specific protocol sequencing methods for different protocol types and suites such as Novell and TCP/IP. For the purposes of this discussion, it is important to understand that there is an exact technique for measuring end-to-end interpacket timing that enables an analyst to quickly determine how various workstations and servers are responding to each other in terms of performance across the internetwork. The process of using a protocol analyzer is used for illustration.

When using a protocol analyzer for end-to-end interpacket timing analysis, it is first important to set the proper thresholds that will trigger alarms when an excessive response time occurs between a workstation and server. Many network analyzers and management systems have threshold settings that set off an alarm when a server or workstation responds over a certain time period. Normal internetwork end-to-end channel communications on a LAN with multiple segments should take no more than 10 to 15 milliseconds (ms), and in fact it is common to see response time well under 5ms on most internetwork infrastructures. Across WAN infrastructures, interpacket latency for end-to-end sessions can be as high as 50ms. A response time of less than 20ms is more typical, however. Some WAN designs are based on different deployment design criteria, such as whether servers are centralized or decentralized across an infrastructure. The server positioning design must be considered when deploying several protocol analyzers against the end-to-end channel.

An example of this process includes a multiple protocol analyzer data-capturing session against an Ethernet end-to-end channel that involves three segments including a WAN. For example, a multiple analyzer positioning "map" relative to the complete internetwork layout can be drawn up. Segment 1, for example, involves a shared Ethernet segment, which connects to a router and then connects to a WAN Frame Relay circuit. That circuit interconnects another WAN site noted as the remote location with an additional router, which is connected to another shared Ethernet segment, Segment 2. This mapping involves the following three specific network areas that must be traversed:

- Segment 1
- The WAN Frame Relay cloud, and
- Segment 2

With this example in mind, at least four protocol analyzers are required to examine an end-to-end channel communication session. One protocol analyzer could be placed on the Segment 1 location in the shared Ethernet area. An second protocol analyzer could be positioned at the exterior side of the WAN router connected to Segment 1 and connected to the Frame Relay cloud or the *Frame*

Relay Assembler Dissembler (FRAD) link. A third protocol analyzer could be positioned at the remote site on the exterior side of the WAN analyzer connected to the FRAD link at the Segment 2 site, and a fourth protocol analyzer could be connected to the remote Ethernet shared Segment 2. This setup places four network protocol analyzers in a parallel mode for synchronized analysis.

Figure 10.11 shows how end-to-end channel analysis can be used in a network baseline study.

Figure 10.11: Engaging in end-to-end analysis.

The next step is to synchronize all the protocol analyzers in terms of date and time to ensure that all the relative base measurements for time in each analyzer platform are as close as possible. Some network protocol analyzers offer synchronization of time through GMT synchronization, depending on the manufacturer. Other inband and outbound triggering mechanisms in different analysis tools also enable an analyst to configure synchronization.

After the analyzers have been engaged, application characterization techniques can then be deployed against a network end-to-end channel being timed. An application can be launched from a local workstation at one segment to access a server at a remote site. This would be valid if a distributed server is placed at the remote site. The application, when launched, can be monitored by all four protocol analyzers. With absolute time set as active, it is possible to trace a specific packet, such as a TCP or a Novell SPX packet, by monitoring the sequence number as it travels from the source workstation to the remote server.

It is also possible to track the TCP or SPX response by examining the sequence and acknowledgment number as well as the identification fields of the networks traversed in the network and transport layer protocols of each packet.

By tracking the packets sent and received, the end-to-end network channel interpacket timing measurements can be determined. An analyst can make delta time active on the Section 1 analyzer to examine the request outbound process from the original workstation and to examine the inbound server response. Even by just using the first analyzer, however, the actual time spent across Section 1, across the WAN Frame Relay cloud, across Section 2, and across the remote segment is all compiled into the remote response. By using several analyzers, an analyst can determine how much time is spent on Segment 1, how much is related to the internal turn time of the workstation or delta time on Segment 1, how much time is spent across router one at the local station, now much time is spent traversing the Frame Relay cloud, how much time is spent traversing remote router two at the remote site, and how much time is spent accessing the server on the remote Ethernet segment at the remote site. An analyst can actually determine the amount of time spent in the server, the server turn time, as well as the server delta time at the remote site.

Timing analysis is an extremely valuable technique, but it must be very carefully configured and engaged. By applying this technique, an analyst can examine the appropriate analyzer screens and cross-map high response time or long acknowledgment time errors, as well as other conditions such as slow responding servers. The analyst can check these occurrences against actual timing events in the internal data-trace analysis results. This technique enables the analyst to accurately isolate the cause and results in extremely on-target information.

This process can be coupled with multiple application-characterization techniques, such as launching certain events. It is then possible to determine delays that may be related to the application processing or delay event sequences that take place when packets are traversing routers or switches on large internetworks.

Various tools enable an analyst to process data scripts across an internetwork based on this sequence.

Some of the most valuable tools available for this type of process include the Chariot platform offered by Ganymede Software and Optimal Software's Application Expert. The Chariot tool allows for immediate generation of data scripts across the internetwork; this will quickly show defined data movement, and allows for viewing transaction time, throughput, and response time operation. Chariot tools can be placed at multiple network points.

Network analyzers can also be placed at the same points to extract data. Optimal's Application Expert provides response-time prediction and data analysis in a multipositioning process, but adds a feature to examine an application's thread across an internetwork.

Many different management systems offer unique platforms and features that can engage tests similar to Ganymede's Chariot and Optimal's Application Expert.

The key factor to remember is that timing measurement is a valid process and should be configured and performed very carefully. By so doing, an analyst can isolate delays and perform specific optimization tuning against internetwork transfer.

This is a valid technique and should be used consistently by an analyst in both proactive and reactive analysis situations.

10.8.6 TRANSPORT AND FILE RETRANSMISSION ANALYSIS

When conducting either a proactive or reactive network baseline study, it is important to monitor the transport layer and application layer for retransmission events. A retransmission occurrence can cause an inefficient situation in terms of final data communication. A retransmission is a redundant dataflow event that adds to the amount of cumulative bytes transferred on a network to effect a final transmission of an intended application process or NOS data.

The specific purpose of the transport layer mechanism operation is to ensure connection. Most transport layer protocols engage a connection process that invokes a sequence-and-acknowledgment cycle between two specific end nodes. This sequence-and-acknowledgment maintenance cycle causes, in certain cases, a higher transmission of redundant data. This is common if there are delays or other abnormal occurrences in the communication channel between two end devices. Later in this book, an extensive discussion is presented on various types of transport layer protocol operations and processes.

For the purposes of this discussion, the main function of the transport layer in network communication protocol sequencing is to ensure that there is a transport mechanism in place for transferring data from specific protocol port areas within certain workstations and hosts across an internetwork. In certain cases, the transport layer also generates packet traffic that allows the transport channel created to be maintained for connection.

Protocol analysis enables an analyst to monitor the transport channel that has been established between a workstation and a file server for general operation and transfer of data across the channel. The analyst can also monitor the transport layer for recurrences of transmission of data considered redundant. In this case, the focus would be monitoring transport layer retransmissions.

Because the transport layer is essentially in place to establish a network channel for data port communication and, at times, to maintain the communication channel in a consistent and reliable state, it is critical to monitor this area through a network baseline process to ensure connectivity.

If a transport layer connection is established with TCP, two specific ports for TCP may be opened on a respective end-to-end channel on an internetwork. The endpoints could be a workstation and a file server, each of which would have a TCP port open. The transport layer protocol TCP would maintain the connection. Polling events between the two protocol ports in the two devices would take place that would allow for maintaining the TCP port transport layer channel that is open related to the port transmission activity.

With the aid of a protocol analyzer, an analyst can monitor this channel. If a delay is present in the internetwork, or if one of the two devices encounters a problem, the end-to-end communication may be negatively affected. Again, this might result from internetwork delays or because one of the devices has an internal issue related to resource handling or processing of data. When this occurs in the TCP environment, the transport layer may show extensive retransmissions of data because it is attempting to ensure that the data required for achievement of an application process is sent on a continuous basis. When retransmissions occur, redundant data is sent. One of the endpoints-for example, the workstation-could encounter a situation in which it is not receiving required data responses from the server because of delays. As this occurs, it is likely that the workstation will re-request the data on a continual basis. Under certain conditions, the host may retransmit the data for integrity purposes, based on the inherent operation of the transport layer protocol TCP.

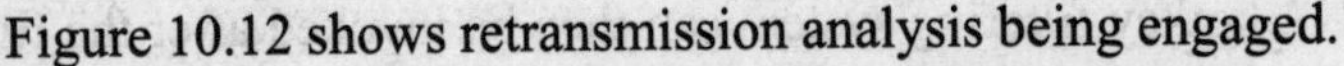

Figure 10.12 shows retransmission analysis being engaged.

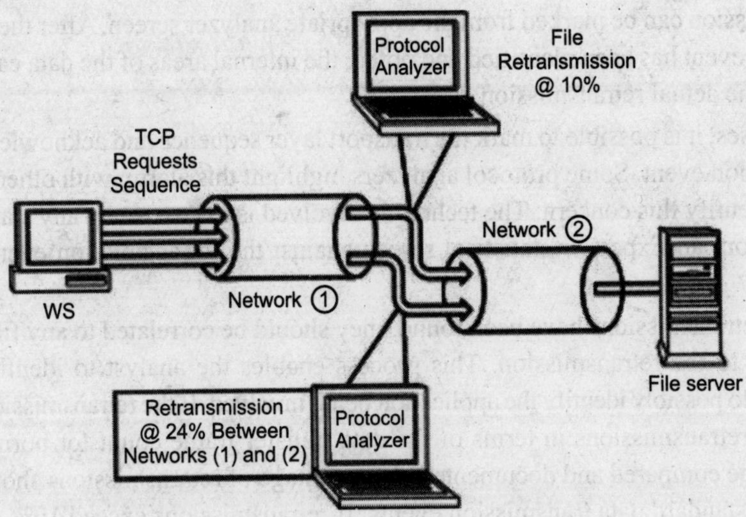

Figure 10.12: Engaging in retransmission analysis.

After a protocol analyzer has captured the retransmissions, an analyst can mark the percentage of data related to retransmissions as related to standard data process transmissions to understand the retransmission level. An extremely high retransmission level, such as 20% or 30% of all frames transmitted, shows an excessive level of redundant communication.

This example clearly shows how transport layer transmissions can become an issue. The simplest way to t monitor transport layer retransmissions is to use a protocol analyzer.

10.8.6.1 APPLICATION-BASED FILE RETRANSMISSION

Application-based file retransmission is another type of retransmission event that can take place in application operations when communication occurs between workstations and servers. In most cases, a complete file retransmission is usually invoked by application operational sequencing, or developers may intentionally code it into the application process for redundant cycles to enable integrity checks in the application transfer.

When a file is sent across a network, a file open and a file close sequence is usually invoked. A protocol analyzer enables an analyst to monitor how often files are opened and closed. If some files are opened and closed on a consistent basis in consecutive order, the application code or the application process may very well be invoking the file retransmissions. When this type of situation occurs, it is critical to monitor the event with a protocol analyzer. Doing so enables the analyst to identify the inefficiently designed applications causing redundant excessive communication on a network.

To monitor transport retransmissions, the network protocol analyzer should first be set for the appropriate thresholds to capture this error. Some network protocol analyzers enable the analyst to set up a predetermined threshold or filter for this type of event. After the network baseline session has been started, if any of the transport layer retransmissions alarms are triggered, the error occurrence and time can then be documented. A hotkey filtering system can then be invoked after the file has been captured and saved. The hotkey filtering system can be engaged or the time of the transport layer retransmission can be marked from the appropriate analyzer screen. After the time event of the retransmission event has been identified and noted, the internal areas of the data capture can then be examined for the actual retransmission event.

In some cases, it is possible to mark the transport layer sequence and acknowledgment fields for the retransmission event. Some protocol analyzers highlight this alarm; with others, only a detailed analysis can identify this concern. The technique involved is to cross-map any statistical alarms on the analyzer from an Expert or statistical screen against the retransmission event inside the data trace.

After the retransmissions have been found, they should be correlated to any file open and close sequence prior to the retransmission. This process enables the analyst to identify the file being transferred and to possibly identify the application being involved. If the retransmissions are excessive, the amount of retransmissions in terms of the data transfer frame count for normal retransmitted frames should be compared and documented. A percentage of retransmissions should be calculated against overall standard data transmission events. If retransmissions exceed 10% of overall traffic, this is a problematic level that could cause redundant communication and additional utilization on the medium. Retransmission levels as high as 20% and 30% could cause application integrity issues and/or application failures. The level of retransmissions should be carefully noted.

Figure 10.13 presents the concept of file fluency analysis.

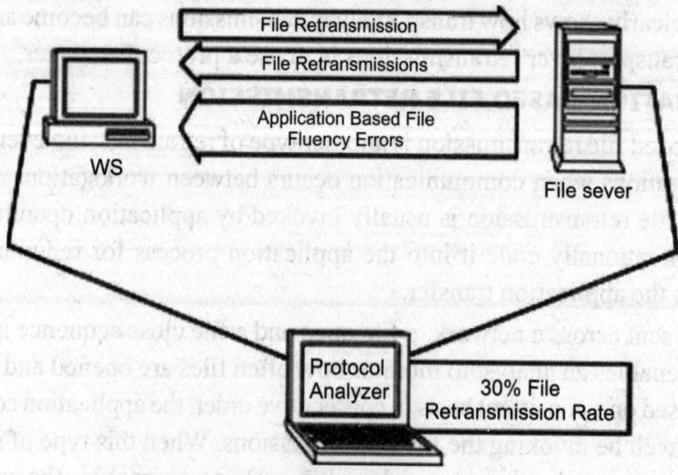

Figure 10.13: File fluency analysis.

When monitoring application-based file retransmissions, it is also important to set up a protocol analyzer prior to starting a network baseline to capture any concerns related to this type of event. Some protocol analyzers enable an analyst to set up a filter or an Expert system threshold to trigger an alarm. If when performing a network baseline session, a file retransmission alarm is triggered, or if a statistic is reported on a screen for an event, the analyzer can then be stopped and the data should be saved for review.

The event occurrence from the statistical or Expert screen should also be noted for the absolute time of occurrence and the devices involved in the file retransmission. It may also be possible in some circumstances to mark the protocol type or application invoked. Usually this is just noted as the protocol layer engaged and not the application type.

After the capture has been saved, the data trace should then be opened and the event should be located by hotkey filtering or matching of the absolute time of occurrence. After the file retransmissions have been located, the type of files being opened should be examined and, if possible, cross-mapped to an application engaged at the site. It is sometimes possible to turn on Hex or ASCII data display views with an analyzer to examine the internals of the file open statement (if the application layer does not report the file type, for instance). This enables an analyst to identify the application access that is occurring.

Next, the file open and close process should be monitored for how often the file is opened and closed in a consecutive manner. A file opened and closed once is a normal event. If a file is opened and closed 25 consecutive times with the same data being transferred, this is an excessive file retransmission event. The application development team should be contacted to investigate whether this is an intended application event or whether this is an abnormal event. In most cases, this issue can be resolved by working in tandem with the application development and NOS server support teams.

Figure 10.14 shows file access-error analysis.

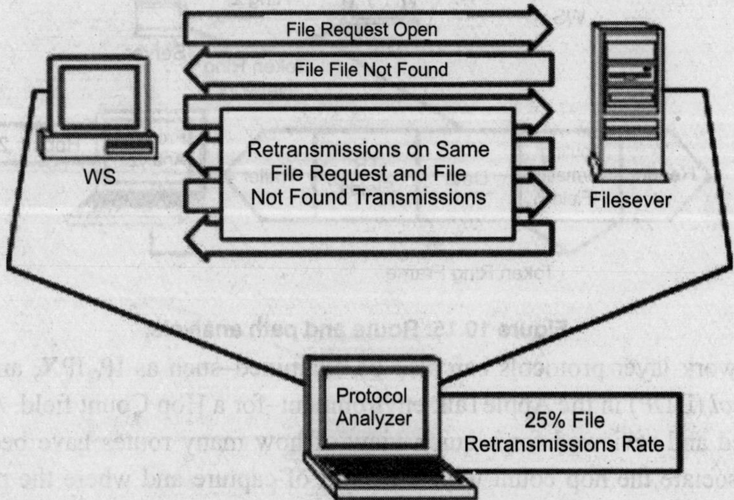

Figure 10.14: File access-error analysis.

Both steps of examining transport and file retransmissions via network baselining are extremely important. These techniques assist in identifying redundant communication that can be eliminated from a communication session. These steps also assist in identifying network-based foundational or application process issues.

10.8.7 PATH AND ROUTE ANALYSIS

During a network baseline, it is important to always investigate the route of packet transfer across a network or internetwork channel. It is also important to determine the number of hops or paths taken across internetwork interval points when transferring information.

The use of protocol analysis in this area is an extremely valuable process. Path route and path count analysis can be used in proactive and reactive network baselining sessions. To examine path route concerns, it is important to understand that within network layer protocols, and also internal to some of the data involved above the physical layer inside a packet, there is information that may identify the route that a packet has taken through an internetwork.

When examining a simple Token Ring frame, for example, it is very common to examine a Routing Information field. The Routing Information field includes specific information as to the bridge, router, or switch that been traversed, and how many hops have been taken related to the Token Ring packet. An analyst can use a protocol analyzer to capture this information.

Figure 10.15 illustrates route and path analysis in a Token Ring network.

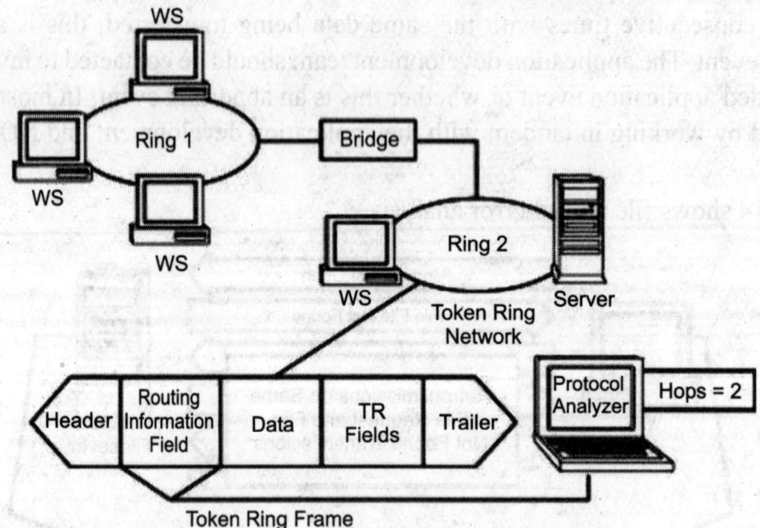

Figure 10.15: Route and path analysis.

Several network layer protocols can also be examined–such as IP, IPX, and even Datagram *Delivery Protocol* (DDP) in the AppleTalk environment–for a Hop Count field. A Hop Count field can be examined and reviewed for a quick view of how many routes have been traversed. It is important to associate the hop count with the point of capture and where the packet is traveling through the internetwork.

Certain network layer protocols, such as IP, provide even more information. The IP protocol provides a Hop Count and combined Time in Transit field, associating how long a packet has spent on a network in the term of actual seconds or time metrics. This a combined field and shows time-to-live (TTL). This field is discussed in detail later in Chapter 7, "LAN and WAN Protocols."

The technique of examining packet, route, packet count, and path count is extremely important and can become intuitive for analyst.

Most protocol analyzers enable an analyst to immediately examine the internals of a packet or frame in a detailed manner. Some protocol analyzers have alarms settings for excessive hop counts or path routes traversed. The protocol analyzer should be set up for any alarms or thresholds required.

After the capture has occurred, if any events take place in a network baseline session, the information related to a path count exceeded or a hop count exceeded field should be noted. The absolute time, the occurrence of the event, and the devices involved should also be noted. The capture should then be stopped and saved. When the data trace is opened, the event should be located through absolute time cross-mapping or hotkey filtering. When the frames showing the event are located, the frames should be opened in a detailed mode. The information related to path route or hop count should be examined. In most cases, this examination focuses on the network protocol involved. Most network layer protocols usually just display the source network, source node, and sometimes the socket or protocol port being communicated to across the internetwork. By examining the source network relative to the destination network, the hop count can be determined for the data communicated across a set of routes.

In a flat internetwork, such as a switched Ethernet environment, a hop count marking in a Hop Count field within a network layer protocol may not be valid or exist. By examining the source and destination network, however, an analyst can determine whether a device is located across an Ethernet end-to-end channel that involves two, three, or four switches. Again, it is extremely important to understand that, in most instances, the network layer protocol holds this information.

Figure 10.16 illustrates route analysis of an Ethernet network.

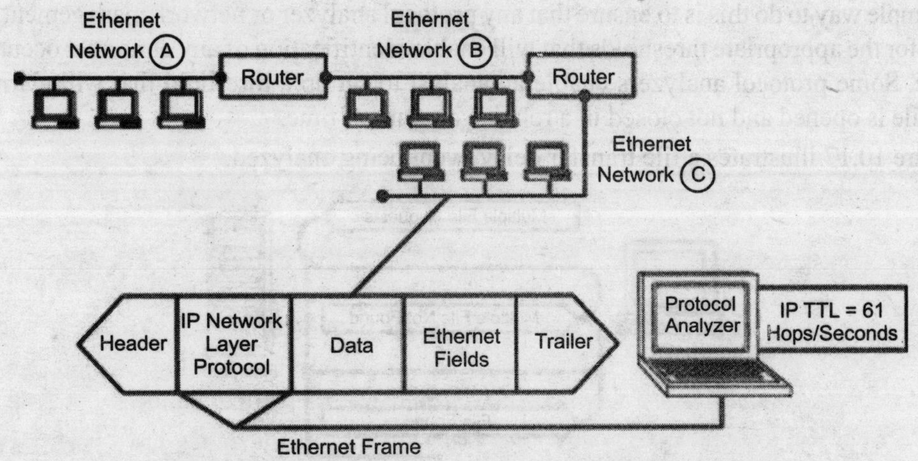

Figure 10.16: Route analysis of an Ethernet network.

The source and destination networks involved should then be marked, and then the devices should be mapped against the physical topology of the network. By just locating the source and destination network, the devices can be reviewed against a physical architecture or topology map. By locating where the devices are positioned on the network and associating this with the route taken, it is sometimes possible to identify inefficient design or incorrect implementation of servers and workstations across an internetwork. Remedies can then be taken, such as relocating a server or reconfiguring switches or routers in such a way that fewer routes are traversed.

At times, excessive multiple-route occurrences can be identified. In some cases, routing loops or delays can be identified in this sequence. Sometimes a pass-through route through a server that provides for IP forwarding or has multiple NICs can be located through this technique.

This is extremely important and allows for route protocol analysis to be used to examine the route that a packet actually takes and the number of hops that the packet encounters when traversing the internetwork from the source to the destination.

The ability to map this to an actual sequence flow or roadmap taken through the internetwork is an invaluable process to a network baseline study, in both a proactive and reactive mode.

10.8.8 END-TO-END FILE TRANSFER ANALYSIS

Another important technique in network baselining is end-to-end file transfer analysis. File access is the main operation of an internetwork. As mentioned earlier, a protocol analyzer can be used consistently to mark a file open and a file close sequence. An analyst can review when files are opened and closed, and can identify the source and destination devices related to the transfer. As discussed earlier, the analyst can examine the internal time sequences between a file transfers and mark the timing related to the file transfer event as well as the amount of data moved.

Taking into account the techniques presented in the application discussion of this book, it is next important to note that a simple technique should be followed during every network baseline study to examine end-to-end file transfer. When performing a network baseline, even with the absence of errors, it is important to constantly monitor file transfer events when examining the internal levels of protocol analysis-based traces captured during a session.

A simple way to do this is to ensure that any protocol analyzer or network management tool used is set up for the appropriate thresholds that will enable identification of any abnormal occurrences of this type. Some protocol analyzers enable an analyst to set up a threshold that will alarm when a certain file is opened and not closed in a relative amount of time.

Figure 10.17 illustrates a file transfer delay event being analyzed.

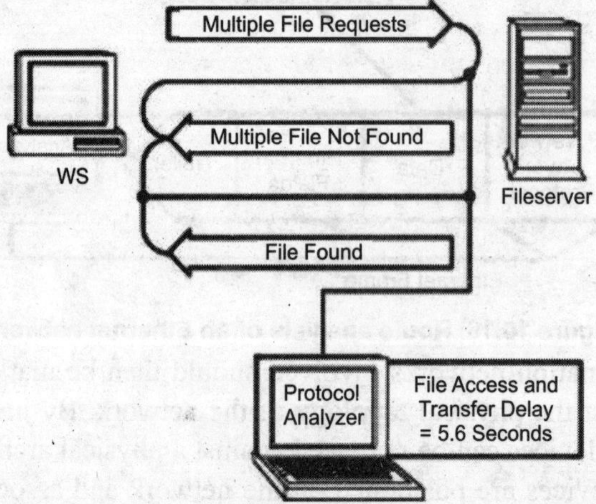

Figure 10.17: Analysis of a file transfer delay.

An analyst can also identify this process by setting specific alarms, such as alarms to a nonresponsive host environment or a slow responding server. In certain conditions, this may enable the analyst to immediately identify any abnormal end-to-end file transfers within a data capture.

A normal process is for a file to be opened, accessed, and closed. In some cases, a file is opened, accessed, and then abruptly stopped. Sometimes the event can be caused by delays on the network or failure of the NOS or failure of the application itself.

Often a device failure in the workstation or file server causes this event. It is important to examine this event on a consistent basis as a thread throughout many network baselining sessions in an enterprise internetwork study.

A protocol analyzer can set up in a predetermined configuration prior to a network baseline session to allow for a threshold alarm to activate upon incorrect file closures or any nonresponsive conditions on workstations and servers.

After the protocol analysis network baselining session has been started, it is then possible to identify any alarms that may be triggered. If any alarms occur related to file transfer sequencing, the devices involved and the absolute time of the occurrence should be noted. After the capture has occurred, the data trace should be saved. The data captured should be opened and the abnormal file transfer located through a hotkey or absolute time cross-mapping sequence.

In the event that alarms are not triggered, a page through the trace exercise enables the analyst to examine file open and close sequencing. If the error is located, the file open and close process can be examined. Once marked, the open and close process should be considered the start and stop point for a file transfer. The packets should next be examined from the open state to the close state for redundancy or abnormal retransmission events. In some instances, the trace data will show an abnormal stop and file close as even be present in the trace.

The key factor here is that normal consecutive file open and close sequencing is essential to a positive network communication process. It is also the main reason that we have file open occurrence, an access event such as a data transfer, and a file close. Most of the time, the application layer protocol is monitored for this type of cycle. Application layer protocols include such types as NCP and Windows NT's SMB. Further information on application layer protocols appears later in this book.

In closing, it is important to examine end-to-end file transfer in every network baseline study session.

10.8.9 TRACE DECODING TECHNIQUES

When performing a network baseline, the final technique is the actual method used by the analyst to identify specific events and perform trace decoding. Earlier in this book, a brief discussion was presented on a process termed "paging through the trace."

When moving through a data capture, the data must be examined on a consecutive basis and reviewed closely by carefully moving through the trace information. Large data captures can include multiple frame sequences that can involve thousands of frames. Some network baseline capture sessions involve anywhere from 30,000 up to 100,000 or more frames. Because of this, it is important to have a technique that allows for quick examination of the frame sequencing. One technique is to use an Expert or statistical screen for cross-mapping event errors and quick hotkey filtering to the area in the trace that shows the problem. At times, an Expert or statistical screen may actually show the frame number prior to stopping the capture when an error event occurs.

When performing a network baseline, careful notes should be taken from the Expert system or the statistical screen prior to stopping the capture. If critical information is noted, such as absolute time of occurrence, devices involved, or frame numbers related to error occurrence, an analyst can move through the trace more quickly after the capture has been saved for review. Even if an Expert system is not available, there are ways to page through the trace to obtain important information that is essential for a network baseline session. This is an extremely valuable step in network baselining.

Figure 10.18 illustrates the concept of trace note taking during a network baseline study.

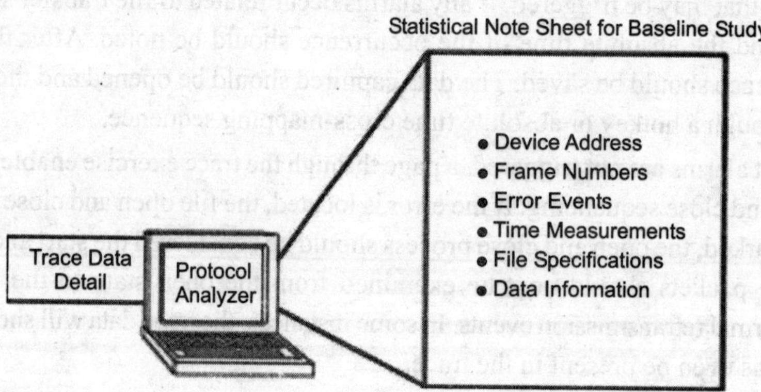

Figure 10.18: Trace note.

The following is an example of using a protocol analyzer to page through the trace. First, the analyzer must be preconfigured for the proper metric thresholds to ensure that event alarms will trigger and show absolute time and areas of occurrence for frame category marking prior to the error event. Watching the protocol analyzer closely while the capture is occurring will also allow for marking this type of event.

After the capture has been started, the analyst should closely monitor the protocol analyzer. This is extremely important when performing reactive troubleshooting analysis for rapid cause isolation. If an error alarm for a retransmission is triggered on the analyzer statistical screen when frames are being received into the analyzer NIC and the analyzer is showing an inbound frame count of 5,325 frames captured, the frame number 5,325 can be quickly noted as a possible frame area in the data trace as associated with the retransmission error.

The error and the devices involved with the error should be recorded on a statistical notebook, along with the frame area within the trace that is inbound. Thus, when the data capture is saved and the event examined, the analyst can swiftly move to frame 5,325 for cause isolation.

Figure 10.19 illustrates the concept of frame marking during a protocol analysis session.

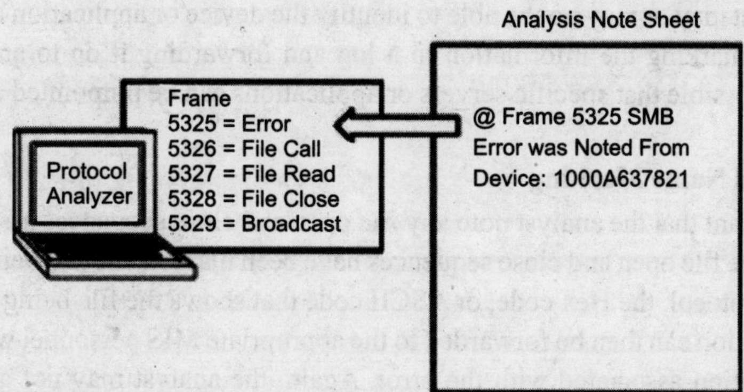

Figure 10.19: Frame marking.

This is just one example of this type of cross-mapping of an ongoing rapid dynamic process throughout a network baseline session. Again, the analyst must be extremely involved with the protocol analyzer while the capture is occurring for this technique to be helpful.

After the protocol analyzer has been stopped, whether an Expert is active or inactive, the analyst can move through the data in a page through the trace process to investigate certain data. If any events are located during the live capture dynamic session, the cross-mapped technique of reviewing the data associated with certain frame numbers or with absolute time occurrence should be followed. Hotkey filtering should also be used, when possible. This will allow for quick use of an Expert system or an artificial intelligence statistical screen to quickly key to the type of error within the data capture.

After a problematic frame or packet has been found, certain types of information should be clearly recorded in a statistical mode by the consultant or analyst performing the network baseline.

An analyst should note information related to the following:

- Address(es)
- File access and name(s)
- Time frame(s)
- Frame structures for field length
- Routing information
- Specific protocol(s)

Address Marking

When examining a trace, it is first important to note the various levels of addressing. The physical address should be noted inside any packet that has an error. The network layer address should also be noted, along with any transport layer ports that are opened. This will assist in identifying any events related to an error frame that could be associated with certain devices or specific network applications.

An analyst might, at times, capture the trace information and identify a specific area of the trace that shows the problem. Depending on the analyst's experience and understanding of the internetwork, however, the analyst may or may not be able to identify the device or application associated with an error. By properly marking the information in a log and forwarding it on to an appropriate MIS person, it is quite possible that specific servers or applications can be pinpointed as the cause of the problem.

File Access and Name Marking

It is also important that the analyst note any file open and close sequences associated with error occurrence. After the file open and close sequences have been marked, the file being called on in the application layer protocol, the Hex code, or ASCII code that shows the file being opened should be noted. This information can then be forwarded to the appropriate MIS personnel who may be able to identify the application associated with the error. Again, the analyst may not always understand which devices or applications are involved. By clearly noting the file sequencing or the file that is opened and closed in an analysis log from a protocol analysis standpoint, however, other MIS team members may be able to identify the application or area of the internetwork related to file server location causing the problem.

Time Frame Marking

As discussed throughout this chapter, it is important to record the time frame of an error event. The absolute time frame of a packet is usually marked within the upper-layer physical header inside the detail level of a packet area. It is also possible to turn on the absolute time within the data-trace summary screen to review the absolute time of any error frame occurrence. Each time an error is noted in a baseline session, the network analyst should always record the time frame occurrence in a statistical analysis log.

Frame Structures for Field Length Marking

Occasionally, a network baseline analyst will encounter a frame structure error. Frame structures are usually designed for a specifically defined operation. For example, a typical Ethernet frame is based on a frame size ranging from 64 bytes to 1518 bytes. A 4Mbps Token Ring frame is limited to 4096 bytes. An analyst should always mark the frame size associated with any error frame occurrence captured.

Specifically, if an error frame is detected when examining a data trace, the frame size and protocol layer sizes should be noted, as well as the data payload. Each packet will always have a certain maximum transmission unit (MTU) size and specific amounts of data will be associated with the protocol layers. It is important to mark the payload of data transferred in any frames where errors occur. This information should be recorded in the analyst's statistical log.

Routing Information Marking

Another key area to monitor is the Routing Information field. As discussed earlier in this chapter, frames contain specific information that indicates to an analyst the route taken or the path hop count achieved. When performing a data-trace analysis session that involves cause analysis or standard network baselining for error mapping, the analyst should clearly mark any critical routing information, such as the route or path taken. If routing update sequences are captured between routers or switches, or other key devices on the network such as servers or hosts, the analyst should also record any routing update sequences when performing error-mapping analysis.

Specific Protocol Marking

Specific protocol marking is also important. This book does not discuss certain event occurrences. These are abnormal occurrences that do not fit any specific profiles, such as an abnormal error from a certain application, or an abnormal type of protocol event that has not been seen before in a network baseline session. If any abnormal event occurs, the analyst should document as much information as possible about the event. This would include the absolute time of occurrence, the devices involved, and any protocol sequencing taken.

When performing a network baseline session, it is extremely important to be in a constant review mode, which involves statistical documentation of the occurrences. Statistical documentation involves recording and documenting information prior to stopping the data capture. It is also vital that information be saved to a trace file save mode or a Common Separate Value (CSV) file format when possible so that the information can be reviewed later in the network baseline process.

Some of this information will be extremely critical to the final data-acquisition decoding and final reporting process of the network baseline study.

It should never be assumed that information is not required or is unimportant. All information should be documented in a concise and detailed basis. When performing a large internetwork baseline involving several baseline areas, such as a 10 to 15 segments in an Ethernet environment, for example, some of the information found in Baseline Session 1 may be relevant in Baseline Session 7. It is important that every network baseline session be consistently documented through statistical save modes for trace file captures, along with general note-taking and statistical marking during a trace analysis session.

EXERCISES

1. What do you mean by network optimization?
2. Explain the terminology of network optimization?
3. Explain the various examples of using network flows?
4. What do you mean by generalized networks?
5. Explain the various goals of network optimization?
6. Explain the various measurements for network optimization?
7. Explain the various network optimization tools?
8. Explain the various network optimization techniques?

OTHER USEFUL BOOKS BY THE AUTHOR

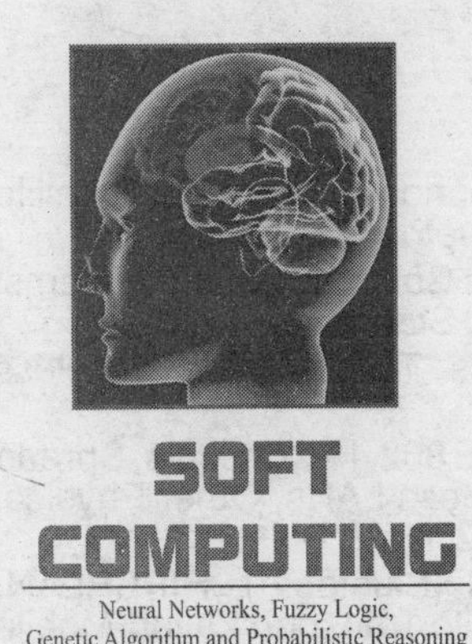

SOFT COMPUTING

Salient Features

- Detailed explanation of soft computing concepts.
- Extensive coverage of fundamental concepts of artificial neural network.
- Description on fuzzy logic techniques.
- Concepts of neuro-fuzzy and genetic algorithm are included.
- Detailed analysis of each and every type of probability.
- Demonstrates the concept of fuzzy logic and probability.

ISBN : 9789380016979 Pages (Approx.) : 670

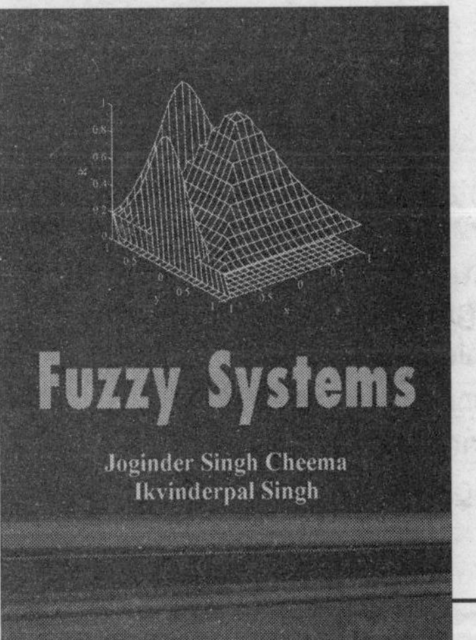

FUZZY SYSTEMS

Salient Features

- Simple and easy language.
- Description on fuzzy logic techniques.
- Discusses on the introduction to fuzzy sets, fuzzy relations, fuzzy graphs and fuzzy rules.
- Concepts of neuro-fuzzy and genetic algorithm are included.
- Demonstrates the concept of fuzzy logic and probability, fuzzy implications and reasoning.
- Covers concept of fuzzy identification model, fuzzy databases, and fuzzy SQL.
- Fundamental ideas on Artificial intelligence and pattern recognition are discussed.

ISBN : 9789380016498 Pages (Approx.) : 496

DISTRIBUTED DATABASE SYSTEMS

Salient Features

- Description on Design and Architecture of Distributed Database Systems.
- Fundamental ideas on Query Processing and Optimization.
- Concepts of Distributed Transaction Management explain in a lucid manner.
- Detailed explanation of Distributed Concurrency Control and Reliability protocols are given.
- Gives the Distributed Deadlock Detection Algorithms and Recovery Schemes.
- Demonstrates the concept of Distributed Database Administration.

ISBN : 9789381068168 Pages (Approx.) : 510

MOBILE COMPUTING

Salient Features

- Detailed explanation of Cellular Telephone Systems, Satellite Communication, Wireless LANs and Bluetooth.
- Fundamental ideas on Modern Wireless Communication Systems: 2G/2.5G/3G/4G Wireless Networks and Standards.
- Detailed explanation of Multi Access Technique & Wireless Standards.
- Gives the Wireless LAN standards: IEEE 802.11 Concepts, Spread Spectrum Wireless LAN, Infrared Wireless LANs, Other Physical Layer Protocol (IEEE 802.11b, IEEE 802.11a).
- Extensive coverage of Wireless PAN (Bluetooth), HIPERLAN, Mobile Network Layer (Mobile IP), Mobile Transport Layer (Mobile TCP), Mobile Data network (GPRS).

ISBN : 9788190698236 **Pages (Approx.) : 470**

DIGITAL IMAGE PROCESSING

Salient Features

- Extensive coverage of fundamental concepts of Digital Image Processing.
- Gives mathematical development when it provides a guide to proper implementation of image signal representation.
- Covers all Image processing techniques.
- Presents hardware architecture for image processing.
- Covers all techniques of color image processing.
- Provides examples of simple applications.

ISBN : 9788190744214 **Pages (Approx.) : 530**

NETWORK OPERATING SYSTEMS

Salient Features

- Description of various Network Operating Systems: Windows 2000/2003/XP, Unix/Linux.
- Overview of Network Operating System and Some Special topics.
- Provides a detailed treatment of Disk Management and Servers.
- Covers the concept of User, Group and Computer Accounts
- Detailed explanation of the Managing active directory, Performance Monitoring and Security.

ISBN : 9788190744199 **Pages (Approx.) : 700**

Introduction to MICROPROCESSORS 8085 and 8086

Salient Features

- Extensive coverage of microprocessor basics, architectural advancement of microprocessor and typical microprocessor development schemes.
- Presents analysis of 8085 and 8086 microprocessor and its internal architecture, interfacing and programming in enough detail.
- Gives detailed description of peripheral interfacing devices includes 8237 DMA Controller, 8255 programmable peripheral interface, 8253/8254programmable timer/counter, 8259 programmable interrupt controller, 8251 USART and RS232C
- Covers addressing modes and interrupts of both 8085 and 8086 microprocessor in enough detail.
- Detailed analysis of Assembly language programming based on intel 8085/8086.

ISBN : 9789381068573 **Pages (Approx.) : 465**

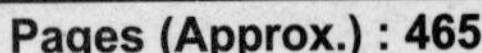

NETWORK DESIGN AND PERFORMANCE ANALYSIS

Salient Features

- Discusses on the introduction to Requirements Analysis and Specifications.
- Detailed explanation of the Traffic Engineering & Capacity Planning.
- Covers the concept of Choosing Service Provider, Vendor and Service Levels.
- Design and Architecture of Access Network Design and Security.
- Detailed explanation of Documentation and Network Management.
- Demonstrates the concept of the Network Optimization.

ISBN : 9789381068410 **Pages (Approx.) : 320**

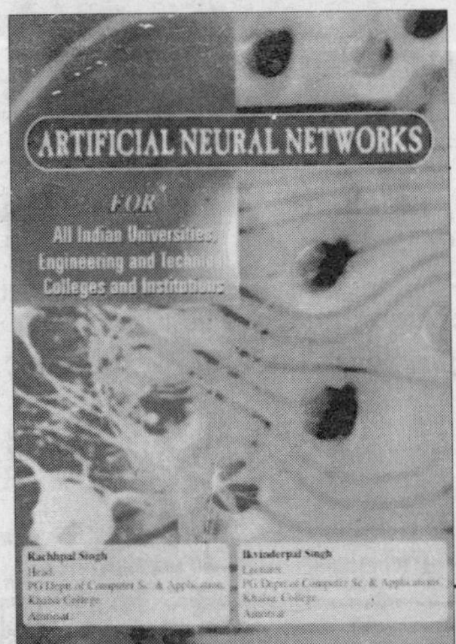

ARTIFICIAL NEURAL NETWORKS

Salient Features

- Extensive coverage of fundamental concepts of Artificial neural network.
- Presents architecture and algorithm of every net in enough detail.
- Provides examples of simple applications.
- Gives mathematical development when it provides a guide to proper implementation of net.
- Covers all supervised and unsupervised learning methods.

ISBN : 9788190698207 **Pages (Approx.) : 300**

DATA STRUCTURES An Algorithmic Approach

Salient Features

- Extensive coverage of Data structure basics, pictorial representation of each and every Data Structures is given in detail.
- Demonstrates the development of algorithms in a lucid manner.
- Includes numerous illustrative examples to understand the topic easily.
- Demonstrates the implementation of algorithms in a good programming style.
- Objective-type questions have been provided.
- Around 300 algorithms are included.

ISBN : 9789380016702 **Pages (Approx.) : 680**

DATA STRUCTURES An Algorithmic Approach with C

Salient Features

- Extensive coverage of Data structure basics, pictorial representation of each and every Data Structures is given in detail.
- Demonstrates the development of algorithms in a lucid manner.
- Includes numerous illustrative examples to understand the topic easily.
- Demonstrates the implementation of algorithms in a good programming style.
- Objective-type questions have been provided.
- Around 200 solved C programs and algorithms are included.

ISBN : 9789380016696 **Pages (Approx.) : 960**

DATA STRUCTURES An Algorithmic Approach with C++

Salient Features

- Extensive coverage of Data structure basics, pictorial representation of each and every Data Structures is given in detail.
- Demonstrates the development of algorithms in a lucid manner.
- Includes numerous illustrative examples to understand the topic easily.
- Demonstrates the implementation of algorithms in a good programming style.
- Objective-type questions have been provided.
- Around 200 solved C++ programs and algorithms are included.

ISBN : 9789380016856 **Pages (Approx.) : 940**

SOLVED PROGRAMMING IN C

Salient Features

- Includes 1600 solved programs.
- Includes system-level programming.
- Numerous examples are included to illustrate concepts and techniques.
- Each and every program given in the book is perfectly working.

ISBN : 9789380016191 Pages (Approx.) : 530

ADVANCED COMPUTER ORGANIZATION AND ARCHITECHTURE

Salient Features

- Describes the introduction of Advanced Computer Architecture and Parallel Processing.
- Covers the Paradigms of Computing like Synchronous and Asynchronous.
- Detailed explanation of the Flynn's classification, Kung's taxonomy and Reduction Paradigm.
- Provides a detailed treatment of Abstract Parallel Computational Models like Combinational Circuits, Sorting Network, PRAM models, Interconnection RAMs.
- Covers the Parallelism in Uniprocessor Systems and Parallel Computer Structures.
- Covers the concept of Pipelining Processors, Superscalar, Superpipeline Design and VLIW Processors.

ISBN : 9789381068694 Pages (Approx.) : 400

DATA MINING & WAREHOUSING

Salient Features

- The order of topics is very logical.
- The choice of topics is quite appropriate for a comprehensive introductory book.
- The subject matter is logically structured, with chapters covering essential components of the data mining and warehousing field.
- The sequence of topics is well planned to provide a seamless transition from design to implementation.
- Within each chapter, the continuity of topics is excellent.
- The figures appropriately enhance and amplify the topics.

ISBN : 9789381068700 Pages (Approx.) : 400

ADVANCED COMPUTER ORGANIZATION AND ARCHITECHTURE

New Release

Key Features of the Book

- ❖ Describes the introduction of Advanced Computer Architecture and Parallel Processing.
- ❖ Covers the Paradigms of Computing like Synchronous and Asynchronous.
- ❖ Detailed explanation of the Flynn's classification, Kung's taxonomy and Reduction Paradigm.
- ❖ Provides a detailed treatment of Abstract Parallel Computational Models like Combinational Circuits, Sorting Network, PRAM models, Interconnection RAMs.
- ❖ Covers the Parallelism in Uniprocessor Systems and Parallel Computer Structures.
- ❖ Covers the concept of Pipelining Processors, Superscalar, Superpipeline Design and VLIW Processors.

ISBN : 9789381068694 Pages (Approx.) : 400